Bridging Art, Design and Technology: My Lifetime Work

Aaron Marcus

Bridging Art, Design and Technology: My Lifetime Work

 Springer

Aaron Marcus
Principal
Aaron Marcus and Associates
Berkeley, CA, USA

ISBN 978-3-032-04341-2   ISBN 978-3-032-04342-9   (eBook)
https://doi.org/10.1007/978-3-032-04342-9

This Springer imprint is published by the registered company Springer Nature Switzerland AG
The registered company address is: Gewerbestrasse 11, 6330 Cham, Switzerland

If disposing of this product, please recycle the paper.

Dedicated to my beloved wife Sandra Bassman Speier, who has helped me during the past 10 years to become a better person and who reviewed the chapters of this book during the final years of its preparation.

Foreword

I am honored, as Aaron's friend, admirer, and one-time collaborator, to write a Foreword for *Bridging Art, Design and Technology: My Lifetime Work*. Aaron was a true pioneer. His story is fascinating. It gives a vivid sense of an important period in the worlds of art, design, and technology—a time in which the digital computer enabled these worlds to converge and allow new forms of creativity. Aaron is as much responsible for this as any other single individual.

Aaron is an artist. Over time, he progressed from early work cartooning and sketching in a variety of styles to abstract creations made by programming a computer (as early as 1967). These often involve clever combinations of type or geometric shapes (see Chaps. 4–6). His work is playful and graceful. His visible language designs are imaginative and evocative. The computer in Aaron's hands is a deft instrument. The reader should particularly look at the striking set of four images "Shades of Hades," "Radioactive Jukebox," "Evolving Gravity," and "Urbane Nova" (Figs. 5.40–5.43).

Aaron is a graphic designer. His art and his posters evoke the work of a sensitive designer with skillful use of evocative typography and graceful page layout. See, for example, his work on a modern Swiss poster exhibit he mounted and designed (Figs. 5.30–5.35) and his "digital hieroglyphics" (Figs. 6.43–6.47). Aaron has also done lovely book designs. The reader should look and read about his work (Figs. 5.2–5.5) designing the 12th edition of *Perspecta*, a publication of the Yale School of Architecture, in which he researched and chose nine different kinds of paper, seeking to match the kind of paper to the content of each of the articles.

In 1980, Aaron proposed to speak at the annual SIGGRAPH conference, the world's premier venue for presenting novel computer graphics research results and striking new computer imagery. Much to his surprise, he was invited to deliver a lecture in the opening keynote panel and a full-day tutorial. (I first got to speak with Aaron at the conference reception on a boat in Lake Washington.) This was followed by increasing interest in his challenge to the computer industry to produce more effective visual communication and to design better computer "*innerfaces*, interfaces, and *outerfaces*" (Aaron's terms). And so, at age 39, for a variety of reasons mentioned at the end of Chap. 5 and [shameful plug follows] discussed at greater length in my new book, *Reinvention: Meaningful Ventures in Later Life*, Aaron reinvented himself as an entrepreneur. With little background in business, he had the courage to create and build what was arguably the world's first information-oriented, computer-based graphic design firm.

Aaron Marcus and Associates did consulting, design, and training for 242 clients beginning in 1972 over a span of more than 40 years. He and I worked together on what became his firm's first project (Figs. 7.10–7.13), the graphic design of the appearance of computer programs written in the C programming language, work documented in the book *Human Factors and Typography for More Readable Programs*. Aaron's client list reads like a Who's Who of important firms, educational institutions, and government agencies from all parts of the globe. Among them were the American College of Physicians, Apple, AT&T, the Bank of America, Eastman Kodak, the Ford Foundation, General Electric, Hewlett Packard, the IIT Institute of Design, Intel, the Japan Patent Office, Microsoft, NASA, NIH, the National Institute of Design (India), Oracle, Random House, Samsung, SAP, Visa, and numerous agencies of the US government including the Federal Reserve Bank.

One early and important project was for Motorola. Between 1989 and 1992, AM+A designed the complete look-and-feel of a new "smart-car" navigation system that made novel use of GPS for vehicle navigation (Figs. 8.11–8.20). Another was for American Airlines, which AM+A did between 1994 and 1997, a project redesigning the user interface for the Sabre air travel reservation system (Figs. 8.31–8.55, 8.56, and 8.57–8.61). Sabre's original design, done 20 years previously for a 24-line × 80-character display with hard to remember input codes, had to be redesigned for the GUIs (graphical user interfaces) of the late 1990s. Also significant was the work in 2000 creating 100 concept designs for advanced functions/features of future Samsung mobile phones to be introduced into North America in 2003.

Chapters 7–10 present numerous other examples of the elegant and effective interaction designs and visual communications produced by AM+A. The reader should pay particular attention to Aaron's whimsical design of FaceBucks presented in Figs. 10.28–10.34.

Finally, let me speak of Aaron as a trailblazer, evangelist, and mentor. Aaron has given hundreds of tutorials about his work and his wisdom to tens of thousands of students worldwide. I will never forget Aaron's first visit to me in Toronto, long before we had laptop computers. He was schlepping about 20 slide trays containing hundreds of slides in two giant suitcases for one of his tutorials. He has also mentored over one hundred employees, contractors, and interns who worked or assisted at AM+A.

We will be forever indebted to Aaron for his important role in advancing the importance and the body of methods that allow us to design technology for human comprehension, speed of learning, and ease and enjoyment of use. This book is a fine testament to his lifetime of work aimed at these objectives.

University of Toronto   Ron Baecker
Toronto, ON, Canada
Columbia University
New York, NY, USA

Preface

Bridging Art, Design, and Technology: My Lifetime Work surveys my lifetime's work in several fields of art and design, especially, but not exclusively, works using or emphasizing technology, in particular human-computer interface design. The works also include graphic design and visible language experimentation. The pages show many factual details, images, and stories covering a wide variety of disciplines and media during approximately 1953–2025:

- Cartoons
- Computer art
- Computer graphics
- Conceptual art
- Concrete poetry
- Drawings and paintings
- Graphic design (books, exhibits, logos, posters, signs/symbols, etc.)
- Human-computer interface (HCI) design (for desktop computers, mobile phones, supercomputers, vehicles, etc.), including user-experience design, human factors, and ergonomics
- Information design and information visualization
- Photography
- Visible language experiments

I decided early on to organize the chapters for this book into a roughly chronologically order, with examples from the professional topics listed above. In the text are comments and solutions to these questions:

- What obstacles did I face? How did I overcome them?
- How did my upbringing in the Midwest; my years spent in Princeton, New Haven, Honolulu, Berkeley, and Jerusalem; or my travels in Europe, the Middle East, and Asia influence me and my work?
- What influences of the 1950s were most important for me? How? Why?
- What art and/or design ideologies most affected me or influenced me? How? Why?

- Which people (teachers, family members, friends, professionals) influenced me the most? How? Why?
- What childhood experiences influenced me the most? How? Why?
- What particular incidents stand out as signposts of later interests, career activities, professional attitudes, etc.?
- Who were my major mentors or helpers? In what way? (Examples: Emilio Ambasz, Umberto Eco, Gillette Griffin, Armin Hoffmann, Zenaide Luhr, Thomas Maldonado, Josef Mueller-Brockman, Paul Rand, Peter Simlinger, etc.)
- What events made me interested in computers, signs/symbols, technology, graphic design, typography, and writing systems (e.g., discovering pasigraphy, early interest in the history of the alphabet, learning Hebrew at an early age, comic book collecting, cartooning, etc.)?

This book is intended as a bridge or gateway between worlds. All my life I have been a kind of Janus-figure standing between two cultures, much as C. P. Snow discussed in decades past (see Snow, C. P., *Two Cultures*): between the humanities and the traditional art and design communities (specifically typography, printing, and traditional graphic design and visual arts) and the world of technology (computer graphics, computer-based telecommunication, and human-computer interaction).

The book's examples, themes, and issues reflect those combinations. Preparing the book has been a challenge, because many of the images are low-resolution, technical images, far from the pristine, crystal-clear images of many graphic designers. The user-interface projects are typically, and inevitably, of a technical, complex, and practical nature whose communication and/or semiotic requirements are more complex than many traditional graphic design projects whose primary objective is aesthetic appeal. The visible language experiments, concrete poetry, and conceptual artworks that appear are not the typical work of traditional graphic designers. The conceptual projects and the mobile persuasion-design projects described in the book required extensive text to explain their objectives, process, and accomplishments, more than a portfolio book for traditional graphic designers or artists.

Of particular importance for me is an emphasis on process: where I began on a project, what I did, and where it ended. In fact, this could be said of my entire life. Some of the initial fascinations with sign-communication began in my earliest childhood years and have endured during my life of 82 years.

It is to the publisher's credit that they permitted me this opportunity to recollect, to consider, and to contribute a perspective view about my life's work. I am grateful for the opportunity. It is also important and valuable that this book opens up communication to audiences beyond traditional "platforms" or "reach."

My hope is that audience for this book will include those interested in the following:

- Early human-computer interface design and computational/digital art
- History of computing
- Research and development centers of the twentieth century, e.g., Bell Labs, Microcomputer Technology Consortium (MCC), etc.

- Big Technology firms (our clients Apple, HP, Microsoft, Motorola, etc.)
- Twentieth-century digital design process
- Information design and information visualization
- Graphic design, its history, its impact
- Typography, symbol design, semiotics
- Conceptual art and typographic art (not necessarily digital)

My book's orientation and offerings are these:

- While most books on early technology focus on its application to science and defense, my book showcases the less-explored creativity and experimentation posed by early computer programming, decades before it exploded online.
- For early technology fetishists, the book offers a peek at obsolete yet very cool computers and technological processes of earlier eras, appealing to an emerging cult fan base.
- For those interested in the history of graphic design, the book offers insights into Swiss-German-oriented graphic design, information design and information visualization, visual/concrete poetry, typographic conceptual art, and more.
- In the era of Big Technology this book traces the hand-to-hand development of technology and design, demonstrating how advancements in technological tools opened up creative opportunities for a new generation of designers.
- The book also documents the practices and tools of early HCI design, a popular contemporary career field with few published histories.

What is my legacy? I would offer the following contributions:

- Improved how people interact with computer technology.
- Improved how graphic design and human-computer interaction design/experience design intersect.
- Contributed during many decades of professional practice, training, and creative innovation to what people experience today.
- Established links between my early work to what some people might take for granted today.
- Showed how I carried out my company's motto: "We help people make smarter decisions faster."

Berkeley, CA, USA   Aaron Marcus

Acknowledgments

I thank my many past clients for creating the opportunities to work on our many projects, and I thank my associates of AM+A for their help in completing the many projects.

Regarding the project figures: I have made every effort to determine permission for all figures, but in some cases I have not been able to locate or secure permission. I have done my best and am happy to correct the permissions in future editions of this book.

More specifically, among others, many of whom are now gone, who helped me to pursue my path through a life in visual communication, I acknowledge and thank the following:

Baecker, Ron, noted computer scientist, who patiently helped me to be a better writer and thinker.

Becker, Leslie, my second wife, who encouraged me to do good and opened my eyes to many aspects of design, art, and life.

Crumb, Robert, Cartoonist, whose publications helped me to see what could be drawn.

Eco, Umberto, Princeton Visiting Professor in the 1970s, who opened my eyes to visual semiotics.

Eisenman, Alvin, Chair of the Yale Graphic Design Department during my graduate years, who decided to take a chance on accepting me into his Department.

Firstenberg, Jean, formerly, head of Public Relations, Princeton University, who allowed me the freedom to take on and learn from many graphic design tasks.

Friedman, Rabbi Manis, who taught me about love and about religious commitment.

Griffin, Gillett, Princeton Curator of Graphic Arts Collection, who encouraged me as a photographer, calligrapher, and drawer and encouraged me to apply to Yale.

HaShem, who was there all along helping me, but I did not always realize it.

Hoffmann, Armin, Swiss graphic designer, who helped me to see how typography could dance.

Klass, Michael, UC Berkeley mathematician and friend from childhood, with whom I have enjoyed a lifetime of philosophical and religious conversations.

Luhr, Zenaide, my high-school art teacher, who taught me the basics of color and drawing, and encouraged me to explore.

Marcus, Libbie Burstein, my mother, who encouraged me with the greats of literature, art classes, a love of language, and a devotion to religious Judaism.

Marcus, Nate, my father, who was tolerant and, in the end, supportive of my pursuing personal and professional interests in which he did not share and in some ways did not understand.

Marcus, Stephen, my brother, who shared my first story-creation, science, and science-fiction interests from earliest childhood.

Marcus, Susan Wightman Douglas, my first wife, who was a partner in bringing two children into the world, who helped me to become more sophisticated, and patiently accompanied me on my first adventures in becoming an adult and parent.

Noll, A. Michael, Bell Labs Researcher, who enabled me to experiment with computer graphics and computer art in the 1960s.

Rand, Paul, Yale Graphic Design teacher, who opened my eyes to systems of form and visual play.

Rosenberg, Dan, Human Factors and UX leader at Kodak, Ashton-Tate, Oracle, SAP, who gave me many opportunities to explore while earning money to keep my efforts going.

Speier, Sandy, my wife, who helped me to become the best of myself through her patient, loving care and who helped review chapter texts for this book.

Tscholkowsky, Rabbi Chaim, Diasporah Yeshivah, Jerusalem, who stimulated and challenged me to learn about Rabbi Chayim Luzatto's (Ramchal's) theories of knowledge.

August 2025

Aaron Marcus and Associates   Aaron Marcus
Berkeley, CA, USA

Contents

Chapter 1
Origins in Omaha

Takeaways

This book is intended as an accounting of, explanation for, and analysis of the meaning/significance of my own work in visual design and visual art, specifically in the use of visible language, the physical forms of language expression, especially as computer technology enabled that expression to expand and achieve worldwide scale in the late twentieth century.

The book features many personal, memorable, funny, weird, and sometimes zany stories about my achievements, failures, successes, mistakes, interesting people I've met, obstacles encountered, and lessons learned along the way during the past three-quarters of a century.

Before Beginning…

Naturally, you're asking: Who, What, Why, When, and Where?…or, as my late brother Stephen (a″h) expressed it: What? So What? Now What?

This book is intended as an accounting of, explanation for, and analysis of the meaning/significance of my own work in visual art and visual design, specifically in the use of visible language, the physical forms of language expression, especially as computer technology enabled that expression to expand and achieve worldwide scale in the late twentieth century.

The book features many personal, memorable, funny, weird, and sometimes zany stories about my achievements, failures, successes, mistakes, interesting people I've met, obstacles encountered, and lessons learned along the way during the past three-quarters of a century.

A. Marcus, *Bridging Art, Design and Technology: My Lifetime Work*,
https://doi.org/10.1007/978-3-032-04342-9_1

Some of the themes I'll be discussing include the following:

- Digital art (an alternate word is "computer graphics" or "computer-assisted artwork")
- Computer graphics
- Computer (hardware and software) technology for human-computer interaction and communication
- Information-oriented graphic design, information design, and information visualization
- Applied visual semiotics
- Perceptual and conceptual visible-language art (perceptual are the Letraset images, conceptual are the conceptual pieces like Zero-Circle Around the Earth)
- Cartooning (I was a cartoonist for the Princeton Tiger, published my cartoons a few times, and have drawn hundreds, if not thousands, of cartoons in my diaries)
- Religious Judaism
- News media

I decided early on to organize the chapters for this book into a roughly chronologically order, with figures illustrating relevant work from the topics listed. Among the threads or themes woven into the text are comments, answers, or solutions to these questions:

- What obstacles did I face? How did I overcome them?
- How did my upbringing in the Midwest, my years living in Omaha, New Haven, Princeton, Jerusalem, Honolulu, and Berkeley, or my travels in Africa, Asia, Europe, Central America, the Middle East, South America, and North America influence me and my work?
- What influences of the 1950s were most important for me? How? Why?
- What art and/or design ideologies most affected me or influenced me? How? Why?
- Which people (teachers, family, friends, professionals) influenced me the most? How? Why?
- What childhood experiences influenced me the most regarding my future career? How? Why?
- What particular incidents stand out as signposts of my later interests, career activities, professional attitudes, etc.?
- Who were my major mentors or helpers? In what way? (e.g., Zenaide Luhr, Gillette Griffin, Paul Rand, Armin Hoffmann, Josef Mueller-Brockman, Emilio Ambasz, Thomas Maldonado, Umberto Eco, Peter Simlinger, etc.)
- What made me interested in computers, signs/symbols, technology, graphic design, typography, and writing systems?

In the Beginning

Like some American children born during/after World War II, I grew up in a typical, Midwestern, nuclear family, prepared for possible thermonuclear war. In 1954–1955, in the fifth grade of Belle Ryan School, Omaha, Nebraska, we all were compelled to learn to sing this song:

I like the United States of America.
I like the way we all live without fear.
I like to vote for my choice, speak my mind, raise my voice,
Yes, I like it here.
I like the United States of America.
I am thankful each day of the year.
For I can do as I please, 'cause I'm free as the breeze,
Yes I like it here.
I like to climb to the top of the mountain so high,
Lift my head to the sky,
And say how grateful am I
For the way that I'm working, and helping, and giving,
And doing the things I hold dear.
Yes, I like it, I like it, I like it here.
[Source: www.Angelfire.com. Copyright unknown. Fair use claimed]

At the same time, we practiced how to protect ourselves in case an atomic bomb were to be dropped on our school, or nearby: We were to crouch under our desks, which would provide us, we were told, with adequate protection. There was a high degree of probability that this nuclear attack might occur, because we were about 11 miles from Offutt Air Force Base, home of the US's Strategic Air Command, which kept a fleet of B-52 bombers circling the world ready to launch a counter attack upon any enemy (that would be Russia) foolish enough to send intercontinental-ballistic missiles (ICBMs) toward the USA.

At the same time, I was launched into Jewish airspace through "Conservadox" Sunday school, Hebrew school, religious service, and family practices.

My reading pleasures included most of DC Comics and almost all of science-fiction and horror comics, *MAD* magazine, and black-and-white television. When traveling in our family car, I always calculated in advance the estimated length of car rides and divided by 12 min, the approximate time necessary to read a 52-page, ten-cent comic book in order to know how much "literature" I needed to bring along to pass the time, in fact to make outside time and space disappear.

From my earliest years, I was fascinated with letterforms, alphabets, symbolism, and visual expression, including cartoons, illustrations, drawings, calligraphy, and, later, other forms of visual design and art.

My parents, Nate and Bebe Marcus (a"h), my younger brother Stephen Marcus (a"h), my Aunt Eva Marcus Ivener (a"h), my Uncle Maxie Marcus (a"h), my Aunt Saemi London Marcus (a"h), in fact all my aunts and uncles save one, are all dead (a"h). I mention those who have died with the Hebrew expressions *alav ha-Shalom*, *alehah ha-Shalom*, or *aleihem ha-Shalom*, peace be upon him/her/them, so that they may be duly honored upon first mentioning them in this text. May their memories be a blessing to those who knew and loved them.

I also acknowledge my teachers and mentors, and friends, such as Zenaide Luhr (RIP), my high-school art teacher (who taught me basic color theory and introduced me to famous artists through their published images), Gillett Good Griffin (RIP), who encouraged me to study/practice graphic design, Paul Rand (a"h), a noted graphic designer (who taught me about spatial layout grids) in graduate school, all of whom have died, and A. Michael Noll, a noted researcher in computer graphics at Bell Labs (who helped start my career in computer-based graphic design). Likewise, I wish to duly honor the living and the dead upon first mentioning them in this text. May their memories be a blessing to those who knew and loved them.

All of these people helped to influence me and, in part, to make me who I am. I am grateful to them.

Where We Are Headed

This book is intended as a gateway among worlds, especially design, art, and technology. All my life I have been a kind of Janus-figure standing between cultures, as C. P. Snow analyzed in decades past (see Snow, C.P. (1959). *The Two Cultures*, Cambridge, Cambridge University Press): between the world of the humanities; the traditional art and design communities, specifically typography, printing, and traditional graphic design and visual arts; and the world of technology, computer graphics, and computer-based telecommunication.

The book's examples, themes, and issues reflect this multi-valent combination. For Springer's publication series, the book has been a challenge, because some of the images are low-resolution, technical images, far from the pristine, crystal-clear images of most graphic designers. The user-interface projects are inevitably of a technical, complex, practical nature whose communication and/or semiotic requirements are more complex than many traditional graphic design projects whose primary objective is aesthetic appeal. The visible language experiments, concrete poetry, and conceptual artworks are not the typical work of many traditional graphic designers. The conceptual projects and the Machine (mobile persuasion design) projects described later require extensive text to explain their objectives, process, and accomplishments, more than a portfolio book of traditional graphic designers or artists.

Of particular importance is an emphasis on process: where I began on a project, what I did, and where I ended. In fact, this could be said of my entire life. Some of the initial fascinations with sign-communication began in my earliest childhood years and have endured during the past 70 years.

It is to Springer's credit that they permitted me this opportunity to recollect, to consider, and to form a perspective on my life's work, for which I am grateful.

The title of my book originally was going to be *Way Ahead of You in Another Direction: The Lifetime Work of Aaron Marcus*, from an expression of my beloved, late Executive Assistant, Ms. June Simonsen, a true British eccentric, who worked in my home office for about 5 years shortly after Aaron Marcus and Associates (AM+A) began in 1982. She was about 10 years older than me, had run her own public relations firm, taught herself to use an Apple Macintosh computer in about 1984, had outlived three husbands, had help to run guns from Toronto to Israel in 1948 (although she was not Jewish), and smoked small dark cigars, which she left half-unused hidden under my mailbox on the front porch. We were often engaged in debates about communication effectiveness of our marketing messages and project descriptions. She demanded that AM+A documents be "cr-r-rystal cl-l-lear" which she pronounced with distinct British clarity. When I tried to argue about her logic, she replied on more than one occasion, "I'm way ahead of you in another direction." I laughed. We battled passionately and then ended our debates to return to our desks. She was usually right, and I later had to admit that to her. Although we disagreed on some matters, I had much respect for her experience and wisdom.

The present title, which more clearly touches upon the book's content, better expresses my lifetime interest in and involvement with design, art, and technology.

Chapter 2
Beginnings in Art and Design

Takeaways
The origins of my lifelong interests in design and art came from artistic talents that I think I inherited from my father. From my mother I inherited my lifelong interest in books and languages. As a young child, I had many curious theories about the origins of babies and the functioning of my own eyes. I grew up as a nerdy geek, with a strong interest in science and art and very little knowledge of graphic design.

0–18 Years Old

Threads of my life have remained constantly important and prominent through eight decades.

What interested me as a small child continued to evolve through my school years, through my teaching years, through my professional design-studio years, and even are present and powerful in my life to this day. Consider my interest in and activities in science, mathematics, science fiction, art, typography/symbol systems, philosophy, languages, and religion.

Alas, to the chagrin of my father, I had little interest in sports and athletic/physical activities, except for ping pong, bowling, and ballroom dancing (which we all had to learn as grade-school students in the seventh grade). While I enjoyed reading, written literature was not as important to me, either reading or writing it, as it is for some of my peers. Although I self-published a small book of poems, *Songs*, I never considered these areas my strength. I love to sing and sang in school and synagogue choruses, but I did not push hard into singing, playing musical instruments, or going to musical performances…and regret it now. I never became devoted to theater and film, although I love to watch movies and have enjoyed going to theater performances. With my first wife, we once watched three movies in a row in New York City theaters. Two of them were *Taxi* and *Nashville* in about 1969.

A. Marcus, *Bridging Art, Design and Technology: My Lifetime Work*, https://doi.org/10.1007/978-3-032-04342-9_2

The preceding is a quick profile. I shall return to many of these themes in the chapters ahead.

My fascination with science fiction runs through many of my activities. As noted by other writers, what is exceedingly advanced may appear as magical. One might describe that as science fiction. What appears as science fiction may eventually become, through science and engineering, everyday reality. So it was with my own life. I designed/drew/built imaginary rocket ship control panels. Little did I realize I would one day help to design air traffic controller interfaces or control panels to help millions of people navigate through data space. It is interesting to note that Yuval Noah Harari in *21 Lessons for the 21st Century* (2018) states that science fiction is the most important genre of literature today because it deals with the issues/challenges of artificial intelligence (AI) and robotics.

Early Years: My Parents

My father, Nathan Marcus, was an immigrant to the USA in 1916 at the age of eight from Lvova, a small Ukrainian (Russian) village of about 300 people. He fled the pogroms against the Jews with his mother and older sister Essie to meet his father in the USA, who had been a wandering Jewish tailor in Russia. His father had already departed for the USA and had already settled in Omaha, Nebraska. I was told the location was determined by a throw of a dart onto a map in a Hebrew Immigration Aid Society (HIAS) office and/or else that the landscape and the weather were similar to the area east of Odessa: flat, cold in the winter, and near a river (Fig. 2.1).

My father, my Dad, had to fight a lot to keep from being picked on. He eventually hung around with Italians, East Europeans, Irish, and African Americans. He finished only two years of high school before he began to work for his father in the dry cleaning, pressing, and tailoring shop his father had established, The Bee Hive Cleaners. Dad ran away several times from Papa and Mama (Harry and Anna Tankelevich Marcus) (a″h) and rode boxcars/hitchhiked/walked to California, returning to Omaha when his money ran out. He phoned home for funds to be sent via Western Union to pay for his bus ride home. He even ran off to Chicago and, according to my father's stories, hung around with friends of Al Capone. He went to the scene of the St. Valentine's Day Massacre, 14 February 1929. He was good in sports and played semi-pro baseball as a young adult (Fig. 2.2).

Nine decades later, I saw a movie based on Al Capone's life. All the men in Capone's gang were dressed in a distinctly spiffy way. I was amazed. They all looked exactly like my father as he headed to my Aunt Sara's and Uncle Ruby's wedding in 1932 (Figs. 2.3 and 2.4):

Scarface was a barely disguised story of the rise, and death, of Al Capone. In the movie, Paul Muni plays Antonio "Tony" Camonte, who rises to the top of the South Side gangs, taking control of bootleg beer and wiping out the competition. George Raft plays another hoodlum.

Fig. 2.1 My father (center), about 8–10. His elder sister Esther, my paternal Aunt Essie (a″h) (left), and his younger sister, my paternal Aunt Sara (a″h) (right), in the USA. (Source: Photo in Aaron Marcus' collections, about 1913, Omaha, NE, photographer unknown. Used with Fair Use)

I marveled at the dapper duds of these hoodlums, thugs, murderers, and miscreants…and realized that Paul Muni and George Raft looked just like my father did!!! I assume that my father saw this movie and probably modeled some of his life path, behavior, and speech patterns on these guys. I do recall that Dad had a beautiful pair of brass knuckles that I occasionally had a chance to see, and he kept a 32-caliber revolver in his bedroom nightstand, just in case some "boogoolars," as he called them, might break in.

Fortunately, he had my mother to "save him" from a "life of crime" (my interpretation), from a path that would have led him from juvenile delinquency to possibly adult delinquency. At least that is my inherited wisdom/mythology of their marriage and life paths. It was a different era….

I looked again at the dashing fellow (see Fig. 2.3) dressed for paternal Aunt Sara's marriage in 1932 to Uncle Ruby, at which I believe he was photographed, and

Fig. 2.2 *Chicago Daily News* reports on the St. Valentine's Day Massacre. (Source: Internet, source not found, fair use claimed)

Fig. 2.3 Photo of Nate Marcus, dressed up for a wedding in 1932 of his younger sister, Sara Marcus to Irving Ruben (a"h). (Source: Photo in the collection of Aaron Marcus. Photographer: Nelson Studios, Omaha. Unlocatable, Fair Use Claimed)

Fig. 2.4 Photo of Nate Marcus in the 1930s. (Source: Photo in the collection of Aaron Marcus. Date, photographer, and occasion unknown. Fair use claimed)

I was bathed with a warm glow of nostalgia, sadness for all those who are not with us any more, with admiration for all the good that he managed to do in his life, and the happiness that my children could know him for some years of their childhood. He and Mom certainly did love my own children madly…:-)…

My mother, Libbie Burstein Marcus (a”), was born in Omaha in 1916, the year my father arrived in the USA from Ukraine (then part of Russia). Her mother Jennie Gerstein Burstein Turkel had grown up in Kiev, Ukraine, and had come from Russia with her mother Pearl Gerstein (a″h) and her brother Harry (a″h) to the USA via

Hamburg, Germany, to Galveston, Texas, the USA's second largest immigration port, where many East European Jews were processed, because Ellis Island was too busy and New York was thought by some German Jews there to be too full of (East European) Jews. Her father, Aaron (Archie/Harry) Burstein, had emigrated from Kolnow, Poland. Mom grew up as a quiet girl, studious and serious. She had several siblings to help care for, being the firstborn. She advanced several grades in grade school and consequently graduated from Omaha Central High School at the age of 16. She did well, studied Latin, took photography extracurricular courses, and liked literature. She had a small collection of the *Wizard of Oz* books. She read many of her books and children's books to my brother Stephen and me as small children.

She met my father through his sister, my paternal Aunt Eva (a″h). My Mom and Aunt Eva somehow met, played together, and were friends after high school. Mom encouraged me in my studies and artistic career throughout my growing-up years. And my father was a natural-born, self-trained folk-artist.

My father served in the US Army during World War II. He was stationed at an army camp in Dothan, Alabama. He never went overseas but was involved in Alabama with aircraft maintenance. I did not see him much for several years after my birth. Later, he took over running the Bee Hive Cleaners from his father. My mother sometimes assisted with bookkeeping and taking orders from walk-in customers. He ran that business until he retired (Fig. 2.5).

All during his life, my father carved and made "artworks" as folk art. Sometimes he used bullets, artillery shells, and aircraft parts to design lamp bases. Sometimes he carved signs and photo frames. Sometimes, in later life, he glued hundreds, perhaps thousands, of small kitsch objects, like miniature people, cartoon characters,

Fig. 2.5 My father, mother, and myself, about 1945. (Source: Family photos, photographer unknown)

and "googly eyes" into the small spaces intended for pieces of hand-set type in California job cases, which once had been standard devices that printers used to hold hand-set type. Making construction artworks like these occupied much of his time after he retired.

In retirement, my mother volunteered at the Omaha Jewish Community Center Library, returning to the world of books.

My Early Years

I was told that I did not begin speaking until the age of three...unusually late it seems.

(A Google search states: Most (but not all) toddlers can say about 20 words by 18 months and 50 or more words by the time they turn 2. By age 2, kids are starting to combine two words to make simple sentences, such as "baby crying" or "Daddy big." From: Delayed Speech or Language Development—KidsHealth, m.kidshealth. org/en/parents/not-talk.html, retrieved 9 Jan 2018.)

For what was I waiting? Was this delay a sign of autism? I am not sure. I more than made up for the delay by loving to learn new words throughout my childhood and using them whenever I could.

From my earliest years, I seem to have enjoyed inventing stories of imaginative fantasy-fiction. When my late brother Stephen was five and I was seven, we shared a single bedroom near 30th Street and Capital Avenue in Omaha, Nebraska, and we slept in bunk beds. I was in the upper bunk. We had a nightly ritual: when our mother had read to us and turned out the lights, Stephen and I would talk quietly and ask each other if we wanted to tell Katzy and Baby stories, about our two teddy bears, who were characters in adventures that we would make up.

I know for certain that some of the stories involved flying to other planets, including to one planet in which we observed a strange phenomenon: babies grew on trees, like fruit. First their heads appeared; gradually they grew larger and longer, with complete bodies, until they were "ripe" and consequently "were born" by falling from the tree limb and running around on the ground. We had invented a birth narrative that, perhaps, satisfied our curiosity about the origin of babies. I remember that our mother was 32 years old at the earliest date I can remember. This would have been in 1948, when I was five.

Another of our childhood stories involved an advanced rocket ship that Katzy (my teddy bear) piloted, with Baby at his side. At one point, needing to make a navigation decision, Katzy had to consult his *Big Book of Knowledge*. This document was a very thick book, like a very large paper dictionary or very large Bible of the time, with its two curved mounds of pages sweeping downward from their crests around the spine toward the left and right edges, like great waves. In this book could be found the answer to *every* question. Katzy searched, then read, then determined the solution to his query. This was about 1948–1950. We had invented a form of Google, or at least a paper version of something like the ideas introduced by

Vannevar Bush in the 1930s, the Memex project. I do not know if we had been introduced to such concepts. Probably, we just invented them ourselves from everyday life experiences. What is curious to me is the focus on documents, book design, information design, and a document that helped people make smarter decisions faster, the slogan of my own design firm 34 years later.

[In 1945, Vannevar Bush published the essay "As We May Think" in which he predicted that "wholly new forms of encyclopedias will appear, ready made with a mesh of associative trails running through them, ready to be dropped into the memex and there amplified".…. The memex influenced generations of computer scientists, who drew inspiration from its vision of the future. [Source: Wikipedia, including the reference: Bush, Vannevar (July 1945). "As We May Think." *The Atlantic Monthly.* Retrieved 20 April 2012.]

I remember several odd theories I had when I was about 5–8:

• I thought that my eyes were two cameras. I knew about cameras, their lenses, and the rolls of film they required. Perhaps this awareness came from my seeing my mother's Kodak Brownie camera, which she had used in high school during an extracurricular photography class (I did not see her photos until about 60 years later). In any case, I decided that my eyeballs had two lenses and the "film" was the whites of the eyes. I had to keep the eyes in synch with regard to using up the film, or I would go blind in one eye (I didn't consider the end result of going blind in both eyes when I ran out of film). Consequently, by intuition, I "felt" which eye was more advanced and would blink the other shut to even out the use of film in each of my eyes. I don't know what people thought when I would occasionally slip into an "eyeball film-balancing" ritual.

• I distinctly remember thinking that my maternal Grandma Jennie was "downstairs" in a small hole in the cement runner to the left of the steps leading up to our duplex on Capital Avenue. Why I formed this notion, I cannot say. As a result, I always knew if she were not around, that she must be down there "doing the laundry," and I could talk with her. I held numerous one-sided conversations with her. I don't know what people thought if they observed me talking to a hole in the ground.

• I had a maroon topless (convertible) toy car about one meter long, moved by my pushing its two pedals. I guess my father had bought it for Stephen and me. I recall that I considered it the funniest thing in the world to pedal furiously, sending the car hurtling down the pavement in front of our duplex. I would then drive it up onto Ms. Beckman's small lawn, which lay directly west of our duplex and crash it gently into a bush or a tree or the tall grass, stopping my madcap trip. I laughed uproariously every time I performed this ritual; I repeated the process numerous times, so much so, that my sides ached, and I was in danger of falling out of the car at the end of my trip. Ms. Beckman, sometimes sitting on her front porch, would begin to laugh with me, caught up by my manic laughter. She would ask me what I was laughing about. I would tell her between gasps for breath that I had no idea why I was laughing.

Regarding my interest in science, especially astronomy, my paternal Uncle Maxie Marcus, my father's younger brother, who was then unmarried and who had no children, took a great interest in my brother and me. As a gift in 1952, when I was nine, he presented Stephen and me with a three-inch reflecting telescope, a SkyScope™, which I have kept and use occasionally to this day. Even though the telescope was simply a cardboard tube fitted with some metal bands and a concave mirror at the bottom end, and small metal viewing tubes, its 60- and 120-power lenses provided excellent views of the moon, Mars, Jupiter, and Saturn, and some of the latter's moons, as well as occasional views of my neighbors. These exciting experiences furthered my interest in science and mathematics, which influenced my schooling for decades.

For example, with the help of my father and mother, in about sixth grade at Belle Ryan Grade School (1954–1955), I made a puppet theater out of two wooden orange crates (one for the stage and one for the pedestal that supported the stage. I painted white pinpoint stars on a black stage background. With permission of Ms. Harrison, my teacher, I presented a trip through the solar system. I drew, then painted colored images of each of the planets, glued them to cardboard, and mounted a black coat-hanger wire to the back of the cardboard so that I could deftly make them sail by the "porthole" of the spaceship viewed by the audience. I wrote the script, also, with whatever facts I could find about each of the planets, ending with Pluto. Pluto had not yet been demoted from planet-hood in those years.

Sometime during high school in an after-school course in electronics, I built a crystal radio from scratch. I did not have enough money to buy a prepared kit from Heathkit Electronics, but it was fun, and exciting, to recreate the steps taken in the first years of AM radio broadcasting.

Regarding typography and printing: At the age of about eight or nine in the third or fourth grade (1951–1954), I already had been given a small "toy" metal printing press. On the cylindrical printing-press drum, I could set rows of rubber letters in order to print and publish "newsletters" of neighborhood news. I think I circulated these publications around my block. I left them on the porches of neighbors up and down my street of white clapboard houses. On another occasion at around that time, I took Grandma's old Victrola phonograph apart, removing the large wooden, lami-nated sound-horn from the main equipment, namely, the heavy-headed reading arm with its sharp, removable needles. Placing the end of the sound-horn against my lips, I simply announced the news and made-up radio programs as I walked along the streets. I must have been something of a nuisance. These early and simple con-nections to typography, printing, publishing, and news no doubt led to my later interests in professions that combined these techniques and disciplines. Certainly, it seemed to lead to my becoming the editor of my high-school newspaper and art edi-tor of my college humor magazine.

Around this same time of third to sixth grades, my parents, who could not afford to purchase an entire encyclopedia, had acquired just one volume of the Funk and Wagnalls *New World Encyclopedia*, probably a giveaway incentive from Hinky Dinky's, a grocery store chain in Omaha, Nebraska.

(*Internet note*: "Unicorn Press, later known as the Standard Reference Work Publishing Co., obtained the rights to publish the encyclopedia, and by 1953 that firm began to sell the encyclopedia through a supermarket continuity marketing campaign, encouraging consumers to include the latest volume of the encyclopedia on their shopping lists." Source: Wikipedia, checked 9 January 2018.)

Our volume, the first, naturally devoted its contents to many of the words beginning with the letter A (perhaps Aardvark to Azimuth). Even though I possessed but one book, the subject matter fascinated me. Two special components stand out in my memory. Under Anatomy, there appeared an explanatory image of the full human body in layers printed on full-page sheets of plastic so that one could lift off the skin and upper organs to reveal lower organs, muscles, bones, etc. I remember being startled by the beautiful colors of the interior of the human body. This kind of information visualization inspired me, I think, to focus decades later on information-oriented graphic design.

The other image that captured my imagination was under Alphabet. A full-page table showed the letters A to Z along the left, with about five columns of earlier forms of the writing signs going back thousands of years to Hebrew and Phoenician symbols, Egyptian hieroglyphs, and Babylonian Cuneiform writing. I was fascinated by the idea that letterforms had evolved with such elaborate twists, turns, substitutions, and other transformations. This single image has intrigued me for almost 70 years. In some ways it inspired or catalyzed some of my visible language artworks decades later.

I remember in my earlier years, perhaps when my younger brother Stephen and I were about six and eight, and even later, that my father would dress us and himself in exactly the same clothes, including dress slacks and sport jackets. We were miniatures of him, "Mini-me's." That was the way wholesome, Midwestern, nuclear families did things. Another facet of our "training" was that, whenever my father whistled using his two baby fingers, when we heard the piercing noise, we were to stop whatever we were doing and run immediately to where he was and stand in the military "at-ease" position in front of him, with our hands linked in back of us, to await his report and/or our orders. We thought this was normal and fun. It was a sign of respect to obey his requests. I'm not sure when that practice ended. I do remember that at some point, perhaps when I was ten, that my mother, putting me over her knees to deliver a spanking, realized that I was laughing or at least not much in pain. We both knew then that this particular era of discipline was over. It was the early 1950s.

In later years of elementary school, perhaps seventh through eighth grades, I loved working with Speedball lettering pen sets. I had a large number of pen points. One of my favorite shopping stores was Brain's Art Supplies in Omaha, Nebraska, where the smell of Arabic gum erasers, new pencils, oil paint, and turpentine was exhilarating. I would usually come away quite high, literally, or at least giddy from the experience of all these mysterious and wonderful art supplies and pieces of equipment. I bought as much as my small allowance permitted.

I loved comics, as seen in the Sunday paper, the *Omaha World-Herald*, and in comic books, which I started reading at an early age. I also went to see Superman movies in serial form at a nearby theater where my maternal grandmother sold tickets...

When I was in about third grade, or perhaps fourth, at Henry W. Yates grade school, I got into a fight with a fellow student Danny Keenan. The subject of our dispute was whether Captain Marvel was stronger or not than Superman. I thought it was so obvious that Superman was the superior superhero. One thing led to another in our shouting and scuffling, and, unfortunately, I shoved him. As he turned around, he collided with a flagpole, chipping one of his front teeth. Alas, it might not have been a baby tooth. I felt terrible, embarrassed, and guilty about my behavior. I apologized to him and his mother who came to help him. Nevertheless, I privately thought he was ridiculous for championing Captain Marvel....

I used to go to the drugstore at 30th and Dodge Streets often, perhaps that was the West Dodge Pharmacy. It was on the northeast corner of the intersection. I enjoyed reading the comic books on the revolving wire comic-book holder. Perhaps at that time I began my lifelong interest in comics and to collect comics. This passion became somewhat all-consuming during my later grade-school years and into high school. I used to wonder how I could collect 18 brands of comics monthly when I received only 50 cents per week allowance or maybe $1.50 per month. I am not sure how much. It seemed like I was paying out more than I was receiving from my parents....:)...

Grandma at times also lived in her own house on Turner Boulevard, where once Stephen (a″h) and I accidentally set fire to things in the storage compartment under the stairs. I had somehow found some matches and thought it was exciting and fun to strike them and let them burn out. One of them must have fallen on papers or textiles. Fortunately, someone smelled smoke and came to investigate. We were admonished, chastised, maybe even spanked. I can't recall.

As for frightening movies, one of my earliest memories is seeing the *Wizard of Oz* in a theater in Omaha, Nebraska. Because it was released in 1939, I am not sure how old I was when Mom took Stephen and me. All I can recall among other images is the amazing change of black-and-white into color imagery when Dorothy alights in the Land of Oz, and the scene with the Evil Witch commanding her Monkey Warriors to fly to attack the good foursome heading to the Oz Palace. This scene of flying monkeys was so terrifying to me that I had to hide my head under my coat or maybe Mom's coat, and I might have been crying. Even today when I see the scene, as I have numerous times in the past recent decades, the scene evokes a certain shudder in me.

I can't recall the first movie I saw. I do know I relished the Saturday morning or early afternoon serials at the Circle Theater where Grandma was the ticket seller. In those days, as some may recall, the theater would have some kind of live entertainment before the kids movies. Prizes would be lined up along the front of the stage, and kids would be selected by some means to answer questions. At one point I was selected, and I won some kind of toy. I don't recall what.

I also remember that Mom would take Stephen and me to some movies, perhaps to help pass the time while she did downtown shopping or some other errand. She would leave us in the back row of the Orpheum movie theater, where Grandma worked, just in front of the velvet curtains that ran along a short wall defining the back limit of the movie theater. She would bring in (sneak in) hamburgers and French fries with lots of ketchup (yum yum) with a beverage for us to enjoy during the movie, and then depart, picking us up later. I am not sure how old we were. Perhaps 6 and 8. Today, this might seem a bit reckless on her part, although deemed necessary under her circumstances, but then it seemed perfectly OK and safe. What I remember most vividly was that when the hero and heroine involved in some caper or activity became romantically entwined and hugged and kissed, Stephen and I both thought that was so "mushy," "yucky," and embarrassing that we hid our faces behind the velvet curtain so we would not be subjected to such passion! Tee hee.

Another memorable, formative moment was when, in some black-and-white movie, I saw an attorney in court rustling some documents he held up for the judge saying something like, "I have these documents, your Honor." I was so impressed by the two or three sheets of paper, and the sounds the paper made while rustling against each other, that I was overcome with desire to have documents of my own. How odd. When I went home, I asked Mom for several sheets of typing paper and resolved to make my own documents. At the top of the first sheet I wrote "Document A" and at the top of the second sheet, I wrote "Document B." Now came the question: What exactly does a document contain? I had no idea and left them blank. However, I did raise up the two sheets in front of me, as I had seen in the movies, and rustled them together. They made a satisfying sound of paper sheets crinkling and scraping gently against each other. I was satisfied! Ahhhhh.... I had created my own documents and relived that glorious sound experience seen in the movies....

Perhaps that experience led to my interest in documenting everything. So much so, that my friends and family later made fun of me for being so obsessive-compulsive about it. Many decades later, after I had met in 2009 Bruce Robertson (RIP), the co-founder of the Diagram Group (Diagram Visual Information, Ltd.) in London, at the Vision+09/DD4D conference in Paris, 18–20 June 2009, he sent me a cartoon he had drawn of myself photographing the toilet where I had just made a bodily deposit (Fig. 2.6).

Even to this day, I have black 9 × 12-inch bound drawing notebooks that act as my diaries of everything that has happened and everyone I have met since about 1964. This represents about five running feet of bookshelves in my home office.... but I digress....

In the fifth through eighth grades, because of my interest and early drawing ability, I had taught myself to draw comic characters in the style of many popular comics: Al Capp's Li'l Abner and Daisy Mae; the Disney characters, such as Donald Duck and his family, Huey, Dewey, and Louis; Minnie Mouse, Goofy, Pluto, Scrooge McDuck, and others. I noticed carefully the different ways in which the cartoonists used thick and thin lines, shading, textures, lighting, and positioning of a character's body. For some reason, I did not attempt to create comic books, as the famous R. Crumb had done in his own childhood. I think I was fascinated with the ability to capture emotions, of creating characters or personalities, and the ability to create spaces and contexts at will.

Fig. 2.6 Cartoon by Bruce Robertson, 24 June 2009. (Source: Personal collection of author)

In later years in high school, I learned to draw in the style of several artists on the staff of *MAD magazine*, especially Basil Wolverton, whose grotesque faces were popular among readers of *MAD* and other publications (Fig. 2.7).

I also learned to draw in the style of illustrators of science-fiction magazines and comic books (Figs. 2.8 and 2.9).

As I mentioned earlier, by the time I reached high school, I was a comic-book addict and collected about 18 brands. I especially loved the science-fiction/horror fantasy comics of EC Publications. I had also discovered science fiction. I seem to recall that somewhere in my junior year, I finally figured out how to draw girls/women, either clothed or not, and could study/draw faces that I thought were especially attractive. I also drew men, often Marlon Brando or Elvis Presley-style "hoodlums" with large pompadours of shining hair with remarkable highlights. I suppose their dangerous behavior fascinated me.

During these years, also, I had fallen in love with automobiles, and I was overwhelmed when the *Saturday Evening Post* published *all* the 1957 cars viewed from the side. My heart-throb was the 1957 Chevrolet Impala, with its sweeping tail fins

Fig. 2.7 Fantasy political poster by the author based on *MAD* drawing by Basil Wolverton, about 1960. (Source: Author's photo documentation of his early artwork)

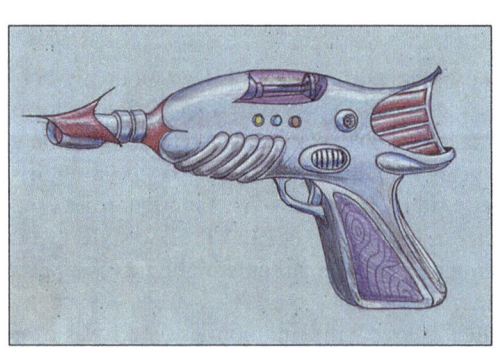 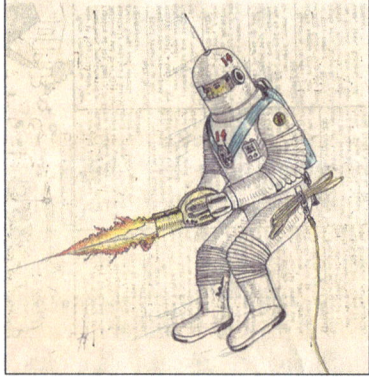

Figs. 2.8 and 2.9 Science-fiction drawings by the author, about 1960. (Source: Author's collection of original drawings)

and its hooded eyes, the front head lights. Of course, I was also partial to the Ford Mustang and the Chevrolet Corvette. I was fascinated by "Cars of the Future" or "dream-cars" that were featured in news stories and advertisements. I even sent away to different companies requesting publicity photos, which I received and collected. Like many youngsters (and adults) I was fascinated with these images of the future. America was headed to an awe-inspiring realm of future cities with amazing gadgets, homes, and means of travel. They inspired me to continue to draw images of the future.

Beginning when I was about eight, or possibly a year or two earlier, I was fascinated by dinosaurs, astronomy, and science fiction. I read with devoted interest Jules Verne's *Twenty Thousand Leagues Under the Sea*, probably my first science-fiction novel. I also read Edgar Rice Burroughs' *John Carter of Mars* and, later, Robert Heinlein's *Stranger in a Strange Land*. As with so many other youngsters, "grok" (to deeply understand) became one of my favorite buzzwords. My favorite authors included Arthur C. Clarke, Ray Bradbury, C.K. Dick, and Isaac Asimov.

I enjoyed immensely reading and collecting pulp science-fiction magazines like *Galaxy*, *If*, *Amazing*, and others. Because I was/am an inveterate collector, I still have most of those magazines and pocket books, including my treasured copies of Ace "double-feature" books that included half the book printed upside down with two "front covers." Chesley Bonestell and Virgil Finlay were some of my most beloved illustrators, and I succeeded in copying their drawing/painting styles. I made hundreds of drawings of space ships, orbiting satellites, men in space suits, ray guns, robots, damsels in distress, alien creatures, other-world landscapes, future vehicles, and future cities (see Figs. 2.9 and 2.10). Fortunately, my mother saved many/most of these drawings.

I loved *LIFE* magazine's articles and later illustrated books about the origins of life on earth and the origins of humankind. I adored poring over these large-scale illustrations with all of their lavish, detailed full-color illustrations.

(*Note*: "The World We Live In" appeared in the pages of *LIFE* magazine from December 8, 1952, to December 20, 1954. A science series, it comprised 13 chapters published on an average of every 8 weeks. Written by Lincoln Barnett, *The World We Live In* spanned a diverse range of topics concerning planet Earth and the universe and employed the talents of countless artists and photographers. These included, among others, cameramen Alfred Eisenstaedt and Fritz Goro, and artists Rudolph Zallinger and Chesley Bonestell.... For the gatefold, Rudolph Zallinger's "Age of Reptiles" mural was used; however, the version in *The World We Live In* was Zallinger's preliminary, detailed study. The actual mural in the Peabody Museum is significantly different." [Source: Wikipedia, accessed 9 January 2018.]) (Figs. 2.10 and 2.11).

(*Note*: "The Epic of Man" article series in *LIFE* magazine ran from 1955 to 1957 and appeared as a book in 1961, published by Time, Inc. for *LIFE* magazine, and written by the editors. The fold-out painting on pages 51–52 of "Fishing and Fowling" was painted by Caroll Jones and Larry Burrows, courtesy of the Danish National Museum, except the mace head at the right of the picture. Larry Burrows courtesy of Gothenburg Museum.)

Figs. 2.10 and 2.11 Illustrations from *LIFE* magazine's articles and later Time-Life books about prehistoric times. (Source: Author's photos from his copies of the books from Life/Time-Life. "The Age of Reptiles," a mural by Rudolph F. Zallinger. Copyright Yale Peabody Museum. Courtesy of the Yale Peabody Museum)

I remember meeting decades later Rudolph Zallinger, the artist who painted the dinosaurs in the museum and in the book, at Yale's Peabody Museum of Natural History when I was a graduate student. I was in awe of him and overcome with emotion at meeting someone who had had such an emotional impact on me as a child. It was like anyone as an adult meeting a childhood hero in real life later.

Beginning at the age of eight in 1951, I became a lifelong reader of *Scientific American*, because my parents bought me my first subscription, perhaps recognizing my slightly out-of-the-ordinary interest in science and art. I have maintained my subscription to that publication for more than 70 years.

Already by the early 1950s, I had become an unofficial member of the Young Nerds of America (if such an organization exists).

While peer males in my cohort were beginning to memorize baseball statistics and to collect baseball cards, I inherited from my Uncle Al (later Dr. Alvin Burstein) books about algebra and my first copy of the *CRC Handbook of Chemistry and*

Physics, which contained countless mathematical expressions, statistics, measurements, and formulas. Sometime around the age of eight, my Uncle Al taught me the elements of algebra, which I thought was exceedingly interesting and exciting. While my peers could rattle off sports teams and players, my passion was memorizing the value of pi to 50 decimal places:

3.14159265358979323846264338327950288419716939937510…

Even today, I can still remember the value and recite it to 21 decimal places.

I also loved obscure, cryptic technical terminology. While my peers learned a basic four-letter-word vocabulary for use with insults, I fashioned my own scathing epithet to be used in confrontations:

You radical, oxidating Cro-magnon, masticating Neanderthal protoplasm, with the body of a brontosaurus, the head of triceratops, and a brain that is a cross between a protozoa and an amoeba!

There. That took care of the situation. Ahh, I would probably wait smugly, confident that my opponent was so overcome with shame, or at least astonishment, that I could walk safely away, unaware that I was about to be pummeled to the ground.

My nuclear family was an early participant in the world of television beginning in about 1953. Television began broadcasting in the USA in 1948. My parents had to go to New York City to speak with US Military or government officials to enable my father to avoid being drafted for the Korean War. He had already served in World War II and was now a family man for almost a decade (they were successful). While they were away, they *rented* a television set, the only one on the block. The apparatus was a large wooden cabinet, perhaps 2 ft wide and 4 ft tall, with a small black-and-white screen about 6–8 inches measured diagonally. Despite the small size, we were hooked. When we moved into our new home in the summer of 1954, we had a newer television. Over the next decade, I became a regular viewer of the changing seasons of *Howdy Doody*; *Kukla, Fran, and Ollie*; *The Hit Parade*; *I Love Lucy*; *The Twilight Zone*; *The Milton Berle Show*; Phil Silvers; Red Skelton; Ed Sullivan; Sid Caesar; Ernie Kovacs (one of my favorites); Dinah Shore; Disneyland specials; and of course the *Mickey Mouse Club*. I had no idea I was being brainwashed into American culture. I lapped it up happily.

(*Note:* 1948: Four television networks (NBC, CBS, ABC, and DuMont), broadcasting over 128 stations, began a full prime-time schedule (8–11 pm, Eastern Time), 7 days a week. Source: 27 December 2016, from *Television in the US: History and Production*, Northern State University, [www.northern.edu/wild/th100/tv.htm, accessed 9 January 2018.])

I should mention, as a side note, that my family was a test family for Tang, the breakfast drink of the US astronauts. The orange-powdered bottles were a staple of our family for a while. Only about four decades later did I read about the questionable characteristics of this chemical concoction and noted that it was reported to be an excellent dishwashing-machine stain-remover. I found it was still available in some stores and tried it. Yes, my dishwasher was sparkling clean…as perhaps was my stomach decades earlier.

In about 1954–1955, I had begun to construct a rocket ship control panel in the basement of our new home, further west in Omaha; I fashioned my first device out of electronic and mechanical parts affixed to a wooden fruit or vegetable box. I had scavenged the components from my father's basement workshop or found and collected them many years earlier, 1952–1954, searching diligently through the trash bins of my neighbors along an alley behind our former home. The trash bins were all conveniently aligned along a back alley separating our side of the block from the other. I even found thermometers and broke open the tubes, fascinated by the mysterious liquid metal inside, which I combined into large blobs and played with the substance in the palm of my hand. I had no idea that the mercury metal was seriously poisonous and should not be handled.

In the basement of my new home, I had an assortment of knobs, dials, gauges, radio vacuum tubes, household light bulbs, flashlight parts, electrical wire, and even small buttons purchased at novelty stores to make lights blink on and off when inserted into the bulb bases. I could then build my first rocket ship control device, to which I gave the official name of "Radical hydroscopic lunar-dimensional sinuspectrum tabulating bi-trometer ratio communicating radio." I called it my "Googoo Machine" for short. I gradually built the walls of my rocket ship control room out of bed sheets stretched around a corner of the basement outside of my basement study room (called the MAD Room after the disliked names of my two friends and myself, *Maurice* Jerome Frank (RIP), *Aaron* "Buddy" Marcus, and Richard *Durland* Clark (RIP)) (Fig. 2.12).

My disliked name was Aaron. Until I graduated from college, I was known as Buddy. That moniker may come as a shock to those who have met me later in my life. The name Buddy was, supposedly, derived from the letters BUD on a wrist

Fig. 2.12 The Googoo Machine, a "rocket ship control panel." (Source: Author's family photos, photographer: Aaron Marcus, probably 1955–1956)

bracelet used by the hospital in Omaha, Nebraska, in which I was born, to identify myself as a baby. Naturally, my father, born in Lvova, a small village of about 300 east of Odessa in the south Ukraine, or Russia at the time, an army veteran, and representative of the 1940s and 1950s, probably came to call me his little buddy, and the name stuck. In fact, there were a number of names in my mother's family all starting with B: My mother Libbie Burstein Marcus was called Bebe (a″h). My Aunt Ethel Burstein Bernstein (a″h) was called Bubbles as a girl. My Uncle Alvin Burstein (a″h) was called Bingo as a boy. So it went… (Only after high school did I "upgrade" my name to my given name.)

With the rocket ship control room, my brother Stephen and I could take imaginary flights to other planets to "to boldly go where no one has gone before," as *Star Trek* would conceive such adventures decades later.

Unlike many of my Jewish peers, I liked afternoon Hebrew school. The ability to learn a new writing system, a new language, and to absorb the history of the Jewish people and the land of Israel was interesting, engaging, significant, meaningful, and absorbing. Around the age of 12, I recall becoming very devoted to attending synagogue services and observing *mitzvoth*, or commandments. Although I could take the bus, I preferred to walk the 36 blocks from my house on the south side of Dodge Street, which was the east-west bisector of the city, to the north side. It was almost a straight journey north, but jogged from 58th Street west of the Missouri River to 52nd Street, a few blocks east. I think, also, the system of thought, of debates about the meaning of life, the nature of good and evil, and the cycle of time, all appealed to my philosophical and religious interests. It was to be a lifelong devotion.

As a fitting bar mitzvah gift at the age of 13 in 1956, I received from my Uncle Al a very lovely pocket slide rule, complete with leather holder and pocket clip, by which I could quickly do varied mathematical functions with an accuracy of three decimal places. I still have this treasured gift. As one can easily understand, I was a young nerd, or geek. In high school and college, I even used plastic chest-pocket protectors for my many pens and pencils. To complete the image, I had very thick black-framed glasses of the style that Buddy Holly also favored until his early death.

Throughout my later years in grade school and high school (7th through 12th grades, 1955–1961) I continued to involve myself with letterforms, typography, graphic design, and publication design. The odd thing was, I never learned that there was a profession of graphic design, although I was aware of Disney animation artists, typographic/lettering artists, and someone who drew and lettered comics.

In grade school, there were art classes in which I learned basic color theory while I stumbled through self-discoveries of cartooning, lettering, and designing/preparing newsletters. I attended art classes as a young child at Joslyn Art Museum in Omaha.

High School, September 1957–June 1961

On 4 October 1957, the Soviet Union successfully launched Sputnik 1, the size of a beach ball, into low earth orbit. The Space Age had been launched, also. The USA was worried about its technological leadership. One result was the creation of

Advanced Placement courses in science and mathematics in high schools. I was fortunate to participate in these courses at Central High School. The focus fit in with my interests in science and mathematics and seemed to lead me to a future career in science, or so I thought.

I also took 4 years of studying Latin, which I enjoyed immensely. My mother had studied Latin at Central High, also, graduating in 1932, and I had her pocket Latin dictionary. My friend Jerry Frank and I became so devoted to our studies that we would speak Latin to each other in his father's car as we drove 30 min from home to school. Our using this "alien" language would sometimes infuriate his father, who could not understand what we were saying, and he would demand that we speak "American."

In high school, I also always took art classes and befriended Ms. Zenaide Luhr (RIP), the art teacher, one of my favorites. She was a blonde, European in many ways, outspoken, zany beatnik-type of person, who upgraded my earlier study of color and composition and encouraged me in many of my art and design activities. Unfortunately, there was then little instruction or education in design per se. At home, I designed scores of posters mimicking content and themes from *MAD* magazine and covered with my posters the walls of my study room in the basement and even its ceiling when I ran out of wall space. I designed wall mural decorations for my Rayim Jewish boys' club parties; designed posters for high-school events; became the editor of the *Register*, the Omaha Central High School (CHS) newspaper; and drew countless cartoons. I still was ignorant of the serious study of typography and layout, the history of visual communication, and the profession of graphic design.

Beginning in my sophomore year, I enrolled in the Reserve Officers' Training Corps (ROTC); this was actually a choice to avoid having to sign up for athletics, in which I had little interest. As a result, I was required to dress every Tuesday and Thursday in a complete ROTC uniform, a hot, scratchy wool material, which began quickly to smell badly. Although Central was a meeting place for many races and cultures, I did not normally socialize or meet with Black kids. I did not encounter many Blacks in my advanced placement classes. However, in ROTC I did meet with many and had practice sessions/classes. The classes were led by white men in uniform who sometimes showed movies about military preparedness and extolled the virtues of military life. What I remember most were the oddity of watching our leader in front of the class occasionally scratch his testicles as he spoke and the chance to practice shooting with an M1 rifle in a firing range. I learned how to take apart my M1 and put it back together quickly. I still can feel the excitement of placing cartridges into the top opening after pulling back the handle with a little knob on the end. I think this ROTC adventure went on for perhaps my second and third years, after which I was exempt.

Among my memorable CHS events: Listening to a lecture in the Math Club by boy genius Saul Kripke, son of Rabbi Kripke, leader of the Conservative synagogue Beth El. Saul was clearly in a league (and mental world) of his own. I think he had already published an article in a peer-reviewed mathematics journal by the time he was graduated. I seem to think it was hard for us to follow his lecture, not surprisingly, but also because we were all so distracted by his facial tics, manner-isms, and nasal snorts that we had a difficult time stifling our giggles, even we math nerds. Years later, *The New York Times Sunday Magazine* featured a front-cover photo portrait of him labeled "The Smartest Man Alive." Well, well. I guess we might have predicted it. I was amazed decades later that I became somewhat friendly with Saul at Princeton University and even invited him over for dinner with his then girlfriend or wife. Saul's snorts and speech oddities were also in evidence with our physics teacher, Roy Busch. I am sure he was very smart, but we used to have a bet-ting pool on the number of snorts that he would make per class. I don't recall if I ever won.

Another memorable high school event: dressing up in a Roman toga for the annual Latin banquet. My mother made my white toga, with a purple stripe edge, from an old bed sheet material. I was allowed to wear the toga as a senior, and younger students acted as slaves; a rare moment of patrician excess. My mother loaned out that toga for decades of future students after I graduated. I still have that costume to this day.

I also recall during those years that we would drive by the millionaire investor Warren Buffett's home sometimes on the way downtown, and my mother would point out that a very rich, smart man lived there. That was the extent of my contact with Mr. Buffet until decades later when I tried to interest him in one of my concep-tual art projects. His then executive secretary prevented my proposal from being shown to him, alas.

I am embarrassed to admit that I was a geek/nerd when it came time to apply to colleges, I thought it best to have a more "well-rounded" biography, so I signed up to be bat-boy for the high-school baseball team. I think the coach realized what I was doing and looked down on me with some disdain. I braved my way through the period of training and games and was awarded my white "letter sweater" with the large purple O. I have kept that sweater to this day.

In June–July 1957, I first visited Disneyland (which opened on 17 July 1955) during a family trip to visit Marcus-family relatives in Los Angeles. I remember vividly being amazed and excited by seeing Tomorrowland most of all, with the inspiring rocket ship standing ready for blast-off outside one of the exhibits/rides. The rocket is no longer there. No doubt that visit energized my continuing interest in science fiction, but it also coincided with my exposure to many superhero and sci-fi comic books I read, like those published by DC, Marvel, EC, and other pub-lishers. I also read sci-fi pulp magazines like *Galaxy*, *If*, *Astounding*, and others, many of which I still have in my varied collections of memorabilia, along with all the issues of *MAD* comic books and the first magazine issues up to Issue Number 24. At some point, I began to think that I, too, like Superman, had been deposited on earth from another planet and was quite different from those around me, especially my parents.

Sometime in my middle years in high school, because I was interested in phi-losophy and analytical thinking, as well as cultural and religious differences, I helped form a "secret" group called ICON (Intelligent Conversation on Nothing) with a few of my classmates, like Bruce Bernstein, Norm Bleicher (a″h), Richard

Fig. 2.13 Business card for the ICON group formed in high school. (Source: Author's memorabilia)

Friedman, and Howard Chudacoff. We met about once per week or at least once per month. I even helped arrange printing of business cards (see Fig. 2.13).

Besides meeting in our homes to watch medical movies about operations (one of our members was the son of a doctor), we discussed "deep thoughts" about society, divine beings, the universe, and girls. On one occasion, we organized a "people-watching event." With permission of the 72nd Street Crossroads Mall, we set up folding chairs and a sign announcing we were people watchers and proceeded to "examine" and "analyze" the shoppers. The *Omaha World-Herald* even sent a reporter, and our photo and a short article appeared (see Fig. 2.14). I think we were pleased.

Sometime about the age of 15–16, that is, 1958–1959, I think I began to think about death, and my own death. I suppose it was an inevitable aspect of changing hormones and the social and psychological pressures of the time. I did not contemplate suicide, but I did do a large oil-paint-on-masonite painting of a Roman-like Legionnaire stabbing himself in the abdomen with his own sword. I think my mother was concerned because I would paint such images. She may have even asked me if I thought I needed psychological counseling. Perhaps I did, but none was provided. The painting stood against a wall in my father's basement workshop room near the furnace, with my other larger format paintings, for some years. I don't know what happened to it. The thoughts about death and my own death continued to be a constant companion for the rest of my life, sometimes a troubling one, sometimes a comforting one.

After my freshman year in high school, I joined a Jewish boys' club, Rayim, which was an alternate to the AZA chapters then active (American Zionist Organization, founded in Omaha and consequently home to Chapters 1, 100, and 1000). I was strongly influenced to join Rayim by appeals from Bill Horwich, my lifelong friend. It was typical for Jewish boys to join such clubs as a way of

Fig. 2.14 Newspaper article about the people-watching event of the ICON group. (Source: *Omaha World-Herald*, 14 July 1961, used with permission of the publisher)

maintaining Jewish identity; learning a little about Jewish history, traditions, culture, and religion; participating in social-good activities and synagogue events; and developing relations with members of girls' chapters of similar clubs, namely, Bnai Brith Girls (BBG) and Rohanu, an independent organization. It was something of a surprise to me that in my senior year, I was chosen to be "Dream Boy" by Rohanu girls. I was flattered and also embarrassed. At some point in the weekend ceremonies, probably during May or June, I had to stand on a conference table, dressed in a sport jacket, slacks, dress shirt, and tie, while a crowd of about 20 girls around the table sang songs of appreciation/adoration. I think I was supposed to slowly turn around in a circle, so that no one would feel left out. Considering that I looked like a lame Buddy Holly in my black-rimmed glasses, suffered from acne, was tall and somewhat scrawny, I could not imagine why I was standing there. I tried not to cry.

Also in my senior year, I was elected President of Rayim. I had helped to decorate walls with murals for parties, participated in some events, and generally had good but slightly distant relations with most members. I was not a politically oriented, activist type of person. I did accept my responsibilities. For example, one Sunday morning in the spring of 1961, the Jewish Community Center (JCC) athletics co-ordinator called me at home to inform me that the person from our club scheduled to represent us had called in sick to the inter-club wrestling matches. He led me to believe I had to find a replacement immediately. I didn't know what to do. I did not know who of us had interest in or capabilities for wrestling, not being a sports-oriented person…as I mentioned, to the disappointment of my father who had played semi-professional baseball, wrestled, fought, and excelled in sports in general. In desperation, I told the caller I would come down and attempt to replace the missing person. I hoped something in my father's DNA might come through and would guide me.

As my friend Bill Horwich recently reminded me at a dinner party in retelling the event, I apparently was looking for any possible exit from the center of the ring when facing my opponent, a skillful athlete in Bill's class, Danny Hollis. After assuming the standard start position (I had to be instructed about what that was), Danny quickly arranged to lift me above his head, twirling me around in triumph, and even somehow managed to wave to the appreciative crowd. Alas, he tripped at some point in this stance, and I fell on him, both of us falling flat, his back on the mat, my weight snapping his collarbone. The referee lifted my limp arm and declared me the winner! I was mortified and felt terrible. During the next round of opponents, I was quickly eliminated and was grateful to be headed home. Danny, I learned later, had eliminated himself from baseball for the season, for which he had trained extensively.

When I was a senior in high school, I had the opportunity to participate in a sketch comedy program sponsored by the Omaha Jewish Community Center but shown in the Central High School auditorium across the street from the JCC. In the particular sketch in which I appeared, I played Fidel Castro, complete with fake cigar and fake beard/moustache. The facial hair intrigued me, and I decided then and there that I wanted to grow a beard as soon as I left high school and Omaha. At that time, it was only "weirdos," beatniks, artists, and some occasional professors/philosophers, or the like, and the Smith Brothers on the cough-drops box, who would have beards. In the late 1950s and early 1960s, it was quite unusual.

Because of my good science, math, and verbal test scores, I could apply to a number of good universities on the East and West Coasts of the USA. I applied to MIT, Caltech, and Princeton University. I was influenced to attend Princeton by my childhood friend Bill Horwich again, whose opinions I valued. Coincidentally, he lived about seven blocks from me throughout 7th to 12th grades; he continued to live about seven blocks from me for much of the next 64 years! He was graduated in 1960 from Central and went to Princeton.

The California Institute of Technology and the Massachusetts Institute of Technology accepted me. Princeton also accepted me as an undergraduate but also offered me a partial scholarship, which was important. My parents had worked hard all of their work lives to save money for my brother's and my education. Regarding the California Institute of Technology and the Massachusetts Institute of Technology, because of my interest in art (and design) I was concerned about becoming merely "a slide rule at CalTech and MIT," as I expressed it at the time, that is, too deeply immersed in science, technology, engineering, and mathematics (STEM, as we would term it today). I thought I would acquire a better education through studying liberal arts at Princeton. I was graduated from Central High School and entered Princeton in September 1961.

Concluding Comments

By the time my high-school years finished, many aspects of my personality had been formed. I was definitely interested in typography, letterforms, languages, "art" (which might have included some aspects of graphic design, even though I did not know the term, and my exposure to artists focused on Jackson Pollack, Salvador Dali, and Walt Disney illustrators), documentation, religion (especially Judaism), philosophy, and writing poetry (I used my own feeble efforts to chronicle my emotional turmoil). It was clear that I loved systems of thought and not the practical world of problem-solving. I liked to assemble things and take them apart, but I did not develop a strong orientation to woodworking as my father had.

I was not as interested in making or studying music (I knew almost nothing of classical composers, but did react very strongly to some rock-and-roll music) and politics (I viewed the Cold War, the struggle for African-American civil rights, and current presidential campaigns between Eisenhower-Stevenson, and Kennedy-Nixon from afar). I knew a little about the Holocaust, the creation of Israel, and Jewish holidays and rituals, but nothing very deep. I had no role models to inspire me to further study or action.

At some point in my childhood, I had been exposed to the children's story of the City Mouse and the Country Mouse:

(*Note: The Town Mouse and the Country Mouse* is one of Aesop's Fables. It is number 352 in the Perry Index and type 112 in Aarne–Thompson's folk tale index.[1] Like several other elements in Aesop's fables, "town mouse and country mouse" has become an English idiom. [Source: https://en.wikipedia.org/wiki/The_Town_Mouse_and_the_Country_Mouse].)

For some reason, that story affected me deeply. I decided I would rather be a country mouse than a town mouse. For the rest of my life, even though I achieved some aspects of Ivy League education, fame, professional achievement, and financial success, I always felt I was a minor player, quietly sitting in a smaller city in the USA, not in the middle of Manhattan or Los Angeles. I looked on with wonder, and a bit of disdain, at the personalities of Richard Saul Wurman and the founders of

IDEO, who continually pushed the business and professional boundaries of their worlds. I was more content with limited academic success and achieving what small accomplishments I could make in my chosen fields of specialization. I suppose in some way, the limited exposure to business that I had through my father and mother led me to a kind of Mom-and-Pop variety of professional achievement.

Leaving Omaha, Nebraska, was a challenge. I had grown up in this city from birth, and my formative views about the world came from here. I knew my way around the city, my high school, and the culture. I knew my friends and had only a few enemies, I loved my teachers and subjects of study, even if I was socially awkward and seemed to find it hard to date and nearly impossible to have a girlfriend. All in all, Omaha was a world I knew and whose rules I understood. I was headed for a new world, full of opportunities and challenges but also many unknowns. I was so overcome with nostalgic loss that I built a small altar (about 12 inches high) to my old self in commemoration of all that would no longer exist. I understood well the inexorable forward movement of time. There was no going back, except in memories.

All my life thus far, I had never been east of Chicago. I had never been outside of the USA. I had never been on an airplane. I was 18 years old. I remember driving to Princeton with my parents and coming for the first time to view New York City. The city seemed magical, surreal, as I first saw its enormous skyscrapers.

My Omaha study room desk, many books, and other belongings were in a small rented carrier attached to our black 1957 Chevrolet Impala station wagon. A new phase of my life was beginning.

Chapter 3
Studying Physics at Princeton, Reaching Escape Velocity to Yale

Takeaways
After 4 years studying physics and mathematics, with a minor in philosophy at Princeton, I decided to take the risk and apply to graduate school to study graphic design at Yale Art School. I was accepted at the last moment before graduating, and my career path and life changed dramatically.

Freshman Year, at Princeton, 1961–1962

All summer long in Omaha, I anticipated with excitement the glorious future in a new environment, experienced nostalgic sadness for the loss of Omaha, and carried out practical preparations for changing my home after 7 years in my current house and all my life in Omaha. Princeton University would be a shock for me. I had never been east of Chicago. The East Coast of the USA was unknown to me.

As a child, I had traveled mostly westward to visit Marcus family members in Los Angeles. Many decades later, in about 1973, when I was 30, I opened a letter I had written when I was 16 addressed to my future self. In the letter, I told my future self about the struggles I had, being a socially misfit, lonesome for the attention of girls but seemingly unable to find someone to be a girlfriend, my interest in art, and my aspirations to study science. I asked my future self questions about his life, but of course was not able to answer them. After the end of the typed letter I had written by hand: "I think you will live in California." How right I was, but it took me decades of wandering the earth and of living in Germany and Israel to find my second home in the USA.

My parents had driven me to Princeton, I think accompanied by my brother. They had attached a small U-Haul wagon to their car, containing my Omaha basement MAD Room desk, some books, and supplies of various kinds, like my drawing

A. Marcus, *Bridging Art, Design and Technology: My Lifetime Work*, https://doi.org/10.1007/978-3-032-04342-9_3

equipment. I remember the afternoon/evening after they dropped me off in August 1961. I had organized my desk area shared bedroom with Bill Whitehead (RIP) from Webster Groves, MO. I remember Bill had said then or shortly later that he had never met a Jew before.

My year was the first that high school graduates outnumbered, perhaps slightly, the number of graduates of expensive private schools, which had dominated Princeton's student body in the past, as they had at other Ivy League schools. The university was all male students; no females appeared as undergraduates until 1964–1965.

As soon as I came to Princeton, I started to grow a beard. I was reliving my joy of playing Fidel Castro in a high-school comedy skit. I was also connecting "spiritually" with the Beatniks and with my ancestors in ancient Israel and millennia later in Europe. As with every year, whenever I went back home to Omaha, I would shave off my beard, because I knew my father did not like beards. He expected men to be clean-shaven, as he was all of his life, although for generations earlier in Europe, not only Rabbis and devout Jews, but most men had grown beards and/or moustaches, as his father had. Thanks to Gillette and other corporations in America, men had been convinced that, like Native Americans for centuries, faces free of facial hair were more manly and/or appealing.

From numerous minor humiliations, I had a rather skeptical view of the quality of the student body. These events populated my introduction to Princeton undergraduate life. On the positive side, I found many of my classes stimulating and challenging in physics, mathematics, philosophy, and German, with a few others. I embarked on a 4-year course in German. For a future profession in physics, I had to take either German or Russian. Both were competitors to the USA in the sciences. I decided to study German to become better at understanding Yiddish, which my parents had spoken whenever they did not want my brother and me to understand them.

During my freshman year, or perhaps the next, I began to take extracurricular classes in painting offered by the Visual Arts Program. My teacher was Joe Stefanelli. I sat in his studio drawing and painting courses for several years.

(*Note*: Joe Stefanelli (March 20, 1921–September 27, 2017), also known as Joseph J. Stefanelli, belonged to the New York School Abstract Expressionist artists whose influence and artistic innovation by the 1950s had been recognized around the world. [Source: Wikipedia, https://en.wikipedia.org/wiki/Joe_Stefanelli_(painter), accessed on 15 January 2018.])

At the close of my freshman year, when we had completed a mathematics book by Thomas, I remember realizing that I knew the theorems and their mathematical/logical derivations so well that I could reconstruct almost any proof possible. It gave me great pleasure that my brain could comprehend, contain, and construct anything necessary within this complex system of thought. That was a source of satisfaction, giving me a sense of achievement, and appreciation of conceptual beauty (Fig. 3.1).

During the year, I came to know, respect, revere, and love my roommate Bob Cover (see Fig. 3.2), from Brookline, Massachusetts. He remained my roommate for 4 years (as did Bill Whitehead). He was a familiar kind of Jewish persona, very

Fig. 3.1 The author's undergraduate roommate for 4 years, Robert M. Cover, about 1962. (Source: The author's photographs. Photographer: Aaron Marcus. Used with permission of Diane Cover)

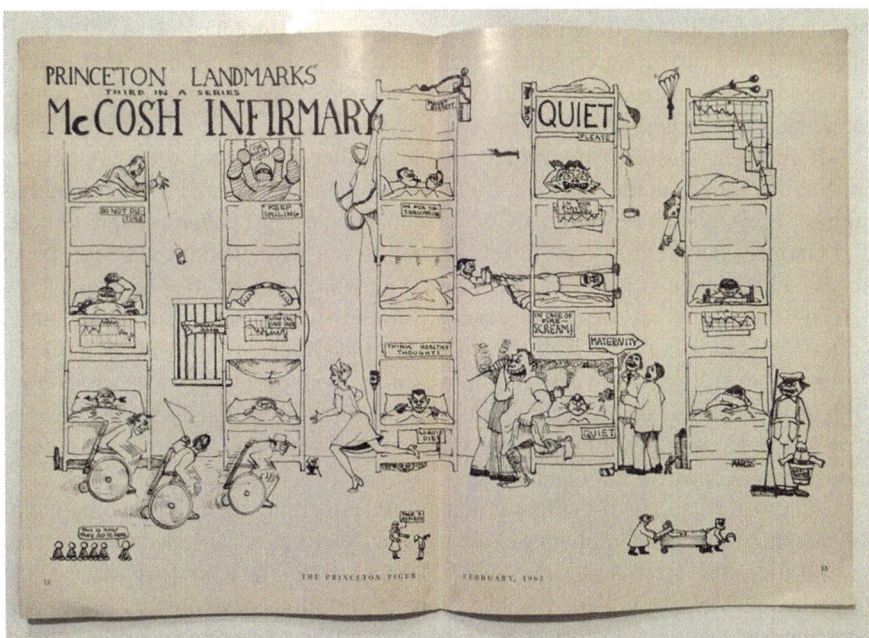

Fig. 3.2 Cartoon by Aaron Marcus in *Princeton Tiger*, 1962. (Photo by Aaron Marcus, used with permission of the *Princeton Tiger* magazine)

likable and informal, also incredibly smart. In his later Princeton years, he would often skip class, unless there was an interesting lecture scheduled, would read all the books he was supposed to have read for a course within a few days at the end of the semester, then sit down at his typewriter, smoking cigarettes and drinking cans of beer, and type a long term-paper at a single sitting, taking out the last page, turning the first and only draft of the report in, and getting an A. In his second year, he decided on a whim to study Chinese. In his third year, he became involved with the efforts to enroll Blacks in elections in the South and dropped out of school to help people there. This was at the time that Medgar Evers and others were shot and killed for doing such work. I attended his wedding in Brookline years later. He went on to study law at Columbia, then taught at Yale Law School. I remember walking with him around Yale about 1982, discussing Judaism, family, education, his life, and mine. By that time, I believe he was already having heart problems and knew his time on earth was limited. He was dead at 42 in July 1986, a brilliant life cut short. I understand that he contributed a specific new realm of constitutional law, that annual conferences are still held in his memory and to further his contributions. Many thought he would eventually wind up on the US Supreme Court. I was privileged and honored to have spent a short time with him, his wife/widow, and his two children.

My first year enabled me to begin my connection to New York City art museums, including my favorites, the Museum of Modern Art (MoMA), with its design collections; the Metropolitan Art Museum, with its Egyptian collections; the Guggenheim; the American Folk Art Museum; as well as others. I suppose the design collections of MoMA were my first exposure to significant examples of poster designs, industrial product designs, and other graphic design works, as opposed to painting, sculpture, and printmaking.

My first year was also my introduction to another language and culture besides the English spoken in the Midwest, Latin, Hebrew, and Ashkenazic Jewish religious culture. I was introduced to East Coast language and Ivy League preppie culture, and German and Germanic culture. I learned to not wear white socks with black shoes and to wear a gray or blue sport coat with white shirt and tie and jeans.

Near the end of my freshman year, my friend Bill Horwich introduced me to Gillett Good Griffin (RIP), then the Curator of the Graphic Arts Collection (GAC) at Princeton. Bill had been assisting him as a work-study student. I was to follow. Gillett was a jovial, somewhat roly-poly man with an infectious laugh and a winning smile. He was given to frequent punning and wordplay. To me, he was enormously well-educated in art and design.

Gillett had been one of the first graduate students, if not the first, to come out of the Graphic Design Department of Yale University, which was headed then, and for several decades afterward, by Alvin Eisenman (RIP), who had started the Department. Meeting Gillett was an extremely fortuitous development in my personal and professional history. I had exposure to the collection of prints, photographs, books, pamphlets, typographic specimens, etc., that the GAC possessed. By working there, I could informally acquire an education in many aspects of graphic design.

Moreover, Gillett encouraged me with my budding interests in typography, calligraphy, and photography. I bought my first camera, a Pentax 35 mm. He ran a campus photography competition, and one of my black-and-white photographs was a winner. He invited me to join him in his home to sip sherry and listen to classical music. I discovered his collection of pre-Columbian sculpture and other *objets d'arte*, which he had collected on numerous trips to Mayan and other sites in Central America. He was friends with many experts in the arts, like the eminent pre-Columbian and Meso-American art historian Michael D. Coe (RIP), with whom I spent some occasions, and Mike Parker (RIP), a noted typographer at Lonotype.

Only later, especially at his death, did I fully realize Gillett's contributions to Princeton and the world of art history. He was a gifted painter himself and encouraged others in all forms of painting, typography, photography, and other arts. He had befriended Albert Einstein when Gillett was only 25 and Einstein was 74, living at 118 Mercer Street in Princeton. Gillett had later helped to build up Princeton's pre-Columbian art collection as a world-class resource, and he himself had co-discovered ancient Olmec cave paintings, the oldest paintings then discovered in the new world [*Note*: Source: Saxon, Jamie, "Gillett Griffin, Collector, Curator, and Scholar, Dies at 87," Princeton Art Museum Web site, http://artmuseum.princeton. edu/story/gillett-griffin-collector-curator-and-scholar-dies-87, accessed on 23 January 2018.]

Gillett was a gifted storyteller, often laughing infectiously at his own raucous adventures. I recall that he told me a story once about being in a remote part of Mexico driving his VW bug when some unfortunate man leaped or fell in front of his car. Gillett instantly hit and killed the man. They were in the middle of nowhere. Gillett was traumatized and did not know what to do. Finally, he decided that the best thing would be to tie the body to the hood of his car and take him to the nearest town many miles away. Gillett feared he would be imprisoned in a Mexican jail for years, but felt he was doing the responsible thing. Imagine the sight of a VW bug with a corpse attached to it like some trophy of a deer hunter. I think Gillett was released by the police after he explained his situation.

On numerous occasions during my undergraduate, graduate, and later years, Gillett would invite me on weekends to drive up to Colrain, MA, to a cabin that he and fellow Yale graduates Jack Marmaras (RIP) and Mike Parker (RIP) had purchased some time shortly after their graduation. Jack became a senior graphic designer at CIBA-Geigy, an international pharmaceutical concern with offices in New Jersey. Mike Parker became a noted typographer and entrepreneur at Mergenthaler Linotype and elsewhere eventually as Director, adding 1000 typefaces to their catalogue, including Helvetica. Jack sent me the Ciba-Geigy little red pocket calendar that I used for decades, and I would occasionally visit with and talk with Mike over the coming decades.

The cabin had been built in the early 1800s, and the team of three Yale graduates had restored it to that time, including providing a cast-iron sink, which had to be thoroughly dried each time it was used or it would rust through and fail. We pumped water from a well outside the building. The bedrooms were decorated with early nineteenth-century prints and bedding. The floors and furniture were very old wood.

We would sit in front of the fireplace. Drink sherry and wine and eat good meals at the simple wooden-plank table.

Being in the company of Gillett was a great relief from the challenges and frustrations of the rest of my life at Princeton. He was very kind and generous to me; I always felt comfortable and relaxed with him. And he was terribly funny, capable of telling the most amazing tales, like those of the person who had originally owned the cabin and other strange locals. After my years at Princeton ended, I would continue to be in contact occasionally with Gillett, always calling him on his birthday in June, until just after his death in 2016.

Sophomore Year, 1962–1963

In my sophomore year, I had to choose a departmental major. I chose physics, with a minor in philosophy. While I continued my studies of physics and mathematics, I relished the study of Hume, Locke, Plato, Quine, Whitehead, and Wittgenstein, among others. I also continued my informal studies of painting and drawing. Around this time, I discovered the Dover books showing the drawings of Heinrich Kley, a wonderful, engaging, and skilled illustrator of people. I was much influenced by him and started to keep drawing-book diaries with my sketches, which I have continued to keep for the remainder of my life. The 42 books in 2024 now take up more than 5 ft of my office shelves. Not surprisingly, after 1982 when I started my design firm, the books began to be filled with business cards more than drawings.

In the Graphic Arts Collection over the course of several years of working with him, Gillett introduced me to *How Prints Look*, the 1943 book by William M. Ivins, Jr., former curator of the print collection at the New York's Metropolitan Museum from its beginnings in 1916 until 1946. This book helped me to understand the full range of graphic arts media. He also introduced me to Ivins' 1953 book *Prints and Visual Communication*, which detailed the different emphases that print media (e.g., woodcuts vs. gravure printing vs. photography) gave to capturing reality. I found both books fascinating and kept them with me for decades in my personal library, which began growing that year with books other than my physics and mathematics texts.

At Princeton in my sophomore year, I was having a good time in my studies. I was doing well but was concerned about my future profession. By the end of the second year, I think my grades were good enough that I was number nine in my class. Not bad for a Yiddish yokel from Omaha, Nebraska. I mention this fact with a little happiness, but also to compare with what happened by the time I was graduated 2 years later. My grade average had plummeted to about 450 out of 750 because of emotional problems and dislike for my chosen field, to be discussed below.

By the end of my sophomore year, I had already learned about the Rhode Island School of Design (RISD), and I thought how wonderful it would be to switch out of Princeton to attend that school in Providence, RI. However, I did not have the courage to make such a break, and I was frightened about how I would earn a living. My standard dismal fantasy was this: I thought I would die in the Bowery of New York City, a starving artist, wearing a black beret and a black turtle-necked shirt, unable to sell my artworks. In contrast, my imagined science career included the completion of my study of physics at Princeton, the inevitable graduate study in physics somewhere, and the inevitable job in some corporate or government research laboratory for the rest of my life. This alternative was secure but equally frightening to me. I was caught in a dilemma that became increasingly traumatic over the next 2 years.

Summer 1963 Internship in Wetzlar, Germany

In my sophomore summer of 1963, I took on a new challenge. After months of negotiation with the Princeton German Department, I was awarded a summer internship in Germany. I flew for the first time out of the USA, to Paris, and then by train on to Wetzlar, Germany. I remember looking at commercial signs on the way to the TWA terminal in New York City trying to imagine what it would be like to see everything in another language. Princeton had arranged for me to work in an office of Buderus Eisenwerke, a factory for steel and mechanical products production in the hometown of Leitz (Leica) cameras. In Wetzlar, Goethe had written *Die Leiden des jungen Wehrters*, the sufferings of this young fellow. My "intense, demanding" job was to sort delivery slips in alphabetical order. I believe I accomplished my task well, although it did not use much of my Princeton education. I also improved my German; by the end of the summer, I was fluent in German and knowledgeable about German culture.

During my stay, I traveled around Germany, especially in the state of Hesse, which included Frankfurt. I noticed throughout Germany that many men who were missing arms or legs used crutches to get about. Much of Germany still looked gray and monochromatic, somewhat dismal, pockmarked with bullet holes and bombed-out buildings here and there. I was a little frightened to go to Berlin on the one highway in and out of East Germany, but I overcame my anxiety. I remember that, on the bus looking out the window as I headed east, the beautiful blue afternoon sky was filled with many puffy white clouds beginning to turn shades of pink and gray as sunset approached, while Beethoven's Ninth Symphony played on the bus's public address system. It was all quite magnificent and impressive.

Crossing Checkpoint Charlie from West Berlin to East Berlin in the morning during my visit, I nervously walked around East Berlin. Many buildings still lay in ruins from World War II in the summer of 1963; others, while standing, still suffered the wounds of many bullet holes and artillery shells. Everything was gray, brown-gray, or brown. Very little color broke this limited spectrum. It was all quite depressing. I made a special point of visiting the synagogue on *Oranienburgerstrasse*. Although originally a large, magnificent building with ornate double towers, it, too, sat half-destroyed.

At that time, people would stealthily and cautiously approach me, asking me if I were from the USA. Learning that I was, they would swiftly hand me small notes to send to relatives, then disappear back into the small crowds mingling about before someone could notice and report or arrest them.

The time spent in Germany impressed me and filled me with awe. I had done some drawings of the people, buildings, and places, as well as taken many photos. I was moved by the kindness of families toward me and the friendliness of the young people with whom I had worked.

At the end of my summer in Europe, my paternal grandfather, Harry Marcus (a"h), paid for me to fly to Israel, for my first visit. I was able to tour much of Israel with my step-aunt Hanna Kashtan (a"h) who acted as a tour guide and translator. I visited Jerusalem and was impressed by the Western Wall of the Temple Mount, the ancient stone buildings, the beautiful archeological artifacts in the Israel Museum, and the Dead Sea Scrolls in the Dome of the Book. I visited, albeit somewhat rapidly, Tel Aviv/Yaffo, Haifa, Herzilyah, Caesaria, the Herodion, Eilat, Beersheva, Tzfat, and Hazor, among other cities and sites. Hanna explained as much as she could in English. My Hebrew was very limited at the time. I remember once seeing David Ben Gurion (a"h) out on the street somewhere in the middle of Israel with a small crowd of people around him, as we traveled by bus from one city to the next. The visit was extremely moving for me and led me to connect further with my Jewish roots, my Jewish identity, my Jewish religion, and with the State of Israel more strongly than ever. I had just turned 20.

I remember that on one occasion, I drove with my step-cousin Drora Kashtan (a"h) northwest of Tzfat. What was memorable was the music broadcast on Radio Luxembourg, the strongest AM station of Europe, which could be received in Israel. As we drove along at night in about August 1963, I heard rock-and-roll music unlike anything I had heard before. It was musically sophisticated harmonies with catchy lyrics in English by a new group that had just emerged from the UK. I sensed immediately that the song would be a hit. The song was "I Want to Hold Your Hand" by the Beatles.

I returned after the summer's exciting adventures to begin my junior year at Princeton.

Junior Year, 1963–1964

What made the first months of my junior year especially memorable was the assassination of the President of the USA, John F. Kennedy (JFK, RIP), on 22 November 1963. Like many people in the USA, I can remember exactly where I was standing when I heard the news.

I was working in the Princeton University Graphic Arts Print Shop in the C-level basement of Firestone Library, which was run by Carol Stoddard (see References below). She was a chain-smoking, growly-voiced, wiry individual with a strong sense of humor. She introduced me to the joys of hand-setting type for a Vandercook proving press, making and printing from lithographic stones, and printing from the large wooden type that was housed in the collection of the Print Shop. (Little did I then realize I would return to this shop as its Director within 5 years!)

The news of the death of JFK hit me very hard. The reality of death, the violence of an assassin, and the loss of the future of JFK all were frightening. The foundations of my world seemed to be knocked out from under me. From the moment I heard the news, I could not speak; I had so much shock and grief. Then, out of respect for the emotional impact of the occasion, I resolved not to speak until I had gone to Washington, DC, seen the president's coffin, and watched the funeral procession, which in short order I did. My roommates supported my silence. I wrote notes whenever those of us who went on our immediate train trip to Washington needed some comment from me. I wrote on a small piece of paper, which I pinned to my chest, that I had laryngitis and had lost my voice. This explained my lack of utterances. In Washington, I joined thousands of mourners along the route of the funeral procession. I was amazed, standing somewhat at the back of the crowd (I could see because I was tall), that just as the caisson pulled by a horse moved by, many of the onlookers in the back, unable to see well, had turned around, with their backs to the dead president, in order to see the image being broadcast on a display of multiple television sets in an appliance store window: which showed the casket clearly going by! I thought: How bizarre is this, that in the presence of the real thing, however imperfect, citizens chose to watch a media-image of the real event right in back of them.

My shock at JFK's death left a long shadow on my life. For many decades, every year on 22 November, I would fast, as on Yom Kippur, the memorial/mourning fast day in Judaism, which I also partially practiced in later years. This JFK-Day practice carried on for perhaps 30 years. My abstention was a way of making my body and my mind remember that day and its significance for me.

My experience in the Graphic Arts Collection, the typography and printing hands-on experience I was getting in the Graphic Arts Print Shop, and my extracurricular painting, drawing, and printmaking courses in the Visual Arts Program all gave me more experience with visual arts and visual communication, a place to safely feel my emotions, and increased skills in typography, color, drawing, composition, and graphic design.

I had started submitting cartoons to the *Princeton Tiger* humor magazine, which was readily available on campus. My earliest entries were two-page cartoon spreads similar to the epic drawings from *MAD* magazine I had seen years earlier. They depicted life on the campus. The editors liked my submissions, and I came into contact with Frank Deford (RIP), who became the Editor-in-Chief, and later a novelist and nationally known NPR sports commentator and essayist, and MacKinnon (Mac) Simpson (RIP), who later published one of the first books created with desktop software on the Apple Macintosh. I kept in contact with Mac until shortly before his death, because he continually kept me updated on the world's humor. Some of my Princeton cartoons were published in a book about campus humor: one cartoon depicts a group of cows in a field with a sign that says "Our cows are scientifically bred." One of the cows is accompanied by a speech balloon containing only the

Greek letter *mu*, which is often used in scientific equations. To my surprise, I eventually became the Art Editor in my senior year and drew the color covers for many issues. The experiences with the *Tiger* magazine gave me additional experience in magazine publishing, deadlines, working with a team, focusing on the market, etc.

In my junior year, I began to have more serious concerns about my future in physics. Concerns notwithstanding, I was required to prepare a junior paper for the physics department. I decided to focus on the development, meaning, and significance of Einstein's theory of special relativity. What impressed me about Einstein most was the fact that the ideas of special relativity were metaphorically floating in front of the faces of his contemporaries at the beginning of the twentieth century. Others had almost stumbled on the key concepts and equations, like H. A. Lorenz, but it was Einstein's daring brilliance to pose the then-inconceivable notion that time might be a fourth dimension of our universe similar in some ways to the three spatial dimensions. In other words, Einstein tried to imagine the previously unimaginable. I found this approach impressive and influential, and I tried to carry on this same approach in a smaller way with my own minor accomplishments. I was also impressed by his devotion to engagement with the outside world later in life, which even came into conflict with the Director of the Institute for Advanced Study at Princeton, who wanted isolation for its participants. As a teenager and young adult, I had always imagined an ideal way to live was in a special glass-enclosed apartment at 42nd Street and Fifth Avenue in Manhattan, where I could observe the world going by and participate as I chose. This was a kind of combination of my childhood fantasy of preferring the quiet of the country mouse to the city mouse.

That summer following the 1963–1964 academic year, I arranged through Carol Stoddard to work in Manhattan running a print gallery located at 1603 York Avenue in the Germantown area near East 86th Street, which was owned by Carol Stoddard's sister. That summer was a remarkable and eye-opening experience. I toured thoroughly museums, galleries, bars, and other sites that summer. The Free Speech Movement had started at the University of California at Berkeley. The nation was in something of an uproar politically, and society had started to shift its gender, drugs, racial attitudes, behavior, and social norms.

I remember attending the New York World's Fair and being amazed that "countries" like General Motors and Disney had their own pavilions. I took hundreds of Kodachrome and Ektachrome slides that summer trying to improve my photography skills. The tall towers and the earth globe symbols of the fair had a special attraction for me, and I was delighted to see them featured in a *Men in Black* movie decades later.

Also that summer, riots broke out in Manhattan's Harlem. I was surprised and concerned about them. I had never been so near to social unrest. The circumstances seemed disturbing and led to suspicions about the police. The entire urban experience of the summer was so different from my Omaha upbringing, although there had been racial tensions in Omaha (including riots in earlier times) and in the staid environment of Princeton.

At the close of the summer, I returned for my final year at Princeton.

Senior Year, 1964–1965

For my final year, the Physics Department required that I write a thesis. At that time many departments did. I settled on an experimental physics project: Raman scattering from a gallium phosphide crystal using a ruby laser. I was attempting to study the particular characteristics of the scattering of the unusually aligned light waves impinging on this crystal.

The consequence of my decision was that I had to spend most of my senior year in a small room approximately 6 ft by 9 ft, about 8 ft high, with walls painted matte black, no windows, and a single door. In that room, I was trying to arrange my spectroscopy-related apparatus, which included a new kind of invention, a ruby laser. Lasers (light amplification by stimulated emission of radiation) had been invented in 1958 as a means of stimulating light rays to emit a strong, collinear beam of synchronized waves by bouncing them between mirrors. Originally masers (microwave stimulated electromagnetic radiation) had been invented. My work in trying to arrange for the proper setup and desired results required that I undertake numerous attempts to capture the scattered radiation. After many months, I failed.

Well, such things happen, and one writes up the failure, which I did. Nevertheless, I spent much of the time depressed and frustrated. I had not wanted to do a thesis in experimental physics, and I did not look forward to a future career in experimental physics with so much time spent on fiddling with physical apparatus. I had wanted to do more conceptual projects, like studying gravitation or the origins of the universe. I also did not feel particularly supported emotionally by my thesis advisor. As the year wore on, I sought psychological counseling and soldiered on, nearing the point of emotional breakdown from the stress of my nonworking thesis project, and the uncertainty of what to do about graduate school and my future career. At some points, I even contemplated suicide as a way to exit from these dilemmas. My challenges seemed fundamental and existential. One development stood out: I had gone through life somewhat narcissistically, solipsistically, and hermetically, with little empathy and connection to people. I spent many dreary and somber days and evenings in Fine Hall's Mathematics Library as my place of quiet and refuge, the same place that John Nash, the famous schizophrenic mathematician, had spent his days and nights and as depicted decades later in the movie *A Beautiful Mind*. I remember seeing him wandering the campus continually. I did not know then who he was, but I thought it odd that a professor seemed to have nothing better to do than to continually wander the campus.

I was deeply emotionally troubled and kept having a vision of a black raven or buzzard with yellow eyes sitting on a black, dead tree in an empty landscape. This seemed to be a symbol of my pending death. During these years, I had learned that within some branch of Chassidism or Kabbalistic Judaism, it was known that the souls of all Jews would be gathered together at the time of the coming of the Moshiakh or Messiah, and that all buried bodies would burrow underground to Jerusalem to emerge re-animated. For this reason, it was recommended to keep track of and retain all body parts. I decided, in my demented state, to start saving all hair clippings from my head and all nail clippings, which I kept in a large glass jar in my bedroom. My roommates and Bill Horwich seemed to think this was disgusting and signs of mental deterioration. They were probably correct. At some point, I abandoned my ritual and the bottle, but I carried on the practice for several months and perhaps most of that academic year.

In my own case of enlightenment, at some point mid-year, perhaps, I had a vision of a "thousand points of light" in a black void, and realized I was looking at the souls of other human beings, and that I was one of these creatures. The vision empowered me to understand my connection to people and to join humanity on my trek through life. It was a slow, painful process, but I had begun, albeit decades late. For that positive change at a fork in the road, I was later to be very grateful.

I have to admit that two people stand out in the physics department as persons I liked and who seemed to like me: Profs. Aaron Lemonick (RIP) and Allen Shenstone (RIP) (see References). Aaron Lemonick may have been an advisor to students at that time. I think I had spoken with him about my career ambivalences, including experimental physics vs. theoretical physics, as well as physics vs. art/design. Allen Shenstone, formerly head of the Physics Department, was then an emeritus professor. Because he was an expert in spectroscopy, he may have been a thesis project advisor. I recall that he took me on a tour of the Physics Department building attic, where generations of equipment used for teaching and experiments were stored. To rummage through these unused and forgotten items moved me and filled me with nostalgia. It felt as if I were poking through the ruins of my career in physics if I left that field and moved on into a new and relatively unknown and uncertain field of graphic design, toward which I seemed to be heading.

As the year progressed, I finally decided I *must* consider the option to study for at least 1 year in an art/design school. Eventually I applied to several good schools: Cooper Union in New York City, the Art Institute in Chicago, Pratt Institute, also in New York City, all of which required me to re-enter as a freshman. Some of my courses in advanced undergraduate physics and mathematics did not count very much in placing me within their curricula. I did not look forward to experiencing a second undergraduate education.

Through my mentor, part-time employer, and friend Gillett Griffin, one of Yale School of Art and Architecture's first graphic design graduates, I knew that Yale could provide me with a graduate education. Yale offered a special MFA program with an extra year for those students who were coming with undergraduate degrees outside those of typical art/design schools. At the same time, I was applying for graduate study of physics at the California Institute of Technology, the University of Pennsylvania, and the University of Michigan.

What was the result? A cacophony of stressful experiences in rapid succession. Each of them reverberating through my psyche and affecting my scheduled activities. I limped through my thesis defense and oral exams in physics. The graduate schools of physics accepted me and were wanting a decision. Was I coming or not? What was I to do? At the same time, all of the art/design schools had accepted me and were wanting to know: Was I coming or not? What was I to do?

Well, not all the art/design schools had accepted me: At Yale, I was placed on a waiting list and was told I would be informed "soon."

At the same time, as an emotional precaution or award, I had applied for special permission to return to Germany as a summer intern for a second time, to perfect my language skills. This was not usually done. I was delighted to be informed that the internship would be granted, and I had to make plans soon to graduate and to depart. But I had no idea to what career or location I would return! My parents were coming within a few weeks for the graduation ceremony, but I had no clear idea of what path I should take! I stumbled through their visit and graduation in an emotional daze.

Suddenly, I received a letter 5 *days* before my graduation ceremony: Yale had decided to accept me, allowing me to join the few people in the world (15 people) who would begin next fall in the Graphic Design Department. I was too stunned and numb from my emotional upheavals of the year to react.

In short order, I finished the forms for my summer internship in Augsburg, Germany, working for Maschinenfabrik Augsburg-Nürnberg (MAN), one of the largest automotive engineering companies in the world. Their trucks were seen everywhere in Germany. I attended the graduation ceremonies with my four roommates accompanied by one of my roommate's girlfriend, a pretty, kind, local woman named Susan Douglas (who would later become my first wife!), my parents, and my younger brother Stephen, who by now was an undergraduate at Brandeis University. Stephen had gone on from high school to study chemistry, as I had gone on to study physics. Within a few weeks, stumbling through each moment of time in a daze, I found myself in Germany again.

During my stay in Augsburg, I traveled once to visit Dachau, one of the Nazi death camps nearby. I arrived late in the afternoon by bus, the only way for me to get there. When I arrived at the ticket booth, the cashier said I was too late for the last tour, and she pointed to a sign about 1.5 m high with many rules and regulations. I marveled at this example of German attention to detail. I tried to convince the woman selling tickets that, because I was an American Jew and this was the only occasion I would have to visit the camp, could she not let me in, and I would join the last group of visitors and see what I could see? Her answer: a firm "Nein." Dejected, and rejected, I slunk away to my left and around the corner to look into the windows to see what I could see. I noticed the last tour group making its way through exhibits in that building before moving on to other buildings on the grounds of the site.

A man in the group noticed me looking intently into the window, came over, opened it, and asked what I was doing. I explained my predicament. He looked to his left and right, and behind, and seeing no one said, "well, why don't you just sneak in through this window." I smiled and agreed, entering head and shoulders first, rolling on the floor, getting up, and proceeded to join their group. I realized, with sad irony, that I was one of the few Jews in the history of Dachau to sneak *into* the camp, not someone trying to escape *out* of the camp. As I walked around the camp, I waited for some divine word to come to me about what I was seeing, which was more terrible and frightening than anything I had ever experienced. Suddenly, in the middle of an open walking area, I realized the Divine Words had arrived: "Do not hate all Germans for what the Nazis have done here. If you do, you will be no better than the Nazis, who hated all Jews." I was struck with the sense of this maxim and resolved to live my life by it.

After my work period in Germany, I bought an inexpensive German car and drove around northern Italy to add to my cultural experience, then flew back to London and headed back to the USA, to the unknown world of graduate school. All during my travels, I filled pages of my diaries/drawing books with sketches. I had seen much baroque and rococo architecture and painting that summer and had sketched/painted with watercolor many drawings of buildings, people, and landscapes. Of note were the strangely dressed young men in London with "winkelpicker" (pointed) shoes, tight black stove-pipe pants, and long hair, and the young women with short skirts, wild hair, and black, heavily netted stockings. The times they were a-changing.

What had I learned at Princeton during my 4 years? I was glad of my mathematics, physics, and philosophy education. The subject matter challenged and intrigued me. I appreciated the opportunities I had to explore my interests in drawing, typography, photography, publication design, and calligraphy. I was uncertain about how all of this would fit together at Yale. Little did I realize that it would all come together in unexpected ways, as I shall explain in the next chapters of my life.

References/Notes About People

Deford, Frank: "Benjamin Franklin Deford III (December 16, 1938–May 28, 2017) was an American sportswriter and novelist. Over the course of four decades, he was a regular sports commentator on NPR's Morning Edition radio program (from 1980 to 2017)." [Source: Wikipedia, https://en.wikipedia.org/wiki/Frank_Deford. Accessed on 24 January 2018.]

Harlem Riot: "The Harlem riot of 1964, or Harlem riots of 1964 occurred between July 16 and 22, 1964. It began after James Powell was shot and killed by police Lieutenant Thomas Gilligan. The second bullet of three fired by Lieutenant Gilligan killed the 15-year-old African American in front of his friends and about a dozen other witnesses. Immediately after the shooting, about 300 students from a nearby school who were informed by the principal rallied. The shooting set off six consecutive nights of rioting that affected the New York City neighborhoods of Harlem and Bedford-Stuyvesant. In total, 4,000 New Yorkers participated in the riots which led to attacks on the New York City Police Department, vandalism, and looting in stores. At the end of the conflict, reports counted one dead rioter, 118 injured, and 465 arrested." Wikipedia, https://en.wikipedia.org/wiki/Harlem_riot_of_1964, accessed 24 January 2018.

Ivins, William M., Jr. (1943). *How Prints Look*. New York Metropolitan Museum of Art.

Ivins, William M., Jr. (1953). *Prints and Visual Communication*. Cambridge: Harvard University Press.

Lemonick, Aaron: "Aaron Lemonick (February 2, 1923, in Philadelphia, Pennsylvania–June 19, 2003, in Princeton, New Jersey) was a Princeton University physics professor and administrator who served as Dean of the Graduate School from 1969 to 1973, and as Dean of the Faculty from 1973 to 1989. Joseph Taylor, winner of the 1993 Nobel Prize in Physics, attributes his decision to study physics instead of mathematics to Lemonick's freshman physics course at Haverford.[1] Princeton awarded him the President's Award for Distinguished Teaching when he retired in 1994, and he received an honorary degree in 2001." [Source: Wikipedia, https://en.wikipedia.org/wiki/Aaron_Lemonick, accessed 24 January 2018.]

Savage, Carol C-B. (1964). "Graphic Arts Printing Shop." *Princeton Alumni Weekly*, v.65, p. 254ff (p. 09ff), 10 November 1964.

Saxon, Jamie (2016). "Gillett Griffin, Collector, Curator, and Scholar, Dies at 87." Princeton Art Museum Web site, http://artmuseum.princeton.edu/story/gillett-griffin-collector-curator-and-scholar-dies-87, accessed on 23 January 2018.

Shenstone, Allen: Allen G. Shenstone (RIP). 1925–1980. "Assistant Professor to Professor of Physics (1925–1938); Class of 1909 Professor of Physics (1938–1962); Chair, Department of Physics (1949–1960); and Class of 1909 Emeritus Professor of Physics and Senior Research Physicist (1962–1980), Princeton University, Princeton (N.J.)." [Source: American Institute of Physics, https://history.aip.org/phn/11609019.html, accessed on 24 January 2018.]

Stefanelli, Joseph: "(March 20, 1921–September 27, 2017), also known as Joseph J. Stefanelli belonged to the New York School Abstract Expressionist artists whose influence and artistic innovation by the 1950s had been recognized around the world. New York School Abstract Expressionism, represented by Jackson Pollock, Willem de Kooning, Franz Kline and others became a leading art movement of the post-World War 2 era. He died in September 2017 at the age of 96." He taught at Princeton: 1963–1966: Princeton University, Princeton, NJ. [Source: Wikipedia, https://en.wikipedia.org/wiki/Joe_Stefanelli_(painter), accessed 24 January 2018.]

Chapter 4
Another World: My Three Years in Graduate School

Takeaways

I spent 3 years at Yale. My first seemed dreamlike, because everything was new. I gradually honed my skills/knowledge and began work as a graphic designer. I left New Haven in 1968 and returned to Princeton University, unexpectedly, in terms of what I had imagined I would do after my Yale experience. My years as a graduate student ended and I prepared for marriage and becoming a Princeton faculty member.

Yale, First Year, 1965–1966: Baby Graphic Design

In August 1965, I moved to New Haven, CT, to begin three years of professional study at Yale. The first year consisted of catching up with other classmates, because I was an outsider, an alien to graphic design. I found a modest apartment at 45 Whaley Avenue, which was located on the edge of the African-American neighborhood to the east, and the whiter, university-oriented stores and shops to the west. The street was a major thoroughfare with constant traffic. I continued to rent this apartment for all my 3 years at Yale.

My bedroom floor was just larger than the size of a double bed mattress, which took up the entire floor! The window was large and faced the street, which meant the traffic noises were constant. To solve this problem, I found a large door, sawed it down to size, and affixed it on hinges to cover the window and to block out the light and sound. A thin line of light slipped through along the fore-edge of the door, which meant that on sunny mornings or afternoons when I was sleeping with the door closed, the room acted as a camera obscura, and a thin slice of the world appeared on the opposite wall at my feet, but upside down. I could clearly observe people and cars moving along in the outside world as I fell asleep.

A. Marcus, *Bridging Art, Design and Technology: My Lifetime Work*, https://doi.org/10.1007/978-3-032-04342-9_4

During the course of three years, I had several roommates, including Bill Horwich, who was then attending Yale's Law School.

Behind the apartment building lived a sign painter, Mr. Cornelius Benson, with his dog Corkie, a friendly collie. Mr. Benson had lost part of one leg and hobbled on a crutch as he continued to paint signs on Masonite or cardboard for local stores. He lived simply. He once invited me to dinner and served corn on the cob, from which he had removed most, but not all strings of husks. I appreciated his kindness, but that was a challenging evening.

I recall in those years, the price of a loaf of inexpensive bread, a quart of milk, and a gallon of regular gas were each about the same price: 25 cents.

My apartment was only a few blocks from the Art and Architecture building, which Paul Rudolph, the head of the Architecture School, had designed. Built in 1963, *The New York Times* architecture critic Ada Louise Huxtable declared it to be the best piece of architecture that year…before anyone had yet entered and used the building on a regular basis. I found it to be a piece of sadistic architecture for several reasons:

- The Graphic Design studios, where I would soon be spending my time, had lighting along an open, unwalled corridor for people passing by the studio, on their way to somewhere else, but no overhead lighting for the area where we had our desks, which made the area dark and gloomy, except where lit by our desk lamps, which the dark space required us to use.
- Outside our few windows was a small area, perhaps a meter on each side, in which a large ceramic planter sat holding a dead plant. The glass walls around that area meant that no one could get to the plant, which at one point was presumably alive, and there seemed to be no means of irrigating the plant. What an odd, macabre architectural gesture, I thought.
- The lighting fixtures in the building's stairwell, which we often took from ground level to the basement, were spotlights affixed to a track. The light fixtures, bulbs and bases, were so long that even when bent at an angle, I would continually bump my head on them, sometimes burning the top of my hair slightly. I had to hunch over at 6'2″ to avoid breaking many of them in a row as I moved down or up the stairs.
- The outside of the building had been designed in a special way with wood slats in a form that let the cement coating the building to ooze out between the wood pieces to make a unique cladding. Italian stonecutters had been imported from Europe to knock off the extra cement to make a special texture of chipped-off cement. It looked good from a distance. However, if one casually rested against the building, one was in danger of slicing open one's arm or hand, depending on what body part came into contact with which knife-sharp edge of broken cement. I could not believe that an architect would be allowed to design and have built a building that endangered people's lives in this way. Did I forget to mention that Rudolph was the head of the Architecture School and had given himself and his students the grandest, best places in the building?

- The building was supposed to bring all students of all the disciplines of art and design "together" by encouraging them to enter/exit one grand entrance space. It did nothing of the kind. Different groups came and went without interacting. The Graphic Design students tended to use a small side door that led directly down to the basement, because it was a faster access.

In August/September 1965, I began my studies of graphic design in Yale's Graphic Design Department. Actually, what I began was called "Baby Graphic Design," and the only three students of that group, as I recall, were Peter Salter, Bruce Michel, and myself, both from the East Coast. Peter had been a Yale undergraduate, and Bruce was, I believe, from some other discipline. We were required to catch up in 1 year on all the courses and knowledge that the regular undergraduates from art and design schools had acquired in 4 years. This might seem to have been impossible, but we did not have to take academic or humanities courses; rather we had to focus on typography, basic design, color, printing, photography, and the history of these disciplines.

The terminology and concepts were, in many cases, completely new to me. During my first semester, when a teacher or a fellow student said, "That works!", I had to ask myself privately, what is it that is working? I did not know at first. In fact, for a short period of time, I wondered to myself if I had had a complete nervous breakdown. I recalled that I had been studying quantum electromagnetic theory the previous semester at Princeton, and now I was cutting out little pieces of colored paper and rubber-cementing them to larger sheets of paper. I wondered if I were in an asylum and just imagining that I was in a graduate design school (Fig. 4.1).

Gradually, meaning filled in behind the words, like a photographic lens gradually focusing, and I began to understand what people meant, but the process took about 6 months. Over the period of the first year, I was surprised and delighted that graphic design, for me, seemed to be something like my experimental physics laboratories. One studied the philosophy, principles, and techniques of the discipline, and then tried things out in a "laboratory situation." I was doing the same thing in graphic design. The difference was that I did not like to do that work in physics, but I loved doing it in graphic design.

In fact, I was having more fun than I had ever had in my life, because everything was new, fresh, mysterious, and full of potential. As a result, I slept almost not at all for three years, usually from 2 am or 3 am to 6 am or 7 am. I wanted to get back to the design studios and my desk as fast as possible.

I noticed an odd circumstance: I did not have to buy many tools; I already had a camera. I already had many graphic design instruments: pens, pencils, protractors, French curves, brushes, papers, etc. I was surprised. It seemed as if some part of me knew all along in my life that I would end up here and had been quietly collecting all the necessary equipment and preparing myself with some of the skills. I had taught myself chancery cursive calligraphy, so I did not have to take a special calligraphy short course, for example. Previously, I had not even known what graphic design was as a profession. Now I was immersed in it.

Fig. 4.1 Sample color study from Sy Sillman's color course using small pieces of Color Aid™ paper. (Source: Author's photo slide archive)

Especially enjoyable was the drawing class taught by Richard Lytle, I practiced drawing ovals, flower pots, chairs, and umbrellas, objects of increasingly complex spatial form. I learned how to depict shadowed sides, highlighted sides, and curved surfaces and how to draw chairs by drawing the spaces between the parts, not the parts themselves. My eyes were being opened and my vision sharpened. We even were asked to draw the front page of a newspaper with pencils so that, from a distant reading position, it was impossible to tell if one were looking at a real newspaper or not.

Dieter Roth was my teacher of basic design (see https://en.wikipedia.org/wiki/Dieter_Roth). He appeared to be from another planet. He spoke in an enigmatic manner suitable for a cult leader. He dressed like no one else: playful and bizarre. So different from my Princeton Ivy League experience. He encouraged us to "think crazy," not just to "think different," as Apple promoted decades later. His design challenges of document making and small booklet design were mind-opening.

In a color course taught by Sy Sillman, a student of Joseph Albers, who had once taught at Yale, we learned basic color theory, to pay attention to a multitude of nuanced differences of black or white, each of which we previously had thought was just "a single color." Our teacher held class sessions that were almost like church or temple worship rituals, with hushed tones and serious, reverent demeanor.

I foolishly agreed with a fellow Baby Graphic Designer to play a joke on our teacher and to come dressed as our homework color-study assignment. I arrived the next morning dressed all in black except for a bright chartreuse tie. My co--conspirator had bailed out of the plot and came dressed normally. No problem, he said. He would introduce me as *his* color study. He went in first, made the public announcement, and I then burst into the room with open arms, expecting my fellow students to break out into laughter. There was not a titter. We had broken the sacred decorum. I shrank as small as I could make myself, creeped to my desk, and began nervously to work as hard as I could on the morning's assignment. Later that morning, Mr. Sillman came by my desk, leaned closer, and with a comforting smile whispered, "Good joke, but very bad timing." I felt slightly better.

Throughout the year, I attempted to absorb from Prof. Alvin Eisenman, the Chair of the Department, and from others as much as I could learn the How-Tos of the following:

- Making paper, literally, from raw wood pulp and/or cloth
- Making a book, literally from cardboard, twine, glue, and book cloth
- Typesetting by hand and printing type (more detailed than my Princeton experience)
- Drawing letterforms with Plaka paint and India ink, pens/brushes
- Preparing working layouts for offset printing
- Arranging varied basic design compositions with colored paper, typography, and other elements
- Correctly spacing letters with Letraset press-on lettering
- Taking and printing carefully composed, compelling photographs
- Understanding and using color
- Designing signs and symbols
- Understanding the histories of letterform design, typographic layout, and print media

I began to see that I could use my physics/math background: to use basic principles I had learned or discovered. Given a design problem, I could go backwards to first principles, figure out what the design challenge was, then take a path forward playing with the principles to arrive at a solution that was different from my fellow students, in some cases very different.

The Baby Graphic Design year had given me enough skills and experience, to the extent that I approached the New Haven Redevelopment Agency about a summer job for 1969 as a graphic designer. My boss was named Woody. I showed up on my first day excited about what my first job might entail. My first day's assignment, I discovered, was to help pack up folding chairs from some civic event on the New Haven Commons that had taken place the night before. Not exactly how I imagined my professional skills would be utilized.

During the course of my summer job, however, I did have occasion to design and supervise the printing of several pieces, including the design of icons/symbols, logos, brochures, posters, booklets, and leaflets. I felt excited that I could carry out the work for which I was being trained/educated. The summer was soon over, and I prepared for my second of three years.

Yale, Second Year, 1966–1967: My First MFA Year

In my second year, I began to have more significant graphic design tasks, including assignments by Bradbury Thompson, a noted traditional book and magazine designer, to design historical two-page-layout spreads that utilized specific typefaces like Baskerville, Garamond, and Bodoni, together with illustrative elements suitable for the time of the content portrayed. I also had graphic design classes with the renowned graphic designer Herbert Matter and photography classes with the renowned Walker Evans. I began to photograph scenes in New Haven, the architecture of new buildings on the Yale campus, and people in various stages of life, as I had begun to do even in New York City during the summer of 1964. Previously, I could work most easily with color slide film. At Yale, I had access to a black-and-white darkroom, where I spent countless hours, night and day, through all the seasons, watching my photographic images spring to life in the development pans of chemicals and learning to control with my eye, my camera, and with the darkroom equipment the success of the final results.

In the course of Bradbury Thomson's classes, Alvin Eisenman's, and others of my teachers, I became familiar with the history and visual characteristics of many typefaces. I enjoyed using about a half-dozen in particular: Baskerville, Bodoni, Futura, Garamond, Helvetica, Times Roman, and Univers. Who would not get excited by the almost erotic beauty of a Baskerville capital E, or the elegant "soaring" verticals of Bodoni? Nevertheless, after looking at them, setting them, and printing them, I focused on two of the typefaces in particular:

- Times Roman, designed in 1929 by Stanley Morrison for the London *Times*. Morrison led the project to design a new text type for the paper and supervised Victor Lardent, an advertising artist for the *Times*, who drew the letterforms. I loved the swells, curves, and serifs, especially the shape of the lower case e and o:
  AaBbCcDdEeFfGgHhIiJjKkLlMm
  NnOoPpQqRrSsTtUuVvWwXxYyZz
  0123456789 &!?
- Helvetica, designed in 1957 by Max Miedinger with Eduard Hoffmann of the Haas'sche Schriftgiesserei (Haas type foundry) in Münchenstein, Switzerland. Haas wanted to design a new sans-serif typeface that could compete with Akzidenz-Grotesk in the Swiss market. I loved in particular the shape of the lower case a, g, and y.
  AaBbCcDdEeFfGgHhIiJjKkLlMm
  NnOoPpQqRrSsTtUuVvWwXxYyZz
  0123456789 &!?

I decided during this year that they were my favorite typefaces, and I would devote my life to exploring these two faces, not others, because I felt there was enough to learn from working with these letterforms to keep my interest for a long time. I would occasionally use others, but these were my "closest typographic friends." I also decided that the three-column grid on an 8.5 × 11 sheet of paper was ideal for complex, varied layouts, and I figured out the exact measurements that would work best.

My influences came from the Swiss-German school of graphic design, which had started in the 1950s, had seen success in Europe, and was imported into US corporate graphic design throughout the 1960s. I found its cool, rational, systematic approach very compatible with deep yearnings and feelings of peace and calm in myself.

John Hill taught my photography class. I mastered the ability to render shades of black and white and created photo sequences. One of my favorite challenges was recording the Omaha stockyards before they were shut down and turning my photos into a sequence in a photo book (Fig. 4.2).

Over the next decade, my teacher/professional graphic design heroes came to be some of the leading figures from Basel, Zurich, and Ulm, where the Ulm School of Design was located, and even earlier from the Bauhaus. People that I've met or communicated with included the following (all have died!). I thank them for their inspiration, education, assistance, advice, and pleasure of their company while they were alive:

Otl Aicher
Josef Albers
Max André
Saul Bass
Gui Bonsieppe
Aaron Burns
Will Burtin
Ivan Chermayeff
Wim Crouwel
Seymour Chwast

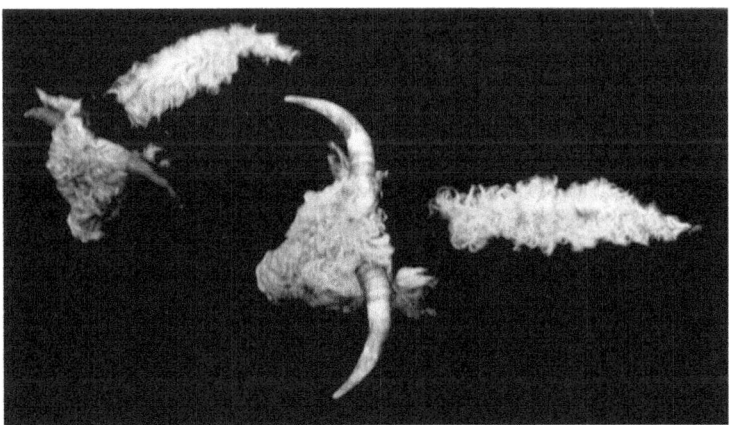

Fig. 4.2 One of several images of the cattle in the Omaha stock yards, (Photos by Aaron Marcus, 1966. Author's photo archives, used with permission)

Adrian Frutiger
Shigeo Fukuda
Milton Glaser
André Gürtler
Walter Herdeg
Armin Hofmann
György Kepes
Thomas Maldonado
Herbert Matter
Josef Müller-Brockman
Dieter Rams
Paul Rand
Emil Ruder
Bradbury Thompson
Massimo Vignelli
Wolfgang Weingart

I began to collect books and examples of the work of most of these teachers and professionals. I communicated with a number of them and met with several of them several times, like Aicher, Bonsieppe, Hoffman, Müller-Brockman, Maldonado, and Weingart, over the next three decades.

I also began to learn about the international concrete (visual) poetry movement, which also appealed to me on the "right side of my brain." I read about Mary Ellen Solt, Dick Higgins, Richard Kostelanetz, and many others worldwide and corresponded with some of these artists/poets over the next three decades.

During this year, I met the team of students creating PULSA, a technology-oriented group of artists. I was invited to design for them event graphics, their logo, and other print pieces that were silk-screened or offset-printed. I attended some of their exhibitions/showings and photographed the events. I also attended an artist's exhibition, whose name I forget, who showed images projected onto artificial fog that filled a room. The three-dimensional, undulating forms (because of the movement of the fog clouds) created beautiful, ethereal, dreamlike forms and landscapes.

In this same year, I began to audit French for a semester, took a semester course by George Kubler in the history of art, a course in architectural history by Vincent Scully, and audited a one-semester course in the essential logic of digital computers. This last course was deeply impactful for me.

I loved learning the essential logical-mathematical operations of a digital computer's central processing unit and how data were stored from programs input to computers and processed. By the end of the semester, I realized I had understood all of the fundamental workings of a digital computer. Next, I audited a course in FORTRAN programming given by the Yale Computer Center (YCC). The equipment was "state of the art" at the time but primitive by today's standards. I had to submit Hollerith-hole punched-card decks at an intake desk for the mainframe computer (an IBM 360) at the YCC. One day later I would get the results back as line-printer records of my program, including my errors, and, occasionally, successful printouts of my typographic/visual results. Even then in the spring of 1967, I was trying to figure out how to get the computer to print out visual patterns and compositions, to draw recognizable abstract objects and compositions, or to use random number generators to inject playful and/or unexpected results into visual compositions.

My Interview with AT&T Bell Labs Recruiters

My classmates knew about my interest in computers and my (limited) skills in programming. I was one of two or three students (another was Murray Milne in the School of Architecture, whom I knew) in the entire Yale School of Art and Architecture who took up the invitation of the Yale Computer Center to use their equipment for free, because they were seeking to build up interest and expertise in any and all disciplines of the university. The "baby graphic designers" had now advanced to join other first-year students with traditional art/design backgrounds. Robert (Bob) Nix (RIP), one of my studio classmates, who had come from Kansas City and had already been employed by Hallmark Cards, had somehow learned that AT&T Bell Labs recruiters were on the Yale campus looking for summer interns. He suggested to me, even encouraged and cajoled me, to go for an interview. Finally, and somewhat reluctantly, I said yes. I did, after all, need a summer job.

I should mention in passing that Bob Nix was very authoritative and thorough about the band of crazies at Hallmark Cards in Kansas City, in the late 1950s and early 1960s. These were the artists, illustrators, and graphic designers who designed the safe, bland, polite greeting cards for America that were successful and well-known throughout the country. These erratic, idiosyncratic professionals were carefully corralled and controlled by Hallmark, according to him, so as not to mix with other staff of the company. That was fine with them. The artists/designers gathered in private parties and events, smoked marijuana, drank, ran around naked, and created film and slide-show extravaganzas viewed only by themselves and fueled in part by LSD and other hallucinogens available to them. Anything went. As long as it did not get out and "infect" the safe precincts of the Hallmark "funny farm." Bob said that, at that time in Kansas, all of the extravagances of the USA in the late 1960s had already been done in Kansas City, at Hallmark, about 5–10 years earlier!

Well, I had decided to go for the interview. I may have taken a few graphic design and computer art pieces with me. I wasn't sure how to dress, what to show, or what to say. I entered a small room in an engineering building on campus with just a small office table and one chair for me. On the opposite side sat two engineer-looking fellows several years older, dressed in dark jackets, white shirts, and dark ties. They looked almost like the two protagonists of the film *Men in Black* exactly 30 years later (1997), only they were not wearing black sunglasses and did not have any strange equipment/weapons with them.

I began the interview by saying exactly what someone should *never* say: "I have no idea why you would want to hire me. All I can tell you is that I spent four years studying physics, mathematics, and philosophy at Princeton, and now I am studying graphic design, typography, color and symbol design at Yale Art School." The two men silently stared at me, unblinking and unsmiling, for a minute, then turned their heads toward each other without moving their bodies. One of them then smiled discreetly; they turned back to face me, and the other said, "Well, as a matter of fact....we are looking for someone *exactly* like you!" I was speechless, flabbergasted, overjoyed, slightly unbelieving, but beginning to think I was in a dream world.

That dream moment was the beginning of my journey into the world of computer technology, computer graphics, computer art, computer-assisted design, and the world of the next century.

My two interviewers were Dr. A. Michael Noll, who had already begun to program computer art and computer dance, and to theorize about the use of computers by artists and designers. His boss sitting next to him was Dr. Peter Denes (RIP), head of the Acoustics Research Department at Bell Labs in Murray Hill, NJ. They were looking for someone to bring in for the summer to explore ideas about computers and design and the potential for computers to produce exciting, useful displays. My internship was signed, sealed, and delivered within a few weeks, and I ended my second year's courses with a move to Murray Hill, New Jersey.

Summer 1967 Internship at Bell Labs

I had no idea what AT&T Bell Labs was: namely, the foremost research facility of the civilized world, long before the rise of Silicon Valley by way of Stanford University. The history and activities of the Labs are summarized well in Michael Noll's detailed memoir [Noll]. Because of an "Experiments in Art and Technology" (EAT) initiative developed by Billy Kluever, I had occasion that summer, and during two years of later consulting with Bell Labs during 1969–1971, to meet and talk with many artists and scientists interested in visual/acoustic experiments who were working with computers and who were on staff or visiting Bell Labs:

Stan Brakhage, a noted experimental filmmaker.

Virgil Finlay, a noted science-fiction illustrator. As a child, I had known and treasured his illustrations, and I was awe-struck to meet him.

Bela Julesz, who was developing his theory of human vision and publishing a book about "Cyclopean vision," that is, what the brain could process and know about the world with just information from one eye, before binocular vision in the brain combined the data from both eyes.

Ken Knowlton, who had begun to program the world's first computer-animated movies.

Max Mathews, a researcher in sound-generation with computers, who developed the "Daisy, Daisy" voice segment representing the advanced computer HAL's mind decomposing in the movie *2001*, which was used by filmmaker Stanley Kubrick and author Arthur C. (I kept audio magnetic tapes of Max's early experiments to perfect that voice segment for many decades before donating them to the Computer History Museum, Mountain View.)

Benoit Mandelbrot, a world-famous mathematician who was developing his mathematics of fractals, visual patterns that repeated themselves continuously at every scale of viewing.

Nam June Paik (RIP), a national treasure of South Korea, who was a pre-eminent video artist.

Around the corner from me, Bryan Kernigan and Dennis Ritchie were inventing the UNIX operating system, and other researchers were perfecting typesetting systems for printout (TROFF).

The roster of people whom one could meet in the hallways was intoxicating. I had never before, or since, been in such an environment of stimulating people.

My assignment for the summer was quite simple: Get to know the equipment and its capabilities and explore how computers could be used for art and design.

To accomplish my assignment, I had access to a GE-645 mainframe computer (in those days General Electric competed with IBM to make and sell such large computers). Many large metal cabinets held all of the electronics, including central processing units, card deck readers, magnetic tape readers/recorders, line printers, Stromberg-Carlson 4020 microfilm recorders, and other components, all of them sitting on raised platforms that covered the floor of the large computer room. Cables could snake around the space below the electronics as necessary. Many of the cabinets had small lights that glowed white, yellow, green, and red, many of them blinking. All the while, the hum of fans muffled all other sounds from human voices and office life outside of this one room. It was a surreal environment.

At one point that summer, I realized no one else was in this computer room. I was alone. I wandered into an area among the gray cabinets in which I was cut off visually from anything else. I was surrounded by this behemoth, which seemed like some human-made, artificial creature that was, in some manner, alive and breathing... I sensed this creation was destined to take over humanity, to take over the earth. I was having a religious moment, in contact with spirits unlike any others I had witnessed....as if a caveman were suddenly placed inside a Ford Galaxy automobile with the motor running and the dashboard lights on...

There was also an IBM 7090 computer in the area, but the GE-645 was the machine I used. Noll describes the history of that time (Fig. 4.3):

Note this history of Bell Labs, in [Noll], pp. 32–33:

Bell Labs believed that time-shared computing was the future. A project was initiated to create a time-shared computer facility with terminals in laboratories. It was believed that IBM was not up to the challenge, and therefore a project, named MULTICS (Multiplexed Information and Computing Service), was initiated, with GE to supply the computer hardware (GE 645), MIT the system software, and BTL the systems integration. The MULTICS project was initiated around 1964. Although GE had not up-to-then made a large mainframe machine, it did deliver its GE-645 to Bell Labs as a replacement for the IBM 7094.

It became apparent that the system overhead for time-shared computing was substantial, and the project seemed doomed to failure. BTL abandoned its involvement around 1969. IBM then supplied its IBM-360 mainframe computer to BTL to replace the GE machine. The failure of MULTICS ultimately led to Unix and C.

Fig. 4.3 A computer center at Bell Labs around 1963 consisted of an IBM 7094 computer. Input and output were on magnetic tape. The operator monitored the operation of the computer at a console. (Photo from Alcatel-Lucent USA, Inc./Bell Labs and used with permission of Nokia Corporation and AT&T Archives)

Getting expert assistance to understand the errors in my programs added to my significant religious and cultural/anthropological experience. I went to the system programmers who would look over the 50- to 250-page printouts filled from top to bottom, from side to side with hexadecimal numbers representing the binary code that in turn represented the programs and statements of the errors. These uber-geeks would flip among the pages, examining carefully the gray texture of full pages of alphanumerics, then suddenly point to some spot and pronounce, "Aha! Here is your error!" Then, they would proceed to explain what set of errors in functions, data values, or variables had caused the crash. I realized immediately that they were the modern equivalent of ancient high priests, pouring over the entrails of some goat to discern signs of reality or the future.

During that summer of 1967, I was able to use the microfilm recorder to experiment with many variations of abstract geometric forms. These all appeared as white lines and alphanumerical symbols on black 35 mm microfilm. The images were usually individually mounted on Bell Labs cardboard cards. I had hundreds of them by the end of my summer at Bell Labs.

One art project that I particularly enjoyed was displaying the mathematical output from a mapping of values for a relatively simple function similar to that which had been suggested by another researcher, I believe Manfred Mohr, a colleague at Bell Labs (Fig. 4.4).

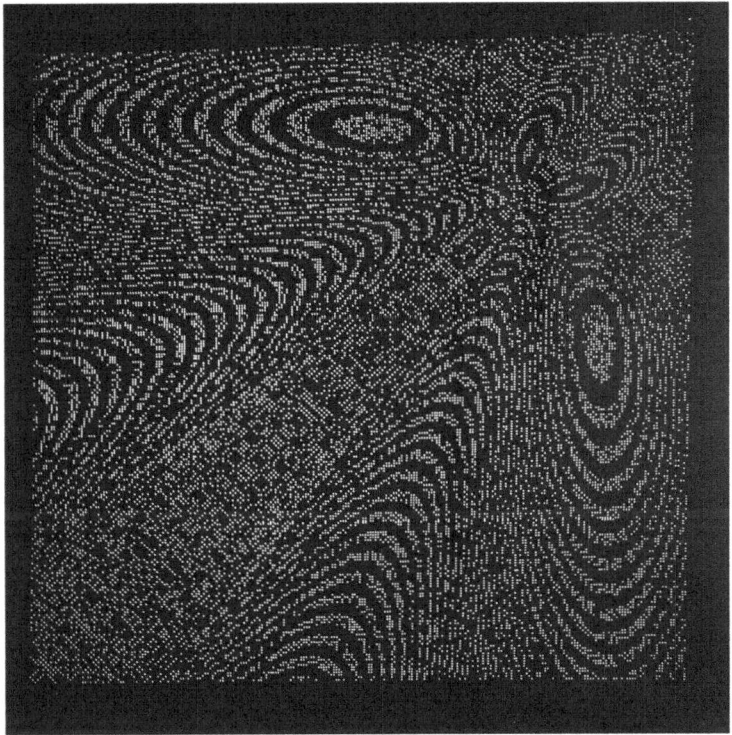

Fig. 4.4 Mathematical expression visualized in computer art, Aaron Marcus, 1967. Based on functions similar to those developed by Manfred Mohr, AT&T Bell Labs, Murray Hill, NJ. Most of these images are in the collections of the San Francisco Museum of Modern Art, the Letterform Archive/San Francisco, the Computer History Museum/Mountain View, and/or the Victoria and Albert Museum/London. (Source: Author's collection of original photocopies of artwork)

I was intrigued with what random numbers could do in programming displays, to give them a "human touch" and to avoid a boring repetition of visual characteristics. I also tried to create a representation of the light-button displays that I saw on many of the metal cabinets of the mainframe computers (Figs. 4.5–4.7, 4.8, and 4.9).

My mistakes in programming were sometimes more interesting than the straightforward images that were successfully coded, because odd lines, numbers, and bursts of light might appear against the black background of the microfilm images. I was fortunate to be able to experiment repeatedly with programming of visual images, creating hundreds of images, many of which were variations upon themes.

During that 1967 summer, riots broke out in Newark, NJ. A summer of social unrest rolled across the USA. About 5.5 miles south of Bell Labs in Murray Hill, NJ, riots broke out in Plainfield, NJ, where I had rented a room in a clapboard boarding house. For the first time in my life, I went to bed with the sound of gunfire drifting to my window. It was not Fourth of July fireworks. I realized that the USA had entered a new stage of its history in the 1960s. This was 1967. In the morning, I

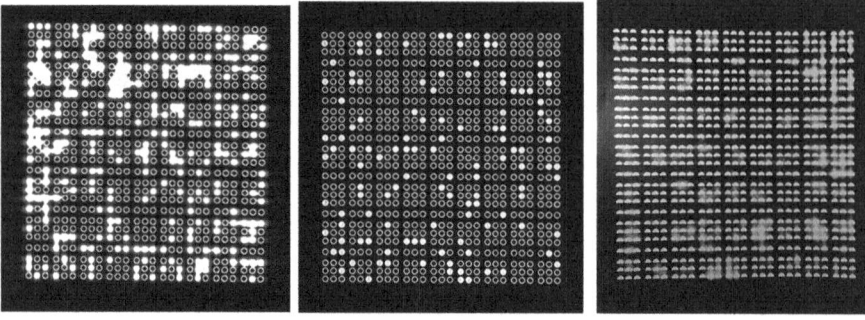

Figs. 4.5–4.7 "Light Buttons." Several of many light-button-oriented displays programmed by Aaron Marcus in 1967. Based on experiments of A. Michael Noll, AT&T Bell Labs, Murray Hill, NJ. Most of these images are in the collections of the San Francisco Museum of Modern Art, the Letterform Archive/San Francisco, the Computer History Museum/Mountain View, and/or the Victoria and Albert Museum/London. (Source: Author's collection of original photocopies of artwork)

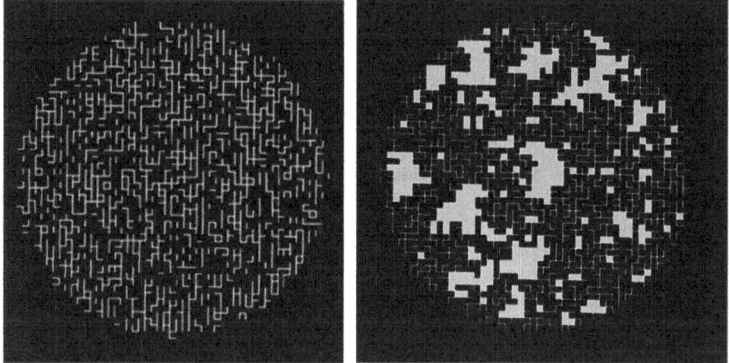

Figs. 4.8 and 4.9 "Random Line Segments." Computer graphics artwork programmed by Aaron Marcus, 1967. Inspired by the work of A. Michael Noll, ATT Bell Labs, and Mondrian's artworks. (Source: Author's collection of original photocopies of computer art, used with permission)

could not get to Bell Labs because US Army Jeeps and other military vehicles had blocked access to my usual route through town. I had to seek alternative, longer routes to get to the Labs. At the Labs itself, the buildings and people seemed sealed off from the turmoil elsewhere outside nearby and throughout the USA.

Over the course of the summer of 1967, in my professional life, I had used my earlier programming skills, learned at least one new programming language, had access to state-of-the-art equipment, had experimented with typography and abstract visual forms in several media (microfilm recorders, ink plotters, and line printers), and had engaged in discussions and debates about art, design, technology, and even religion. For me, the internship at Bell Labs was a fortunate, thorough, and successful introduction to the world of computer technology. As far as I knew then and since then, I had become the first professional graphic designer in the world to work full-time with computers.

What did I learn from working with computers that summer? Here are summary observations:

- Programming was challenging. It took time to figure out how to accomplish even simple objectives. There were no ready-made tools in those "ancient years." I needed to build almost all of what I wanted to see and to take place, except for the most primitive functions.
- As a general rule, it was difficult working with computers if one had specific things in mind. It was easier if one went with the flow and made compromises, or followed the paths of what computers "had in mind" to let one do. In other words, the computer won the competition.
- It was indeed possible through skillful programming and/or use of random number generators to generate "human-like" or "natural artifacts," signs, gestures, forms, movements. Still, the context seemed very technological. One was aware that it was computer art, not some other medium.
- The computer was a medium like no other for art and design. The computer was a manipulator and manager of all other media. For that matter, it was a manipulator of the programmer/artist/designer who was "using" the computer. *The computer was also "using" the human being.*
- The spread of computers into everyday life, thought, communication, and visual/verbal form was inevitable and unstoppable. Even in 1967 it was possible to foresee this trend. How exactly computer technology would accomplish all of this takeover was only vaguely known to me at the time, and perhaps to the others working with computers. Artificial intelligence (AI) was in its infancy (starting in 1956 with the work of John McCarthy and Marvin Minsky) and was decades away from being "real" or commercialized.
- Most people had an outdated view or limited understanding of computer technology, either viewing it as monolithically evil or monolithically benign.
- Computer technology seemed to require extensive government and big-industry support to move it forward. In 1967, the concept of personal computers was unknown to me, I think, except for random mentions in sci-fi literature. In the movie *2001*, Stanley Kubrick and Arthur C. Clarke did not depict this kind of computer at all, with perhaps a rare exception. Kubrick and Clarke had not anticipated or visualized mobile phones in the film, which today have more computing power than the supercomputers of that and the following decade (1960s and 1970s).
- It seemed likely that computer technology would have dramatic impacts on typography, typesetting, type design, graphic design, and most forms of media communication.

I returned in the fall of 1967 from Bell Labs for my final year at Yale.

Yale, Third Year, 1967–1968: Graduation, Two Degrees

During my last year at Yale, I was recruited, or volunteered, to help with the production of *Eye* magazine, a Yale Art School publication about art and design. I recall that one of my assignments was to interview Anni Albers, the wife of Josef Albers. Her husband, the noted Bauhaus painter and teacher, had come to the USA and had taught at Yale for some years. At that time, Josef Albers had little to do with the Yale School of Art. I went with my list of questions, sat with both Josef and Anni Albers, and photographed her for the interview.

During my third year, and possibly even beginning with my second year, I began to design posters for events of Yale's Hillel organization on campus, a Jewish group, headed by Rabbi Richard Israel. We became friends, and I recall attending a Passover (Pesakh) seder in his home in April 1968 (Figs. 4.10, 4.11, and 4.12).

In April 1968, Martin Luther King, Jr. was assassinated. On 6 June 1968, Senator Robert F. Kennedy was assassinated. These events made the spring and early summer seem threatening and tragic. The mood of all students in the department seemed somber. After JFK's assassination and now these two other leaders, we thought we were headed for a national catastrophe.

Rob Roy Kelly, a Yale graduate, has written a fine summary of the education at Yale and mentions many of my teachers ([Kelly], in his article available online. He comments on the history of the Graphic Design Department from the early 1950s to

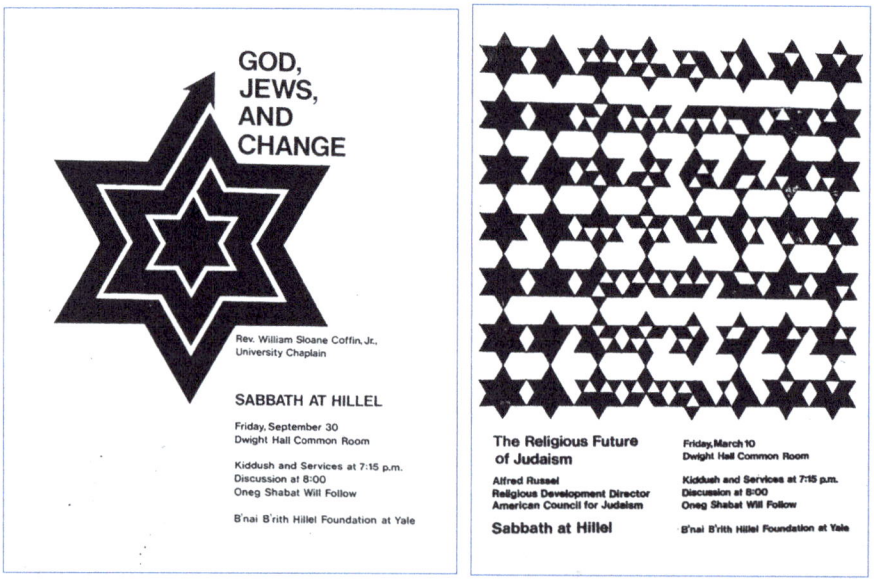

Figs. 4.10 and 4.11 Hillel poster designs, 1967–1968. (Source: Author's design archive; used with permission)

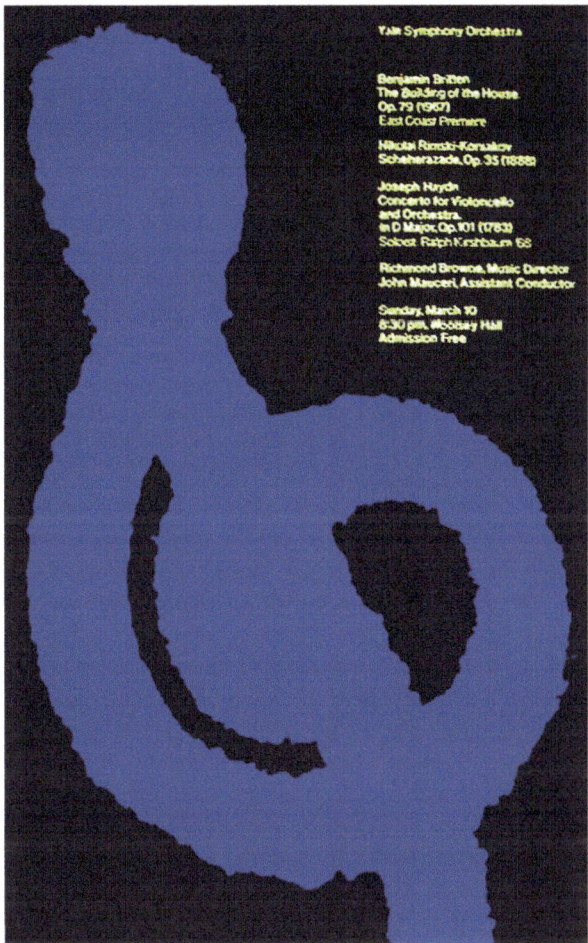

Fig. 4.12 Yale Symphony Orchestra Poster, 1967–1968. (Source: Author's design archive)

about 1965 when I joined the School [Kelly, Rob Roy, "The Early Years of Graphic Design at Yale University," *Design Issues*, Volume 17, Number 3, Summer 2001].

> ....type, photography, printmaking, and printing production, they were required to take Albers's color class. A number of design students elected to enrolling drawing classes taught by Albers or Bernard Chaet. As I remember, art or architectural history were required and students chose other electives from the Yale College curriculum. Herbert Matter taught photography and, on occasion, design. [Alvin] Eisenman was responsible for typography and printing production; Ives concentrated in design. [Gabor] Peterdi instructed in print-making, and the Visiting Lecturers gave students either short or extended practical problems. In their last year at Yale, graduate students were expected to find a manuscript (or write one), and then to design, print, and bind an edition of fifty books. By the time of the second generation of instructors—the late 1950s—book projects were no longer required.

Critiques and reviews were conducted by several teachers working together, which broadened the scope of criticism and discussion enormously. Teachers worked as a unit, so there was no pigeon-holing of classes in separate rooms with separate instructors. Students were expected to perform competently in all the areas of design, typography, printmaking, and photography. To fail in any one area was to fail the program. (I do not remember any student ever being failed, but we were told, and we believed, that to fail one course was to fail them all). Treating the program of study as a whole strengthened the interrelationships between the various areas and, combined with team-teaching of sorts, made graphic design at Yale different from design instruction at the majority of other schools during that period.

Grading was done at the end of each semester by review. Eisenman, Ives, and one or more of the Visiting Critics would occupy the front office. Students would come into the room one at a time with their portfolio. A timer from the photography lab was set for fifteen minutes. The reviews were conducted by Alvin Eisenman. They consisted of all faculty members present examining and discussing the student work along with some general counseling. When the timer sounded, the review was over and you were out of there.

The new design program at Yale was unique in several other respects. The curriculum of design, typography, photography, and printmaking was exclusive to it. The faculty and the Visiting Lecturers constituted the most prestigious concentration of designers teaching at one school in the country.

In my third year, my graphic design studio courses increased in complexity, detail, and demand for thinking, research, analysis, and formal construction. My graphic design teachers included Herbert Matter (RIP), who would smoke nonstop in our presence, his cigarette ash growing longer and longer at the end of the cigarette in his mouth, until it fell off onto the work shown in front of him. My photography teacher was Walker Evans (RIP). He would tell engaging stories and produce a large collection of pharmaceutical bottles during class and "take his pills." Norman Ives (RIP) seemed a saintly figure, devoted to the high art of typographic construction of compositions that paid attention to the visual interactions among large letterforms. Gabor Peterdi (RIP) provided me "media relief" by engaging us in lithographic and intaglio printmaking. I seem to recall having modestly good relations with all of my teachers, whom I liked and respected.

My most demanding graphic design teacher was Paul Rand (a"h), (born Peretz Rosenbaum, 15 August 1914, died 26 November 1996), from whom I learned a certain playfulness about visual form, for which he was famous, but also learned to design using carefully thought-out spatial grids to control the layout of all pieces of visual content on the page, poster, exhibit panel, or two-page spread. Paul Rand was so hard on students during his "crit sessions" that men as well as women would be reduced to tears. For some reason, he did not intimidate me, even if he might have occasional harsh words for my work.

I assume he knew, by the end of my third year, that I was involved with programming computers and generating computer graphics. I tried communicating with him for decades after Yale, sending him Jewish New Year (Rosh Hashanah) cards that I had designed, because I knew he was Jewish. He never replied, as far as I can recall. Once, in about 1994, decades after Yale, and shortly before he died, he was fêted at the AIGA/California College of the Arts in San Francisco and interviewed on stage by Steve Heller, noted author/design critic and art director for *The New York Times*. As Paul Rand approached me on his way out, wading through the crowd offering congratulations and compliments, including my own, my ex-wife number two, Leslie Becker, like Paul, a graduate of Cooper Union, mentioned me to him and introduced me to him. "Yes," he said, "I remember you. Are you still doing that shit with computers?" He might have been smiling ever so slightly. Still the same old Paul.

In the autumn of 1967, shortly before it closed in October1967, several of my classmates and I arranged to visit the 1967 World's Fair in Montreal, Québec, Canada. We drove in several cars and stayed in inexpensive hotels. We were amazed by the Buckminster Fuller geodesic dome that was part of the USA pavilion; we noted the clear communication of its information and exhibition graphics; we marveled at Moshe Safdie's Habitat structures, and we enjoyed other country pavilions, particularly the Czech pavilion with an innovative multimedia presentation. We planned to return to New Haven after about 2 days roaming the grounds.

As it happened, in the Medical Pavilion, as I was wandering among medical displays, I began to feel a significant pain in my left chest, with tendrils of pain creeping down my left arm. I had never felt such pain before. Soon, the pain was so severe that it interrupted my breathing. I could not stand up, and eventually I could not even sit up. I thought for sure that I was having a heart attack. Why at 24 would I have a heart attack? I could not reason very well as I attempted to endure the pain. I thought to myself: I don't want to cause a scene and interrupt the experience of the other tourists. I shall just crawl behind one of the large medical exhibition display cases and quietly die. Someone will eventually discover my body when the janitors are cleaning up.

But because I was a bit hasty and clumsy in hiding myself during my forthcoming demise, my feet were sticking out from behind the display! A passing tourist became curious and peaked around and down at me. Shocked, he asked me if I needed an ambulance. I said weakly, "yes!" Within a short time I found myself in a local hospital's emergency room, where the doctor had diagnosed that I had suffered a 15% collapse of my left lung, a painful, but not fatal event. Apparently, this situation is more common among tall, thin people (which I was then), who have thinner tissues and linings within their bodies. The doctors required me to stay in the hospital, but when I protested and said I needed to go with my colleagues back to Yale University in the USA, they allowed me to ride back with my colleagues if I promised to check in at the Yale Infirmary, which I did. I stayed a week, by which time my lung had begun to re-inflate. This notable misdiagnosis is memorable in my life because of an event 30 years later, in which just the opposite circumstances occurred (see Chap. 7). In any case, my medical condition would later keep me out of being drafted into the Vietnam War, but I did not realize my condition's impact at the time. I continued with my final year.

One of my most exciting learning experiences was working with architecture students in a joint course led by the renowned duo Robert Venturi (RIP) and Denise Scott-Brown (RIP), who had made names for themselves by their eclectic inclusion of architectural references to past styles in their work and their interest in popular forms of architectural design. They had just published *Learning from Las Vegas*, in which they popularized the idea of designing buildings for the viewers driving by on the highway, and recognizing that buildings could be "sheds" or "ducks," in which binary architectural universe, ducks were decorated sheds that provided visual imagery at large scale suitable for drive-by viewing.

Our assignment was to design signage and architecture for the Herald Square subway station in Manhattan. Here was an ideal environment that was both built form and signage that advertised and guided movement. For me, sitting with an architect and learning what made sense to him was enlightening. I hoped the reverse was true for my project partner. The value of this kind of cross-disciplinary learning stayed with me for decades and inspired my own multidisciplinary-student and multidisciplinary-learning courses that I designed at several universities and art/ design schools.

Departmental policy required final-year students to select a thesis project in consultation with faculty and to work for a semester on achieving research and design objectives. I decided to write/illustrate/design a book about the history of number forms. I have been interested in sign and symbol systems all of my life, and my interest was unabated. I was able to use Yale Library as well as Art School Library resources. One could not use the Internet/Google. They had not yet been invented ("ARPANET adopted TCP/IP on January 1, 1983, and from there researchers began to assemble the 'network of networks' that became the modern Internet. The online world then took on a more recognizable form in 1990, when computer scientist Tim Berners-Lee invented the World Wide Web." [Source: www.history.com/news/ask-history/who-invented-the-internet, Dec 18, 2013, accessed 6 February 2018]).

Eventually, I produced a simple survey of many number-writing systems as diverse as Hindu-Arabic, Mayan, and Chinese. I took time to design a classic book layout in Times Roman and Helvetica, and even to make the book covers and binding. My typesetting machine was an IBM Selectric™. I hoped the document would interest a reader in the subject matter and inspire her/him to study further (Figs. 4.13 and 4.14).

At the close of the year, I had completed my intense, three-year introduction to color design (especially the work of Joseph Albers), typeface design (especially Times Roman and Helvetica), typographic composition (especially abstract type-form layouts, asymmetric page layout, and flush-left/ragged right text and title setting), Swiss-German graphic design (the work of Jan Tschichold, Armin Hoffman, Josef Mueller-Brockman, the Ulm school of design), corporate graphic design (the work of Paul Rand, Herbert Matter, the Container Corporation of America, and the Vignelli studio, among others), concrete/visual poetry, and the emerging world of computer graphics and computer-assisted art and design.

Invitation to Join Princeton's Faculty

Although I was being prepared for a corporate graphic-design-studio entry-level job, probably on the East Coast, I did not feel comfortable with that career path. I felt I wanted to do research of some kind and to teach, but how might this be

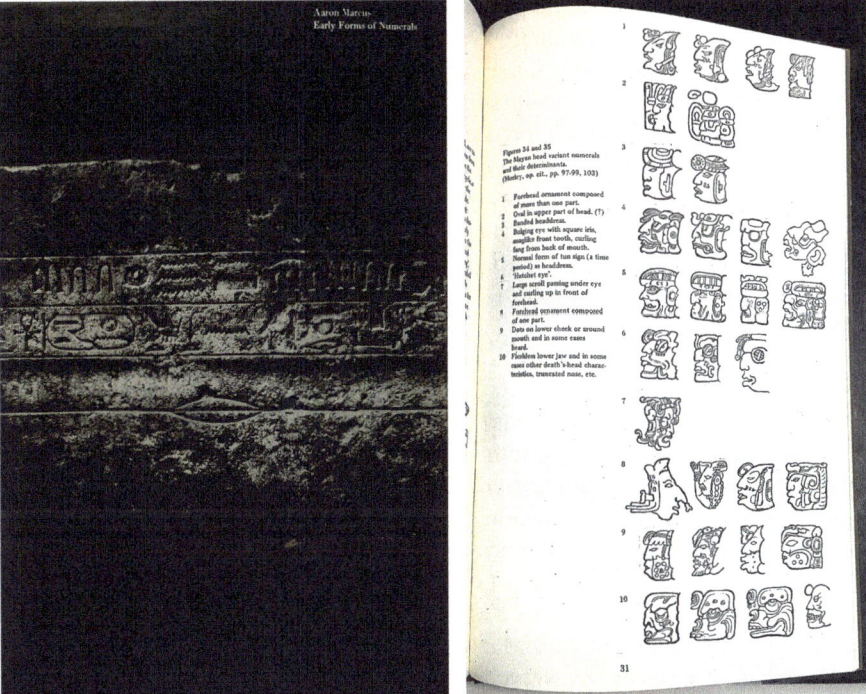

Figs. 4.13 and 4.14 Master thesis by Aaron Marcus about the history of numerals, 1968. (Images from the author's copy; used with permission)

accomplished? One path that I discovered to postpone a decision, and to avoid being drafted into the Vietnam War (about which I had my skeptical beliefs), was to seek a post-graduate year's study at some institution. I discovered that I could apply for a Fulbright Scholarship award through a German exchange program (Deutsche Akademische Austausch Dienst, DAAD). I did so and learned to my delight in May 1968, shortly before graduation, that I had been accepted, and I could go to study at the world-famous Ulm School of Design in Germany for a year. This would be heavenly. But wait! The very day I received a formal letter from the German organization DAAD that I had won the Fulbright, *The New York Times* featured a front-page story that political unrest at Ulm's design school had caused the governing powers to close the school! What was going on? Did the left hand not know what the right hand was doing? Did I want to arrive in Ulm only to be told there was no school, and would I be so kind as to leave? This situation did not seem desirable. I was confused, anxious, and slightly miserable, because I had made no other plans!

A day or two later, my class colleagues told me that there was a phone call from someone, for me, on the payphone at the other end of the class studio. Odd. Who would even know to try to reach me at Yale? I walked to the phone and somewhat timidly replied, "Yes, I'm Aaron Marcus, who is calling?"

The caller was none other than Emilio Ambasz, a former student colleague from Princeton. We had become friendly as first-year undergraduates. Emilio was bright, ambitious, the son of a humble father, which made him a likable person in my book. We both had started out as undergraduates in our first year. Four years later, by the time I finally achieved a BA in physics, Emilio had not only completed his undergraduate degree but had gone on to get a Master's, then a PhD!! How was that possible!? I don't know, but Emilio was brilliant, eloquent, and persuasive, that I knew. By this time, three years later, he had been on the Princeton University School of Architecture and Urban Planning (SAUP) faculty as a Professor and was leaving to become Associate Curator of the Design Department at New York's Museum of Modern Art!

He asked me simply and straightforwardly if I would like to take over his course at Princeton!

Out of the blue, this extraordinary opportunity had come like a bolt of lightning. I hesitated for only a few seconds; then, having no alternatives, I meekly, but enthusiastically said I would gladly assume a position at the SAUP. My career dilemma was solved. I had entered the world of university education, with the unexpected location of Princeton University once again.

To complete the formal process, I had to be reviewed by the SAUP faculty. Now, how was this to be accomplished? I was asked to arrange quickly to travel to Max's Kansas City restaurant in Mid-Manhattan, where the relevant faculty members would assemble to meet me. Nervously I prepared my portfolio notebook, dressed up as well as I could, and took the train to Manhattan. I had never been to this restaurant, but I found it and entered. Inside, even at mid-day, the restaurant was almost pitch black, with small candles at each table. I was shown to the group from Princeton University seated at a long table. Emilio greeted me and showed me where to sit to the left of Dean Robert F. Geddes, with Emilio sitting to his right. I bowed as graciously as I could to each of the people to whom I was introduced. I cannot now say who was there. Probably young leaders of the younger intelligentsia, like Ken Frampton, Anthony (Tony) Vidler (RIP), Michael Graves (RIP), and some senior members of the Old Guard. I would guess there were about 10–12 people including myself.

We made light conversation, I answered questions as best I could, I asked a few questions about the position (Lecturer) and the course (an introduction to visual communication and visual thinking), and I inquired about my responsibilities to set up a visual studies workshop/lab to help undergraduates and graduates gain visual design and communication skills. Time for the meeting was running out, and I hesitatingly asked the Dean if he did not want to see some examples of my work. "Ah, yes, of course, please show me." I had calculated which train I needed to take to get back to New Haven. I had perhaps less than 10 min to display my life's professional work, and only the light of one candle by which anyone could see anything in the darkness. I felt a bit embarrassed, frustrated, and confused. Nevertheless, I flipped through my works, trying to summarize the design assignment and my approach. We quickly said our goodbyes, and I rushed back to the train station to catch the return train to New Haven. On that trip, I agonized over my performance and whether the entire event might have been some elaborate joke or charade. The entire process and perhaps the job I hoped for was perhaps a dream of mine, or a mistaken identification of me. However, within a day or two, Emilio called to tell me all was OK, the faculty had approved me, and, without a search for a faculty member other than that phone call to me, I had been selected. Only later did I realize, of course, that Emilio had hand-picked me as his successor and that the entire faculty (or most of it) had simply accepted his decision. I was in.

I quickly completed my graduation activities at Yale and prepared for a move back to Princeton.

Summer 1968

Shortly after graduation, I moved to Pittsburgh to attend a special workshop at the Graphic Arts Technical Foundation. My workshop appointment was sponsored by Champion Papers. I am not certain, but I think it was Alvin Eisenman's decision as to who would go. Perhaps he thought the technical content would be better suited to me than some of the other students. I was the winner from Yale, and I met students from other graphic design schools and university departments. We studied printing technology and practiced preparing all the necessary pre-production materials for offset printing. Some of the classes in the history and details of printing were interesting.

That summer I also prepared to become married. I had been dating my college roommate's former girlfriend Susan Whitman Douglas, a native of Princeton, and we had decided to get married, as it happened in September 1968. How convenient. I would begin married life, begin teaching, and return to Princeton. Just one of the several times when the anxiety level of my life was off the scale. In addition, I was marrying someone not Jewish, which caused my parents, and also myself, some concern. However, I was hopeful that somehow everything would work out….

I left New Haven and returned, unexpectedly in terms of what I imagined I would do after Yale, to Princeton University, thus ending my years as a graduate student and preparing for marriage and becoming a Princeton faculty member.

Bibliography

Kelly, Rob Roy (1989). "The Early Years of Graphic Design at Yale University." Source: http://sheltonography.com/resources/Articles/GraphicDesignAtYaleUniversity.pdf. Accessed on 31 January 2018.

Noll, A. Michael (2015). "Memories: A Personal History of Bell Telephone Laboratories." Quello Center Working Paper, Michigan State University. Source: http://quello.msu.edu/wp-content/uploads/2015/08/Memories-Noll.pdf, accessed 1 February 2018.

Chapter 5
Wandering in Academia for 13 Years

Takeaways
For 9 years, 1968–1977, I taught at Princeton University and helped students learn about visual communication and publication design. I also made progress in using computers to generate computer art. I seemed to be working simultaneously each week in three different centuries: the nineteenth, twentieth, and twenty-first.

Princeton University, Year 1, 1968–1969

In the autumn of 1968, I moved with my new wife Susan Douglas Marcus into faculty housing by Lake Carnegie, on the southern edge of the Princeton University Campus. I had met Susan at a Joan Baez concert at Princeton; we dated in graduate school, and upon her graduation from New York University and mine from Yale, we decided to marry.

I began joint teaching responsibilities in the School of Architecture and Urban Planning (SAUP) (under a Danforth grant) and in the Visual Arts Program (VAP). In the SAUP, I taught basic design, graphic design, and publication design to undergraduates and graduates. In the VAP, I was in charge of their letterpress printing equipment, which I had used when I was an undergraduate student.

At the university, one of the most shocking things that had changed in my three years away was that there were now women students on campus. It was a breathtaking improvement, making life for the male students and the mostly male faculty more humane and normal. In my last undergraduate year 1964–1965, there were only the five first women undergraduates at Princeton, so-called Critical Language students studying Russian, perhaps Chinese, etc. Now, in the School of Architecture and Urban Planning, there were many women students. There were also some women faculty members, like Suzanne Keller, who taught about

A. Marcus, *Bridging Art, Design and Technology: My Lifetime Work*,
https://doi.org/10.1007/978-3-032-04342-9_5

73

sociology and architecture (she became Princeton's first tenured female professor), and Galen Cranz, who taught about the social and cultural bases of architectural and urban design.

Within the building, I became familiar with my faculty colleagues. A friendly benevolent fellow was Ernst Jandl (RIP), a Beaux Arts architect who represented the generation of gentlemen architects who designed grand pavilions, villas, and buildings suitable for Princeton's elite alumnae. Their work was presented in large, elaborate, beautiful drawings, some of which are still to be seen as framed works of art.

At the other end of the scale was the building technology construction advisor Leon Barth, a socialist Jew from the fabled Northern New Jersey farming Jewish communities (perhaps Roosevelt, NJ) that had emerged outside of New York City in the 1930s. We developed a mutual liking for each other, and I would enjoy going to his workshop outside but near the Architecture Building where he helped students build models. Over the years, Leon chose to give me collections of old folk songs, 3D cameras, and other items from his vast holdings, because he thought I would like them. I did.

One of the faculty members I did not get along with was Michael Graves, who seemed, over the years I spent there, to dislike me and to ridicule me, even to my face. This was not unusual behavior for him, as he spent a fair amount of time at a giant conference table at the opposite end of Dean Geddes ridiculing him and laughing at private jokes with his cronies. Fortunately, over the years, I developed good relations with Ken Frampton, Tony Vidler, Colin Rowe, Lance Brown, and graduate students like Stephanos Polyzoides, Gustav (Gus) Escher, and others. These people helped me to survive the pressure and the clashes with others less friendly to me.

During my first year, I did not teach at all. The Danforth Grant that had brought me to the campus and paid for my time enabled me to prepare for new courses and facilities. I had several primary challenges. I had to catch up on the world of design. The faculty referred to numerous concepts, terms, professionals, and critics, with which I had no familiarity. Semiotics, Roland Barthes, Umberto Eco, Tomas Maldonado, the Russian Constructivists, Vitruvius, architectural design theory, community-oriented design, Christopher Alexander, among others, all crowded together in my brain. I audited several of Ken Frampton's fine courses on architectural history. I read everything I could find. I tried to absorb many theories, concepts, principles, and techniques. My brain was being stretched in every direction, just as it had been in my first graduate school year.

At the same time, I was studying all the documents of Emilio Ambasz's course introducing visual communication, visual thinking, and visual design. The lecture topics and exercises were a *tour de force* of powerful subject matter and eloquent language. I could understand why the students were in awe of him, feared him, and possibly understood him. It seemed as if Emilio wanted to erect a wall of words as a fortress around himself, so that only the most sophisticated and brilliant might pass through. I had a different approach: I was trying to explain things that so almost all people could understand, and I had sympathy for those who might not have been exposed to the topics before (like *myself*!).

   Sometime that year of 1968, I bought a Sony portable 13-inch color television for about $300, the first-ever portable device made for consumers, and placed that set on my desk, which was a flat door painted white and supported by file drawers. I have used such desks for the rest of my life. I realized even then in 1968 that someday, almost everyone would have televisions (or some kind of screens) on their desks, and that being connected to the world through desktop computers (there were none then) and/or desktop televisions, together with other media, would be the norm. At the time, I was the only person I knew with such a television. Amazingly, after more than 50 years, that very television set still works! In those days, Sony, and other manufacturers, actually made products that were meant to last (see Fig. 5.1).

   During that one year, I developed a set of lectures and exercises that were an introduction to simple theories of design, basic design principles (so-called spots and dots exercises), and an introduction to graphic design, especially typographic design.

   But I had other responsibilities.

   I was supposed to set up a facility in the basement of the Architecture Building that would provide equipment and training in visual design and visual communication, so that SAUP students would be better able to communicate their architecture and urban planning ideas in posters, leaflets, books, magazines, and photographs, that is, modern mass communication media. That challenge underlay my being selected to come to Princeton. What was I to do? I had only my 3 years of Yale education to provide professional experience.

   I decided that I would build a miniature version of the graphic design facilities at Yale. I laid out the rooms and spaces made available to me in what I called the

Fig. 5.1 1968 Sony desktop television still in use, originally with "rabbit ears" VHF antenna and a circular UHF antenna but now connected to an analogue-to-digital signal converter. (Source: Author's photo collection; used with permission)

Visual Studies Laboratory in the basement, and I filled it with equipment of the kinds that I had used at Yale: silkscreen presses, back-and-white darkrooms, photo studios, graphic design preparation rooms, typesetting equipment (expensive variable-width-type IBM typewriters), a book-trimming machine, and even a Nu-Arc carbon-rod lighting cabinet used for making photo-silkscreen imagery. After ordering, receiving, and setting up all the equipment and supplies, I also had to write detailed instruction manuals for using every piece of equipment that the students could use. This project itself took several months of part-time effort.

Princeton University's Visual Arts Program

At the same time, I was expected to teach in the Visual Arts Program (VAP) (formerly called the Creative Arts Program) half-time. This collection of facilities, equipment, and staff had emerged more strongly in the years that I was away and now was collected into one building, the old Nassau Street Elementary School, where my wife (born and raised in Princeton) had herself gone to school as a child!

I was to take over immediately the Printing Room and to teach any undergraduates, graduates, and faculty who had interest the basics of hand-setting type, how to print from a Vandercook proving press, and preparing lithographic stones or intaglio metal plates for printing on a special press, just as I had done several years earlier. The room in which I would work two days per week would be the former kindergarten room, which meant the space was large, well-lighted, and airy, with many windows, and equipped with a unisex bathroom with tiny toilets and sinks for the former wee ones who had to "make pee-pee." It was all quite bizarre and charming.

During that year, and in later years attending VAP faculty meetings, I would have occasion to meet several visiting artists and writers, including George Segal, who created paper-maché life-like sculptures of people in daily life situations (several of which are in the NY MoMA collection), and Jerzy Kosiński, noted author of *The Painted Bird* and *Being There* (which was made into a fine movie with Peter Sellers). Decades later, I read almost all of his novels. These were two people I particularly enjoyed seeing and conversing with. The secretary of the Program was Kate Kuhn, the wife of Thomas Kuhn, the noted author of the *Nature of Scientific Revolutions*. I met with him several times over the next years. (When he gave a lecture in the 1990s at the University of California at Berkeley, where I later lived, I went to see/ hear him. I was delighted, as I told him, that he had begun to include diagrams of scientific theories as a significant visual token of the underlying metaphors of scientific theories, like the drawing of the Bohr atom or Maxwell's interlocking rings representing electromagnetism.)

Finally, at the end of my first year of preparation, I had most of my teaching materials and knowledge ready to impart to students. I was as prepared as I could be, but still very nervous, because I was only a few years older than my students. I suffered from the Imposter Syndrome: I thought they would see through me, that I knew almost nothing, or at least only a little more than they did.

One other project that kept me busy during 1968–1969 was designing the 12th edition of *Perspecta*, the publication of the Yale School of Architecture. Peter Papademetriou and Stuart Wrede were the editors. I arranged with Champion Paper Company to get the paper for the edition donated, which allowed me to carry out my idea to use a different paper for each article in the book. To my knowledge, this variation of paper had never been done. It was extremely expensive as a design concept, but considering the paper was free, I decided to carry it out.

The book used about nine different papers, repeating some throughout the book, and attempting to match the kind of paper to the content of the articles. For example, an article by Kenneth Frampton on the work of the French architect Chareau's Maison de Verre (the house of glass), which used much glass throughout the building, was printed on bright, white glossy stock. An article by Antonio Hernandez about the architectural theory of J.N.L. Durand, who was born in the late eighteenth century, used a traditional laid-finish paper. The covers of the book were prepared using heavy-weight black cover stock with stamped disks to look like a specific kind of flooring in favor in Europe and among architects: Pirelli rubber flooring, a surface with a regular pattern of raised disks (Figs. 5.2–5.5).

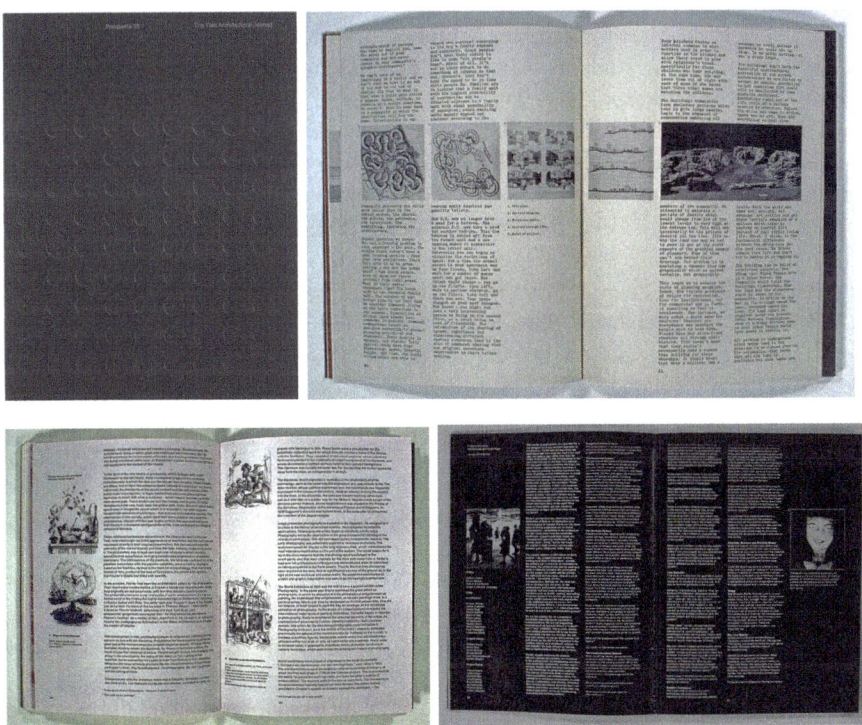

Figs. 5.2–5.5 Page designs from Perspecta 12, 1968. (Source: Pages photographed from the author's copy of the publication he designed, copyrighted by Yale School of Art and Architecture. Used with permission)

I designed a three-column grid, which also allowed for occasional two-column layouts, and used Helvetica and Times Roman fonts as primary text/display titles, almost always flush-left, ragged right, often simply in black on paper color, but occasionally in other printed type colors. I also used typewriter type simulating a standard pica type font, reversed pages with black background and white type for an article on communal architecture. I was quite happy with the outcome of this significant, challenging design project, and the editors were also pleased.

Summer of 1969

For the summer of 1969, I had arranged for funding from the SAUP that enabled me (with my wife Susan) to visit many design schools in Europe in order to study their curricula, meet with faculty members, and gather materials as best I could that might help my own teaching and the Visual Studies Laboratory. Among the schools I visited were the Royal College of Art in London, the School of Design in Ravensbourne, UK, the London School of Printing, and, ironically, the Ulm School of Design in Germany. That last school visit was perhaps the most moving and bizarre of these experiences. Here I was finally at the most famous school of design in my world, the one I had hoped to attend after graduating from Yale. I visited the campus, met Prof. Martin Krampen, who had been teaching there, and received a tour by two remaining students. Almost all other faculty and students had departed.

I saw the very storerooms in which the famous 3D design compositions of students and teaching aids were stored, and I was given copies of rare student publications and saw many artifacts that had been published in the Ulm Design School magazine sent around the world. All of this material was in heaps, ready to be trashed. What a waste! What a calamity! I could do nothing about it but weep quietly to myself. I managed to salvage a large collection of publications and eventually donated these to the San Francisco Museum of Modern Art (SFMOMA).

In Munich, I visited the graphic design studio of Otl Aicher, a former lead faculty member at Ulm, who also led the design team for all of the graphics and signage of the 1972 Olympics games. I was in awe of their work. Their designs seemed stunning in their beauty, geometric sophistication, and rationality. They had thought of everything and had published their design guidelines in numerous booklets and posters, which I collected from the studio and sent back to Princeton.

What I found very amusing and revealing was an anecdote that Otl Aicher or one of his assistants in their studio told me: They had been using computer software to manage all of their projects' schedules, dependencies, and deadlines. The computer had calculated the date by which everything would be finished: about 1974, two years after the Olympics!! They decided to abandon the use of that program and just work as hard as they could to finish everything on time. They did.

(*Note*: Decades later, in 2016–2017, I donated all of my posters and publications from Ulm and the 1972 Munich Olympics to the San Francisco Museum of Modern Art thanks to the interest of Joseph Becker, Associate Curator for Design.)

During my visit, I also met among their studio staff the German graphic designer Heiner Jacob. We were born in the same year, 1943. I remained friends with Heiner for perhaps two decades, corresponding and occasionally meeting him in London, Germany, and Princeton, but we drifted out of contact. I always felt we were very compatible in our thinking about design. Alas, when I tried to find him on the Internet in about 2014, I discovered that he had already died the previous year.

During that summer, Susan and I spent some time with Bill and Mijo Horwich in Cordelle, France, the small village in which Mijo had been raised near Lyons. Her father and mother (RIP) had the only television set in the village.

Consequently, on 20 July 1969, with others in the village who had come by, we watched Apollo 11 astronaut Neil Armstrong (RIP) become the first man to step out of the lunar module Eagle and walk on the moon. It seemed especially moving and a little bizarre to me to witness this demonstration of advanced technology from that French locale. As two American citizens, Susan and I were viewed as somewhat unusual and a little suspicious. We went out to help pitch hay in local fields. A rumor circulated that I was an agent for NASA searching for a Frenchman to capture and launch into space on a future flight. One man became frightened and did not show up the next day to continue with pitching and bundling hay.

Princeton University, Year 2, 1969–1970

With the beginning of my second year, I began my primary formal teaching at Princeton. I took over Emilio Ambasz's undergraduate introduction to visual studies. I remember once again being so nervous, even frightened at the prospect of addressing students only a few years younger than me. I feared, they would see through me and realize I knew barely more than they did. Consequently, I typed out all of my lectures and read these scripts. It must have been excruciating for the students. I am sure that I droned on in a monotone voice that would have put almost anyone to sleep. However, I did use 35 mm slides to illustrate my points, like Wertheimer's principles of the organization of visual form (proximity, similarity, common fate, etc., which he first published in 1923), or basic proportions (square, square-root-of-two rectangle, golden rectangle, etc.). For some of the images, like those just mentioned, I would draw by hand abstract imagery of the desired phenomena and photograph them with my Nikon F 35 mm camera. In other cases, I would photograph works from printed versions in books, or in rare cases from objects that I possessed. Still today, I have about 10,000 of these teaching slides in my collections.

As part of my duties at the SAUP, I was assigned the design of many School publications, including a School newsletter, a School poster, and lecture posters. I was also in charge of designing and putting up all exhibits in the lobby of the building (see accompanying figures). For the lecture series, I set up a simple template that would work for most occasions and printed the poster on diazo paper (a limited set of colors: black, brown, and dark blue) (Figs. 5.6–5.11).

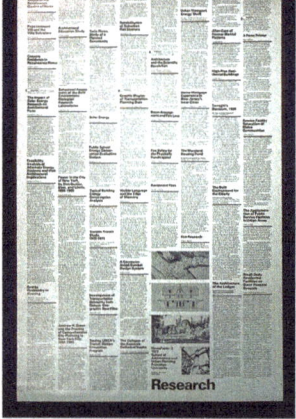

Figs. 5.6–5.11 Princeton University School of Architecture and Urban Planning publication designs, 1968–1969, by Aaron Marcus. (Source: Author's photo archives. Permission granted by Princeton School of Architecture (SoA))

Similarly, in the Creative (Visual) Arts Program, I designed posters for lectures that had a limited circulation on campus. I decided to spray paint illustrations for the texts printed with letterpress type, sometimes changing the ink colors. This technique meant every poster was unique (see accompanying figures) (Figs. 5.12 and 5.13).

Print Magazine Publications

Also that academic year, I began to publish articles in *Print* magazine, a premier non-peer-reviewed professional magazine for graphic designers. The Editor-in-Chief, Martin (Marty) Fox, and one of his chief contributing editors/writers, Rose DeNeve, took an interest in me and eventually made me a contributing writer.

During the next decade, articles appeared about me, and I wrote about a half-dozen articles, including about the coming age of computers and design, the need in professional education for more information-oriented, systematic (i.e., Swiss-German functional) graphic design in addition to the emotion-oriented, eclectic design of graphic designers such as Herb Lubalin or Milton Glaser. The article titles summarize the contents fairly well:

Figs. 5.12 and 5.13 Poster designs for a Princeton University Creative (Visual) Arts Program lecture designed by Aaron Marcus, 1969. (Source: Photos from author's archive. Used with permission of the author)

Byrne, Chuck. (1990, September/October). A Conversation with Aaron Marcus. *Print*, 108–111, 168–170.

DeNeve, Rose, "Aaron Marcus: Communicating with Computers," *Print*, New York, NY, Vol. 27, No. 2, March–April 1973, pp. 41–47.

Marcus, Aaron (1978, March). Routes, Loops, Transfers, and Dead-Ends. *Print*, New York, NY, Vol. 32, No. 2, March–April 1978, pp. 49–54.

Marcus, Aaron (1973). Making Israel Visible. *Print*, 27(5), 54–61.

Marcus, Aaron (1972). New Signs Along the Highway. *Print*, 26(3), 62–67.

Marcus, Aaron (1971). The Designer, the Computer, and Two-Way Communication System. *Print*, 25(3), 34–39.

Marcus, Aaron (1970). Why Today's Design Training is Inadequate and What Can Be Done About It. *Print*, *24*(2), 28–31, 78.

Marcus, Aaron, and Carnese, Tom et al. (1972). "Hands: 35 Interpretations of a Theme: A Special Print Portfolio." *Print, 26*(3), 31–54.

Consulting Work at AT&T Bell Labs, Murray Hill, NJ, 1969–1971

During my first year at Princeton, after some negotiation with Michael Noll, Researcher/Staff Scientist, and Peter Denes, Michael's boss and Researcher/Group Manager, I arranged to become a consultant in design with computer graphics at Bell Labs. This was an exciting opportunity. It meant that at least one day per week, I would commute to and from Bell Labs in Murray Hill, NJ. This trip itself was a challenge. I could drive my 1963 white Chevy Impala sedan, which I inherited from my father when I became married. That trip would last one hour each way and cause me to drive part of the time on the famed east-west Route 22, which was called one of the most dangerous highways in America.

Or, I could take the train.

The train trip would require me to catch the Princeton Junction train, a short train that took people from Princeton a few miles out to the main railroad line of the Pennsylvania Railroad. Andrew Carnegie, I was told, had this spur built so that when he lived around Princeton, he did not have to drive out to the junction but could take his own private train on the spur. Now all of us commuters could enjoy this privilege. I would then take the Amtrak train to Newark and need to walk a block to catch the fabled Erie-Lackawanna line to Murray Hill.

I knew the name of this last train line from my Monopoly game board of childhood on which it appeared. The trains themselves were fabulous and surreal. The conductors seemed to know virtually every one of the regular commuting passengers who comprised perhaps 90% of the travelers. The seats were made of wood and wicker, and the entire décor, which was in very good condition, seemed straight out of the early twentieth century. In fact, once while commuting during the rainy winter season, I needed a place to momentarily hang my umbrella. Without thinking, I hung it on something convenient hanging on the wall. When I reached out to retrieve my umbrella, I realized my hanging post was the speaker tube of a telephone in a wooden box, dating from sometime in the late 1920s. The painted-over electrical cords had been severed long ago. The entire apparatus was held to the wall by two large screws. I was sorely tempted to take the phone immediately but thought the right thing to do was to call the train station manager, which I did after I arrived at the Labs. When I explained what I saw and asked if I might remove the old phone, the person in charge nonchalantly gave me permission! On my next commute home that evening, I simply unscrewed the phone with the screwdriver I had brought with me, wrapped it in a cloth I had brought along, and carried it home. I kept that phone until 2022, always meaning to "renovate" it. Inside were the original last dry cell batteries that had last been installed to power the phone, perhaps sometime in the 1930s–1950s. All through my life I have been a collector of old technology.

At Bell Labs in 1969, engineers had succeeded in connecting for the first time black-and-white television-like displays (raster-scan displays) to computers. Previously, such displays were vector displays of lines individually drawn by the computer. I was fortunate to be able to use state-of-the-art computer graphics displays connected to mini-computers, far smaller than the mainframes that I had used earlier. I was getting access to the latest interactive computer equipment, and I had to learn the specialized graphics language for these computers. My supervisors wanted me to explore computer-assisted graphic design using interactive computer graphics systems....for the first time. Such research was taking place in only a few places around the globe.

I experimented with several possible computer-assisted design tasks. One of them was to start programming an office layout system, by which office workers could try out different layouts of furniture by looking at overhead views of their office space and moving simple depictions of office furniture. I was making only small progress, when I decided a more reasonable project would involve typography and page layout. Fortunately, there was a real-life problem that AT+T faced: designing all the telephone books of all the cities served in the USA. This Herculean task at that time used conventional typesetting and layout systems. I decided, with discussions of my supervisors, especially Michael Noll, to focus on programming a prototype page-layout system that would eventually be used on the Picturephone™, which device had been introduced recently at the 1964 World's Fair in New York City (Fig. 5.14).

The software application would facilitate design but also communication of the telephone book designs throughout the USA to clients, namely, the many different White Pages and Yellow Pages publication groups. I began work on this project in 1969 and completed my work in 1971, publishing a formal peer-reviewed article *in Visible Language* (Marcus, 1971). The publication previously was called *The Journal of Typographic Research*, founded by Merald Wrolstad in 1967. Merald had taken an early interest in my work and later invited me to become a member of the publication's Board of Advisors, which position has continued to this day. I visited him in about 1971 on the occasion of my lecture in Cleveland.

MOD II (Model two) version - From the 1969 "The Telephone Story" poster

Fig. 5.14 AT+T Picturephone™, about 1969. (Reproduced with permission of the AT&T Archives and History Center)

During the next two years, from 1969 to 1971, I realized that each week, I was working in three different centuries "simultaneously": the nineteenth, twentieth, and twenty-first. On one day per week, I would be working in the nineteenth-century print shop of the Princeton University Visual Arts Program. The next day I would be teaching SAUP students about twentieth-century graphic design. On the third day, I would be commuting to Bell Labs and working in a high-tech laboratory inventing the future of twenty-first-century communication. This experience was heady, exhilarating, and a little surreal, but it kept my synapses snapping creatively. I realized at the time how unusual this hopping back and forth among centuries of communication was.

For my Bell Labs project, I used a Computer Control Company DDP-224 interactive computer (much smaller than a mainframe computer) connected to a black-and-white raster display (somewhat like a television set), which connection had just been achieved shortly before I began the project (Fig. 5.15).

The display would mimic the Picturephone's resolution (but would be larger in size). In the process of coding the interactive displays, I was using a "user-centered design" approach approximately 10–20 years ahead of the industry, because I was using knowledge of myself as a graphic designer to judge the efficacy of the functions and data display. At that time, I don't think there would have been a budget for outside user testing. I was also engaged in "user-interface design," although the term had not been developed yet.

Fig. 5.15 Peter Denes using a stylus tablet and knobs to control stick figures programmed by Michael Noll on a DDP-224 interactive computer at Bell Labs. (Source: A. Michael Noll, copyright © 2015 by A. Michael Noll. Used with his permission)

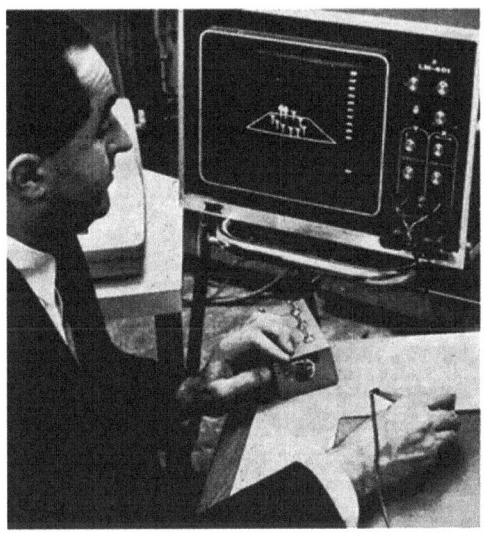

The application I was developing during those two years was a form of desktop publishing, about 10 years ahead of commercial systems. I must admit that the displays were quite primitive. A two-page display, approximately 17 inches wide and 11 inches deep was depicted, although anything smaller might have worked as well, with a three-column grid. The test type could be depicted flush left or justified. The lines of type were quite limited; letters appeared as simply two small white points of light in a vertical arrangement on a black field (or in reverse, black on white). Italic type appeared as inclined points of light/darkness. Display type could be shown similarly at a slightly enlarged scale. Photographs could be shown in only a few gray values within rectangles of assigned size. At the time, when I attempted to find previously published research about the legibility of type depicted on screens with white-on-black or black-on-white lettering, little was to be found. Essentially, I was in new territory regarding computer-based typographic display (Figs. 5.16 and 5.17).

As part of my research, I looked at other advanced layout devices. One of these was the enormous machine engineered at Time-Life headquarters in New York City. I journeyed to Manhattan to observe the giant photo-mechanical device, which consisted of about 10 or more 35 mm slide projectors mounted on a circular metal frame. In the center of the circle were mirrors and pivoting mechanisms that could send the projected beams of light to anywhere needed on a frosted glass screen that showed images and dummy type. Graphic designers needed to determine each week from the latest available articles and color/black-and-white photographs the layout of each two-page spread for LIFE magazine. While very costly to construct and sophisticated in many ways, the approach was inevitably limited and would not be able to accomplish what computer graphics systems would eventually enable.

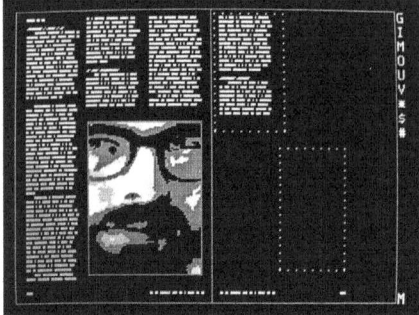

Figs. 5.16 and 5.17 Images of the Bell Labs prototype page-design system coded by the author during 1969–1971. (Source: AT+T Bell Labs. Courtesy of AT&T Archives and History Center. Used with permission)

Sometime in late 1969 or early 1970, after Bell Labs had published an entire issue of the Bell Labs *Record* devoted to the Picturephone™, I realized that not one article in the issue had mentioned anything about the possible social impact of the introduction of this device. I became upset about this seeming oversight and decided on my own to write the Director of Bell Labs to complain. I simply wrote the letter and mailed it, I think using internal Bell Labs mail delivery. Within a week or two, I received a reply from the Director, explaining that such matters were beyond the expertise or responsibility of Bell Labs. I was disappointed, but not surprised. This lack of responsibility, which led to not even mentioning the possibility of adverse

Fig. 5.18 Symbol design for Oxfam America, a variant of which became the symbol for Oxfam. (Source: Author's archive of work; used with permission)

side effects, seemed unethical and undesirable. Today, Apple computer and other companies making highly addictive hardware and software are finally being asked to consider such impacts and to take appropriate action. Fifty years ago, it was rare or unknown for companies to take such steps, as has been shown for not only computer technology companies but for cigarette companies, pharmaceutical companies, and others. At that time, my boss's boss, Peter Denes, called me into his office and criticized me for not informing him or going through him to comment to the Director of the Labs. Apparently, my letter's existence had been communicated to him. Fortunately, I was just rapped on the fingers and not fired.

Academic Year End

On 22 April 1970, the USA and other countries worldwide celebrated the first Earth Day. Many excited, dedicated people created events, marched, and carried out rituals. For my own part, together with my wife Susan, I helped silk-screen t-shirts with a large recycling symbol that we had designed. We also joined with many other SAUP students and a few faculty to participate in the rituals of the day.

In about May 1970, via an invitation arranged by my father-in-law, Paul Douglas (RIP), I was invited to design the symbol for Oxfam America. Oxfam is a British-founded confederation of 21 independent nongovernmental organizations focusing on the alleviation of global poverty. The symbol was adopted and adapted for Oxfam worldwide, which is still in use to this day (Fig. 5.18).

Summer 1970

That summer flew by so quickly, I cannot remember at all what I did, although the daily events were captured, I'm sure in my little red daily pocket calendar supplied each year by Jack Marmaras, head of graphic design at Ciba-Geigy in northern New Jersey. I have kept all of these diaries in boxes for almost 50 years, so that, should my obsessive-compulsive disorder (OCD) require it, I could find out what was on my schedule for any particular day in the last half-century.

Princeton University, Year 3, 1970–1971

I continued to teach my courses in the SAUP and VAP at Princeton. At some point in the 1970s, Ken Hiebert invited me to lecture in the Graphic Design Department at the Philadelphia College of Art. I believe I lectured there several times. One of the most amusing moments came when I arrived on a previously arranged evening to give a lecture and discovered that the students did not know I was to be there, and Ken was absent and not contactable. I did the best I could with available rooms to provide my lecture. Later I learned Ken had simply forgotten about the appointment completely. This was ironic, he said, considering that he was then taking some kind of course specifically to improve his memory!

I continued to design many posters, announcements, booklets, and other publications for the SAUP, for the Creative/Visual Arts Program, and for other university clients (Figs. 5.19, 5.20, 5.21, 5.22, 5.23–5.26, 5.27, and 5.28).

Summer 1971

During the summer of 1971, Susan and I decided to drive across America in our car. We were fortunate to have an academic schedule and the free time in the summer to undertake such a trip. We made many stops, including in Omaha, the Grand Canyon, Las Vegas, and Los Angeles, among other places.

Figs. 5.19 and 5.20 Princeton University School of Architecture and Urban Planning posters designed by Aaron Marcus. (Source: Images by the author; used with permission of Princeton School of Architecture (SoA))

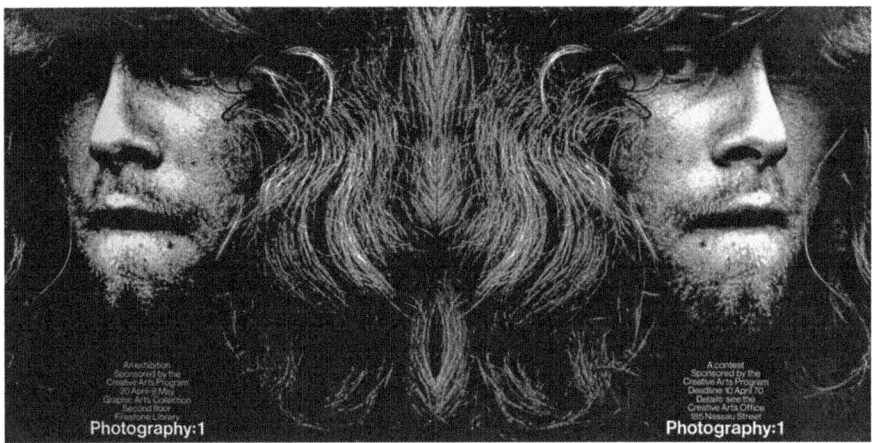

Figs. 5.21 and 5.22 Posters for a Princeton University Creative Arts Program/Visual Art Program photography contest and exhibition, 1970, based on a photograph by Aaron Marcus of a hippie in a New York City Be-in taken years before. (Image source: Author's design archive; used with permission)

To conserve expenses, we slept sometimes by the side of the road in sleeping bags on remote stretches of highway, agog at the enormous collection of stars under a black dome of heaven. In those days, we were not afraid of wandering mass murderers. We stopped to visit my childhood friend Bill Horwich who lived in Berkeley with his wife Mijo. Roaming the campus and streets of that university town, I realized there were only three places I could possibly live in the world: Jerusalem, Cambridge (Boston), and Berkeley.

On the way back east, we drove through the Hopi and Navajo reservations on back roads and visited the ancient towns of Mishongnovi, Shippolevi, and Oraibi, the last being one of the oldest continuously inhabited urban settlements in North America (since about 900 CE). The people and the places were quite eye-opening and beautiful. The tales/records of suffering of Native Americans were quite moving. My mentor Gillett Griffin in Princeton had given me the name of a silversmith Hopi jeweler in the area whom we visited.

We returned, sun-drenched, and full of powerful memories of the USA, to begin another academic year at Princeton.

Princeton University, Year 4, 1971–1972

Throughout the years at the SAUP I arranged for exhibitions in the front exhibition space of the Architecture Building. Numerous collections of architects' and planners' works arrived on an irregular basis to be exhibited there. I also arranged for some graphic design exhibits, such as an exhibit of the MIT Press Graphic Design

Figs. 5.23–5.26 Examples of graphic design for university clients, 1970–1971. (Source: Photo and scan archives of Aaron Marcus. Used with permission of the Princeton School of Architecture (SoA))

Department, including Muriel Cooper (RIP) and Jackie Casey (RIP), which was sent by the AIGA office in New York City, and even an exhibit of my own work. Through these graphic design exhibits, I wanted to help promulgate the importance of graphic design for the education of students of architecture and urban planning.

During all my years with SAUP, I was also in charge of designing SAUP publications, including the SAUP *Newsletter*, catalogues of courses, marketing brochures, and posters. I also designed VAP posters for events. For the SAUP, I decided to make perfect-bound small, precious, silver-paper covered *Newsletter* documents in the Swiss-German style that I had come to love. As for those and for most of the other publications, I used Helvetica type, occasionally Times Roman, and large,

Figs. 5.27 and 5.28   Aaron Marcus with an example of visible language artworks in the form of two-sided cartoon balloons that were hung in space for an exhibit in the Princeton University Graphic Arts Collection, Firestone Library. Visitors could move near the balloons that would then seem to be expressing their speech or thoughts, 1971. (Source: Photo archive of Aaron Marcus. Photos by Aaron Marcus, used with permission)

bold condensed sans-serif fonts for display type of posters. For some of the VAP posters, which were produced in relatively small numbers for posting around the campus, I spray-painted the posters using small objects, such as coils of string, coins, nails and screws, and even cardboard capital letters to make reverse-shadows on the paper (somewhat like Man Ray's Rayograms) that sometimes had been printed with large type or some text type announcing the lecture or other event.

At some point, I was able to arrange for an exhibit of my own work in the Princeton University Art Museum. The works exhibited were wide-ranging, including graphic design, concrete/visual poetry, computer graphics, and some drawings (Fig. 5.29).

The Museum also agreed to exhibit my collection of modern Swiss posters, which I had gathered during my earlier trips to Europe. These included works by my "heroes": Armin Hoffman, Josef Mueller-Brockman, Emil Ruder, André Gürtler, Karl Gerstner, and others. I had personal contact with almost all of them in the preceding years. The Museum permitted me to write and print a four-page brochure explaining the characteristics of Swiss-German graphic design (Marcus, 1971) (Figs. 5.30–5.35).

Experimental Visible Language

I continued to experiment with visible language, exploring in drawings and calligraphy what extra-terrestrial or ancient, unknown earthly languages might have used (Fig. 5.36).

I had been reading the *New Republic* for several years. When the government issued the Eisenhower silver dollar, I became intrigued by its surrealistic image of the US eagle on the moon shown on one of the coin's faces. I was inspired to write and publish in January 1972 an essay about that coin (Marcus, 1972). I tried to make

Fig. 5.29 Photo of Princeton University Art Museum exhibit of Aaron Marcus' works, 1974. (Photo by Aaron Marcus; courtesy of Princeton University Art Museum. © Trustees Princeton University. Used with permission)

a popular, easy-to-read-and-understand semiotics-derived interpretation of the coin's appearance and symbolism. The editors liked the essay so much that soon after the essay's publication, the "TRB"-column writer (I think Richard Strout, who wrote "TRB" from 1943 to 1983) wrote to me and asked if I would like to become the contributing writer of a column about art/design for the magazine. I was too shy and uncertain of myself; I declined his generous offer. I wonder still if that were the right decision.

Symbolic Constructions

These years seemed to be especially busy with creativity. Sometime in 1971, I began to experiment with the graph- or charting-papers that I had begun to collect from my years consulting with Bell Labs. These sheets were used by scientists for many different purposes to chart experimental data. In my earliest years at Princeton as an undergraduate, I had made extra money by hand-plotting data for physicists, something in later years that would be done by the physicists themselves using computers. How curious and coincidental it seemed that once I had been a physics student charting data and later as a graphic designer designed computer graphics–based plottings of data.

In any case, my works of art were later published (Marcus, 1973) as a special insert in *Typographische Montatsblätter* in Switzerland, prompted by the magazine's designer/graphic editor, the noted typographic and graphic design *enfant terrible* Wolfgang Weingart. The text below is adapted from text appearing in my first monograph, *Soft Where, Inc.*, Vol. 1 (Marcus, 1975, pp. 4–6), which in turn was adapted from the original publication in *Typographische Montatsblätter* (Marcus, 1972). (The published text and the figures are reprinted with permission of *Typographische Montatsblätter: Communikation*, St. Gallen, Switzerland.)

Daily experiences from television, film, highway signage, newspaper advertising, and other forms of typographic communication continue to erode our traditional linear means of absorbing information. (Anyone trying to read Charles Morris' *Signs, Language, and Behavior* can appreciate the help that two-dimensional

Figs. 5.30–5.35 Cover of "Modern Swiss Posters" exhibit brochure designed by Aaron Marcus and following pages, which include an essay written by Aaron Marcus, November 1971. (Courtesy of Princeton University Art Museum. © Trustees Princeton University. Used with permission)

Introduction

At the turn of the century the poster rapidly became a vital force in the visual arts. Such artists as Henri de Toulouse-Lautrec, Jules Cheret, and Henri Van de Velde helped to establish the poster as an independent and valuable medium for visual communication in which the artist expressed his aesthetic ideas through the shapes, colors, and composition of typographic as well as illustrative elements. The changing nature of communication within society of the twentieth century demanded a medium with, as James Joyce has said, 'all extraneous accretions excluded, reduced to its simplest and most efficient terms not exceeding the span of casual vision and congruous with the velocity of modern life.'[1] As examples of the 'Swiss' approach to poster design, this exhibit focuses on the works of several artists-designers whose attitudes towards visual imagery and composition have had considerable international influence on graphic design, particularly during the late 1950s and early 1960s.

In the 1920s the Russian and Dutch constructivist artists, among them El Lissitsky, Theo van Doesburg, Piet Zwart, and H. N. Werkman, and the German Bauhaus artists, notably Joseph Albers and Herbert Bayer, offered radically new ideas through the introduction of new typefaces, dynamically oriented typographic elements,

and photographs as integral parts of the poster. With the success of the Bauhaus movement, the imagery of machined forms reduced to 'functional' simplicity received a powerful international impetus. Albers has said, 'to design is to plan and to organize, to order, to relate and to control. In short it embraces all means opposing disorder and accident. Therefore it signifies a human need and qualifies man's thinking and doing.'[2]

Even after the destruction of the Bauhaus in the early 1930s the Bauhaus principles of visual composition and visual education, and the idea of the artist as a designer for modern technological society continued to find validity in and new insights into visual communication. Although there was some work done during the Depression and the Second World War, it was only after the war that increased activity in poster design took place. By this time, the figure of the graphic designer had emerged as an artist committed to the design of posters, books, and other forms of mass communication as his primary activity. This presents a contrast to the earlier situation in which a painter or graphic artist (i.e., printmaker) also worked as a poster artist.

Swiss Poster Design

Switzerland was one of several countries to be influenced by the Bauhaus aesthetic. In 1935 the Swiss typographer Jan Tschichold revolutionized typographic design for books, magazines,

and posters through his book Asymmetric Typography[3] in which he encouraged the abandonment of axial symmetric compositions, experimentation with sans serif typefaces (1), and careful use of 'white' space.

In 1942 the Swiss Ministry of the Interior, in conjunction with the General Poster Company (the national distributor of posters), instituted an annual national competition and exhibited two dozen of the best posters of the year. The posters were judged according to 'aesthetic merit, adver-

1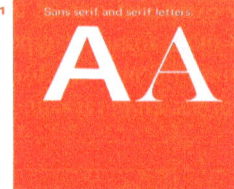

tising effectiveness, and quality of printing.'[4] In addition, Switzerland instituted a standardized format (35 5/8 by 50 3/8 inches) for commercial posters and set up poster kiosks and

---

1 This apt statement from Joyce's *Ulysses* is quoted by Mildred Constantine in her introduction to Allen Fern's history of the poster, *Word and Image*, Museum of Modern Art, New York, 1968, p. 5.

2 Francois Bucher, *Joseph Albers: Despite Straight Lines*, Yale University Press, New Haven, 1961, p. 75.

3 Jan Tschichold, *Asymmetric Typography*, translated by Ruari MacLean, Rheinhold, New York, 1967.

4 Berchtold von Grunigen, 'Swiss Poster Art over the Last Twenty-five Years,' *Swiss Poster Art*, Verlag der Visualis, Zurich, 1968, p. T-43.

Figs. 5.30–5.35 (continued)

other display facilities throughout the country, encouraging an educated and lively appreciation of poster design.

On looking through a recently published collection of these best Swiss posters, it is not surprising to find a wide divergence of styles. By the middle of the 1950s, however, strong, identifiable groups of poster designers had emerged. In an article on the history of posters, Allen Fern describes three parallel developments in poster design: 'imaginitive and amusing posters using painted illustrations' (e.g., Celestino Piatti, Donald Brun, Herbert Leupin), 'moody and powerful surrealist designs' (e.g., Hans Erni, Armin Hoffman), and 'typographic designs' (e.g., Joseph Müller-Brockman, Max Bill).[5] In many ways this serves as a useful and valid analysis. On the other hand, in the late 1950s and early 1960s posters of striking geometrical simplicity and boldness appear more and more frequently. The decade of approximately 1955 to 1965 saw the emergence of a strong design style in posters, books, and magazines which was the work of typographic designers, the last of Fern's categories, but which also includes Armin Hoffman as a formative figure. It is the work of this group of artists-designers that has come generally to be called the 'Swiss' approach to graphic design.

Swiss Graphic Design Principles

Drawing upon the experiences of the 1920s and 1930s, the basic principles of Swiss poster design may be stated as follows:[6]

5 Fern, *Word and Image*, pp. 96-97.

1   Sans Serif Type Styles
Following the precedent of the Bauhaus and the constructivist typographers, the Swiss designers rejected the traditional serif letters in favor of the more simplified sans serif letterforms.

In 1957 Swiss designers introduced two new sans serif typefaces, Helvetica and Univers (2). Because of their frequent use in graphic design work influenced by the Swiss approach, Helvetica and Univers have become strongly associated with the Swiss typographic style. Both typefaces retain the

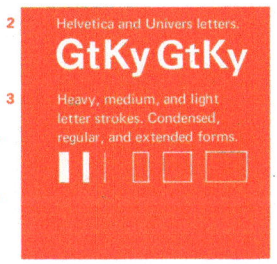

2   Helvetica and Univers letters.
GtKy GtKy
3   Heavy, medium, and light letter strokes. Condensed, regular, and extended forms.

'machined' look and the uniform letter weight that the rougher versions of the 1930s introduced, but add a greater homogeneity and a new elegance to the curves used in their letterforms.

6 The categories presented here draw upon a list by Darrell Hyder in 'Swiss Typography Today,' *Penrose Annual 63*, Visual Communications Books, Hastings House Publishers, New York, 1970, pp. 117-120.

7 Von Grunigen, *Swiss Poster Art*, p. T-45.

2   Simplified Imagery
The standardization of format for Swiss posters prevented the poster designer from relying on the size of the poster to gain impact. Instead, he had to work from 'effectiveness at a distance which belongs to the mural rather than [the easel] painting.'[7] This contributed greatly to an early universal reduction in the amount of primary text presented on a poster as well as the use of one essential image for immediate recognition.

The typographic emphasis of the Swiss poster asserted both the usefulness and the sufficiency of typography alone to attract the eye of the viewer and to communicate, through the basic text of the poster, other abstract symbolic meaning. For such strict advocates of typographic design for posters as Emil Ruder imagery was usually limited to typography. When illustration was included it was often geometrical in form. When photography was introduced it was usually treated in scale (e.g., greatly enlarged size) or in tonal emphasis (e.g., high contrast photographs) so as to immediately simplify the image. In conformity with the choice of modern typefaces, the imagery of Swiss design emphasized reduced complexity, flat surfaces, and images that were technically transformed, without traces of manual operations. 'Handdrawn' images were generally excluded.

3   Open Space
Within the simplified image of the Swiss poster, carefully used negative spaces devoid of both text and illustration establish a geometric subdivision of the poster's field or provide emphasis for the visual elements within the poster.

Figs. 5.30–5.35 (continued)

Given a fixed format, a limited set of typographic elements, and often no other imagery than type, the designer must rely essentially upon spatial composition to make the informative aspects of the poster clear and to provide the arena for provocative aesthetic relationships.

4   Consistency of Design
No mixing of typefaces within a poster is one immediate result of a desire for simplicity. On the other hand, a variation within one type family (bold,

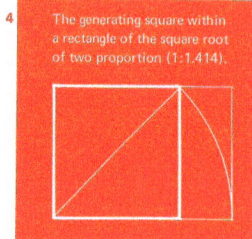

4   The generating square within a rectangle of the square root of two proportion (1:1.414).

medium, or light; condensed, regular, or expanded letterforms) can occur because of the uniform aesthetic features within a type family (3). The number of these changes (in the size, boldness, or proportion of the type) is usually limited to two or three. The proportion of these changes is usually a simple and dramatic factor. For example, for the proportional size of primary to secondary type, ratios of 2:1 or 3:1 are commonly found.
      Strong reliance on a grid of implied lines that organizes and controls

the positioning of typographic and illustrative elements also typifies the Swiss poster. The grid establishes a series of harmonic visual relationships that make coherent the entire field of the poster. A rectangle of the proportions of one: square root of two (1:1.414) is the basic Swiss poster format and also the established norm for the European international paper size system. Within this rectangle lies the primary form of the generating square (4) which is often used as an immediate source of asymmetric division of the field. Primary visual elements can be made to express directly or to imply this basic geometric relationship, thus helping to integrate the poster. In some cases, such as in the work of Müller-Brockman, grids are created that can be used for a series of posters or events. The grid provides many possibilities for the positioning of visual elements, allowing strongly differing variations to occur that are nevertheless clearly related visually.

The Exhibit

The posters exhibited at the Princeton University Art Museum reveal that concert programs and museum exhibitions often provide the subject matter for the most successful Swiss posters. This low level of commercialism has allowed the graphic designer to freely invent the visual symbolism of the poster within the formalism described above.
      Joseph Müller-Brockman's work shows clearly the precise approach to establishing visual rhythms across and within the abstract space of the poster. His nontypographic imagery is usually severe and geometrical, closely related

to the tight organization of elements on the field. Armin Hoffman, on the other hand, is much freer in his use of photographic elements and abstracted forms that convey a subtle humor and lyricism.
      Hoffman, Müller-Brockman, and Emil Ruder have all published rather complete statements of their approaches to graphic design gained from many years of teaching and professional experience in Basel and Zurich.[8] The Swiss graphic designer defends his restricted system of forms and composition by explaining that for him the use of the grid in organizing a field frees him from the countless minor decisions he would otherwise face about placement of material. His choice of simplified imagery reflects the rapid pace of modern society and the necessity of communicating with a mass audience. The designer places greater emphasis on the abstract qualities of the composition rather than relying solely on the impact of literally portrayed objects. Swiss poster design reaches its highest expression in the completely typographic poster where only the rhythms of color, size, and placement of abstract typographic symbols convey the aesthetic qualities of the poster.
      Through their work, their books, and design magazines, the approach of the Swiss designers was carried to England and to the United States. There it found a receptive audience in design schools and in the professional design studios that had begun to develop in the early 1960s. As in most realms of twentieth-century visual arts,

8 The bibliography contains references to these writings.

Figs. 5.30–5.35 (continued)

the style was quickly internationalized.[9] In the United States, Swiss-oriented poster design has been adopted by many of the largest metropolitan art museums, theaters, and concert halls and in some commercial advertising. Because of its emphasis on regularity and multiple variations within a highly organized framework, the Swiss approach to typography has found widespread use within almost every major American corporation's graphic communications.

As with all approaches to visual communication, the Swiss style of design continues to evolve even in the country of its origin, as Darrell Hyder points out in his article on recent Swiss typography.[10] After being a strong influence on American graphic design for more than a decade, the 'pure' form of Swiss design currently faces strong competition in academic and professional areas from more exuberant, less strictly disciplined aesthetic im-

pulses that have developed in the United States during the last decade. The artist-designers shown in the Princeton exhibit, however, continue to practice today and to find liberating vitality in the sophisticated, disciplined approach that constitutes Swiss poster design.[11]

Aaron Marcus
Visual Arts Program
School of Architecture
and Urban Planning

Acknowledgements: Special thanks are due Joseph Müller-Brockman and Armin Hoffman for providing copies of their posters (4,5,16,17,20,22) not in the collection of the author and to Susan Marcus for her assistance in the preparation of the exhibit and of this catalog.

Fern, Allen, Word and Image, edited by Mildred Constantine, Museum of Modern Art, New York, 1968.

Gerstner, Karl, Designing Programmes, Hastings House Publishers, New York, 1968.

Hoffman, Armin, Graphic Design Manual, Hastings House Publishers, New York, 1965.

Hyder, Darrell, 'Swiss Typography Today,' Penrose Annual 63, edited by Herbert Spencer, Hastings House Publishers, New York, 1970, pp. 117-125.

Müller-Brockman, Joseph, The Graphic Artist and His Design Problems, Hastings House Publishers, New York, 1968.

Müller-Brockman, Joseph, A History of Visual Communication, Hastings House Publishers, New York, 1971.

Neue Graphik, Verlag O. H. Walter, Zurich, no. 1-18, 1959-65, no longer published.

Ruder, Emil, Typographie, Hastings House Publishers, New York, 1967.

Stevens, Carol, 'Swiss Design is Alive [etc.],' Print Magazine, vol. 25, no. 1, January-February 1971, pp. 37-49.

Swiss Poster Art, Verlag der Visualis, Zurich, 1968.

Tschichold, Jan, Asymmetric Typography, translated by Ruari MacLean, Rheinhold, New York, 1967.

Typographische Monatsblätter, St. Gallen, vol. 90, no. 3, March 1971.

9 It is interesting to note Allen Fern's remark: '[Herbert Matter] and other American designers were able to bring the clean asymmetry of Bauhaus design into everyday life in this country long before Gropius and Mies Van der Rohe were given an opportunity to do so in architecture,' Word and Image, p. 62.

10 Hyder, 'Swiss Typography Today,' p. 120.

11 Emil Ruder died in 1970, bringing to an end his leadership of the Allgemeine Kunstgewerbe Schule (School for Applied Arts) in Basel, Switzerland. A summary of his work appears in a special issue of Typographische Monatsblätter, vol. 90, no. 3, March 1971.

Figs. 5.30–5.35 (continued)

1 Armin Hoffman
Lace-work
Museum of Applied Arts, Basel
1969

2 Armin Hoffman
City Theater Basel
City Theater, Basel
1958

3 Armin Hoffman
City Theater Basel
City Theater, Basel
1966

4 Armin Hoffman
City Theater Basel
City Theater, Basel
1964

5 Armin Hoffman
City Theater Basel
City Theater, Basel
1967

6 Armin Hoffman
City Theater Basel
City Theater, Basel
1963

7 Armin Hoffman
City Theater Basel
City Theater, Basel
1965

8 Gérard Miedinger
The Poster
Museum of Applied Arts, Zurich
1953

9 Peter Von Arx
The Drinking Glass
Museum of Applied Arts, Basel
1963

10 Max Bill
Documentation of Marcel Duchamp
Museum of Applied Arts, Zurich
1960

11 Emil Ruder
Danish Silver and Hand-work
Museum of Applied Arts, Basel
1962

12 Robert Büchler
Typography
Museum of Applied Arts, Basel
1960

13 André Gürtler
Stacking Chairs
Museum of Applied Arts, Basel
1967

14 Karl Gerstner, Markus Kutter
National Zeitung (Newspaper)
National Zeitung, Basel
1960

15 Pierre Mendel
Professional Work of Former Students
in the Graphics Classes of the School
of Applied Arts, Basel
Museum of Applied Arts, Basel
1967

16 Joseph Müller-Brockman
Concert Series
Concert Hall Society, Zurich
1971

17 Joseph Müller-Brockman
Concert Series
Concert Hall Society, Zurich
1971

18 Joseph Müller-Brockman
Musica Viva Concert Series
Concert Hall Society, Zurich
1963

19 Joseph Müller-Brockman
Musica Viva Concert Series
Concert Hall Society, Zurich
1965

20 Joseph Müller-Brockman
Musica Viva Concert Series
Concert Hall Society, Zurich
1969

21 Joseph Müller-Brockman
Musica Viva Concert Series
Concert Hall Society, Zurich
1969

22 Joseph Müller-Brockman
Less Noise
Conference of City Police-Directors,
Zurich
1960

23 Joseph Müller-Brockman
Opera House Zurich
Opera House, Zurich
1964

24 Fridolin Müller
Theo Van Doesburg
Art Museum, Basel
1969

25 Fridolin Müller
H. N. Werkman
Museum of Applied Arts, Zurich
1966

Printed in the United States of
America.

Figs. 5.30–5.35 (continued)

and, eventually, three-dimensional composition would bring to the limitations of conventional text typography.) As familiar messages have become more complex and numerous, we have also had to simplify them to retain a coherent perspective: from Massachusetts Institute of Technology to MIT to…? At one moment we lose precise definition, but at the same time we gain an ability to conceive of and to manipulate entirely new relationships at a different scale.

These "Symbolic Constructions" are from a series of compositional experiments that attempt to discover aspects of possible symbolic grammar, i.e., rules by which meaningful visual statements may be formed for public communication. The examples in the figures can be read as essentially syntactic structures freed from specific semantic content. The symbols interact in a semi-random fashion, sometimes

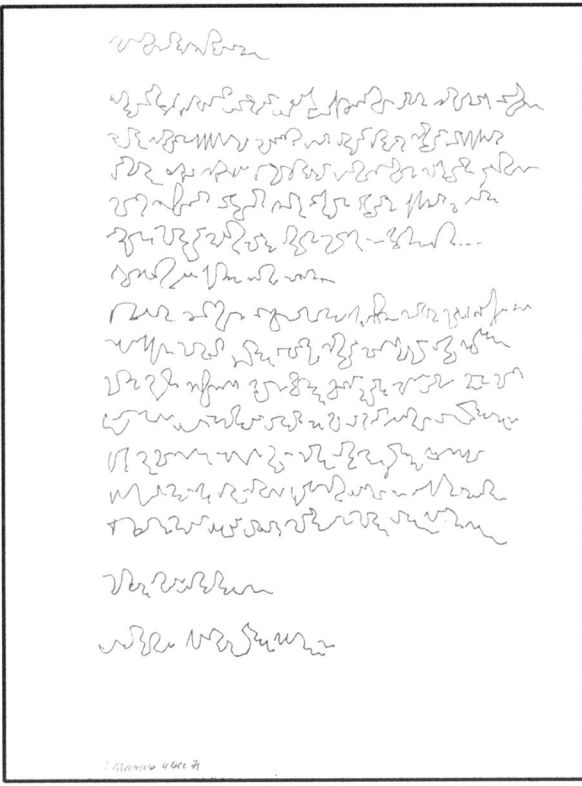

Fig. 5.36 Example of experimental visible language, 1971. (Source: Image by Aaron Marcus; used with permission)

affected by traces of their former roles. At the same time, they interact with grids provided by graphing systems. This work is intended as a metaphor for typography and language itself, which act as nets to catch some realities while letting others slip through. In these figures, the results are sometimes playful; irrationality plays a cat-and-mouse game with rationality.

It is possible that computer programs could be written to organize rules for such formations and to enable alternatives to be displayed. The potential for meaningful compositions could then be analyzed more exactly. For the present they remain enigmatic and diagrammatic. Viewed from the next century, they may resemble familiar symbolic communication (Figs. 5.37–5.39).

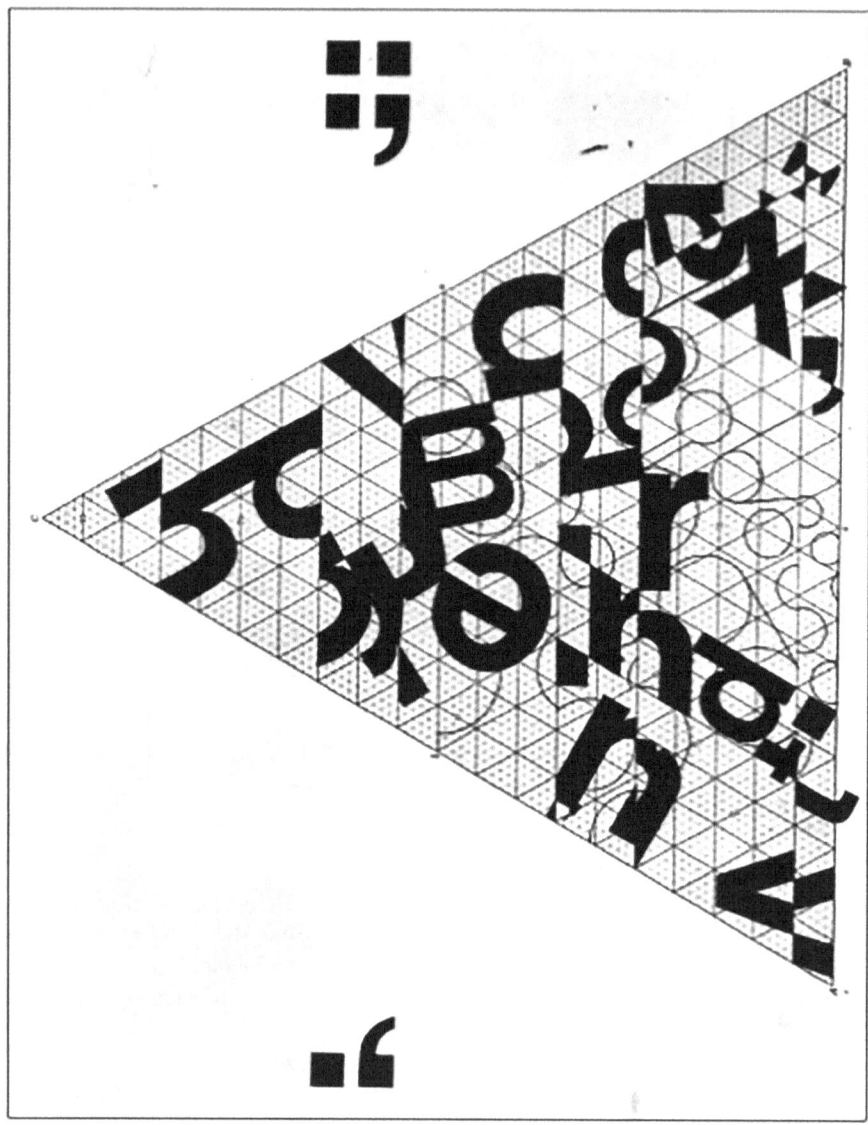

Figs. 5.37–5.39 "Symbolic Constructions," untitled visible-language experiments, press-on lettering and ink on graph paper, 8–1/2″ × 11″, 1971–1972, by Aaron Marcus. (Source: Aaron Marcus'
photo archives, used with permission)

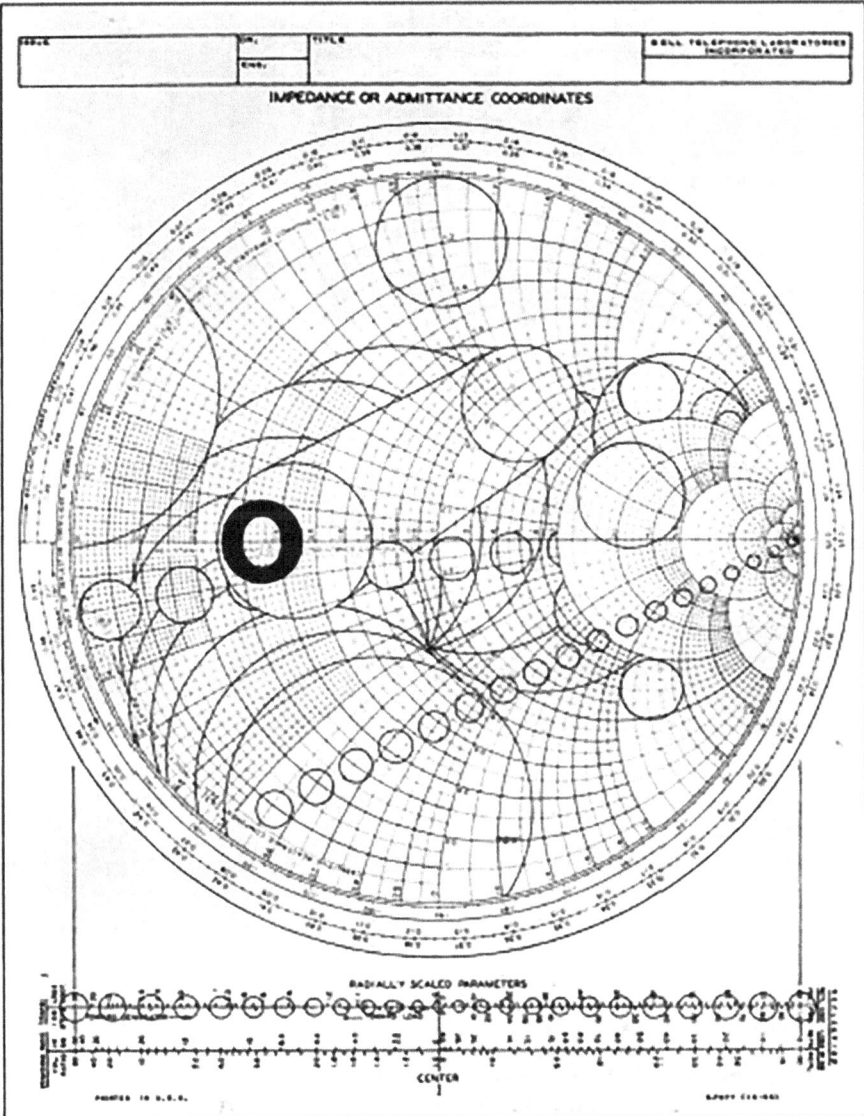

Figs. 5.37–5.39 (continued)

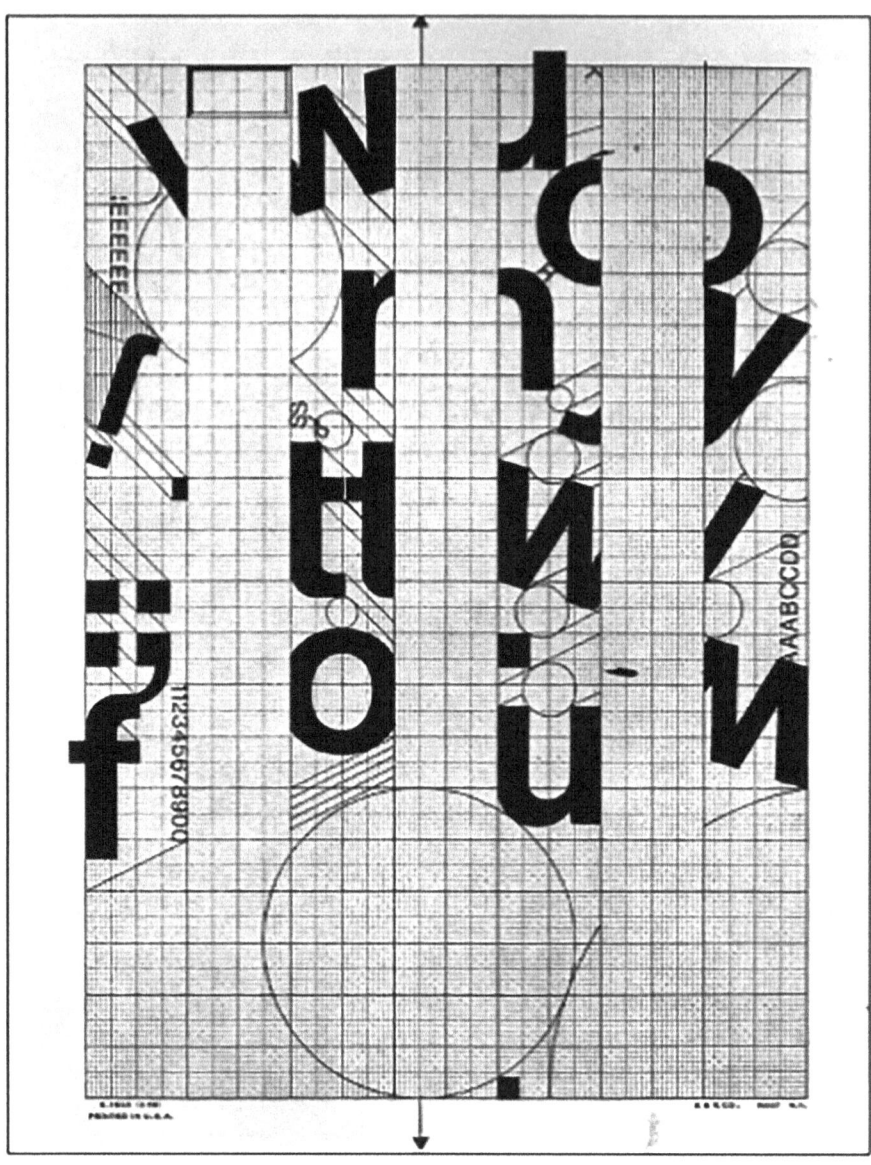

Figs. 5.37–5.39 (continued)

Sabbatical at Yale, Spring 1972

(*Note*: Part of this section of text is adapted from my first monograph, *Soft Where, Inc.*, Vol. 1 (Marcus, 1975, pp. 7–11, used with permission).)

I can't remember why, but I had earned, quite early, a sabbatical, which meant I could take a semester off with full pay. I considered going to MIT to work with Nicholas Negroponte of the Architecture Machine Group. I had met him in the spring of 1968 at Yale, and I was impressed with his work and the facilities for designing with computer graphics that he was building in the Architecture Department at MIT. However, I decided I might make more progress by going back to Yale and working with a Mergenthaler phototypesetting machine that had been set up by Prof. Alvin Eisenman in the Graphic Design Department. I later felt regret that I had not been able to become friends with Nicholas and part of the MIT Visual Language Laboratory in-group, which included Muriel Cooper (RIP) and others.

During the spring semester of 1972, I was a Research Associate in the Arts at the Yale Art School, New Haven, Connecticut. At Yale, the typesetting machine was connected to a PDP-10 computer, one of the first such setups of its kind in the world. Programmers fed in their programs via a punched-paper tape-reader. My wife and I moved to New Haven and lived in a small apartment near the Art and Architecture Building, which enabled me to have frequent access to the equipment. At the time, graphic designer Dan Friedman (a"h) was teaching there. I had many conversations with Dan and remember distinctly walking along York Street in front of the building as we lamented the state of graphic design education. Dan had studied at the *Kunstgewerbeschule* in Basel for many years and was a very gifted graphic designer. (As a reminder, I had lectured there in 1969 in German about the coming world of computer graphics and design.) Dan and I felt, in teaching undergraduates and graduates, that we were both doing remedial education that should have been completed in high school. We sighed. At Yale, I created and taught one of the first courses ever given about graphic design with computers. (Upon returning to Princeton eventually, I began to think about teaching such a course at Princeton, and brought it into being sometime about 1975, publishing an article about the course (Marcus, 1977) and about computers and the humanities (Marcus, 1979).)

At Yale, I had ample time to program the Yale Graphic Design Department's computer, using punched paper tape, to typeset numerous variations of themes of typographic compositions that were abstract typographic poem/drawings. This semester was a fortunate, rich experience for me. At Yale, my intention was to explore new possibilities for typographic and symbolic expression. Through a give-and-take process, through writing programs and examining the visual results of these decisions, I was able to finalize the images.

As with most of my computer-assisted artworks, they were originally meant to be seen as white symbols against dark fields. Therefore, the positive space as well as the negative space is part of the total meaning. I was interested in this kind of computer-assisted image-generation as it relates to the use of light/electromagnetic information display, the primary medium for a computerized, bureaucratized society. I was also interested in relating the most advanced technological-symbolical achievements to the most archaic experiences of humankind. Hence, I felt it appropriate to ponder Genesis 1 and 2 in considering these images: the creation of order out of chaos, the creation of light out of darkness.

Most of the images I designed and programmed used standard typographic signs available on a phototypesetting machine. Some of the compositions resemble more familiar forms of poetic expression in linear typographic form. The images attempt to focus attention on the manifold nature of symbols, as gestures of movement and material, as pictograms, as ideograms, as phonograms, as two- or three-dimensional objects. Conceptual cross-references are the turnpike at night, the starry sky, ritual chants, and typography dreaming.

One set of images became a set. "Shades of Hades" is one of a set of multicolored transformations of the original white on black computer-generated forms. The other images in this set are "Radioactive Jukebox," "Evolving Gravity," and "Urbane Nova." These images were created when I had an opportunity to produce colored versions of four images for a bank in Norfolk, Virginia's, annual report. I arranged to produce, as well, a limited edition of 50 images. Signed, numbered copies of this work are in, among other collections, the San Francisco Museum of Modern Art, the Letterform Archive/San Francisco, the Victoria and Albert Museum/London, the Computer History Museum/Mountain View, and the RIT Vignelli Center for Graphic Design/Rochester (Figs. 5.40–5.43).

"Noise Barrier" is a transformation of the original computer-generated form produced first in 1972. To create more calligraphic signs, I substituted for the phototypesetting machines' glass plate of font characters, a sheet of glass covered on one side with a layer of ink and carbon dust, which I had scratched away with a needle-tipped tool. The resulting "chicken scratches" were selectively projected onto the phototypesetting machine as it tried to typeset and input anonymous text. The gap in the imagery resulted from an error in my programming. In 1974, the Pratt Graphic Center, Manhattan, New York City, an extension of the Pratt Institute, Brooklyn, New York City, commissioned me to produce two signed, numbered editions of 100 of "Noise Barrier" and "Evolving Gravity" for its membership. These works were also produced in a set of 100 artist's proofs of each, which I numbered and signed (Fig. 5.44).

"Meaning Map," another experiment from this period in 1972 explored another direction. "And out of the ground the Lord G-d formed every beast of the field, and every fowl of the air; and brought them unto the man to see what he would call them; and whatsoever the man would call every living creature, that was to be the name thereof" (Genesis 2, v. 19, *The Soncino Chumash*) (Fig. 5.45).

As in a sacred roster, "Meaning Map" presents all combinations of consonant-vowel-consonant listed by a digital computer connected to a phototypesetting machine. I felt that I, a human being, was in a somewhat symbiotic relationship with the machine regarding the final work. I proceeded through my self-created ritual of striking out all combinations which had no meaning for me at the time. As I carried out this ritual, visions of personal experience were called forth from various levels of my mind by the simple combination of symbols, a basic element of connotation and denotation in English and Western languages, similar in some respects to the three-letter word-roots of Hebrew (but also very different from them because vowels were included in my list). I was left with a "map of meanings," a personal collage of English words, acronyms, foreign words, etc., which were available to my

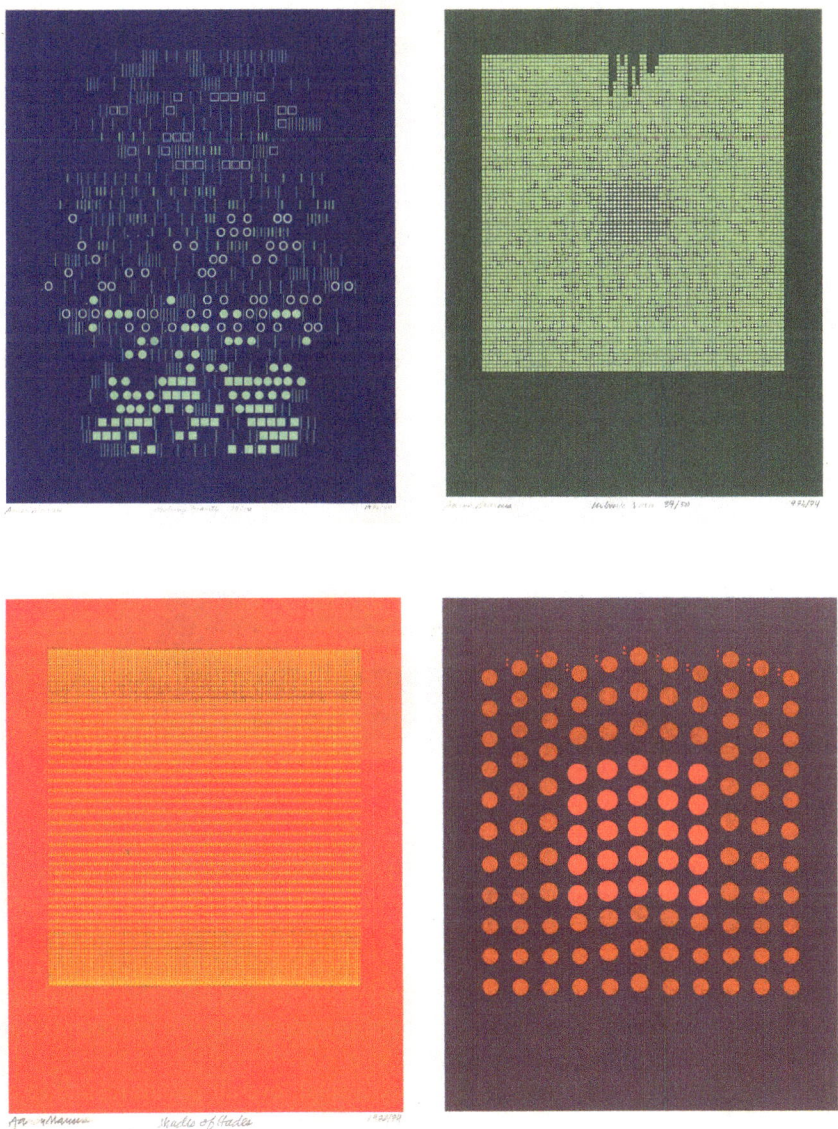

Figs. 5.40–5.43 Four sets of color images produced originally in 1972 in black on white, converted to white on black photocopies to be exhibited, and later converted to color lithographs in 1974. (Source: Images from Aaron Marcus' archive; used with permission)

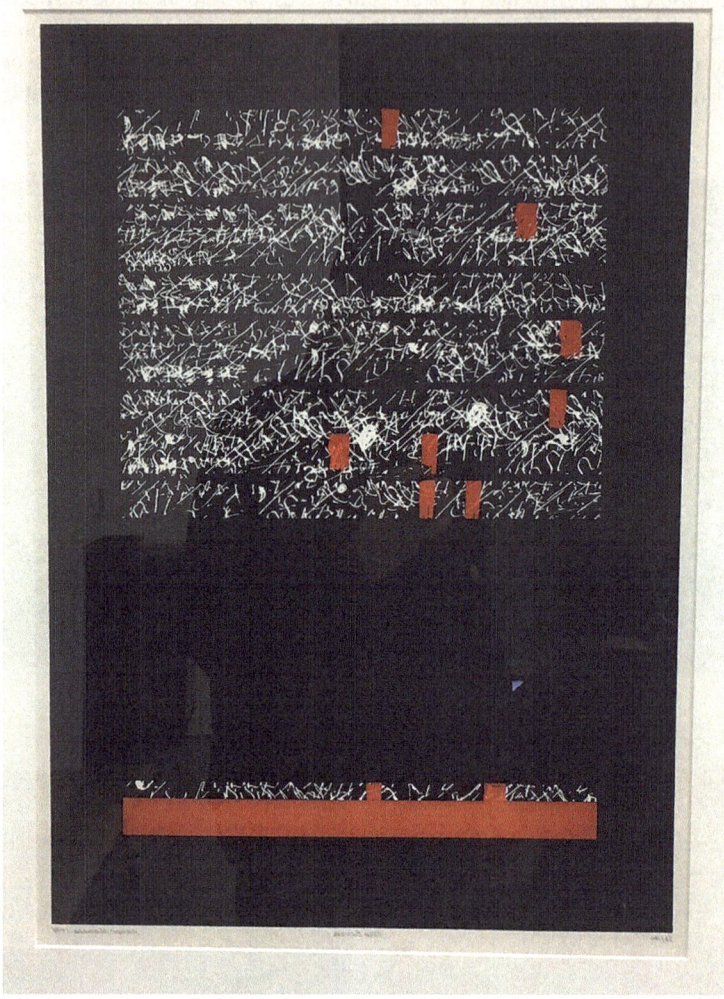

Fig. 5.44 "Noise Barrier," Silkscreen, image 15–1/22 × 22″, Arches 88, edition of 100, Created through the Pratt Graphic Center, Manhattan, New York City, 1974. (Source: Aaron Marcus archive; used with permission)

conscious mind at a particular time and place. As a reflection upon the individual's relationship to the cosmos and the sacred act of naming reality, the important combination of MAN/G-D emerges, the one/all.

The reader is able, at a glance, to perceive a total, overall gestalt related to an individual's language experience, the language history of a society, and the evolution of human language itself. The reader is able to share in the stream of images and emotions embodied in the work and to compare and contrast with his or her own, the contours of my meaning space.

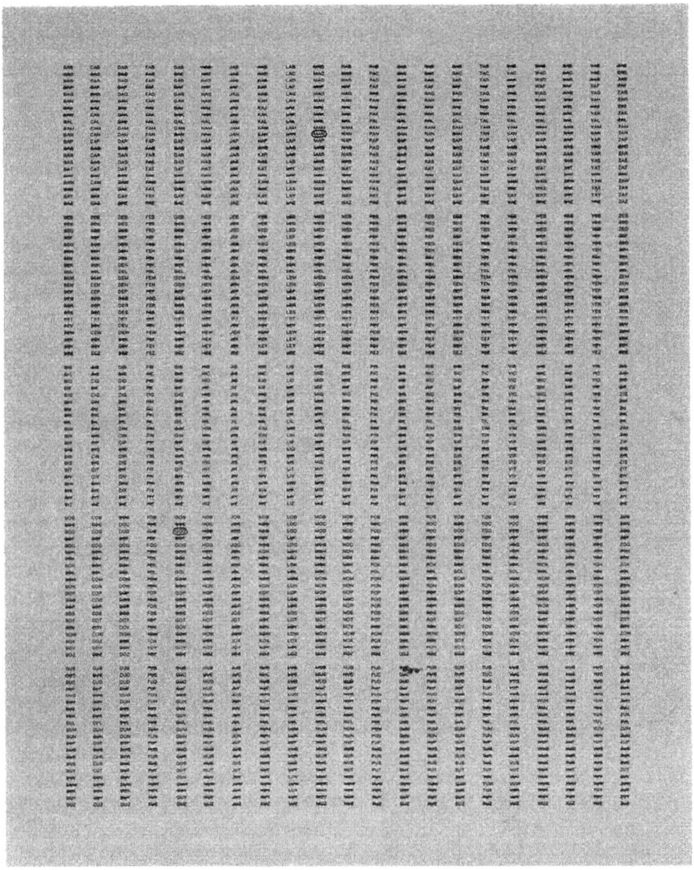

Fig. 5.45 "Meaning Map." 15″ × 19″ Photoprint, 1972. (Source: Aaron Marcus' archives, photo by the author, used with permission)

(*Note:* This above text was scheduled to appear in a book edited by Mary Ellen Solt (RIP), *Semiotic, Trends in Concrete Poetry*; however, to my knowledge, that book was never published. Mary Ellen Solt died in 2007 at the age of 86.)

With the Yale equipment, I also produced some verbally oriented works like "The City Sleeps, but Someone Is Watching," in which the computer simply printed out line-after-line repetitions of letters of the sentence. Each line repeated the given character a number of times according to the order of that letter in the English alphabet, thereby generating "cityscapes" or "skylines" when viewed sideways (see Figs. 5.45 and 5.46).

Inspired by Dan Friedman's graphic design exercises given to graduate students, which required them to lay out skillful compositions based on the day's headlines from *The New York Times* first page, I programmed a computer to lay out semi-automatically the lines of headlines I had entered. I called these works "Weather

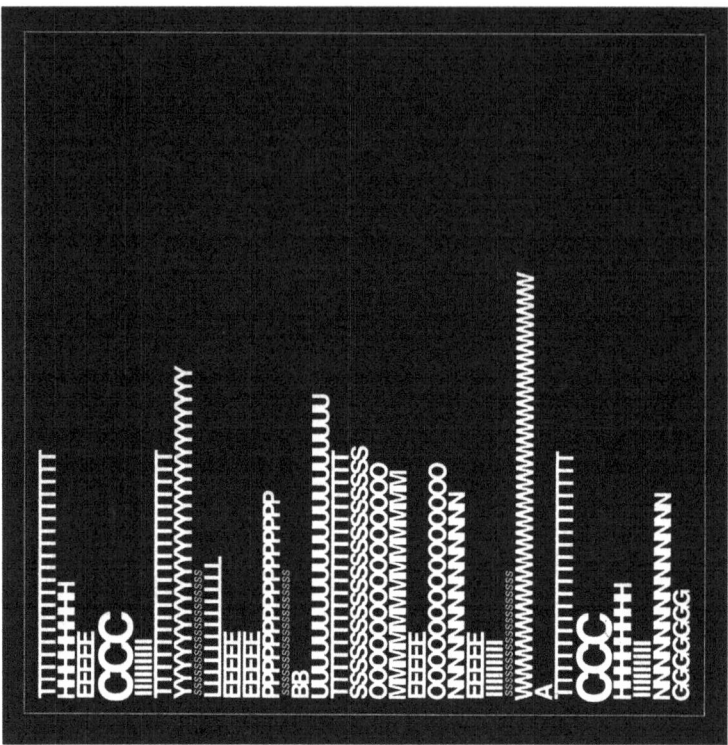

Fig. 5.46 "The City Sleeps, but Someone Is Watching." White-on-black version, 1972. One of many "cityscapes" produced by the phototypesetter's repeating a letter according to its order in the alphabet. The Letterform Archive, San Francisco, possesses the complete set of experiments of this kind. (Source: Photograph from the author's archive, used with permission)

Reports," because they urged viewers to contemplate the general psychological and emotional content of the verbs and nouns in the daily barrage of news. Thanks to the facilities and time, I was able to generate hundreds of variations of output onto photo paper. I exhibited some of these works as they were initially output and transformed others of them into enlarged and/or colored images in 1974 that I exhibited and published worldwide (Fig. 5.47).

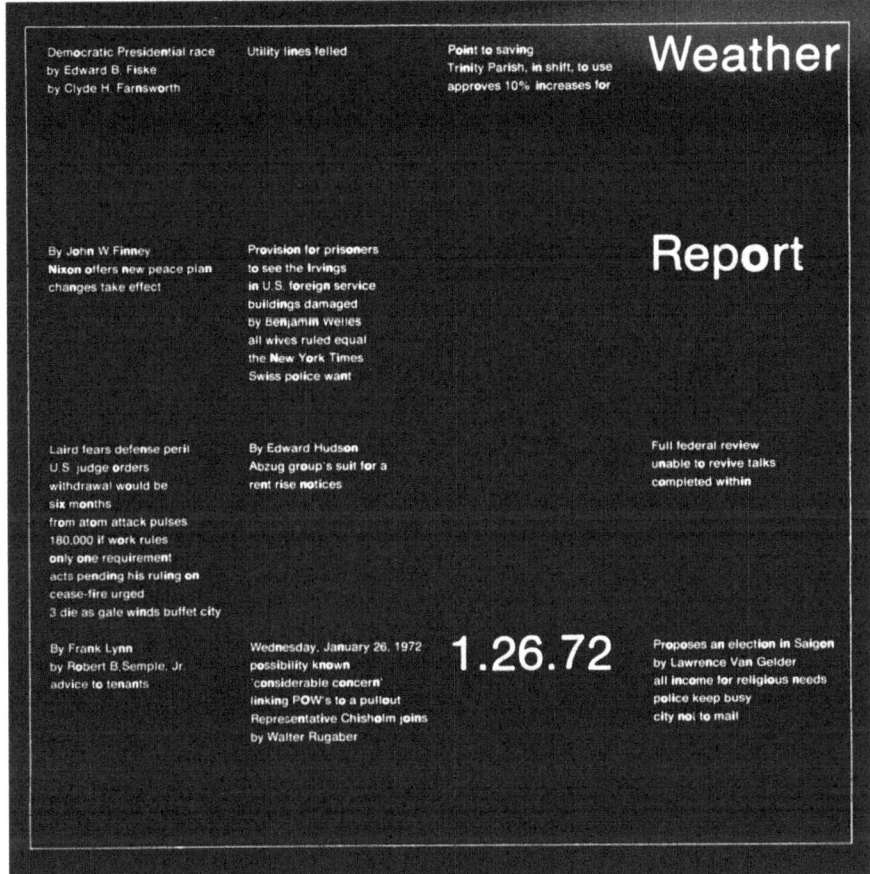

Fig. 5.47 Examples of "Weather Reports" designed, programmed, and generated by Aaron Marcus in 1972 while at Yale University's Graphic Design Department. (Image photographed by Aaron Marcus; used with permission)

Other Works by Aaron Marcus Created at Yale

See Figs. 5.48 and 5.49.

Other Published Work

See Fig. 5.50.

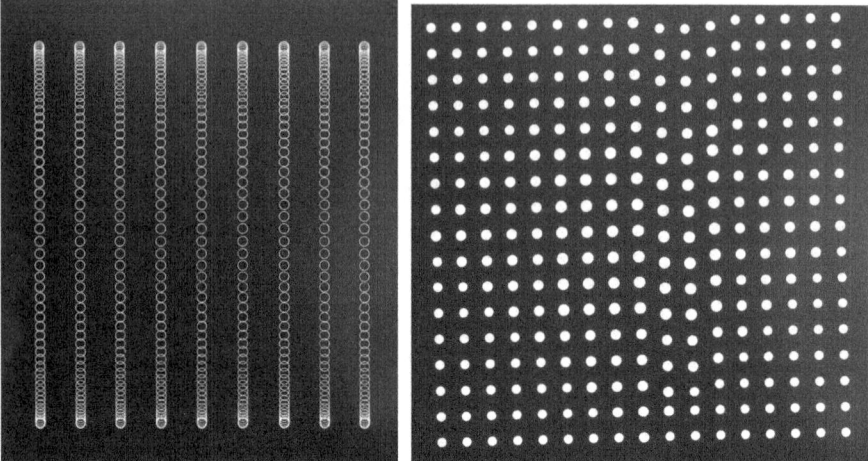

Figs. 5.48 and 5.49 Untitled and "Slight Disturbance." 1972, by Aaron Marcus. (Source: Aaron Marcus' photo archive; used with permission)

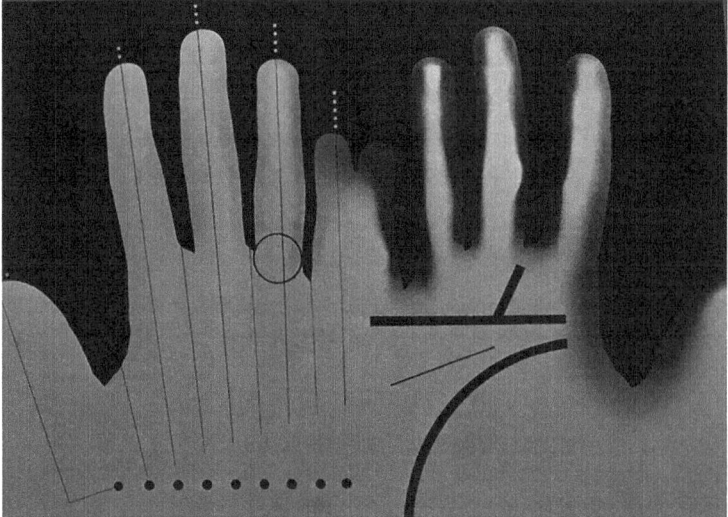

Fig. 5.50 "Hands" project, published in *Print* magazine, May/June 1972, 26:3, p. 37. I was invited by *Print* magazine as one of several designers to design thematic images based on the word "hands." (Source: Aaron Marcus' photo archive, for original artwork. Used with permission of author)

Summer 1972 in Israel with a Stop in Istanbul

In the summer of 1972, Susan and I traveled to Jerusalem, Israel. I helped to finance this trip by selling 1500 comic books from my childhood collections. I found a dealer in New York City who would pay me $1500 based on my list of each issue that I was selling (I still kept 300 comics that I thought would not be worth selling, including many uncovered comics). One dollar per comic; not bad for an investment of 10 cents per comic book (in general, except for the relatively few 52-page special thick issues that cost 25 cents) or less, accounting for the many donated comics from my maternal first cousin once removed upward Herman Burstein in Marshalltown, Iowa, and my paternal first-cousin Alan Rosen, then in Omaha. The most valuable issue was *Flash*, No. 4, which was worth $150 at that time. I was sad to deliver the boxes to the New York dealer, but happy that they were being "sacrificed" for a worthy cause: a visit to Israel again after nine years.

On our way, we stopped in Istanbul. It was my first experience being outside of Western culture, and the sights and sounds were something of a shock. Streets in Istanbul seemed not to have street signs, so even if I had a map, navigation was difficult. We could not read the store signs, even though most were written in Roman characters; none of the words made any sense to us; there were no helpful roots or recognizable cognate terms. In addition, we often could not tell from the shop windows what was being sold. Everything seemed a mystery.

We toured many architectural and cultural sites, like the Topkapi Museum, the Blue Mosque, and the Hagia Sofia. One of my more memorable occasions was when we were viewing calligraphy works in a large room of a museum. Suddenly, at the diagonally opposite end of the great chamber, a gaggle of young girls (or is "giggle" the proper group noun?) in blue uniform-dresses and white blouses entered and, instead of going to look at the nearby display cases as their teachers insisted, they broke away and all ran toward Susan and myself. Why? Not only were we obviously foreigners, and possibly recognized as Americans, but I think also because I had a beard and a long black ponytail, something unusual for a man to wear. They gathered around me laughing, pointing, and wanting to touch my braid. Finally, their teachers got them back into an orderly group to go back to the entrance and to examine and appreciate the calligraphic works of art.

In Israel, after months of negotiations, I had succeeded in being invited to visit Bezalel Academy of Art and Design's Graphic Design Department, then under the leadership of Yarom Vardimon. I gave some lectures and gathered information about graphic design in Israel, which I published as an article in *Print* (Marcus, 1973). After I left Israel, I again felt that there were only three cities in the world in which I could possibly live: Berkeley, Boston (Cambridge), and Jerusalem. I tried over the next few years to move to Israel and live in Jerusalem, but I could not work out a suitable teaching position. I felt Cambridge was intellectually exciting, but I did not like the physical climate. That left Berkeley. It took me until 1979 to discover a way to move there. All three locations are "university towns." That primary characteristic was what drew me.

At the end of our stay in Israel, I arranged for us to visit Greece, including Athens, which I had first visited in 1963, the Peloponnesus Peninsula, Crete, and the island of Paros.

In Athens, from a high point, Susan and I watched as part of the city burned one sunset. We listened to the fire trucks in the distance. It all seemed surrealistic. We visited the standard tourist sites of the Parthenon, the Temple of Zeus, the Archeological Museum, etc. For me, the most exciting and beautiful images were the Aegean sculptures of Cycladic art from 3300 to 1100 BCE, startling in their simplicity and seeming modernity.

In the Peloponnesus, we drove around the entire Peninsula in a counter-clockwise direction, visiting Corinth, Mount Olympus, Kalamata, Tripoli, Nauplion, and other ancient sites. Along the way, we stumbled on an unguarded, open, current dig. I placed my hand onto the sunken relief impression of someone's hand that had pressed into the clay bricks 2000–2500 years ago. It was a moving experience of time and history.

Susan and I sailed from Athens to Crete using the most inexpensive tickets, which meant we spent the night sleeping on the deck of the ship. Tired and aching, we nevertheless enjoyed our stay of about a week, visiting Heraklion, its museum, its picturesque streets, and enjoying the breads and yoghurts that could be purchased in the open markets, some of which were covered. Sometimes we had to travel on the backs of simple wooden carts of farmers, pulled by a single donkey. At other times we could take bus trips. The country was far less traveled by tourists than when I visited it again decades later. We visited several ancient sites, most notably the Palace of Knossos, where we gaped at the reconstructions of earlier decades and marveled at the upside-down tree trunks used as column cores.

Our last stop for the summer: On the island of Paros, Greece, the ex-wife of a Princeton SAUP colleague/friend lived with her three young daughters in a small, white-washed stucco cottage on the outskirts of the main village of the island. The setting was rustic, primitive, beautiful, and appealing. We had to walk for a while to town to buy food. We swam in the clear, warm, blue waters of the Aegean under crystal clear, warm, blue skies. We enjoyed life intensely. When the time came to board the boat that would take us back to Athens, I was sorely tempted to turn around, never to return to Princeton. I longed to escape and to live there. Life at Princeton had already begun to be unpleasant and undesirable for me, with publish-or-perish pressures, the suspicion and disdain of several SAUP faculty colleagues, and my general underlying dislike for Princeton's snobbery.

Nevertheless, the appeal of a faculty tenured position there and my general reluctance to make radical breaks with the past were two carrots tempting enough to make me carry on. I returned to Princeton. I had begun to grow a long black ponytail, which I learned to braid myself into three interlaced plaits that stretched down to my hips. I was perhaps the first Princeton faculty member in several hundred years to wear a ponytail. I was also one of the youngest Assistant Professor faculty members on campus. I had joined the SAUP when I was 25. I prepared to carry on with my career in the next academic year.

Princeton University, Year 5, 1972–1973

I continued to develop my courses. At the same time, I began many experiments to understand the limits of typography and graphic design as communication and expression media.

Post Card Typographic Art

Sometime in the academic year, I began to experiment with applying large Letraset letters into somewhat banal picture postcards. I was struck by the surreal, monumental, powerful, mysterious, and seductive combination of images that were produced. Some examples were published only 45 years later in a book about Letraset (Marcus, 2017) (Figs. 5.51–5.53).

During the course of my years at Princeton, I had contact with several unusual people and several people who achieved significant fame. One of my more notable students was Lisa Halaby, who was graduated from Princeton's School of Architecture and Urban Planning in 1973. I believe she took part in my visual studies course and my course in advanced visual studies SAUP 318. She prepared a significant notebook on her topic of visual design. She later became Queen Noor Al-Hussein of the Kingdom of Jordan. I wrote her from Jerusalem in 1977–1978 to ask if I could attend her wedding to King Hussein. I had to send a letter first by Israeli taxi and then by Jordanian taxi. I never knew if she received it. Only after I had departed Israel and moved to Honolulu in the summer of 1978 did I receive a brief note from her assistant expressing regrets. It was months after the wedding, anyway.

"An X on America," 1972

I continued to teach, publish, design publications, and draw. I had begun to create conceptual typographic artworks, like my "X on America," in which I wanted to make a mark on the USA. Where would I find enough ink or graphite? Where could I find a piece of paper at the scale of the continental USA? I seemed to be creating a variant of Jorge Luis Borges' idea expressed in his 1946 one-paragraph short story "*Del rigor en la ciencia*" (On Exactitude in Science), which describes a map of the world drawn at a 1:1 scale: "… In that Empire, the Art of Cartography attained such Perfection that the map of a single Province occupied the entirety of a City, and the map of the Empire, the entirety of a Province. In time, those Unconscionable Maps no longer satisfied, and the Cartographers Guilds struck a Map of the Empire whose size was that of the Empire, and which coincided point for point with it. The following Generations, who were not so fond of the Study of Cartography as their

Figs. 5.51–5.53 Post Card
artworks, 1973, by Aaron
Marcus. (Source: Aaron
Marcus' photo archive;
used with permission)

Forebears had been, saw that that vast map was Useless, and not without some
Pitilessness was it, that they delivered it up to the Inclemencies of Sun and Winters.
In the Deserts of the West, still today, there are Tattered Ruins of that Map, inhabited
by Animals and Beggars; in all the Land there is no other Relic of the Disciplines of
Geography." Purportedly from Suárez Miranda, *Travels of Prudent Men*, Book

Four, Ch. XLV, Lérida, 165. [As quoted in Wikipedia: https://en.wikipedia.org/wiki/On_Exactitude_in_Science. Accessed on 27 February 2018.]

I decided that only through telecommunications could I write/draw at a geographically large scale. After arranging with AT&T, I initiated a conference call that connected four public telephone booths in the USA: in New York City (where I was); Washington, DC; Los Angeles, CA; San Francisco, CA; and Omaha, NE. People walking by on the street heard the telephone ringing and out of habit or curiosity answered the phones. They found themselves connected to four other people in the USA. We discussed the weather and politics, and the meaning of my artwork. While we talked, an "X" 3000 miles wide was "drawn/written" across the USA. I published the documentation for the work in my monograph *Soft Where, Inc.*, Volume 1 (Marcus, 1977) and exhibited the documentation nationally and internationally for at least a decade (Figs. 5.54 and 5.55).

One of the most exciting events of the year was the birth of our firstborn child, a son, Joshua Marcus, on 5 July 1973. I was able to attend the birth and took photographs. I was amazed and moved by Susan's childbirth and her courage during the painful process. I was amazed to see a new human being that we had produced. Our lives were changed forever, and I felt great love for this sweet, tiny creature of our creation.

My schedule changed significantly, as we now had inserted baby maintenance tasks. Susan did most of the parenting work, but I happily wheeled baby Joshua in

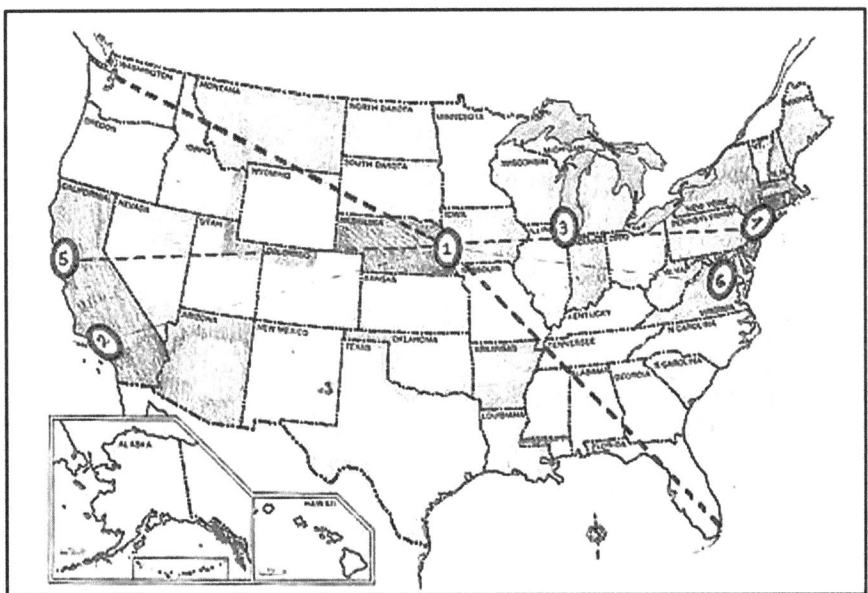

Fig. 5.54 "An X on America," conceptual visible-language artwork documentation map showing possible sites for telephone booth calls, 1972. Work by Aaron Marcus. (Source: Aaron Marcus' photo archive; used with permission)

Fig. 5.55 "An X on America," photograph of Aaron Marcus in a phone booth in Manhattan during the work's enactment, 1972. Work by Aaron Marcus. (Photographer unknown; source: Aaron Marcus' photo archives; used with permission)

a beautiful wicker baby carriage from the early part of the twentieth century, which Susan and I had renovated. I took Joshua from our faculty apartment up to my office for sleeping sessions outside my door.

During these years, I published more articles, created more artworks, and explored more concepts dealing with typography, symbolism, and computer graphics. I also continued to design publications for the SAUP and for the VAP. I think I began to develop a relationship with Joe Rothrock, the new head of the Graphic Arts Collection in the Firestone Library. Joe and I organized one year a course in concrete poetry and used the printing shop facilities to carry out some of the projects. About this time, I also began to develop my course AUP 318, which loosely focused on advanced visual studies and enabled me to give the students the challenge of

Aaron Marcus/graphic designer/Princeton, New Jersey

Fig. 5.56 International Monetary Unit Design by Aaron Marcus for "Designer's Choice: IMU 2073" article in *Print* magazine, 1973, page number unknown. (Source: Original design in Aaron Marcus' photo archive; used with permission)

researching, writing, designing, and producing a book about a particular topic. The topics were extremely varied. I recall that Mali Burgess did a history of light in the visual arts. Other topics explored semiotics, symbolism, typography, etc. That year, a magazine article invited graphic designers to imagine a design for a world currency. I was delighted to put my thoughts together into visual form (see Fig. 5.56).

Cybernetic Landscapes, 1–3

Also, in 1973, I completed art-oriented programming work with the Computer Graphics Lab in the Chemistry Department of Princeton. I had completed a set of major works in virtual reality. My work with Bell Labs had concluded in 1971. At Princeton, I found the Evans and Sutherland Line-Drawing System 1 (LDS 1) connected to interactive, color, 3D display devices exciting and challenging. I learned yet another set of graphic commands to control the device and produced, among other things, the "Cybernetic Landscapes 1–3" (1971–1973), which I exhibited as Polaroid prints of the screen displays and published in my first monograph (Marcus, 1975).

As far as I know, this work was the first virtual reality work to be programmed and designed by a professional graphic designer/visual artist. The landscapes were filled with a "sacred axis" road, along which were signs like those for Burma-Shave, which was popular in the early to mid-twentieth century. The signs featured snippets of doggerel that ended with the punchline of the brand name. My signs were simply verbal commands of life: sleep, eat, etc. Off to the east were sculptures of lines, like a forest of trees, which aligned and misaligned to make interesting visual rhythms as one moved along them. Off to the west was a circling spiral of letters, a dynamic three-dimensional sculpture. Somewhere in the plane was a sole dancing, moving stick-figure representing an unknown person that a visitor might encounter. Controls on the display enabled the viewer to select a speed, path, height, and viewing direction.

Although three-dimensional dynamic display devices like the one I was using had been used for engineering purposes, I thought this was the first one to be used for a visual arts project. I was glad about the results. These landscapes continued to explore visible language. *Note:* The following text is adapted from my first monograph, *Soft Where, Inc.,* Vol. 1 (Marcus, 1975, pp. 12–14). The text was originally scheduled to appear in a book to be edited by Mary Ellen Solt, *Semiotic Trends in Concrete Poetry,* which I believe she never published.

As writing was born, humankind struggled to find ways to compress spatial, temporal, and wraparound experience into abstract, easily reproducible marks on specially prepared flat surfaces. From essentially pictographic images bearing an iconic resemblance to things and actions, abstract forms evolved to provide man with more complex conceptions and a more intricately structured cosmos. After two millennia of relatively stable symbols and 500 years of their mechanical reproduction, the forms of writing, the ideas expressible by the mare changing rapidly. At this moment, with the aid of electronic media and computer-assisted displays, the semiotic parameters of verbi-voco-visual communication are revitalizing long unused possibilities and discovering new combinations of elements for restating the inner and outer worlds of man's experience.

In the late nineteenth century, the poet Mallarmé dreamed of a language and a language space in which everything could be expressive. With music as an ideal abstract formal system, he conceived of and began to make concrete a poetry in which marks, their form and position on a two-dimensional field, as well as their verbal denotations and connotations, contributed to a visual, spatial construction which one must see as well as read and hear. In the middle of this century, the international concrete poetry movement expanded and restructured the visions of nineteenth-century innovators like Mallarmé and Apollinaire. Joined to electronic, computer-assisted communication, the forms of visually oriented expression are beginning to bloom with a new array of ideas, a new dimension in abstract symbol communication and an all-encompassing environmental impact.

At the Computer Graphics Laboratory at Princeton University, I developed a series of cybernetic landscapes utilizing programs in Fortran for a PDP-10 digital computer and an Evans and Sutherland LDS-1 interactive computer graphics display system. The cathode ray tube device permits images in stereo and color as well as two-dimensional pictures that can be altered smoothly and instantaneously.

These landscapes in a simulated space provide a concrete, palpable, spatial experience of abstract visual forms and conventional verbal and typographic elements. As such, the space functions as a poem-drawing environment. Instead of the white field and black letterforms of traditional written symbols, the field is the deep, black space of night, and the symbols have been transformed into glowing filaments of light: a direct extension of the desire for "constellations" which Mallarmé, Gomringer, and others cherished. The "objects" are diagrams for objects, as the letterforms are diagrams for sound/ideas. All are in a dematerialized form. Computer graphics effectively interfaces with human beings via light. The images have no mass, no physical substance in a sense, but they are perceivable and meaningful to the viewer. Most importantly, the statements appear in a three-dimensional space. The viewer/reader/participant is no longer bound to the flat surface of the incised, written, or printed sheet. By using the interactive equipment (a "joystick" and knobs to control the display), the viewer may look at and wander through this aesthetically composed symbolic space at will.

The figures show various views of Cybernetic Landscape I. The small diagrams at the top indicate the location of the viewer on the ground plane (dot in the square) and direction of view along the ground plane (line in the circle). Bars indicate height above the ground plane and a vertical viewing angle. The space is organized with hortatory slogans of the Consumptive Good Life distributed along a sacred axis. At certain locations, other visual elements are to be found in the space away from the main path, and the viewer may explore these as desired. The simple forms near the center of the space symbolize the "I" of the viewer—the vertical presence moving about the horizontal landscape plane. In one quadrant of the space is a kinetic piece, a whirlwind of letterforms rotating silently with a pulsating, varying rhythm independent of the viewer's position or movement. Within the space is a diagrammatic person who moves randomly along the ground plane. This creature is both a "mirror" of the viewer and an indicator that other viewers, other human beings, could be connected to this space, could "enter" it and could "meet" the present viewer "inside" this electronically created environment. The space is cyclically infinite. Each side wraps around electronically to the opposite side so the viewer moving off one edge would emerge instantly into the space again at the opposite edge. To signal the beginning/end of the journey, a canopy of points/stars/periods hovers in space at one terminus of the path.

By means of this computer-assisted display, new relationships and new meanings emerge, depending on the position, movement, and viewing direction of the viewer/reader/participant. As objects of light, the elements in the space convey a distinct and forceful presence combining the mystery of dreams, the awesomeness of the starry night, and the wonder of the modern, man-made urban environment seen at night. Instead of the strict topology of the stele, codex, and later book forms, the linking of elements can be richer and more complex yet is achieved through visually simple elements: points, lines, and planes. These visual components of our familiar forms have been transmuted into light and space. The reader travels through the text as context (Figs. 5.57 and 5.58).

Visible Language Artwork

Throughout 1972–1973, I continued my interest in experimental visible language through artworks on paper. I was particularly interested in creating samples of some "extra-terrestrial" or ancient earthly written forms. Some examples appear below (Figs. 5.59–5.61).

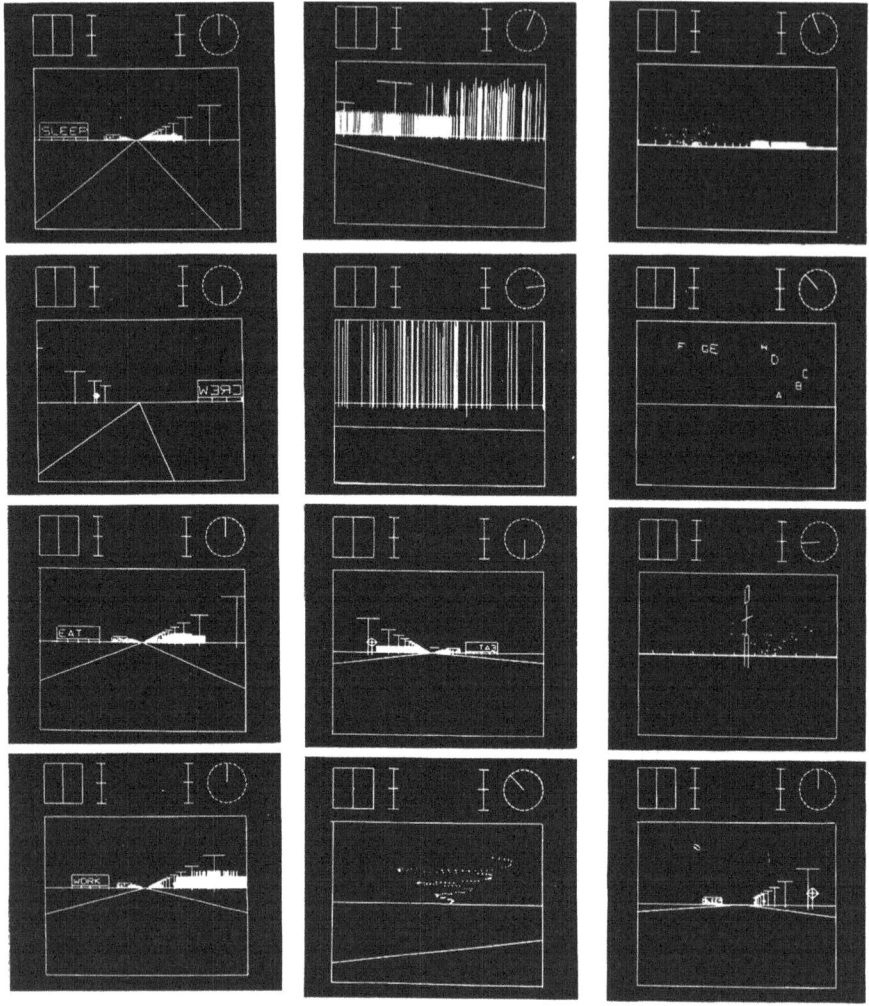

Figs. 5.57 and 5.58 Views of "Cybernetic Landscapes 1–3," 1972–1973. Images were originally produced by the author using an LDS-1 and photographed by the author, later reproduced in *Soft Where, Inc.*, Vol. 1, 1975, pp. 12–13. Original Images are now in the collection of the San Francisco Museum of Modern Art and in the collection of the Letterform Archive, San Francisco. (Source: Aaron Marcus' photo archives, used with permission)

School of Architecture and Urban Planning (SAUP) Graphic Design

During the academic year, I designed and arranged for printing of many SAUP documents, including the SAUP Newsletters, posters, catalogues, even letterheads and symbols (Figs. 5.62, 5.63, 5.64, and 5.65).

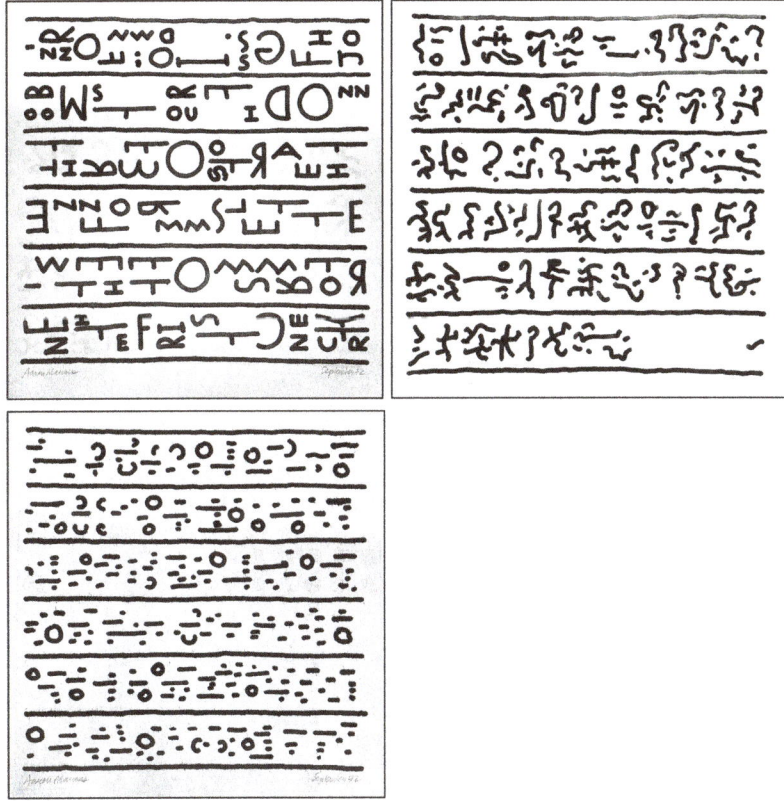

Figs. 5.59–5.61 Examples of experimental visible languages by Aaron Marcus. (Source: Aaron Marcus' photo archives; used with permission)

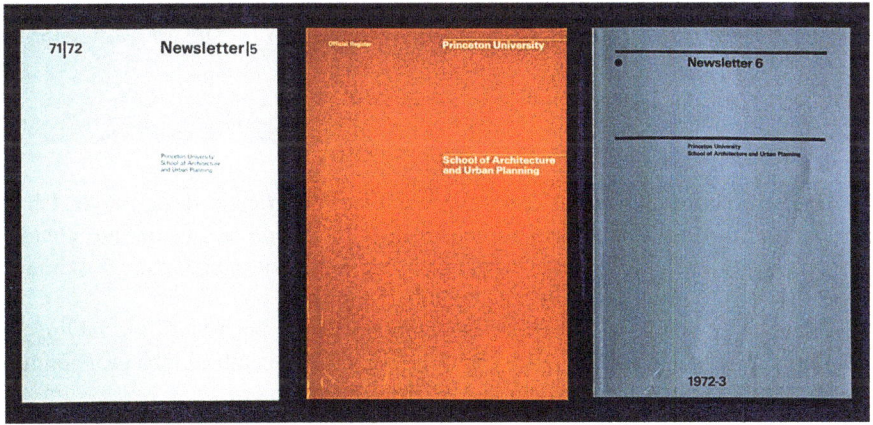

Fig. 5.62 Covers (left to right) for Princeton University School of Architecture and Urban Planning Newsletter 5 for 1971–1972 academic year; Official Register, 1972; Newsletter 6 for 1972–1973 academic year, late 1973, designed by Aaron Marcus. (Source: Aaron Marcus' photo archives; used with permission of Princeton University School of Architecture (SoA))

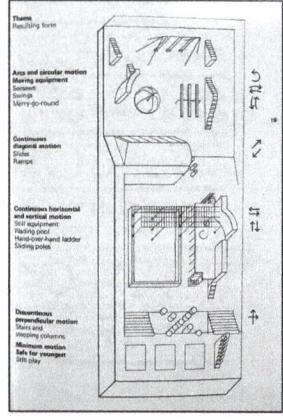

Fig. 5.63 Page designs from Princeton University School of Architecture and Urban Planning Newsletters, 1971–1973, designed by Aaron Marcus. (Source: Aaron Marcus' photo archives; used with permission of Princeton University School of Architecture (SoA))

Fig. 5.64 Poster designed by Aaron Marcus for Princeton University School of Architecture and Urban Planning exhibit of MIT Press publications, 1973. (Source: Author's photo archive, used with permission of Princeton University School of Architecture (SoA))

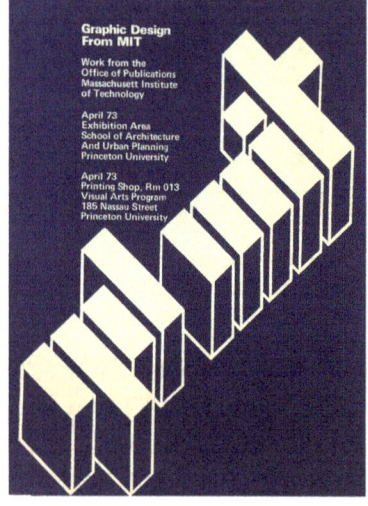

Almost all of these carried on the Swiss-German graphic design style I had learned at Yale and in the years subsequent to that period as I came into contact more and more with some of the creators of that style. I designed many posters for the Creative Arts Program and for an exhibit of my work on campus.

I planned on staying at Princeton as long as I could, but I had little inkling of what the future had in store for me. The final years at Princeton and the years immediately afterward are discussed in the next chapter (Fig. 5.66).

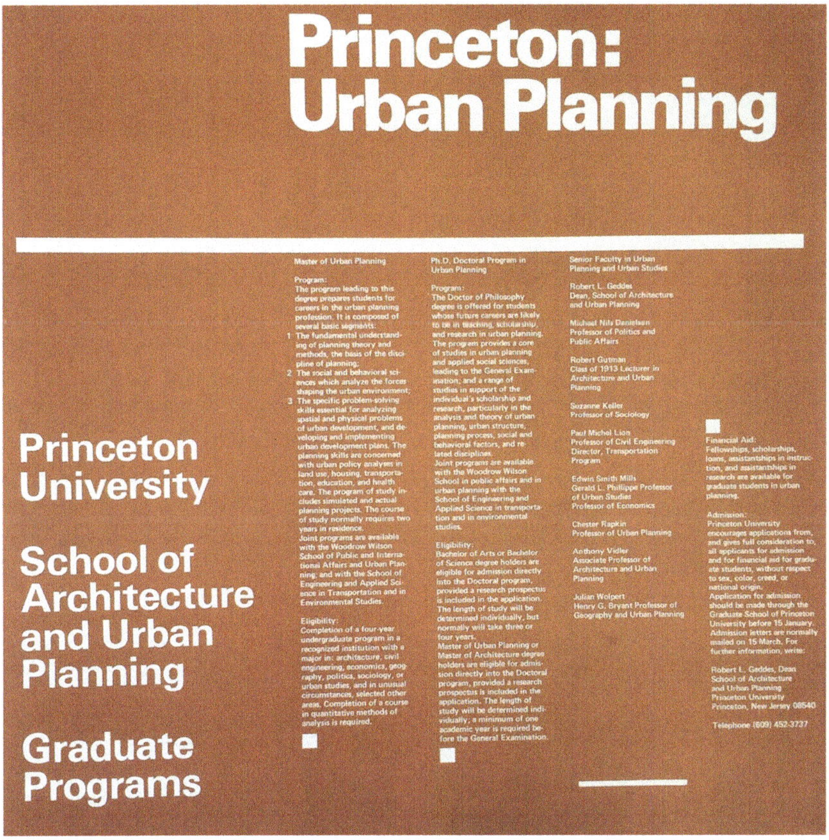

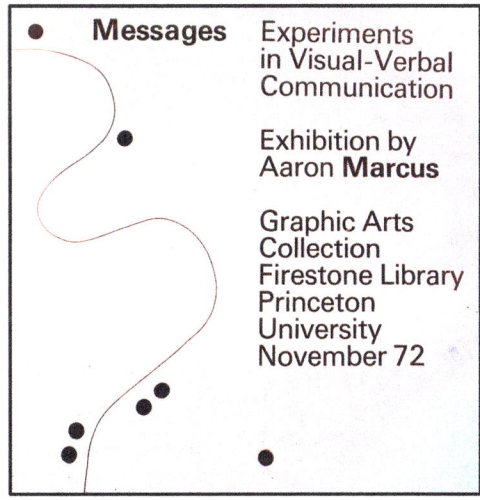

Fig. 5.65 Poster designed by Aaron Marcus for Princeton University School of Architecture and Urban Planning graduate programs, 1973. (Source: Author's photo archive, used with permission of Princeton University School of Architecture (SoA))

Fig. 5.66 Poster design by Aaron Marcus for his exhibit of experimental visible languages in Princeton University's Graphic Arts Collection, 1972. (Source: Aaron Marcus' photo archive; used with permission of Princeton University Library)

Chapter 6
Princeton and Beyond

Takeaways
- *In 1973–1977, I continued to teach and work at Princeton University.*
- *In 1977, I left Princeton and moved to Israel, teaching graphic design, visual communication, and computer cartography at Bezalel Academy of Art/Design and at the Hebrew University in Jerusalem during 1977–1978.*
- *In 1978, I accepted a half-year Research Fellowship to research and design a nonverbal audio-visual presentation communicating information about global energy interdependence at the East-West Center, Honolulu, HI.*
- *In 1979, I moved to the University of California/Berkeley to teach visual communication and computer graphics.*

Princeton, Summer, 1973

The years sometimes blur one into another. I cannot recall what I did during the summer of 1973. I'm sure I did something! Among other things, our first child Joshua was born!

Princeton University, Year 6, 1973–1974

Academic Year 1973–1974

The years blur one into another. I cannot recall much of what happened during the academic year. I am certain that my students continued to produce fine publications in my course on visual studies. I continued to refine my courses in the SAUP, run the

A. Marcus, *Bridging Art, Design and Technology: My Lifetime Work*, https://doi.org/10.1007/978-3-032-04342-9_6

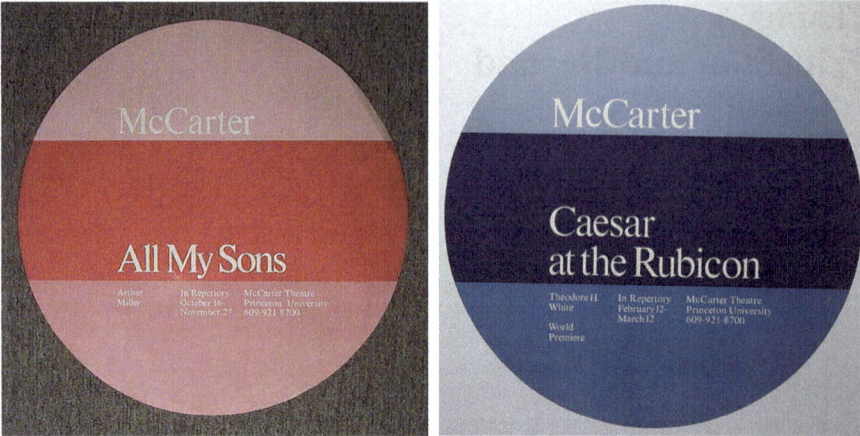

Figs. 6.1 and 6.2 Poster series design for McCarter Theater. The poster was die-cut into a circle so it could be posted at any angle and would seem to be readable and appealing. (Source: Aaron Marcus' photo archive; used with permission of Princeton University McCarter Theater)

Visual Studies Lab, run the Printing Shop in the VAP, create various works of art and design, and publish articles.

I believe I designed book covers and publications for the History Department, the Woodrow Wilson School, and other groups. I also designed posters for the McCarter Theater around this time (Figs. 6.1 and 6.2).

A Zero-Circle Around the Earth

I continued my exploration of conceptual visible-language artworks by planning and executing in October 1973 a work entitled "A Zero-Circle Around the Earth." The work extended my efforts as an artist, graphic designer, type designer, or mark-maker to create a sign at a very large scale, in fact, at the scale of the entire earth. Like "An X on America" I exhibited the documentation in exhibits in the USA and elsewhere and later published the documentation in *Soft Where, Inc.*, Vol. 1 (See Bibliography: Marcus, 1975). The descriptions below are adapted from that publication:

After months of preparation during the summer of 1973 and into the Fall, on Wednesday, 24 October 73, United Nations Day, at 3:00 pm EDT, I placed a phone call from a public telephone booth in the basement of the United Nations building, New York City, to an adjacent telephone booth, by way of Tokyo, Japan, and Frankfurt, Germany. The telephone connection circled the globe, creating a conceptual zero and/or circle around the world (Figs. 6.3 and 6.4).

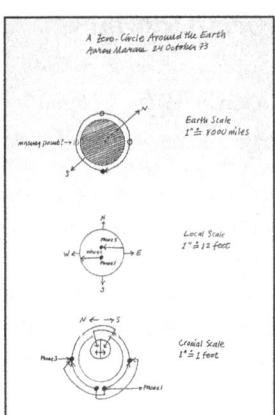

Figs. 6.3 and 6.4 "A Zero-Circle Around the Earth." Photo of Aaron Marcus during the call and diagram drawn by Aaron Marcus to illustrate scale of the work. (Source: Images by Aaron Marcus; used with permission of the author)

I completed the circuit by talking and listening with both telephones. Conceptually, the work is an electronic poem-drawing at an environmental scale. The telephone connection (electricity = fire) went by way of satellite (air), undersea cable (water), and underground cable (earth). The theme of the event was solipsistic unification despite topological deformation. By means of its development over time, its position in space, its intentions, its abstract/concrete ambiguity, and its sensual properties of shape, color, texture, solidity, etc., this work of conceptual art demonstrated the statistical, quantum-relativistic, soft edge of form (see diagram in the figure) with respect to ontological, epistemological, and teleological inquiry. In regard to the single concept of connectivity, one may observe the following aspects of unification implicit in the total work:

1. The unification of humankind via the institutions of the United Nations and electronic communication systems and via the very surface of the planet.
2. The unification of the eastern and western hemispheres, with their corresponding modes of thought, i.e., quality vs. quantity.
3. The unification of the left and right cerebral hemispheres, i.e., the unification of the verbal and the visual/tactile centers.
4. The unification of the rational with the intuitive, of reason with emotion, and the worlds of science/technology with the arts/the humanities.
5. The unification of space and time. My voice as myself encircled the earth while I simultaneously was at a single point in space in New York City. I was calling Tokyo into the future across the International Date Line, and Tokyo was calling back into the past to reach New York. During the phone call, space and time were collapsed into conceptual nodes.

Poem-Drawings

In early 1974, I began to experiment with drawings that expressed the history of letterforms as they transformed over millennia. The descriptions of several works below are adapted from text in my first monograph: *Soft Where, Inc.*, Vol 1. (See Bibliography: Marcus, 1975, pp. 2–3). By using specific conventions of writing and drawing, I am able to examine several aspects of mark making that continue to fascinate me. In each case I begin with a known, standard form and I attempt to copy it. Following a predetermined procedure for contemplation, then action, I am able to outwit certain ingrained writing, reading, seeing, and drawing tendencies which operate within me unconsciously. In the visual results of the procedure, one is able to find traces of mechanical response to spontaneous mutations, and creative intuition as the gestalt of the mark undergoes change. These and others of my alphanumeric time-pieces enable one to indirectly eavesdrop on left-brain/right-brain dialogue. In another sense they allow one to travel backward through time through the generation of successive stages of quasi-primitive forms (Figs. 6.5 and 6.6).

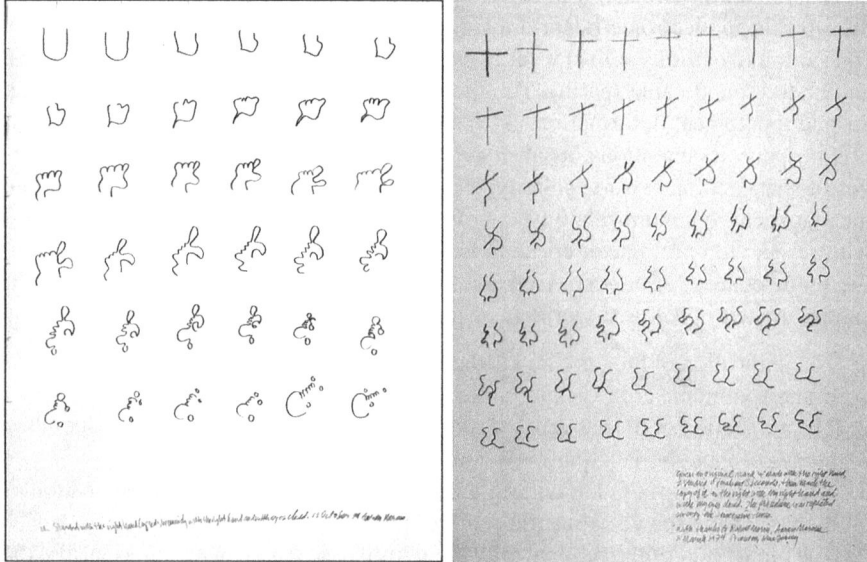

Figs. 6.5 and 6.6 Examples from a set of studies of the complete alphabet, 1974. Each top row mark was made with my right hand and with my eyes closed. After examining a mark for about three seconds, I attempted to copy the preceding symbol with my right hand and with my eyes closed. I repeated this process for each letter seven more times. (Images from Aaron Marcus' archives; used with permission of the author)

Other Graphic Design and Visible Language Works

As in other years, during 1974–1974 I completed many other graphic design projects for the SAUP, Visual Arts Program, and other clients. I also experimented with playful collages of traditional gravure and lithographic prints (Figs. 6.7 and 6.8–6.11).

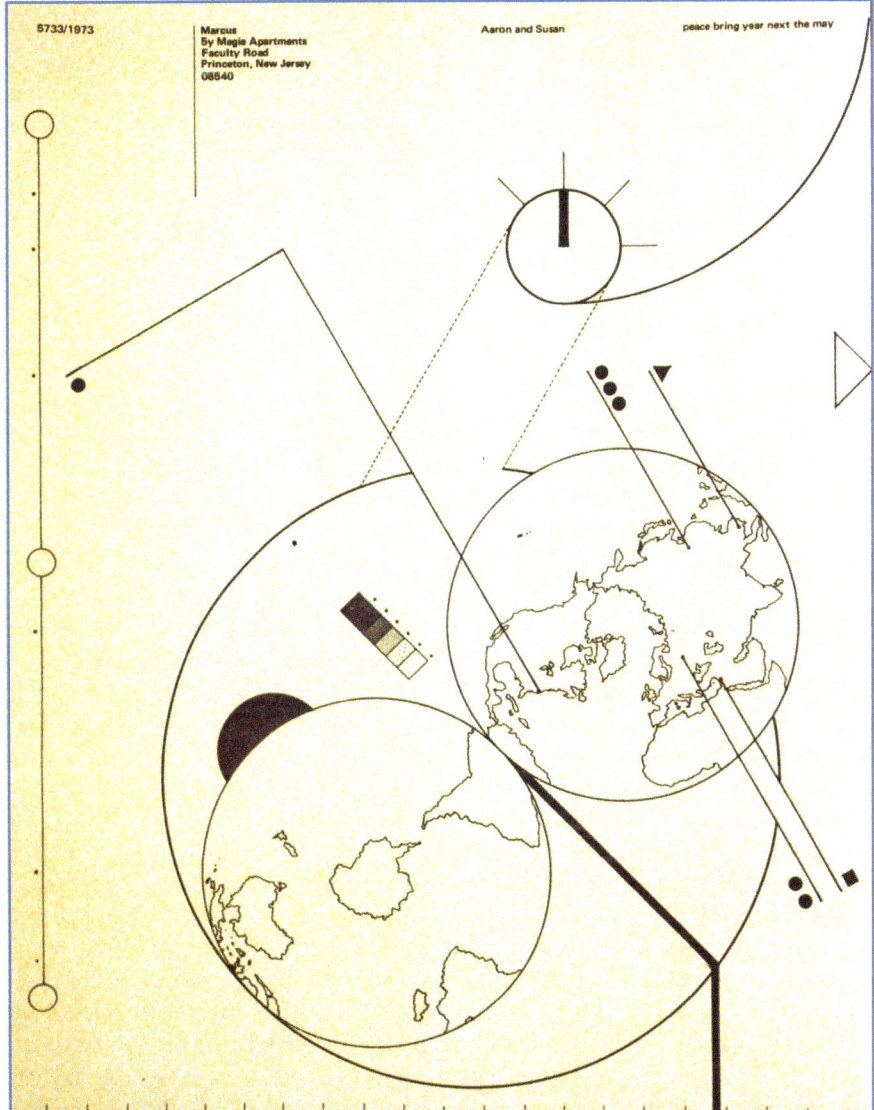

Fig. 6.7 Jewish New Year card for 1973/5733. I enjoyed experimenting with playful abstract layouts. Design by Aaron Marcus (Source: Aaron Marcus archive; used with permission of the author)

Figs. 6.8–6.11   Collages using traditional gravure and lithographic portrait prints from the late nineteenth and early twentieth centuries. Collage design by Aaron Marcus (1973). (Source: Aaron Marcus' photo archive; used with permission)

Princeton University, Summer, 1974

Signing on the Dotted Line

Following is a documentation of "Signing on the Dotted Line," a conceptual artwork involving a light bulb, which I carried out on the celebration of my son Joshua's first birthday. The documentation is adapted from that published in *Soft Where, Inc.*, Vol. 1 (see Bibliography: Marcus, 1975, used with permission).

At noon EDT, 4 July 1974, in Princeton, New Jersey, on the top of a building (the SAUP building in which I taught), I set up a flashing light. For 24 hours, while the earth made one complete revolution the light flashed. In doing so the tiny flashes or points of light created a dotted line in the form of a circle or zero or "o," whose radius was approximately 8000 miles as viewed by someone looking at the work from a location above the North Pole. This art-mark was a sign/light/space work. On 16 December 1973, I had conceived of a conceptual artwork in which I would hold a marker at one place for 24 hours. Because of the revolution of the earth, the marker would trace out a circular form. Of course, not precisely a circle (or zero or "o") because of the movement of the earth about the sun, the sun's movement toward the star Vega, simultaneously the rotation and translation of our entire galaxy, and the expansion of the universe. However, for all intents and purposes, the gestalt image would be circular. When I first began to conceive of this work, I was uncertain whether I could hold during the entire time a piece of chalk or other conventional art marker without falling asleep. Actually, I considered simply tying a pencil or other similar object to my hand for the entire period. The gesture was ritually possible as an unusual binding ceremony, but I eventually dismissed **it** as too representational.

About 15 February 1974, in the February *Scientific American*, I read that 25 years after the first artificial satellite, a man-made object (Pioneer 10) will be on its way to the stars, having passed the orbit of the planet Pluto [then considered a planet!] in

Fig. 6.12 "Signing on the Dotted Line." Photograph of the light bulb fixture, the "mark-maker" with a flasher in its base. (Source: Image from Aaron Marcus' archive; used with permission of the author)

Fig. 6.13 "Signing on the Dotted Line." Photograph of Aaron Marcus placing a light bulb with a flasher in its base on the roof of the Princeton University School of Architecture and Urban Planning. (Source: Image from Aaron Marcus' archive; used with permission of the author)

1983. This seemed to confirm the appropriateness of the expanded scale of my conceptual artworks.

In creating this "circle" of light, I envisioned it, also, a giant set of candles set upon the planet earth as a birthday cake for Joshua (Figs. 6.12 and 6.13).

Princeton University, Year 7, 1974–1975

Academic Year 1974–1975

This year marked the end of my part-time teaching in the Creative Arts/Visual Arts Program (VAP). Instead, I began to work in the Public Relations office of the University under the direction of Ms. Jean Firstenberg, then the wife of the Provost of the University, Paul Firstenberg. I found working for her to be exciting, challenging, enjoyable, and fun. I think she was the best "boss" for whom I had ever worked. She was sometimes moody, unpredictable, but I felt a certain basic trust in her judgment, experience, and instincts. She gave me a lot of respect and responsibility. In this position, I designed the official Princeton University Map, the undergraduate and graduate school catalogues, the campus signage system, the *Princeton Weekly Bulletin*, and all the main signage and maps of the Firestone Library, then the world's largest open-stacked library.

All of these projects emerged from my office drawing board after meetings with clients, printing/construction professionals, Jean, and others. I was changing the image of Princeton dramatically, bringing it out of the eighteenth century or early twentieth century at the latest, and creating a new brand, one more like the corporate graphic design in which I had been trained. Only one project generated mail that complained about my changes. The old "Princeton Weekly Bulletin" was very traditional looking, with narrow paper width and serif type. My design (see Figs. 6.14, 6.15, 6.16, and 6.17) was more like a large poster, with sans-serif lettering (Helvetica again). The design featured a folding pattern that enabled the Newsletter to have its own "mailing page" so that it easily could be mailed to subscribers. An anonymous letter we received said we were ruining the traditions of Princeton. In some ways that was true, but I felt at the time that I was helping Princeton to join other institutions and organizations of the late twentieth century. That year, the "Weekly Bulletin" kindly made space for an article about my work at Princeton.

Spring Semester 1975 in Israel

Fortunately, I was able to take another fully paid semester off, another sabbatical, this time to relocate to Jerusalem, Israel, with my family, during the Spring 1975 semester. Instead of just being a short-term visitor to Bezalel, the foremost school for art and design in Jerusalem, Israel. I was able to teach at least one course in Bezalel in the Graphic Design Department and had contact with many faculty and students. I loved being in the historic building of old Bezalel in the center of the city, not far from Mahane Yehuda, the main marketplace of West Jerusalem. We lived in Bayit Vegan, in the far southeast. For reasons unknown, Bezalel, filled with somewhat rebellious, anti-establishment, secular types, had rented a faculty guest apartment for visitors like myself in a very religious section of West Jerusalem, which meant my family and I could not drive our car in or out of this area on the Sabbath. I had to park just outside the outskirts of the neighborhood. During our stay in Bayit Vegan, our son Joshua began to speak his first language: Hebrew. To be more precise, Yemenite Hebrew, because his caretaker was Ms. Tzivia Hobara, our next-door neighbor on the two-apartment floor of our building. Chaim, her husband, and Tzivia, as well as their son Danny and their daughter Merav, became good friends. I was one of the few people at Bezalel who wore a kippah, a sign of adherence to

Marcus blends talents of artist and graphic designer

If you're looking for information about Princeton, you're likely to find it in something designed by Aaron Marcus. If it's a building or landmark, check his campus guide and map. If it's an event that is scheduled for this week, it will probably be listed in the *Bulletin's* Weekly Calendar. Or if you're just tracking down a piece of information that is tucked away in an obscure recess of the library, refer to his floor-by-floor graphics in Firestone.

A lecturer in the architecture school and graphic designer in the Publications Office, Marcus combines graphic arts talents with those of the visual artist.

As a graphic designer, he's involved with the formulation of the visual/verbal aspects of publications that the University uses to communicate to its many internal and external constituencies.

Among his most visible creations is the design for the *Princeton Weekly Bulletin*, which has been selected by the Council for the Advancement and Support of Education (CASE) for a special design education project as one of 20 outstanding tabloids in the country. Earlier this month, his design for the architecture school's *Newspaper: 2* was chosen by the Type Directors Club of New York for their annual awards exhibition to be held this June.

Among his other recent design projects are the Graduate School Announcement, a course offerings tabloid, and the 1976 Commencement program.

"In all of this work I have tried to stress quality of appearance and good organization in the aesthetic and informational aspects of these publications," Marcus says. He characterizes their appearance as strong, easily identifiable, and consistent. "I've introduced modern sensibilities to the design of University graphics. And while this fresh new look may be viewed with initial discomfort by those who see it as a departure from what they consider "traditional" design, the new approaches will eventually become part of a *new* "traditional" mode for the campus."

As an artist, Marcus has exhibited both his visual design and visual arts work (including computer graphics, visual poetry, and conceptual art) in museums and galleries in this country and in Amsterdam, Sao Paulo, Tokyo, and Vienna. In 1974 his one-man show "Symbologinstructs" was exhibited in the Art Museum, and last year he and his wife, Susan, a freelance designer who also has done a lot of work for the University,

Marcus with (l to r) NewsPaper: 2, library signage, and campus guide and map

exhibited much of their campus-related design work in a show at the architecture school.

Marcus's courses in the Visual Arts Program and in the School of Architecture and Urban Planning reflect a blend of visual and graphic arts skills and have included instruction in typography, printing, graphic design, diagramming, and computer graphics. About his teaching he says: "It is gratifying to me that, although the University offers no convenient program or well-planned route to acquire a liberal education in visual communication, I have been successful in helping a selected number of students to gain a broad, coherent education in graphic design and related subjects."

Marcus further integrates his role as artist and graphic designer by sharing his expertise with the broader community of "students" both on and off campus. He has lectured on his work and related subjects at universities, art and design schools, and professional institutions in the United States and abroad. At the University, he has arranged exhibits such as "Modern Swiss Posters" and "Photography and Modern Society" to help members of the

University community gain a better understanding of graphic design techniques.

For his campus clients who must apply his design principles in a continuing project or publication, Marcus often writes extensive guidelines, critiques the first few issues, and then turns the project over to those who will be caring for it. "I am interested in and enjoy the challenge of creating projects that can be taken over by others to become independent, self-contained sources of good design on the campus," he says.

Marcus says his background in physics as an undergraduate here (Class of 1965) and in visual arts at Yale (B.F.A., M.F.A. 1968) has given him a binocular, rather than a monocular, perspective on visual communication. "I am particularly interested in the possibilities for creative interaction between the two cultures of the engineering/sciences on one hand and the humanities/arts on the other, between the rationalism and fantasy of each of these cultures."

Fig. 6.14 Daily Princetonian article about Aaron Marcus, 1974. (Source: Aaron Marcus' photo archive; used with permission of the Office of Communications, Princeton University)

many, but not all, traditional Jewish values and practices. I called this approach Conservadox Judaism.

I also took a course in spoken Hebrew at Ulpan Etzion, the first Ulpan (fast-track Hebrew learning institution) in Israel in southwest Jerusalem. I recall that one of my classmates was Sana Hasan, an Egyptian, who was a graduate student at Harvard at the time. I believe she was the daughter of a diplomat. We met a few times during the Ulpan classes and talked about the unusual circumstances that enabled her to be

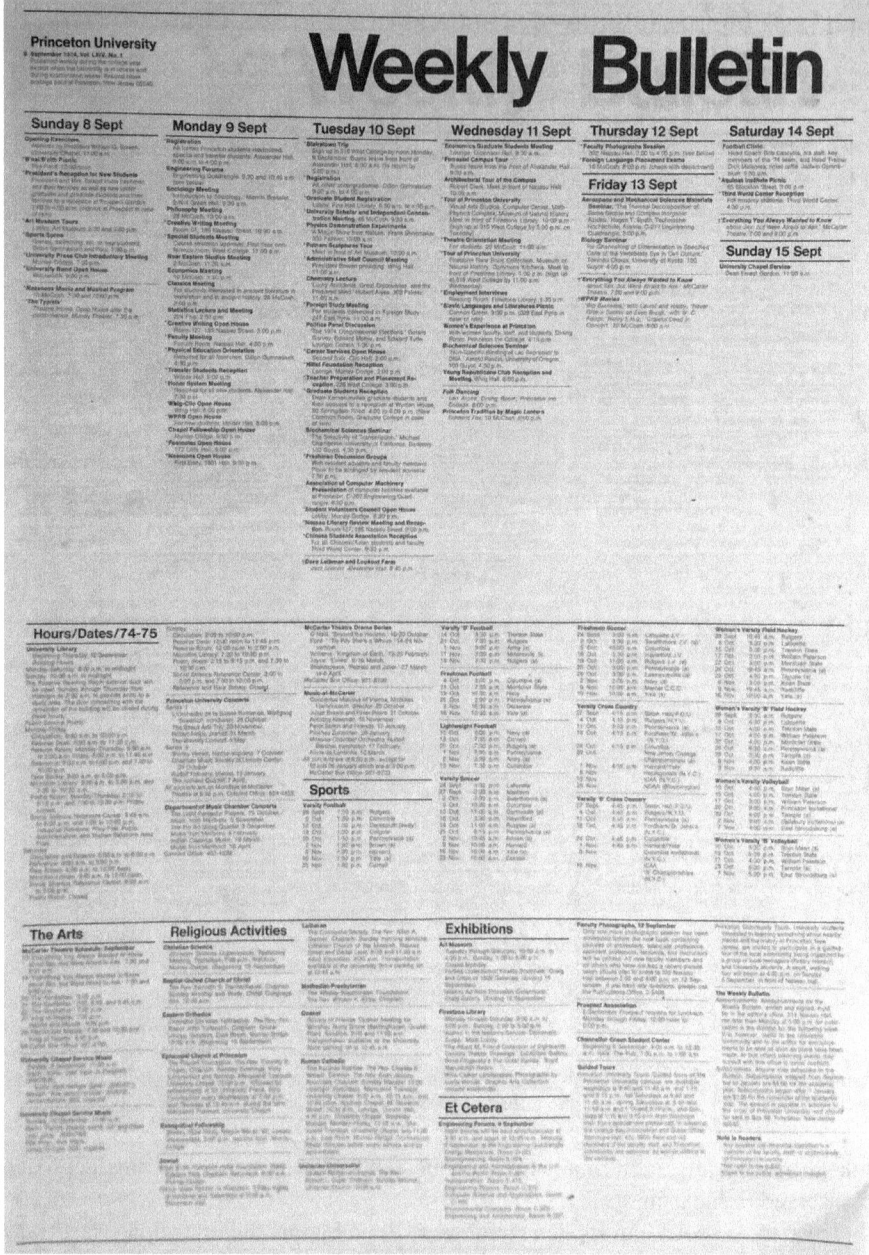

Fig. 6.15 "Princeton University Weekly Bulletin," 08–15 September 1974, redesign by Aaron Marcus, which featured a poster-like layout. (Source: Aaron Marcus' photo archive; used with permission of the Office of Communications, Princeton University)

Fig. 6.16 Poster for
Princeton University Office
of Publications graphic
design work by Aaron
Marcus and Susan Marcus,
exhibited in the School of
Architecture and Urban
Planning 1976. Design by
Aaron Marcus. (Source:
Aaron Marcus' photo
archive; used with
permission of the Princeton
University School of
Architecture (SoA))

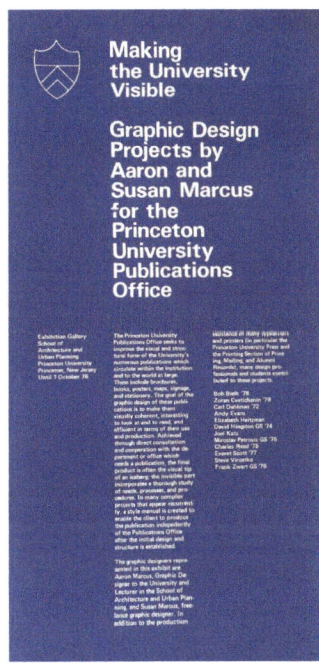

in Israel. She later wrote a book about her experiences in Israel, *Enemy in the Promised Land.*

One of the places that most intrigued me at Bezalel was a computer graphics laboratory set up in the Wolfson Building, elsewhere in Jerusalem by Vladimir Bonacic (RIP), a non-Jewish Croatian computer artist from Yugoslavia, who had somehow convinced people at the Hebrew University and at Bezalel, which was then a separate institution (it is now part of the Hebrew University) to fund his laboratory. I cannot remember at this point specifically what his "research" into computer-based art and design comprised. I do remember that he had a lot of expensive furniture and equipment, which was quite impressive. He demonstrated for me some kind of computer game involving a rocket ship landing on the moon, some of the earliest computer games.

One morning, I had visited the Herodion with my wife and children. The Herodion is an impressive archeological site, an artificial truncated-cone-shaped hill, about eight miles south of Jerusalem and three miles east of Bethlehem. Herod the Great built a palace fortress and a small town there between 23 and 15 BCE. After walking around the ruins, we got back in my car, and my wife dropped me off 45 min later at the computer graphics laboratory. As I played with the equipment there and talked with Vladimir, I could only marvel at the several millennia differences in technology provided by a 45-min trip. Such were the amazing contrasts to be found in Israel.

Several people I met that semester were particularly kind to me, including Dan Hoffner (a"h), the head of Bezalel, Henry Friedlander and his wife (a"h), and

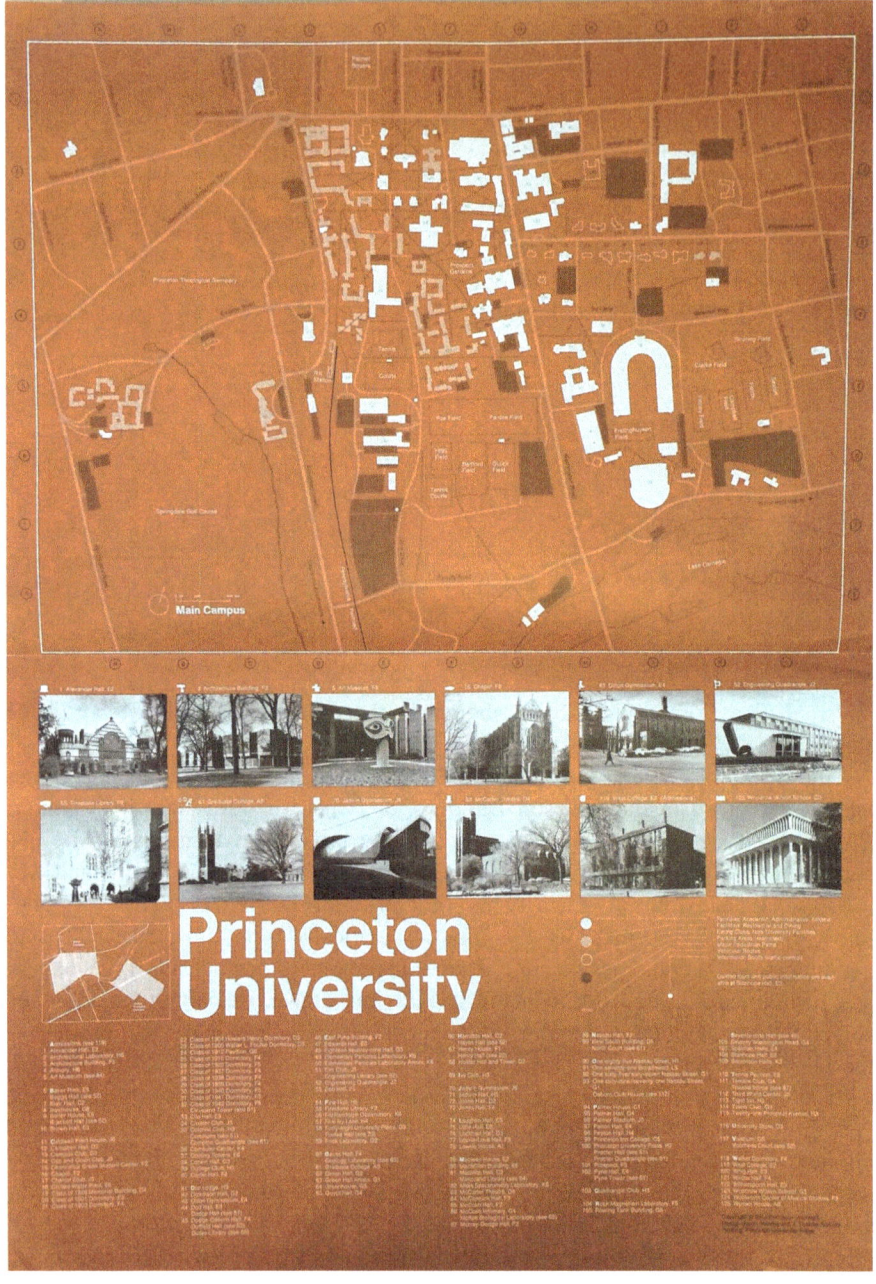

Fig. 6.17 Princeton University Map, designed by Aaron Marcus, 1975. (Source: Author's photo archive; used with permission of the Princeton University Office of Communications)

someone from the Israeli print industry (a"h), whose name I now have forgotten. Henry Friedlander was a Dutch type designer, who designed the popular Hadassah script. My wife and I enjoyed our time with these people, particularly the Friedlanders, who invited us many times to visit their home on the outskirts of Jerusalem.

I tried to make contacts with many different graphic designers, industrial designers, artists, and science/technology people, with the thought in mind that I might wish to return to Israel. These contacts would prove valuable two years later when I decided to emigrate to Israel.

I continued to create conceptual artworks, typographic works, and graphic design works.

Summer 1975

Again, after more months of preparation, my wife Susan, my son Joshua, and I prepared for our return to the USA. We had bought round-the-world tickets for two. Our son Joshua, at his age, traveled for free, fortunately for our budget. As long as we kept heading generally east, we could continue the voyage that first had taken us from Princeton, NJ, to Jerusalem. During the next three months of travel, we visited Iran, India, Nepal, Thailand, Hong Kong, Taiwan, and Japan, and re-entered the USA through Hawaii.

We flew first from Jerusalem (Ben Gurion airport) to Tehran, nonstop, direct, without being shot down. These were the last years for the Shah in Iran. We saw his motorcade drive by at one point as it entered the palace grounds. We toured many mosques, the great Bazaar, and enjoyed the delicious foods, especially the breads and the yoghurt, and the friendly people, as we had in Crete in 1972. From Tehran, we flew to Isfahan and Shiraz, progressively smaller cities, with progressively more beautiful mosques, Kufic calligraphy, and charming people and street scenes. In Isfahan, as I marveled at a Star of David (*Magen David*) in a house and what seemed to be a small niche in the doorpost for a *mezuzah*, a ritual prayer document, some people crept cautiously closer to us, then one blurted out quietly, "Atah m'daber b'Ivrit?" (Do you speak Hebrew?). We had stumbled on a Jewish community in the city and were immediately invited to Friday night Sabbath dinner, which was delicious, and to the local synagogue for services. In fact, there were many Israelis in Iran at that time, helping to bring their knowledge of agriculture and irrigation to the country.

We flew onward to India for 11 days, landing first in Mumbai (then Bombay). The degree of poverty, the number of people, and the number of beggars were staggering. So was the beauty of some local people as well as the numerous local crafts for each region. In Bombay, we stayed in a very inexpensive hotel near the Taj Mahal Hilton. The contrast could not have been greater. Our room was a dreary single gray room with a dreary gray bed, with a single light bulb hanging from the ceiling. The heat at night was so stifling that we had to keep the window open to get some fresh air. During the night, I heard a dull thump of something landing outside our window. To me, it sounded like the sound a dead body might make after falling several stories. In the morning I was relieved to see that it was not a corpse, but instead garbage bags flung into the alleyway behind our hotel. Crawling over the garbage were the largest rats I had ever seen. The scene was unnerving, considering we were inhabiting a first-story room with a window ledge not very high.

In rapid succession, we visited the Elephanta Island cave temples near Mumbai, Ahmedabad (where I gave a lecture at the National Institute of Design's Graphic Design Department), Jaipur, Fatehpur-Sikri (an entire empty town in the Agra District of Uttar Pradesh founded as the capital of Mughal Empire in 1571 by Emperor Akbar, but serving this role only from 1571 to 1585, when Akbar abandoned it, leaving the site completely abandoned in 1610), New Delhi, Agra, the cave temples cut into solid rock of Ajanta and Ellora, Sarnath (the birthplace of the Buddha), and Varanasi (earlier called Benares, the locus of Hindu burials along the Ganges). The overwhelming sensuous cascade of sights, sounds, smells, and touches were richer and denser than anything we had ever experienced on earth. India, as people said, was another planet living on our earth; the USA, to them, was another planet living on their earth. Joshua had become ill in a small village of 800 people in India at the age of two. Fortunately, we could get him treated in New Delhi.

From Varanasi, we flew to Kathmandu, stayed a few days to experience the poverty, beauty, temples, and religious intensity, then flew on to Bangkok, where we stayed with a US banking family in a gated community. The disparity of cultures was extreme. On 4 July 1975, we celebrated with hot dogs, hamburgers, and sauerkraut. Our morning breakfasts were Kellogg's Cornflakes, orange juice, and coffee. No wonder we wanted to escape to the canals of Bangkok to see the local vendors and to experience the amazing Buddhist temple architecture that I thought surely had inspired imagery for alien space cultures in *Flash Gordon* movies of the 1980s and afterwards.

From Bangkok, we flew to Hong Kong for a few days; viewed Communist China from a lookout point near the northern border of the city; experienced the cacophony of sounds, sights, and smells in this cosmopolitan city; and then flew on to Taiwan, where we visited the National Museum in Taipei, among other sites.

Finally, in Asia, we spent a month's sojourn in Japan, the first of many future visits to that country. I gave a lecture at the American Embassy in Tokyo, thanks to Yukio Ota, with whom I had become friends after some years of correspondence and my interest in his LoCoS universal sign language, which he invented in 1964. We traveled throughout Tokyo's many districts, then on to Kyoto and Nara, which had been ancient capitals of Japan long before Tokyo. Everywhere, the beauty of the landscapes, the temples, the calligraphy, the modern designs, as well as ancient crafts astounded us. People were extraordinarily friendly to us and curious and amused by us, as well as charmed by our little son Joshua, who captured people's interest everywhere we went.

We returned to the USA through Honolulu. After a month in Japan, I began to think of myself as Japanese in height and weight, although I was much taller and heavier than most. I could then understand how the Japanese must have felt when they first saw the gigantic Caucasian people of Hawaii. After seeing nearly empty store shelves in India, we were also astounded by the bursting shelves of US supermarket chains. The level of somewhat identical but competing brands of almost everything was overwhelming, a bit depressing, and cause for alarm, considering all of the poverty that we had witnessed.

By the end of the summer and beginning of the fall, I was back in Princeton. I swam laps in the University pool for hours, trying to remember almost every memorable moment that I had experienced during the summer. Certainly, the exposure to so many different languages, cultures, cuisines, religions, customs, and people had sparked my interest in cross-cultural communication like nothing before, an interest and professional activity that remained a lifelong commitment. I also was made acutely aware of the disparity between the riches of the USA and the circumstances in which most of the world's population lived. The contrast was sobering, both making me grateful for what I had, but also committed to being sensitive and to helping others outside the USA.

"Time Piece": Conceptual Visible-Language Artwork

In 1975, I had conceived of another typographic/sign/mark-making conceptual visible-language artwork, which I called "Time-Piece." I conceived of the project during January through June 1975 and executed it during June through September 1975. I documented the work, exhibited the documentation, and published the documentation in *Soft Where, Inc.*, Vol. 2 (see Bibliography: Marcus, 1982). The text below is excerpted and adapted from that publication:

During a trip around the earth by jet, plane, boat, bus, train, car, scooter, bicycle, rickshaw, and foot, I purchased conventional picture postcards in cities, from Jerusalem, Israel to Omaha, Nebraska, USA. On each card I wrote a special text that was temporally specific but verbally ambivalent. I addressed and mailed them to myself. The postcards and I traveled to Princeton, where I eventually received them, read them, and contemplated their images, their messages, and their significance. At that moment, an asterisk- or star-like object was completed in time-space, in which the "lines" from myself intersected myself in a point. The work involves the passage of time, simultaneity, and memory. Resonating conceptually between drawing and calligraphy, it is primarily a "time·time" work, or "time-piece."

15 January 1975: My wife Susan, our son Joshua, and I left Princeton University and the United States for a sabbatical semester in Jerusalem, Israel, where I was a guest faculty member/researcher at Bezalel Academy of Art and Design and at its Program of Art and Science. It was our plan to travel eastward to return to the USA after leaving Jerusalem.

19 March 1975: I had planned originally to continue my telephone-based conceptual art works that explored the nature of late-twentieth-century mark-making

and the bivalent symbolism of writing and drawing in such marks. The earlier pieces "An X on America," "A Zero-Circle Around the Earth," and "Signing On the Dotted Line" were appearing in a special monograph about my work called *Soft Where, Inc.*, being published by the *West Coast Poetry Review* in Reno, Nevada. In continuing the themes of the earlier pieces, I conceived of a conference-type phone call that would connect Moscow, Russia, Washington, DC, USA, and Cairo, Egypt, through Jerusalem, Israel. When eventually connected, the electronic marking would create an arrow-like symbol wrapping around the Western hemisphere and pointing to Jerusalem, the symbolic spiritual center of the West. At the same time the form would be the elemental structure of the "shin," the Hebrew letter associated with "shaddai," one of several names for G-d, and with "shalom," the Hebrew word for peace.

I carried out a trial of this approach to mark-making, but decided I should try something else. Having completed a "sketch project," I began to think of other ways to explore visual communication using postcards, the international postal system, and time, to create a work over which I would have more control in terms of the nature of the end points. I realized that our impending travel through Asia afforded me an ideal opportunity to create such a work over the appropriate physical scale and time scale.

Quickly, the scenario unfolded: I would send postcards with a standard text to myself from a number of points around the globe. Jerusalem would begin the sequence, and Omaha, Nebraska, would end the sequence. These source points had an obvious, close personal relationship to me that enhanced the significance of the work, both objectively and subjectively. I purchased a conventional postcard with a view of Jerusalem. Without much pomp and circumstance, from a post office near our apartment in Bayit Vegan, an outlying south-eastern neighborhood of Jerusalem, I sent the postcard winging its way to the USA and its target, me, at a future time, in another space. From our apartment, we could see the sun rising over the Old City of Jerusalem and the modern buildings of the Hebrew University campus. Because we were near the edge of the city and on a high cliff, in the evening we could watch the bare sand hills of the Judean desert and the distant site of Herod's winter palace, the Herodion, perched upon an artificial hill, gradually merge their somber colors with the warm gray of the darkening sky.

During the next 3 months, I sent other postcards from the cities and countries we visited, eventually collecting them all. As I anticipated, the effect was dazzling when I saw all the postcards at one moment and reflected on the times and spaces from which they had come; it was like a star, a burst of memento-energy, that occurred in my brain (Figs. 6.18–6.22).

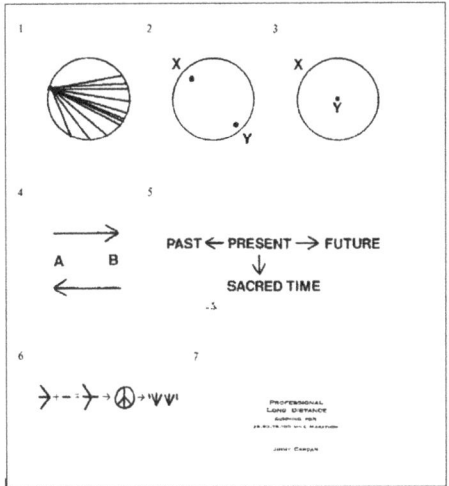

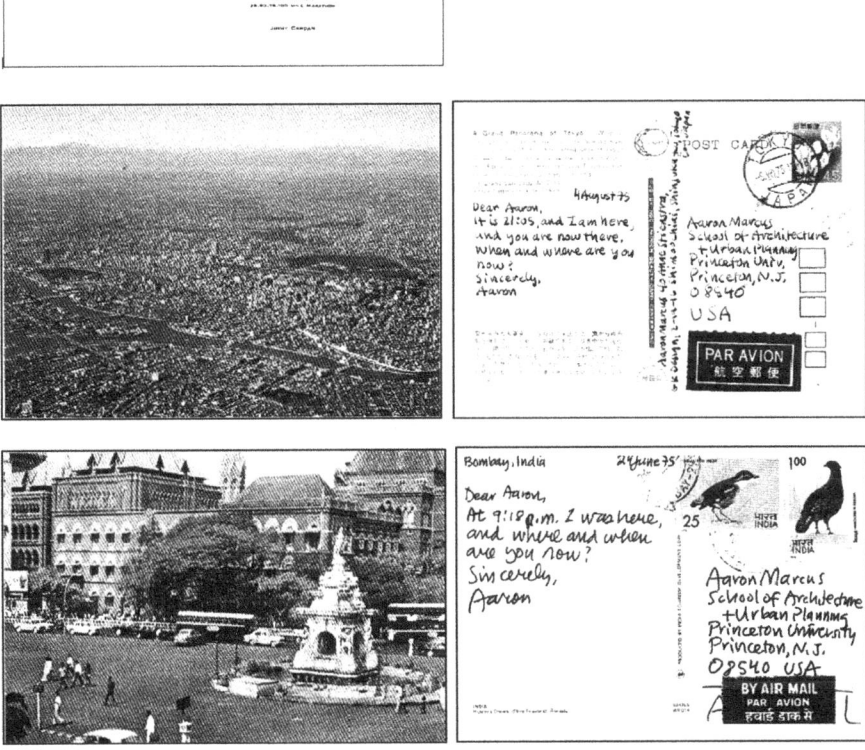

Figs. 6.18–6.22 "Time-Piece." Diagram of time-time space structure and examples of postcards, conceptual artwork by Aaron Marcus, 1975. (Source: Aaron Marcus' photo archive; used with permission of the author)

Princeton University, Year 8, 1975–1976

After the trip around the world, I returned to Princeton for another year of challenges and opportunities.

Soft Where, Inc., Volume 1

I published my first monograph, *Soft Where, Inc.*, Volume 1, at the invitation of William L. Fox, Editor, *West Coast Poetry Review*, Reno, NV, which had published examples of my computer art, visible language experiments, and conceptual art. In 2009, he kindly gave me permission to post electronic versions of this monograph (Marcus 1975) and the second (Marcus 1982), which he later published. The first monograph contained examples of my poem-drawings, computer art, experimental visible language artworks, and conceptual visible-language works documentation. I was very grateful for the opportunity to showcase this work. The cover image showed a "script" or "score" for an invited artwork, a ritual I called "Genesis," which I designed for a summer event at the Rhode Island School of Design. The work was to be performed where earth, air, fire, and water combined: sunset along the ocean near Providence. Groups of men and women were assigned musical changing symbols and followed the script of the chart-like form shown on the cover. I could not attend, but I was told it was very well received (Fig. 6.23).

Princeton University Graphic Design

I continued to work with Jean Firstenberg, head of the Public Relations Department, on publication projects that continued my "make-over" of the traditional Princeton University publications. Eventually the undergraduate and graduate catalogues, the commencement programs, even real-estate development brochures for a new Forrestal Research Park all fell into line with this new program that emphasized flush-left, ragged-right type, Helvetica or Times Roman typefaces, and "modern" approach to typographic layout emphasizing asymmetrical balance, extensive open space, and clean, forceful, geometric imagery. These were personally attractive and engaging to me, and I felt that the Princeton audience might benefit from an introduction to this kind of formal style. Weren't some of them in love with Platonic forms and Platonic love? (Fig. 6.24).

Among the examples of my official university work in 1975–1976 are the Princeton University *Graduate School Announcements* (Figs. 6.25 and 6.26).

I joined the staff, part-time, of the Interactive Computer Graphics Laboratory headed by Yonatan Hazoni in the Engineering School. My responsibilities included designing the logo and collateral publications of the Lab (Fig. 6.27).

Fig. 6.23 *Soft Where, Inc.*, Volume 1. Cover, 1975, designed by Aaron Marcus. (Source: Author's photo archive; used with permission of the author)

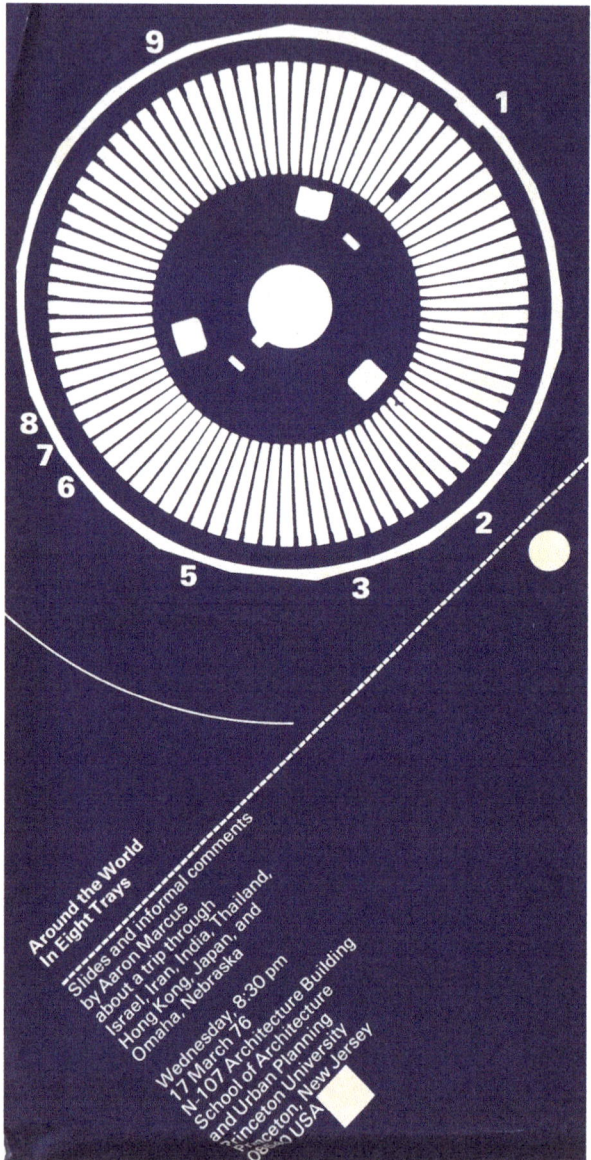

Fig. 6.24 Poster for Princeton University School of Architecture and Urban Planning lecture about our trip around the world, 17 March 1976. Design by Aaron Marcus. (Source: Aaron Marcus' photo archive, used with permission of the Princeton University School of Architecture (SoA))

Fig. 6.25 Princeton University Graduate School Announcement, designed by Aaron Marcus, July 1975. (Source: Author's photo archive, used with permission of Princeton University)

Fig. 6.26 Princeton University Graduate School Announcement, designed by Aaron Marcus, July 1976. (Source: Author's photo archive, used with permission of Princeton University)

Fig. 6.27 Princeton University Firestone Library Handbook for visitors/users, designed by Aaron Marcus, Spring 1976. (Source: Aaron Marcus' photo archive; used with permission of Princeton University Library)

Summer 1976

4 July 1976, I created another conceptual artwork to celebrate the USA's bicentennial: "American Bi-Centennial Tetragram/Tetragon: A Conceptual Visible-Language Art Work." After considering a varied set of theoretical sketches, I created a commemorative marking of the 200th birthday of the United State of America by writing/drawing over time and space in the following manner: electronic-environmental forms were constructed by means of (a) phone calls to blood relatives who, during the calls, ritually clasped hands and joined four points on the continental USA and (b) phone calls to far northern, southern, eastern, and western points of the USA, in which I tried to locate another person bearing my name (Figs. 6.28 and 6.29).

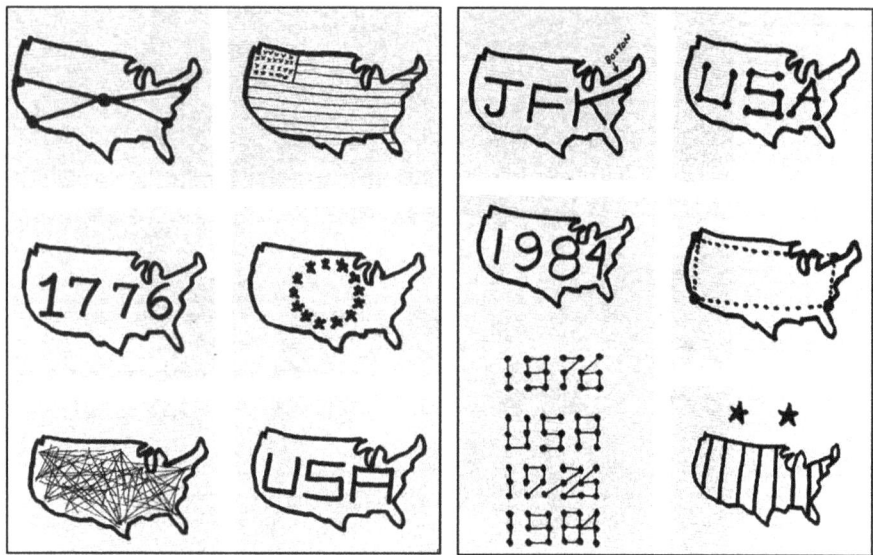

Figs. 6.28 and 6.29 Tetragram-Tetragon conceptual artwork in honor of the USA Bicentennial, sketches created by Aaron Marcus, July 1976. (Source: Aaron Marcus' photo archive; used with permission of the author)

On 14 July 1976, our second child Elisheva was born. I felt happy and satisfied that Susan and I had brought forth a son and a daughter to start, and very likely to complete our family. I had to admit that I felt less secure about how to bring up a daughter, having only my brother Stephen as a sibling. I bravely carried on, hoping that I would somehow acquire Just-in-Time Wisdom.

During the summer of 1976, I arranged to work for Richard Saul Wurman in Philadelphia. This location meant that every day I would have to take a Pennsylvania Railroad commuter train from Princeton Junction south to downtown Philadelphia, then walk to his office. Ricky, as we called him, was an architect gaining some fame as a graphic designer and publicist, mostly for himself. I was impressed by his articles about "making the city observable," the title of one of his books. My interest in this subject was part of my drift toward information visualization and information design in general, which had been present always since childhood, but was more focused now.

According to my work agreement, I had to live each day in the top floor of his office building during the very hot summer of the 200th birthday of the USA. There was no air conditioning to relieve the oppressive heat. My professional task was to research and organize all materials for a second volume of *Making the City Observable*. Working alone, my usual chores were relatively menial, but I did learn much about many projects to visualize urban infrastructure. Alas, as far as I know, after a summer of work, the author and the publisher failed to reach a publishing agreement, and the entire project's materials ended up in document tote boxes, never to see the light of day. It was quite a disappointment. However, I did have enough of a relationship with Mr. Wurman to join in a National Endowment for the Arts proposal the following year to be discussed briefly below.

Princeton University, Year 9, 1976–1977

In the previous year at Princeton, the Dean had decided that the best thing for my academic record would be for me *not* to apply for tenure and be rejected, but to shift back to a lecturer's position while I waited to exit Princeton. Most of the people I liked gradually disappeared from the school as they graduated or left the faculty.

This may have continued into 1976–1977. In 1975–1976, I think, I began to spend half-time in the Public Relations office and half-time as the graphic designer to the Interactive Computer Graphics Laboratory in the Engineering Department. I might have continued to do some work in the Visual Arts Program. I cannot remember too well, because the entire final year was an emotional upheaval for me.

In the fall of 1976, around the time before the Jewish New Year, and in conjunction with the printing of the new Princeton University map that I had designed, I was able to use the extra space at the edge of the sheet of paper for the printed map to print small designs for Rosh Hashanah cards (Jewish New Year cards) for the next eight years. As with many of my designs, they were simple, minimalist, and geometric in nature. These kinds of forms had appealed to me and interested me for many years, and they continued to interest me in my graphic designs and artworks for years afterwards. I sent them to the NYC Jewish Museum gift shop to ask if they were interested in selling them, but they declined. Probably around this time, I also designed two copies of a geometric mezuzah, a ritual object containing written portions of the Torah, that I also tried to get the Jewish Museum to consider whether they wanted to sell copies of this art/design work, but they also declined. I sold one copy to a friend on the faculty of Princeton, and I kept the second, which I have had in my house since then (Figs. 6.30–6.37, 6.38, and 6.39).

My career as a Princeton faculty member was coming to an end, and I would have to re-invent myself. Part of my efforts that year were spent arranging to move out of the USA and to make *aliyah* (emigration) to Israel, where I hoped my new home would be at Bezalel Academy of Arts and Design in Jerusalem. Because one needed at least to be working one-and-a-half positions, I also applied to teaching at the Hebrew University/Jerusalem. I was able, with prodigious effort, to secure a teaching position in two departments of Bezalel: Graphic Design and also the Industrial Design under the leadership of Arthur Goldreich (a"h, a powerful professional from South Africa). I was able, also, to secure teaching lines in two parts of the Hebrew University, the Geography Department and the Institute for Communication under Elihu Katz (a"h). The departure from Princeton was psychologically painful, stressful, and a little humiliating. The University was quick to cut its ties to me, including any lingering health care. My life as a US academic seemed to be coming to an end. I was cutting ties with the USA and moving to a new world, accompanied by my wife and two young children. We all did not know what we would find.

Sometime during 1977, I joined with Richard (Ricky) Saul Wurman to propose to the Design Arts Program of the National Endowment for the Arts the first-ever national, design-oriented, funded competition for information-visualization. We

Figs. 6.30–6.37 Rosh Hashanah (Jewish New Year) cards designed by Aaron Marcus for eight sequential years, each with the right-to-left-reading English slogan: "peace bring year next the may," 1976. (Source: Aaron Marcus' photo archive; used with permission of the author)

secured $5000, I believe, for the winning entry and an exhibit of all entries at the Art Center College of Design in Pasadena, California. Ricky knew some of the leadership there. Ricky had his favorite subject matter in mind for the case study to be given to participants, but I persuaded him finally to make the national energy input/outflow diagram the content of the information to be visualized. After publishing ads and news of this competition over a period of months, we waited for entries to roll in from across the country. To my (and perhaps Ricky's) astonishment, we received only six entries from around the country, most of them mediocre. With some embarrassment, we cancelled the event. We were too far out from mainstream graphic design practice and too early for what would happen 30–40 years later after the advent and spread of computer graphics.

Summer 1977

12 July 1977: In preparation to leave for Israel, I sold most of my childhood comic book collection to a New York City comic book dealer. My parents carried the 1300 copies in their car from Omaha, Nebraska, on a familial visit. Although I

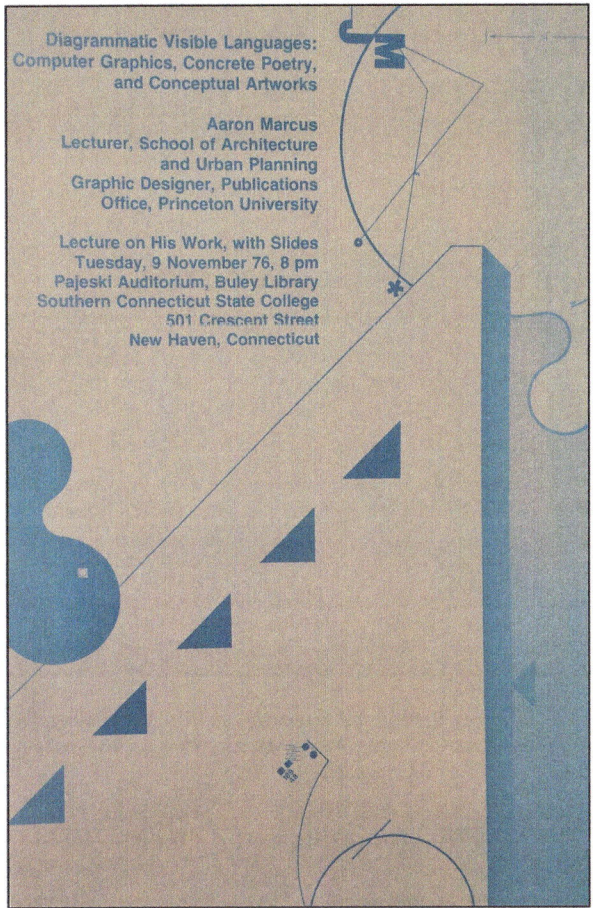

Fig. 6.38 Poster design for my lecture at Southern Connecticut State College, design by Aaron Marcus, 1976. (Source: Aaron Marcus' photo archive; used with permission of the author)

hoped to receive $2000 for my comics (the dealer later admitted that their worth was in excess of this amount), I settled for $1400 for a collection for which the earliest copy dated from 1937 and whose most recent issues dated from about 1957. At various moments after the sale, I brooded over the fact that, in a single transaction, I had "sold away my childhood," leaving only a few remnants for my children to inherit. I repressed deep feelings of guilt and sorrow and hurried back into my life.

That summer after the close of the school year, my family and I prepared for our transcontinental move and transporting ourselves to Jerusalem, Israel.

Fig. 6.39 Princeton University School of Architecture and Urban Planning, NewsPaper 2, early 1977, designed by Aaron Marcus. (Source: Aaron Marcus' photo archive; used with permission of the Princeton University School of Architecture (SoA))

Jerusalem, 1977–1978, Honolulu and Berkeley, 1978–1979

Academic Year, 1977–1978

As the academic year began, my family and I lived in a reasonably pleasant apartment in Moshavah Germanit (the German Colony). Elisheva and Joshua were taken care of in childcare institutions. Susan worked for Izika Gaon (a"h), the head of the Design Department of the Israel Museum.

Through the connections to Izika, we had an opportunity to meet and spend time with Ettore Sottsass, the founder of the Memphis Group in Italy, who was being given a one-man show at the Museum. That occasion was only one of many extraordinary events in the year. Susan also designed a brochure for Teddy Kolleck, the Mayor of Jerusalem, to celebrate a new urban renovation project.

I began teaching in four departments, two each at two different institutions. For that reason, all of my courses had different start/stop schedules during the year. As a result, during two weeks in February of 1978, I was burdened with teaching my ending and starting classes at the same time during those two weeks. I was teaching approximately six to eight courses simultaneously or 40 contact hours per week! I would simply drive from one place to the next as required, playing musical chairs with my lectures and exercise assignments. Fortunately, many of my classes were studio courses of 2–3 hours. In most of them, I spoke Hebrew, which was good enough for the simple advice I was giving the design students. At the Hebrew University, I taught a course in beginning computer graphics in the Geography Department and a course in visual semiotics in the Communication Institute. At Bezalel, I taught a course in visual studies for the Industrial Design Department, and at Bezalel, I taught one or two courses in graphic design and in computer graphics.

My biggest disappointment was the fact that the Bezalel/Hebrew University Computer Graphics Lab had been closed after some kind of scandal with Vladimir Bonacic. No one would talk much about it before I arrived. It was amusing and frustrating. I would write long letters to Yarom Vardimon and others trying to be specific, asking about what my duties were and what I might do with computer graphics at Bezalel. He and others would write back with just a few sentences. It was to be a typical experience of my time in Israel. I was being an over-specific, paranoid, neurotic, too-detailed *Yekki* (Ashekenazic) American Jew (think Woody Allen as a software engineer). They were being shoot-from-the-hip, fly-by-the-seat-of-your-pants, everything-at-the-last-minute Israelis.

The Computer Graphics Laboratory equipment, all new and expensive, all unique and delicate, had been confiscated and imprisoned as a wall-to-wall hodgepodge layer of junk (about 4 ft high) in a store room at the old Bezalel building just inside the guarded gates. Shortly after I arrived, in August or September, it was surreal for me as I entered this *machsan* (store room) and had to climb over computer equipment (CRT screens, keyboards, computers, cables), office furniture (chairs, desks), supplies, etc., trying to find things that I might be able to use during my year at Bezalel. It was a futile attempt to preserve anything of major value. Alone in the room, I could only cry quietly to myself and scream silently. I did the best I could for the remainder of the year.

I strongly felt that the graphic design students whom I taught at Bezalel, although in some ways less sophisticated in their backgrounds, were nevertheless the most creative and smartest students I had ever encountered. Their humor, dedication, and inventiveness made teaching them a pleasure.

On 19 November 1977, Anwar Sadat became the first Arab leader to visit Israel officially when he met with Israeli Prime Minister Menachem Begin, and spoke before the Knesset in Jerusalem about his views on how to achieve a comprehensive peace to the Arab–Israeli conflict, which included the full implementation of UN agreements. I remember when his motorcade drove by us on a downtown street in Jerusalem.

For Jerusalem Day that year in the spring, the Bezalel faculty carried out small projects on the streets of the city. My project was to re-create a form of urban drawing that I had carried out in earlier years at Princeton. With a minimal budget, I found a source of white photo backdrop paper and taped it to a wall on the streets (perhaps it was Ben Yehudah Street in downtown Jerusalem). Interested passers-by on the street, women, men, and children, were handed thick, black magic markers and invited to trace the outline of their family/friends, or I would trace them, and then they could sign the outline image and add comments related to the day.

During the year, I also had an opportunity to have a small exhibit of my conceptual artwork, my graphic design work, and my computer art in the old Bezalel Building.

Once again, I was one of the few faculty members to wear a kippah, and I was considered a weird outsider, as an American, a religious Jew, and as a representative of the high technology/computer graphics world. I was about 30 years too early.

For all of my time in Israel, I tried to befriend and live with Israelis, not with US ex-pats. The Israelis had little patience with our family's sufferings and loneliness. I did not rely on US/Israeli organizations to help us make *aliyah* (emigration to Israel). I was trying to do it on my own, with a first objective of securing a formal agreement for full-time "tenured" teaching at either the Hebrew University or at Bezalel. In the end, I failed. Neither institution would or could make such a commitment to me, even though I was offering them my entire professional career-switch to be in Jerusalem.

Toward the end of the academic year, I had decided, reluctantly, to leave Israel and had begun to wonder how I was going to re-enter the US academic world. Suddenly, unexpectedly, blessedly, Sheila deBretteville contacted me. Sheila is a former Yale graphic design graduate and was then a graphic design faculty member at Otis School of Design in Los Angeles, as well as a famous supporter of women's rights and leader of her own group and building oriented to this objective. (Years later, she returned to Yale as Chair of the Graphic Design Department.) She explained that she had been offered an unusual research/design opportunity in Hawai'i but could not accept it; did I want to go? With little hesitation, I said yes! Suddenly I found my life-vector changing once again. I was quickly appointed a Visiting Research Fellow at the Open Grants group at the East-West Center in Honolulu, Hawai'i, on the University of Hawai'i campus. This was an amazing, fortunate, career-changing occurrence.

On the other hand, Susan and I immediately contracted Hepatitis B, the nonfatal kind. We had taken precautions to inoculate our children against the disease with gamma globulin shots, but we had forgotten to give *ourselves* the same protection. We both fell quite ill and were very weak, taking turns to rise from our bed and feed our children. With only a few weeks left before we had to leave Israel, my kind students helped to sell our car, sell our possessions that we were leaving, and to help us pack and leave Israel.

"Satellite": Conceptual Visible Language Art, Autumn 1977 Until Autumn 1978

Note: The following is an excerpted, edited documentation (see Bibliography: Marcus, 1982) of a conceptual visible language artwork that I conceived during Autumn 1977 and executed during Winter 1977–1978 and completed in 1978. At the time, I spent an academic year 1977–1978 as a Visiting Lecturer, Bezalel Academy of Arts and Design, Jerusalem, Israel, and had just begun a half-year position as a Research Fellow, Open Grants, East-West Center, Honolulu, Hawaii, during the Autumn of 1978.

Summary: On 21 November 1977, I launched a visible-language satellite, a work that circled the earth at an altitude varying from approximately one to 10,000 meters altitude. I accomplished this project by mailing from Jerusalem, Israel, an airmail letter that was forwarded around the globe by friends. The letter was intended to return eventually to me in Jerusalem.

27 July 1977: I decided to create a conceptual artwork for 1977 and to start it in Jerusalem. The work would be called "Satellite" and would involve sending a letter around the earth. I debated starting the work in Princeton, catching the envelope in Jerusalem, then flinging it onward around the earth. I eventually rejected the idea, because it seemed purer to begin and end the low-level earth-orbit in Jerusalem, which for many centuries had been considered the "center of the earth" or at least of Western civilization. The draft text of the enclosed letter was to read as follows:

> Dear Friends, I am sending this letter in order to complete a work of conceptual art called "Satellite." The work involves sending postal letters by regular airmail routes around the earth several times. The letters consist of a small dot and dash, basic markings within most typographic systems. They will circle the earth at an approximate height of one to 10,000 meters. I would like to ask your co-operation in sending out the letters again by airmail to the next address on the list. Please enclose the front sides of all previous business envelopes so that I shall have a record of postage and postmarks to exhibit afterwards. Please do not drop the current envelope or its contents; it should not touch the ground. Thank you. Sincerely, Aaron Marcus

These were the names of the participants (all males) in the order of the travels of the satellite:

Aaron Marcus, Jerusalem
Henry Steiner, Hong Kong, a noted graphic designer and friend
William Horwich, San Francisco/Berkeley, a life-long family friend
Nate Marcus, Omaha, my father
Paul Douglas, Princeton, my father-in-law
Pieter Brattinga, Amsterdam, a noted graphic designer and friend
Wolfgang Weingart, Basel, a noted graphic designer and friend
Aaron Marcus, Jerusalem

20 October 1977: In mid-August, my wife Susan, our children Joshua and Elisheva, and I left for Jerusalem from JFK Airport, New York City, aboard an El Al 747.

During President Anwar Sadat of Egypt's historic visit to Jerusalem in November, I realized that the explicit focus of my work ought to change. I felt the work needed to be dedicated to his outstanding ascent to Jerusalem and to peace in the Middle East. The new text was to read, in part, as follows:

> In order to complete a conceptual visible language artwork, I am sending this explanatory sheet and the enclosed card around the world. The work is intended to be a symbol of international communication and co-operation. I am beginning the work on the occasion of Anwar Sadat's historic visit to Jerusalem. Please help me to complete the work....

The days of Sadat's visit to Jerusalem were like a rare dream. All schools had been closed just before his address before the Israeli Knesset. Susan, Joshua, Elisheva, and I walked over to the King David Hotel where Sadat was staying. I was reminded of Henry Kissinger's visit there three years ago during the period of his shuttle diplomacy. We had also been in Israel for half a year at that time. When Kissinger was at the hotel, he had interrupted my bus route during each morning's trip to Ulpan (Hebrew-language) classes, and his busy schedule had prevented me from seeing the US Ambassador before he died (see "Time Piece," an earlier work, 1975). The King David Hotel was about 15 min by foot from our apartment in Moshava Germanit. We hurried along with other curious well-wishers until we stood as close to the building as the police barricades would allow. Eventually a black Cadillac with darkened windows emerged and hearty cheers from the public greeted the visiting head of a state at war with Israel. Surely this was an unusual chapter in the book of world history.

21 October 1977: I hurried to finish the final text of the accompanying letter and to complete the symbol/mark set that would be launched into space. [Perhaps I felt the same excitement as NASA engineers before a launch.] The final text read as follows:

> In order to complete a conceptual visible-language artwork entitled "Satellite," I am sending this explanatory sheet and the enclosed card around the earth by regular airmail routes. The "letters" I am sending consist of a dot and a dash, basic markings within most typographic systems. They will circle the earth at an approximate height of one to 10,000 meters. The work is a symbol of international communication and cooperation. I am beginning on the occasion of Anwar Sadat's historic visit to Jerusalem. Please help me to complete the work.

The final countdown began. I took the letter to our corner post office station on Emek Refaiim Street where I purchased postage and asked a person waiting in line to photograph me with the letter. He grudgingly complied. The post office personnel were amused at my event.

01 December 1977: While waiting for the letter with its accumulating contents to return, I continued to teach graphic design at Bezalel. I also had a part-time teaching position at the Hebrew University in the Communication Institute and in the Geography Department. As is my custom, while passing between to Computer Center and these other two locations, I examined the contents of the trash bins located behind the National Library. Among the old copies of Hebrew and Arabic newspapers, scholarly and professional journals, and other esoterica, such as a

dental journal from Cuba in the 1930s, I was startled to find a half-year's collection of the international edition of *Penthouse* magazine. Were the sacrosanct chambers of the National Library a "hidden hothouse of lascivious leerers" (as Spiro Agnew, the USA's most ignominious Vice-President) might have remarked? I could hardly imagine a less appropriate place. Ah, the glory of international commerce which brought these images from New York and elsewhere to Jerusalem the Holy City.

21 January 1978: The satellite had successfully returned from its flight. I decided I could not trust the postal system or my friends to enable the satellite to circle a second time without mishap and therefore cancelled my informal plans to have it orbit several times in succession.

01 February 1978: I exhibited the envelope and enclosed sheet in Bezalel's ground floor exhibit case for a two-week period. Most students ignored it, especially those who read English with difficulty. I received a few enthusiastic responses from persons who immediately "grokked" (see Robert Heinlein's *A Stranger in a Strange Land* for a definition of this term) the internal and external content of the work.

11 July 1978: I learned from Prof. I.K. of the East-West Center and Gakushuin University, Tokyo, of the Kura ceremony performed in the Melanesian Islands of the South Pacific. Among these islands, a ritual object is carried by boat from island A to island B, then from island B to island C, and eventually back to island A. The token itself had little intrinsic value. The warriors who carry it from one island to the other faced the possibility of losing their lives at sea as they traversed the great distances among the islands. The ceremony's existence and description was confirmed by the account of L.K., a governmental official from the Kingdom of Tonga in the South Pacific, who was also at the East-West Center. The main purpose in this "chain letter" of the Kura ritual seemed to ensure that each island knows its neighbors still exist and are willing to co-operate in this one activity of communication. I smiled inwardly and outwardly when I learned of this ceremony and considered my project to be completed (Figs. 6.40 and 6.41).

Summer 1978

My mind, heart, and soul were greatly conflicted about leaving Israel, but I felt then I had no alternative and was now committed to moving to Honolulu after a summer in Princeton to recover from our hepatitis illness. Susan's parents had kindly arranged a house-sitting agreement, so we had somewhere to stay near our old friends and family. However, when we entered the USA, the border agents took one look at our yellow skin and eyes and placed us under voluntary house arrest in Princeton. Until we had fully recovered (in about one month), we were not allowed to leave our house or to have visitors. Our friends had to leave care packages for us at the front door. Eventually, before we left for Hawai'i, we were able to be with our friends and have them and Susan's family visit. Then I flew to Hawai'i.

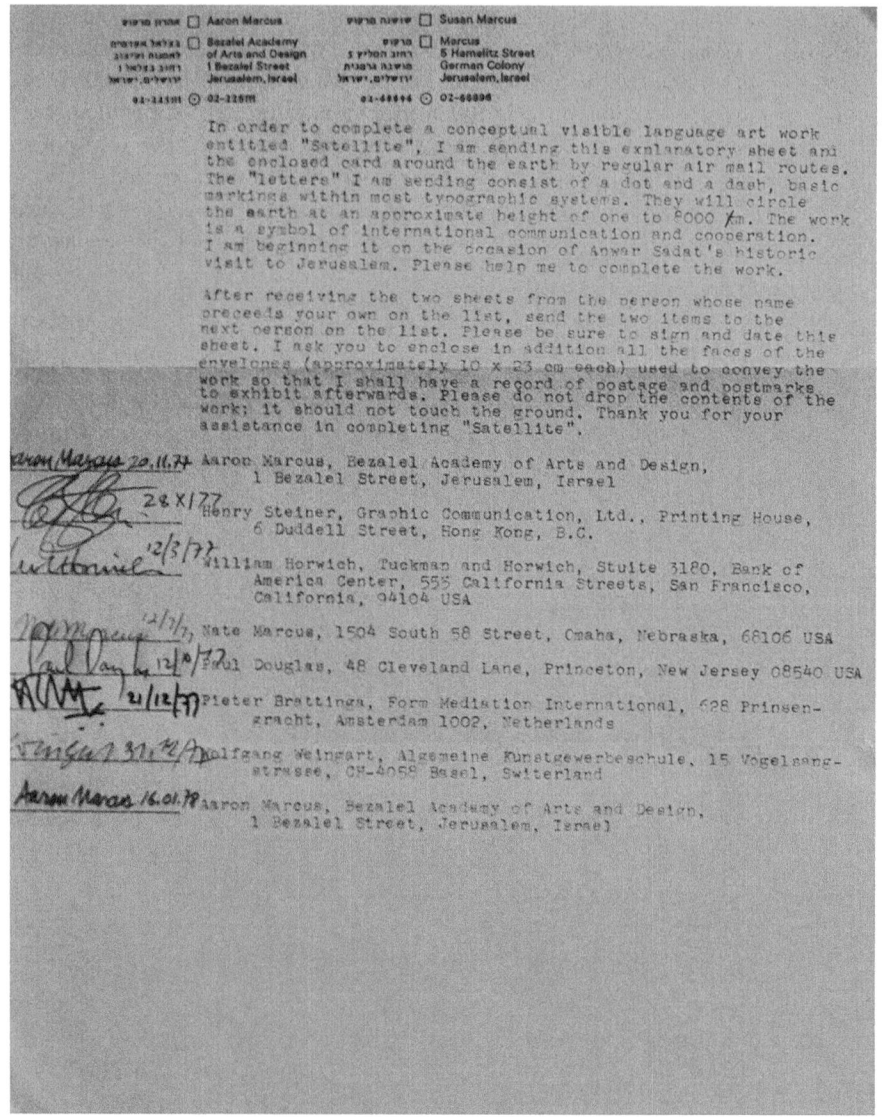

Fig. 6.40 "Satellite." Letter signed by senders, Conceptual artwork by Aaron Marcus, 1977. (Source: Aaron Marcus' photo archive; used with permission of the author)

Fall 1978

I had about one week before Susan arrived with our two children, and all of our possessions, in suitcases and cardboard boxes. We had investigated how to move our household transcontinentally from Jerusalem to Princeton to Honolulu. It turned out

Fig. 6.41 "Satellite." Sheet containing the art mark, Conceptual artwork by Aaron Marcus, 1977. (Source: Aaron Marcus' photo archive, used with permission of the author)

that accompanied baggage was the least expensive. In those days of old, the charges were relatively low and the number of accompanied bags was unlimited. We had about 20 boxes!

I took what I could, stayed at Jefferson Hall dormitory on the campus while I searched for an apartment. I was helped to learn about Honolulu from a Visiting Faculty Guide that was excellent. It included everything about schools, restaurants, and laundries, whatever visiting families would need. The process of apartment-finding was straightforward. Saturday evening just after midnight, one went to one of the few places in Honolulu where the local newspaper was delivered first. One bought a copy, and armed with many dimes and nickels, entered a public phone booth and started calling the first likely apartments advertised, no matter that it was after midnight. I secured several appointments for Sunday.

A kind East-West Center woman helped drive me around to visit the apartments, offered advice on locations, and helped me buy an inexpensive used car, all in one to two days. Because I had secured, then lost an apartment and had to secure another, I was delayed in ordering furniture for the unfurnished apartment. The furniture was scheduled to arrive and be set up at almost the time the airplane with my family touched down! I had to trust that all would work.

I also had to enroll both of my children into either nursery schools or grade schools based on where we were now living, in the top floor of a high-rise at University and King near the campus.

As I drove to pick up Susan and the children, I wondered what I would find back at the apartment. We had to make two or three trips with the kind woman who helped us load all the boxes and luggage into her car, as well as ourselves. We would have to go back for more boxes. I had not told Susan about the tight timing of furniture delivery. We drove to our apartment and walked in. To my amazement, everything was there, looked decent enough, and in about the right place. Only after Susan had inspected and approved everything did I reveal the miracle of the apartment being ready.

During six months in paradise at the East-West Center (EWC), I researched the topic of global energy interdependence and decided with my teammates to create a traditional audio-visual slide show about the issues, using only signs (icons and symbols), maps, charts, and diagrams, almost no words. We also created a multicultural musical soundtrack to accompany the imagery. Most of what we saw during an analysis of comparative designs was too gaudy and poorly designed. For the stark facts that we wanted to explain, we chose a white on black display that was almost like a meditation on the topic (Fig. 6.42).

My colleagues included a visual communications expert from Tehran who was the first to translate Marshall McLuhan into Farsi, a Chinese geographer, an Indian audio-visual expert, and my friend Yukio Ota from Japan. My wife also helped us as well as Jerry Kuyper, who had studied at Basel and was working in Hawaii. We researched the subject matter studied at the EWC, designed thousands of signs and information-visualization sketches, and put together our final storyboard. We checked it for cross-cultural effectiveness by testing it on our own multi-language, multicultural backgrounds. We finished our project, showed it at the EWC, and prepared to take it overseas to our respective locations.

To our understanding the project was a success. We published an article about it in the EWC magazine. I was able to exhibit my work at the EWC, and I was able to find out about an open faculty position at the University of California at Berkeley, which I decided to accept. Once again, my family was on the move.

The EWC experience had convinced me to move my professional center to information design and information visualization. I realized more than ever how important it was to help show people information to help them make effective decisions. In addition, my expertise in computer graphics seemed to direct me to explore charts, maps, and diagrams as a means of combining information-oriented graphic design with the emerging professions of computer-based design and visual communication.

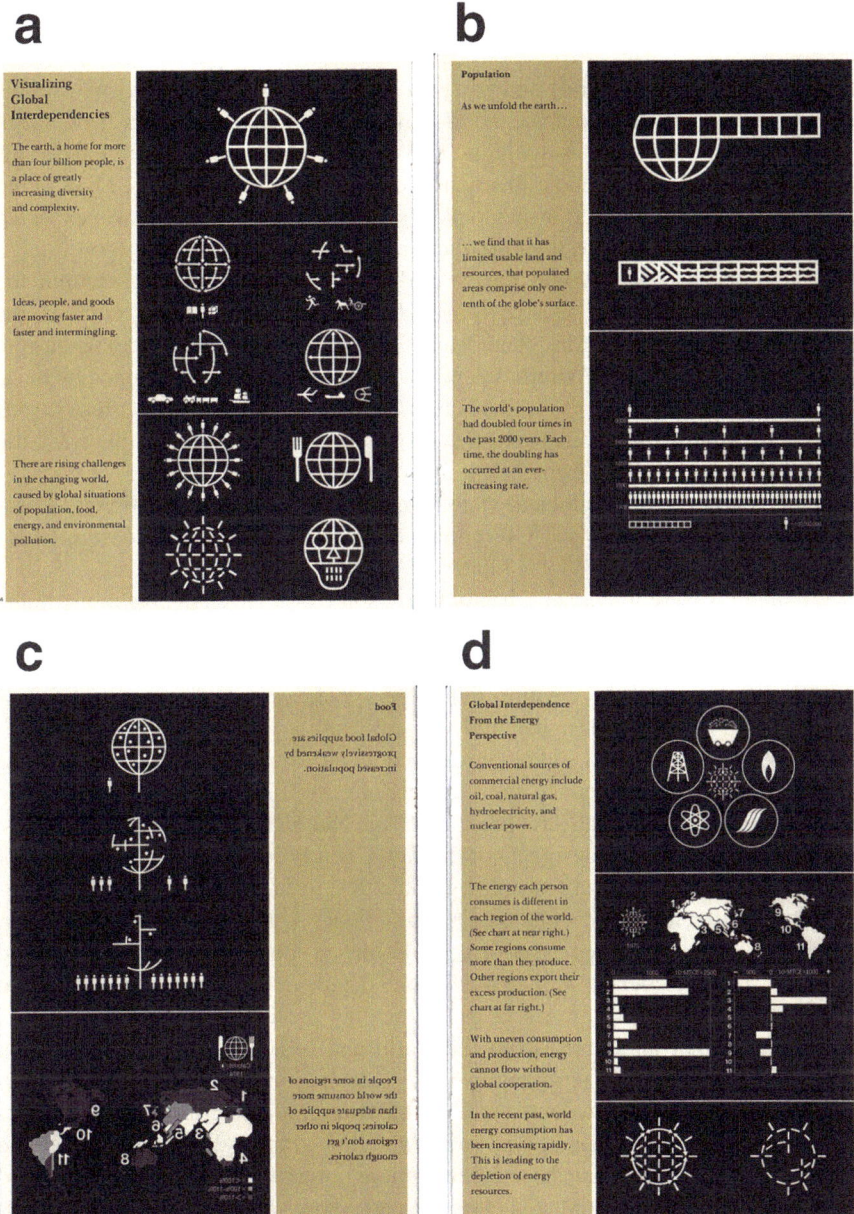

Fig. 6.42 (**a–d**) Images from the East-West Center Project Visualizing Global Energy Interdependencies, 1978. (Images from AM+A Archive, used with permission of EWC magazine)

UC/Berkeley, 1979–1981

On 8 January 1979, my family and I arrived in Berkeley, California, my new home. Little did I realize that I would spend more years living here than anywhere else in my life. Within a short time staying with my childhood friend Bill Horwich and his wife Mijo, Susan and I found a lovely house just north of the campus. I had to bid on the house in a public auction and to pay more than twice what I had ever expected to pay for a house. This was my introduction to California living.

I taught introductory visual design and some computer graphics within the College of Environmental Design (CED) Program, which itself was within the Architecture Department. Alas, there was no strong commitment to graphic design, computer graphics, or me. Within two years, I was more or less abandoned by those who I thought might support me. As before, especially with the budget restrictions imposed by a vengeful President Reagan on the UC Systems, there simply was little support in an Architecture Department for someone "outside the tribe."

I continued to do experimental visible language, trying to create digital "hieroglyphics" by programming UCB computers and outputting the designs onto CalComp plotters (Figs. 6.43–6.47 and 6.48).

My students were good, and I began to use some of them as interns in my home graphic design studio that I ran with Susan. One of the first was Zuzana Licko, a Slovak-born American type designer known for co-founding the graphic design magazine *Emigre* and for creating numerous typefaces with her husband fellow typographer and graphic designer Rudy VanderLans.

In November of 1979, I suddenly received a call from Lance Brown, my friend from Princeton SAUP days. He and Charlie Zucker (RIP) and Michael Pittas were now in charge of the Design Arts Program of the National Endowment for the Arts. One of the major graphic designers of the day, Colin Forbes, one of the founders of Pentagram, one of the most respected graphic design firms in the world, was supposed to give a lecture in Washington, DC, to all Federal graphic designers. However, he had hurt his back. Lance asked if I would like to substitute for Colin? I gulped and said, "Yes! Of course." After I learned the details and had hung up, I went into a deep period of anxiety, hysteria, and dreaming around 22 November 1979. I became somewhat unplugged from the world and basically had a 3-day waking coma, in which ideas and terminology swirled around in my brain. I was trying to understand what I had been doing for 15 years since graduating from Yale, to understand where computer graphics was going, and how graphic design could combine with computer graphics to make something more powerful together than each could do alone. At the end of my introspection, I typed up my scribbled notes. I found lists of terms. I had no idea what my brain had meant. My brain was sending me coded messages, and I now had to interpret them. Out of this dream-time came the concept, among others, of the Three Faces of Computers: innerfaces (visualizations of code), interfaces (human-computer interaction depictions), and outerfaces (visualizations of information output).

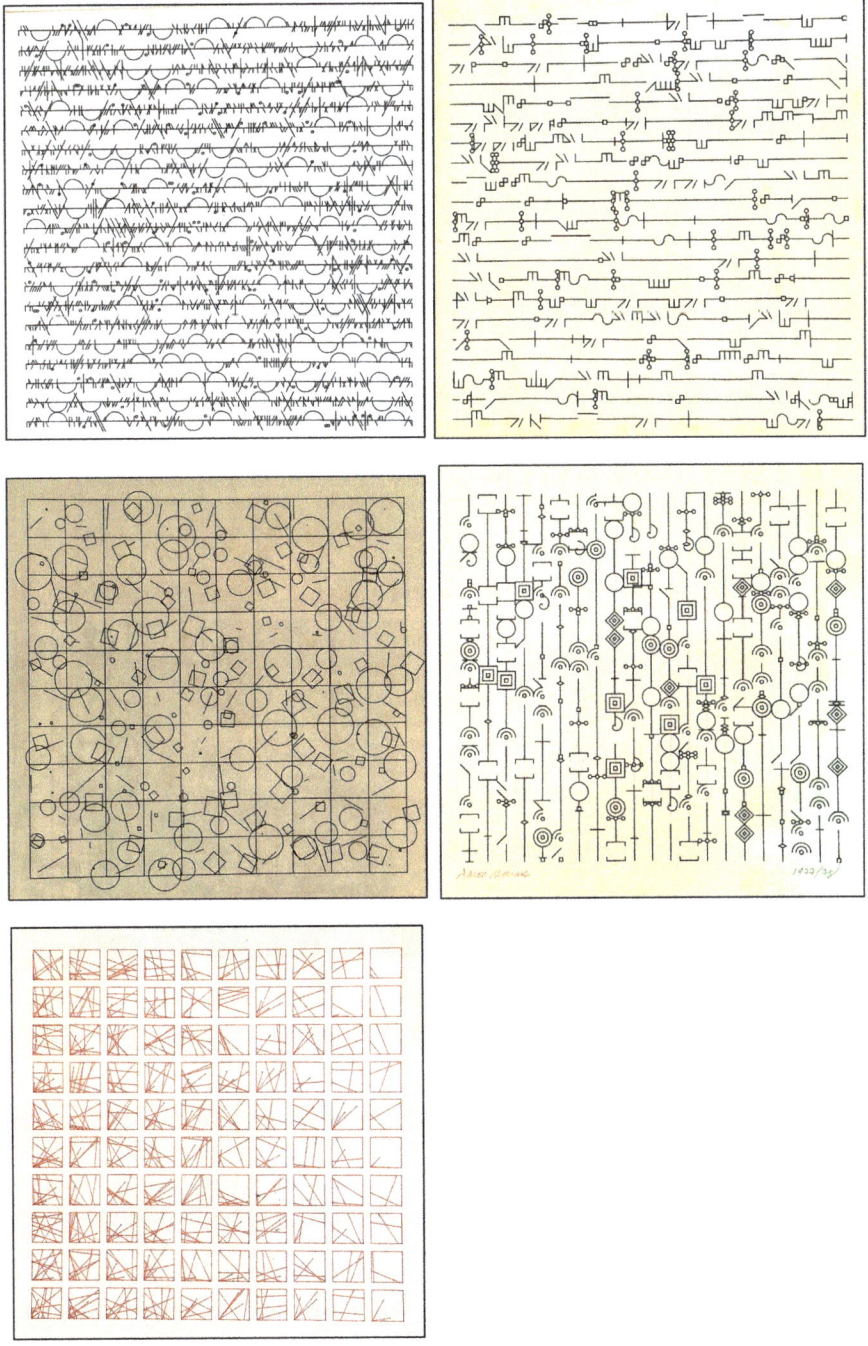

Figs. 6.43–6.47 Examples of "digital hieroglyphics" programmed via FORTRAN on computers, 1976–1980, ink on paper, by Aaron Marcus. Some of these works are in the collection of the San Francisco Museum of Modern Art. (Source: Aaron Marcus' photo archive, used with permission of the author)

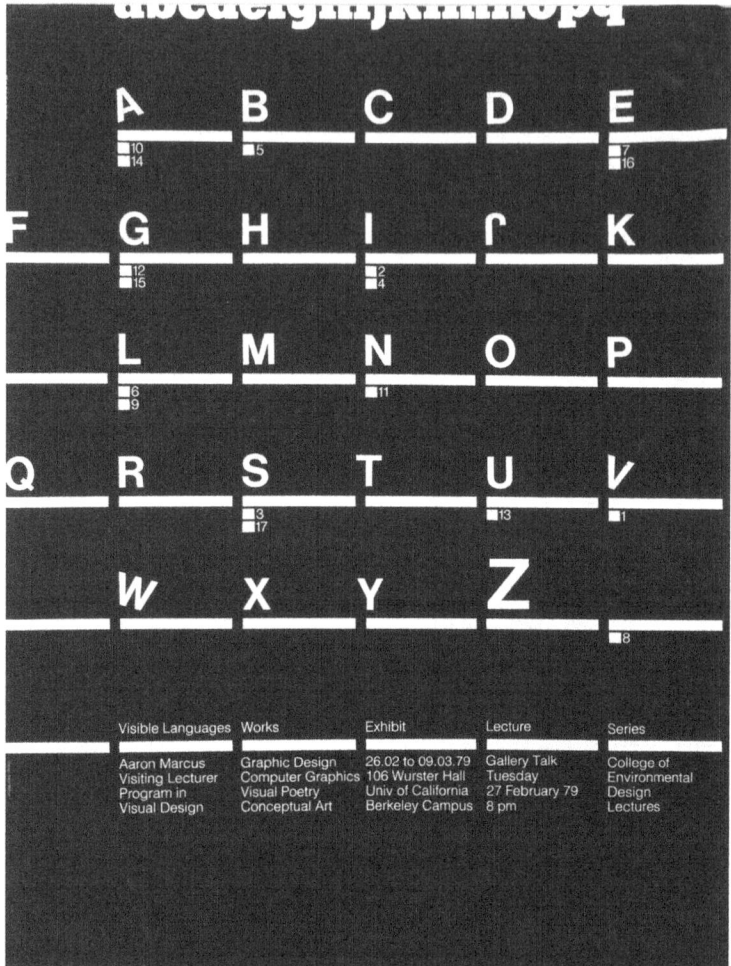

Fig. 6.48 University of California/Berkeley College of Environmental Design Aaron Marcus Lecture Poster, designed by Aaron Marcus, February 1979. (Source: Aaron Marcus' photo archive; used with permission of the author)

From these notes, I organized my lecture, which took place in the National Gallery of Art that fall.

By 1980, the handwriting was once again on the wall. I was about 30 years too early for UC/Berkeley. I began to look for other professional possibilities. For a short while, I worked as the official graphic designer of the UCB Computing Services Center. In this capacity, I was able to redesign many of its publications, especially its *Newsletter*. I was mentored and befriended by Stewart Lynn who headed the Center. Eventually, he became Director of Computing Services for the entire UC System. Later, he retired to southern California.

Once again, I had to find a new home. I did not look forward to moving my family again, especially internationally. It was simply too difficult and out of the question. I explored teaching positions in California, but I did not find anything suitable. I finally decided that I would take any kind of job as long as it was a 15-min bike ride or walk from my house. Suddenly, I realized that Lawrence Berkeley Laboratory (LBL) was within that range. I thought: once, decades ago, I had enjoyed working at AT&T Bell Labs. Perhaps I was destined to return to an R&D environment.

Screwing up my courage, I contacted Dr. Carl Quong, the head of the Computer Science and Mathematics Department of LBL. At my interview, I once again resorted to my confused, seemingly foolish pitch of not knowing if they could use me but feeling that somehow their equipment seemed right for my background, and that I could help them improve the quality of their computer graphics output. For some reason, Carl saw in me a possible good fit and agreed to start me as a Staff Scientist in their lab, since they had no category for a "designer" position.

Within a short time, I realized I *was home*. I had several million dollars of high-tech equipment around me, competent staff technicians, enormous, years-long research projects funded by the US Department of Energy and the US Department of Labor, and significant challenges in developing SEEDIS, a Socio-Economic-Environmental-Demographic Information-System, which was seeking to develop a display-device-independent software system for analyzing and synthesizing such information from 40 terabytes of data in approximately 40 different databases at about 40 different levels of aggregation, from units about the size of a household to entire cities, counties, and states. It was exhilaratingly complex. At the same time, I felt certain that my information-oriented graphic design expertise could help improve their display of user interfaces, screen designs, forms, tables, charts, maps, and diagrams.

During my time at LBL, I learned about fuzzy set theory, fuzzy logic, and fuzzy mathematics of Dr. Lofti Zadeh at UC Berkeley. This approach to logic meant it was possible to work with values other than 0 and 1 in considering statements and that a set of simple mathematical operations could be defined, making it possible for researchers to explore complex data sets of imprecise information. I explored visualizations of fuzzy information, e.g., where would be the best place to live in the USA, taking into account "good" education resources, housing costs, climate, etc., without specifying exact amounts.

Based on my lecture for the NEA's Design Arts Program, I was able to arrange to write and design a booklet jointly published by the NEA and by LBL: *Designing Facts and Concepts*, which introduced graphic designers to the coming world: the Image of Information Age (see Fig. 6.49).

Whereas earlier I had a difficult time explaining what I did and what I wanted to accomplish, I suddenly could now talk about these subjects easily for hours, as I began to do when I started to give tutorials.

There were also a continual series of lectures in the Lab that brought some of the best thinking about artificial intelligence, video games, and the idea of using anthropology to evaluate user needs. Speakers like Geoffrey Hinton, a computer scientist gave a mind-enlarging lecture about how the neurons in the brain were stimulated

Fig. 6.49 Marcus, Aaron (1981). Designing Facts and Concepts. Jointly published by the National Endowment for the Arts, Washington, DC, and Lawrence Berkeley Laboratory, Berkeley, CA. (Source: Aaron Marcus' photo archive; used with permission of the National Endowment for the Arts, Washington, DC, and Lawrence Berkeley Laboratory, Berkeley, CA)

and worked together. All of this discussion occurred years and even decades before they became popular trends topics.

By August 1980, I had already submitted a suggestion for a small panel discussion about graphic design and its value for computer graphics at the annual meeting of SIGGRAPH, the major computer graphics conference in the world, taking place in Seattle, WA, that year. To my surprise, the organizers of SIGGRAPH wanted to make my session the opening keynote event for the conference. I was awed and amazed, but I also sensed that something significant was happening. The computer graphics world was waking up to the power of effective visual communication.

I arranged for two local graphic designers whom I knew, Jack and Gay Reineck, who had designed the Bay Area Rapid Transit (BART) map, and for Mervyn

Kurlansky, a famous London graphic designer and member of Pentagram, to join me in explaining the value of information-oriented graphic design to the success of computer graphics displays of all kinds. I also gave my first one-day tutorial at SIGGRAPH 1980 about using graphic design to improve innerfaces, interfaces, and outerfaces. My wife Susan Marcus as well as Jack and Gay Reineck assisted me. In my tutorial audience were many people who would go on to found some of the great companies of Silicon Valley and elsewhere, including:

Hertzfeld, Andy, Apple Computer, Inc.
Levine, Dr. Stephen R, Electronic Graphics Associates
Metrick, Lee, Tektronix, In.
Moses, Dr. Franklin, US Army Research Institute
Shoup, Dr. Richard, Aurora Imaging Systems
Smith, Alvy Ray, Lucasfilm
Tessler, Larry, Xerox PARC
Whitted, Dr. Turner, Bell Laboratories
Williams, Dr. Lance, New York Institute of Technology
Wizny, Prof. Michael J., Rensselaer Polytechnic Institute

The revolution had begun. Within days of my being at SIGGRAPH, I was beginning to get calls from computer graphics companies, like Tektronix, in Beaverton, Oregon, which wanted to improve their displays.

During 1981 and early 1982, I continued my work at LBL. I wrote one of the first user-interface design guidelines in 1979. I worked on the graphics standards for one of the "largest books" ever designed, about one million pages in length (Fig. 6.50).

These were the 1980 US Census output laser-printed documents that were produced for the first time because of the capabilities of SEEDIS and were made available through the US Government Printing Office. I was designing page layout, chart layout, table layout, etc., for pages too numerous for me to design individually. I was setting up the standards for automatically laid-out pages that were determined by the software based on the data that had to be displayed. Such documents were being produced for the first time in history by computer programs connected to large databases and varieties of output devices.

I also worked on experimental depictions of chart data, trying to find the best way to use bi-variate area color choropleth maps, fuzzy logic depictions of chart data, and other unusual data visualizations. I learned about face charts using depictions of faces depicting multivariate data that had been invented in 1973 by Herman Chernoff. About a year later, I met Al Inselberg then of IBM at a computer graphics conference. He had invented the parallel coordinates method of depicting multidimensional data, in which the familiar x, y, and z axes were broken apart and laid out as parallel lines, to which other parallel lines could be added for additional dimensions needed to depict data. All of this activity was stimulating, challenging, and exciting.

By late 1981 and into 1982, I had connected with Ron Baecker, whom I first met at SIGGRAPH 1980, a Professor of Computer Science at the University of Toronto, and head of his own firm, Human Computing Resources in Toronto. We had

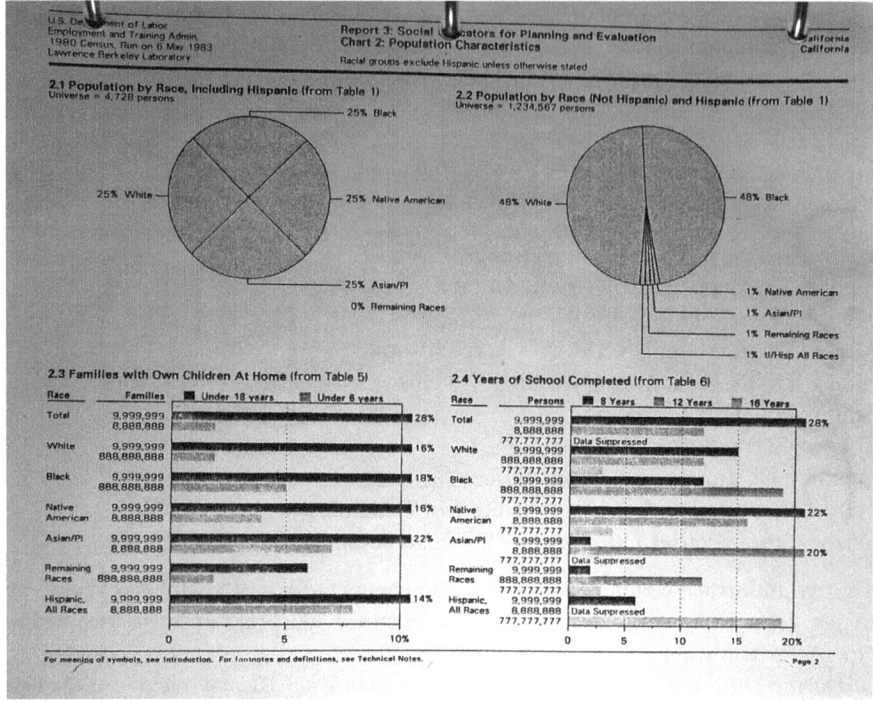

Fig. 6.50 Page from the US Census document automatically designed by the SEEDIS archive software using graphic design techniques designed by Aaron Marcus, then a Staff Scientist of Lawrence Berkeley Laboratory's Computer Science and Mathematics Department, 1980. (Source: Author's photo archive; used with permission of the Lawrence Berkeley National Laboratory)

developed a strong friendship with mutual trust and respect. Ron was far more sophisticated in business and research than I was. Together, we realized we could apply for a research grant from the US Defense Department's Advanced Research Projects Agency (DARPA). DARPA had funded much of the high-tech computer research for decades and had started the Internet years before through ARPAnet.

Ron and I decided to try to submit a proposal to their Program Visualization group, which sought better ways to visualize code. We wrote and rewrote our proposal, then submitted it. Just about this time, we realized that UCB and LBL (a subset of UCB) would, naturally, take a large percentage of the funds as overhead due them for "housing" and supporting the project.

This brought me to a crossroads. I could continue at LBL or I could try to create my own graphic design firm to do the research, without losing the overhead charged by UCB and LBL. With a giant gulp and hope for the best, I decided to leave LBL, which had kindly catalyzed my start as a computer graphics designer. I would start my own graphic design firm focusing on computer graphics and information visualization.

This exciting moment could not have come at a more difficult and challenging time. Susan and I had experienced emotional discord for some time since coming back to the USA (it had started earlier but was more of a low-burn situation). I did not know how to manage the emotional challenges of being married, raising children, seeing my academic career crash and burn, seeing my research career ending, and being challenged by this new world of big-government big-grant-writing.

By 1981, Susan had decided to divorce me. I had to find a new house, which I did one block away, so that the children would not have far to commute during parental exchanges. I had to quickly learn to be a single parent, caring part-time for our children. I had submitted my proposal separately from LBL. Ron and I were successful in the DARPA Program Visualization Research project. We had succeeded in winning a two-year contract to research the improved visualization of the C Programming language. I was also trying to start a new life as a businessman, the head of Aaron Marcus and Associates (AM+A), with almost no experience in business. All of this was happening during the summer of 1982. A new phase of my life was beginning.

Concluding Comments

Looking back now from about 40 years later, I could not have imagined my life would take the paths it took. Life for me at times was intellectually exciting, almost overwhelming. But it was also emotionally overwhelming, challenging me in ways that were beyond my knowledge, beyond my capabilities.

I am thankful for all the patience, love, and understanding shown to me by my parents, my ex-wife Susan, my children, and all the friends along the way. I don't know who could have done much better in my shoes. I am certain that some might have. Alas, I was the one wearing the shoes.

I acknowledge the use of some of my former texts. I appreciate the permissions granted from those who have published my work in the past.

Bibliography

Byrne, Chuck. (1990, September/October). A Conversation with Aaron Marcus. *Print*, 108–111, 168–170.

DeNeve, Rose, "Aaron Marcus: Communicating with Computers," *Print*, New York, NY, Vol. 27, No. 2, March-April 1973, pp. 41–47.

Marcus, Aaron (1970). Why Today's Design Training is Inadequate and What Can Be Done About It. *Print*, *24*(2), 28–31, 78.

Marcus, Aaron (1971a). The Designer, the Computer, and Two-Way Communication System. *Print*, 25(3), 34–39.

Marcus, Aaron, "A Prototype Interactive Page-Design System," *Visible Language* (aka *The Journal of Typographic Research* before 1971), Vol. 5, No. 3, Summer 1971b, pp. 197–220.

Marcus, Aaron (1971c). Untitled Introduction, "Modern Swiss Posters," Princeton University Art Museum, Princeton, NJ: 5 November 1971, pp. 1–4.

Marcus, Aaron (1972a). Pop Goes the Eagle. *New Republic*, *166*(5), 29 January 1972, 24.

Marcus, Aaron (1972b). New Signs Along the Highway. *Print*, 26(3), 62–67.

Marcus, Aaron (1973). Making Israel Visible. *Print*, 27(5), 54–61. "A Computer-Graphics Course for the Two Cultures," Third International Conference on Computing in the Humanities, State University of New York (SUNY), Albany, NY, August 1977.

Marcus, Aaron (1975). *Soft Where, Inc.*, Vol. 1, Reno, NV, West Coast Poetry, 1975 Review Press.

Marcus, Aaron (1978, March). Routes, Loops, Transfers, and Dead-Ends. *Print*, New York, NY, Vol. 32, No. 2, March-April 1978, pp. 49–54.

Marcus, Aaron (1979), Two Cultures and Technology Trends," Invited paper, Conference: The Humanities in a Computerized World, Institute of Humanistic Studies, State University of New York (SUNY), Albany, NY, April 1979.

Marcus, Aaron (1981). *Managing Facts and Concepts*. Berkeley: LBL and Washington, DC: National Endowment for the Arts.

Marcus, Aaron (1982). *Soft Where, Inc.* Vol. 2. Reno, NV: West Coast Poetry Review.

Marcus, Aaron (2017). "Aaron Marcus: Interview with Adrian Shaughnessy" in Shaughessy, Adrian, *Letraset: the DIY Typography Revolution*, Publication 34. London: Unit Press, pp. 288–295.

Marcus, Aaron, and Carnese, Tom et al. (1972). "Hands: 35 Interpretations of a Theme: A Special Print Portfolio." *Print, 26*(3), 31–54.

Chapter 7
Turning Design Theory into Practice at AM+A

Takeaways
I proposed co-leading a DARPA research project and won the contract that allowed me to start AM+A in 1982. For DARPA, we designed new conventions for the C programming language and one of the first commercial graphical user interfaces for Intran. We also completed major projects for HP, Apple, and the Microcomputer Technology Consortium. We were well on our way to becoming a significant design studio for technology.

1982–1990

In August 1982, I had co-written, co-proposed, and co-won a US DARPA grant for at least 2 years to research improved typography and page layout of the C Programming language and to develop a compiler that would automatically lay out pages of superior typographic design, thereby improving the legibility and readability of code worldwide. My Co-Principal Investigator was Prof. Ron Baecker, whom I met at SIGGRAPH 1980, a Professor of Computer Science at the University of Toronto, and head of his own firm, Human Computing Resources in Toronto.

At the same time, I had left teaching at the University of California/Berkeley and a government research position as a Staff Scientist at Lawrence Berkeley Laboratory (LBL). I re-invented myself as a design-office professional and businessman. Susan and I recently divorced, making me a "start-up" in the role of a single parent with part-time access to our children. On the then-current scales of stress published in popular magazines and newspaper articles, I was off the charts. Nevertheless, I soldiered on. I had only $8000 of assets to my name by the end of the divorce, and I had to rely on a "loan" from my parents to make a down payment for a new house one block away from my previous house, on opposite sides of the Berkeley Rose

A. Marcus, *Bridging Art, Design and Technology: My Lifetime Work*, https://doi.org/10.1007/978-3-032-04342-9_7

Garden, to minimize the change of environment for our children. I moved into my new house as I started Aaron Marcus and Associates (AM+A). Now began the process of turning AM+A from a concept into a functioning business entity.

In this chapter and the one following, I am not able to give a year-by-year, event-by-event account, as I could in earlier decades, because AM+A was working with so many different prospects and clients, usually simultaneously, with a group of approximately ten prospects and five clients, and across multiple years of business relationships. In this chapter, I have started a client thread in about the year that an engagement began, and I felt it was more helpful to continue that client thread until the end of our engagements even if it were years later.

In retrospect, it is amazing to me what a variety of projects we had during the 1980s and 1990s. As I describe our process and activities, you will see what I had to explain to our prospects and clients to convince them to hire us, then to help them understand what was happening and why, all through a project. I would guess that 50% of my marketing time was spent trying to educate our prospective clients about what we did and why it was so important to the future of their product/service developments. We were adding a missing ingredient: achieving effective computer-based visual communication.

We researched, planned, analyzed, designed, produced, tested, documented, trained, and maintained the content of our projects. These terms (see Bibliography: Marcus, 2015) were the basic verbs or action words of our user-centered design (UCD) process, which began with our first project. The terms were adapted from my experience teaching with architects and urban planners, and were moved over to the software development world, and then from there to the user-interface development world. The UCD process focuses on users throughout all these development steps, or tasks, which sometimes occur iteratively:

Plan: Determine strategy, tactics, likely markets, stakeholders, platforms, tools, and processes.

Research: Gather and examine relevant documents, including all stakeholder statements.

Analyze: Identify the target market, typical users of the product/service, personas (characteristic users), use scenarios, and competitive products/services.

Design: Determine general and specific design solutions, from simple concept maps, information architecture (conceptual structure or metaphors, mental models, and navigation), wireframes, look and feel (appearance and interaction details), screen sketches, and detailed screens and prototypes.

Implement: Script or code specific working prototypes or partial "alpha" prototypes of working versions.

Evaluate: Evaluate users, target markets, competition, and design solutions; conduct field surveys, and test the initial and later designs with the target markets.

Document: Draft white papers, user-interface guidelines, specifications, and other summary documents, including marketing presentations to help explain and convince others.

Not all projects required all these tasks. AM+A carried out most of these tasks in the development of each of the Machine concepts described in subsequent chapters, except for implementing working versions.

The above analysis describes the essential "verbs" of the user-interface (UI) design, human-computer-interface (HCI) design, or user-experience (UX) design profession. Over the past three decades in the UI/HCI/UX design community, designers, analysts, educators, and theorists have identified and defined a somewhat stable, agreed-upon set of *user-interface components*, or "nouns" on which the above verbs act, i.e., the essential entities and attributes of all user interfaces, no matter what the platform of hardware and software (including operating systems and networks), user groups, contents (including vertical markets for products and services), and contexts.

In the course of our work throughout the first decades of AM+A, we developed user interfaces, information visualizations (tables, forms, charts, maps, and diagrams), books, stationery letterheads, brochures, slide shows, calendars, exhibits, posters, tutorials, and lectures. We decided early on that our fundamental activities focused primarily on user interfaces. During our projects, we realized that all of them required that we act on these objects, nouns, or user-interface components (Marcus 2015).

These UI components can enable developers, researchers, and critics to compare and contrast user interfaces that are evidenced on terminals, workstations, desktop computers, Web sites, Web-based applications, information appliances, vehicles, and mobile devices. Marcus (Marcus and Ziegler 1999; Marcus 2002), among others, provides one way to describe these user-interface components, which is strongly oriented to communication theory and to the applied theory of semiotics (Eco 1976; Pierce 1933; Innis 1985; Hooper 2014). This philosophical perspective emphasizes communication as a fundamental characteristic of computing, one that includes perceptual, formal characteristics, and dynamic, behavioral aspects of how people interact through computer-based media. Expanding upon Claude Levi-Strauss's idea of human beings as sign makers and tool makers (Levi-Strauss 1969) the theory understands a user interface as a form of dynamic, interactive visual literature as well as a suite of conceptual tools, and as such a cultural artifact. The user-interface components are the following:

Metaphors: Metaphors are fundamental concepts communicated via words, images, sounds, and tactile experiences (Lakoff and Johnson 1980). Metaphors substitute for computer-related elements and help users understand, remember, and enjoy entities and relationships of computer-based communication systems. Metaphors can be overarching or communicate specific aspects of user interfaces. An example of an overarching metaphor is the desktop metaphor to substitute for the computer's operating system, functions, and data. Examples of specific concepts are the trashcan, windows and their controls, pages, shopping carts, chatrooms, and blogs (Weblogs). The pace of metaphor invention, including neologisms or verbal metaphor invention, is likely to increase because of rapid development and distribution through the Web and mobile devices of ever-changing products and services.

Some researchers, such as David Gelernter, predicted the end of the desktop meta-phor era and the emergence of new fundamental metaphors (Fertig et al. 1995).

Mental models: Mental models are structures or organizations of data, func-tions, tasks, roles, and people in groups at work or play. These are sometimes also called user models, cognitive models, and task models. Content, function, media, tool, role, goal, and task hierarchies are examples. They may be expressed as lists, tables, and diagrams of functions, data, and other entities, such as menus. They may be tree-structured or more free-form.

Navigation: Navigation involves movement through the mental models, i.e., through content and tools. Examples of user-interface elements that facilitate such movement include those that enable dialogue, such as menus, windows, dialogue boxes, control panels, icons, and tool palettes.

Interaction: Interaction includes input/output techniques, status displays, and other feedback. Examples include the detailed behavior characteristics of key-boards, mice, pens, or microphones for input; the choices of visual display screens, loudspeakers, or headsets for output; and the use of drag-and-drop selection and numerous other action sequences.

Appearance: Appearance includes all essential perceptual attributes, i.e., visual, auditory, and tactile characteristics, even olfactory in some unusual cases. Examples typically include choices of colors, fonts, animation style, verbal style (e.g., ver-bose/terse or informal/formal), sound cues, and vibration cues.

A word or two about information visualization (Marcus 2015):

Crucial to much effective user-experience design is gathering the data, informa-tion, knowledge, and wisdom that must be interactively explored, analyzed, dis-played, understood, and acted upon. Entire professional groups are devoted to information design and information visualization (plus sonification and other rarer perceptual forms of information display). Among the organizations are the Society for Technical Communication (STC), its conferences and publications, and the International Institute for Information Design (IIID), with its *Information Design Journal* and associated conferences such as Vision Plus.

In these professions, similar development steps, especially user studies, task analyses, and careful design of new terminology, schema, querying, forms of reply, and other systematic approaches, lead to higher-level, more strategic solutions to people's needs for, desires for, and uses of information. A discussion of the field in general is contained in (Marcus 2009).

A word about data and information. Computers have been called number-crunchers or data-processing machines. Nowadays, more is required, and people speak of computer-based systems for information processing, and Chief Information Officers have evolved in corporations. The following practical definitions are appro-priate and useful:

• **Data** are significant patterns of perceptual stimuli, e.g., a collection of tempera-ture sensations or readings.

- **Information** is significant patterns of data, e.g., the temperature and other weather conditions, or the traffic conditions for a particular road, for a particular day in a particular city.
- **Knowledge** is significant patterns of information *together with action plans*, e.g., the weather conditions for a city on a particular day, their impact on traffic patterns, and the likely alternate roads on which to drive to arrive safely and on time at a destination, with a likely best choice indicated or in mind.
- **Wisdom** is significant patterns of knowledge, *either in-born or acquired through experience*, e.g., the knowledge of past experience taking certain roads, the likelihood of traffic accidents or repairs along that route, and familiarity with the various route options.

Helping people make smarter decisions faster means helping them to make *wise* decisions, no matter what the subject domain, context, or personal experience and expertise of the user. This expression became the slogan of our firm over the coming decades.

Of special interest are the means for communicating structures and processes, which may be shown in abstract or representational forms. Classically, these may be described as tables, forms, charts, maps, and diagrams. Many fine, classical, and thorough treatises about how to show information have appeared in the past decades, such as the works of Bertin (1967) and others.

The list of graphical communication techniques suggests an approximately increasing complexity of visual syntax. This term and approach, derived from semiotics, the science of signs (see, for example, Eco 1976), identifies four dimensions of "meaning":

- **Lexical:** how are the signs produced?
- **Syntactic:** how are the signs arranged in space and time, and with what perceptual characteristics?
- **Semantic:** to what do the signs refer
- **Pragmatic:** how are the signs consumed or used?

In the context of this book describing our AM+A projects, metaphors may be termed the fundamental concepts. The information architecture comprises the metaphors, mental model, and navigation. The discussion of screen designs will describe, also, the interaction and appearance, especially as the designs move from conceptual designs (so-called wireframe versions) to perceptual designs (so-called look-and-feel versions).

Getting Started

To begin at the beginning of AM+A, I had learned about Michael Arent from my Hawaii colleague Jerry Kuyper, who worked with me on the East-West Center project. Jerry had attended graphic design studies at the *Kunstgewerbeschule* in Basel,

Switzerland, as had Michael, after he graduated from the Graphic Design Department at the University of Cincinnati, both institutions that I respected. Michael seemed interested in the future of computers and graphic design, so I invited him to become my first Associate. We designed our first letterhead and started the firm up officially in my home during August 1982.

We arranged for the delivery of the equipment that DARPA provided, which included the following (see figures for examples of the equipment):

- Three-Rivers mini-computer with vertical black-and-white display at 300 dots per inch (DPI), the same as xerographic printers at the time, which was highly unusual), using the PERQ Accent operating system, at a cost of about $60,000
- Intran Metaform software, which allowed for graphics editing and which could drive our xerographic printer, at a cost of about $20,000. Xerox laser printer, with only two typefaces: Helvetica and Times Roman, at a cost of about $24,000 (Figs. 7.1–7.3)

In other words, to design and print our letterhead with computers, we needed to have about $100,000 of equipment, far out of the reach of most graphic designers at that time!

In the beginning, it was difficult to get high-quality typefaces for the Xerox printer. Only rudimentary typefaces had been made available for government projects. We were finally able to acquire good quality Times Roman and Helvetica, which suited our purposes.

I recall that within 3 years, when our project ended, DARPA had forgotten about this equipment and did not want/need it back. By then, I could not even give it away. Fortunately, the Computer Science Department of the University of California/ Berkeley accepted our donation, sent a crew of two men and a truck, and carted off this equipment. I imagine that all this equipment sat silently abandoned in relatively unused hallways or storerooms until it was sent to China for recycling. Sigh. Such

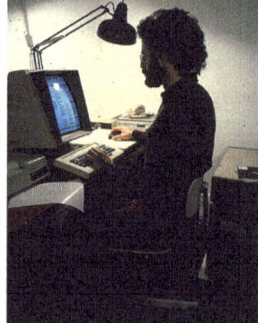

Figs. 7.1–7.3 Aaron Marcus and AM+A equipment funded by DARPA. (Photos by AM+A and used with permission)

is the life of some government research projects (and other corporate projects) that become disconnected and abandoned from supervision.

Our team of two was improved with the hiring of Bruce Browne, a recent graduate from the Rochester Institute of Technology's Visual Communication Department.

As we began our work in 1982, we also were given some basic technology through the generosity of the Atari Institute, which was then headed by Ted Kahn, who had taken an interest in my work and career. We thus had a state-of-the-art high-end workstation, software, and laser printer, but also an Atari 650 game machine and a low-end dot-matrix printer. I discovered that there was a primitive word processing application that could be used with the Atari computer. In this way, AM+A began its business life as a computer-based design firm. I would type and print simple letters and reports for our prospects and clients using this "primitive" equipment. We later improved our office equipment with an Atari 1200 game machine. Thirty-five years later in 2017, I donated some of this Atari hardware, which I had saved, together with software, and documentation, to the Computer History Museum, Mountain View (which AM+A helped to fund as a patron founder of its West Coast location in 1996) (Fig. 7.4).

Over the next decade, approximately 1982–1992, almost every day, I called across the USA, drove frequently to Silicon Valley, and flew around the USA and around the world, looking for new clients to keep AM+A alive, especially after the DARPA project came to its inevitable end in 1985. For many years, I kept in my leather DayTimer vest-pocket calendar holder, in addition to the current month's calendar, a list of all my likely prospects and clients, numbering some 500 names, companies, and telephone numbers (Fig. 7.5).

- To this day, I am amazed that I could keep most of these people *by memory*, in my head, all organized by company, then last name, then first name, then telephone number. I almost never had to look them up! The telephone numbers would magically pop up in my consciousness as I thought of the region of the USA, the company, then the person, then the number. I spent hours and hours on the phone each day calling to check in or making cold calls to make people aware of our services, skills, and track record. For the first 10 years of my firm's history,

Fig. 7.4 AM+A's Atari 1200. (Photo by AM+A used with permission of the author)

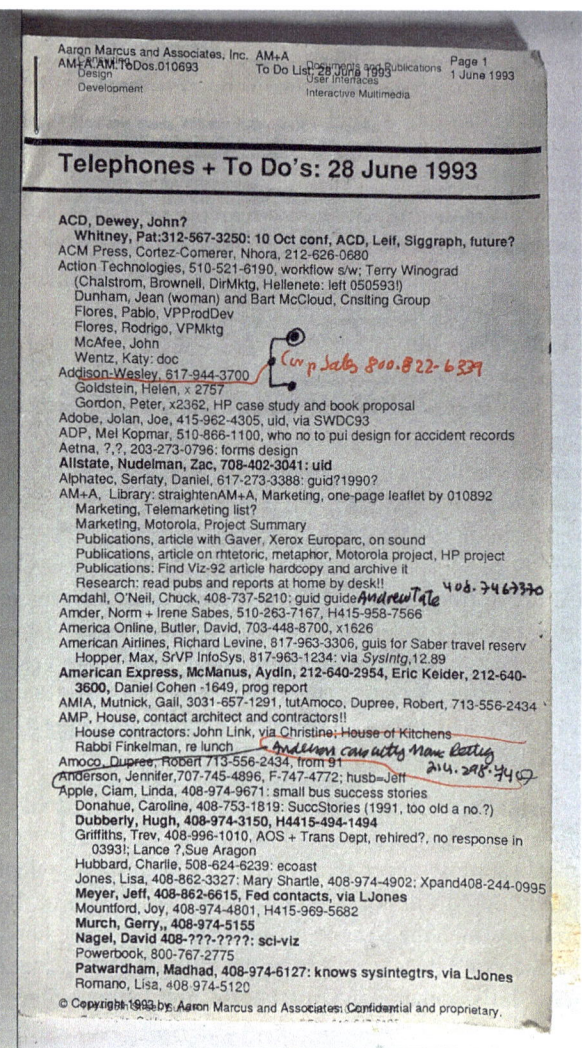

Fig. 7.5 Telephone and to do's list of 28 June 1983, first page of 12. (Source: AM+A archive; used with permission of the author)

I had to *spend half of my time with prospects* explaining not only who we were, but what was it that we did, and why should a prospective client be interested in improving the user interface (a term unfamiliar to many). Over and over again, I would explain how better typography, use of color, layout, symbols and icons, sequencing of information, and information visualization (tables, charts, maps, and diagrams), in short, more *effective visual communication*, would make their products/services easier to learn and use and would reduce users' learning time and user errors, with associated improvements to documentation, training, and performance.

- I also lectured at every conference to which I could get access. Amazingly, my proposals were accepted, seemed to be appreciated, and were successful. During those years of the middle and late 1980s, my message was novel, and it seemed in the business and conference world that wherever I pushed, the doors seemed to open, unlike my experience in academia during the 1960s and 1970s. Among organizations that accepted proposals were these:

  – ACM SIGCHI (Special Interest Group for Computer-Human Interaction) attended by most of the world's user-interface (human-computer interaction) academics, researchers, and professionals
  – ACM SIGGRAPH (Special Interest Group for Graphics and Interaction), attended by the cream of computer graphics programmers for movies, commercials, and industrial use
  – AIGA (American Institute of Graphic Arts), attended by most of the USA's graphic designers
  – HFES (Human Factors and Ergonomics Society), professional home for most human factors and ergonomics professionals, researchers, and academics
  – NCGA (National Computer Graphics Association), a more business-oriented version of computer graphics and user-interface design companies, especially for CAD/CAM/CAE (Computer-aided Design, Manufacturing, and Engineeering)
  – STC (Society of Technical Communicators), the professional organization for documentation specialists.

- I seemed to act as a one-man propaganda machine for user-interface design and information-design and visualization among our many prospects and conference participants. Not the only one, but certainly one of the first and one of the most active. I was also one of the few people who was not part of a large corporation or university. Instead, I was representing a tiny design firm, without major funding for marketing and PR. I loved to teach, so the process was not too painful, but it was tiring and demanding on my schedule and on my personal life.

- In the early days of the 1980s, things were more informal, less organized, less structured, and less directed by Big Business and Big Government. The self-proclaimed geeks of personal computers had their own software development conferences, and I think I saw actual barefoot participants. In those days, the originator of what became Macromedia multimedia software distributed software that enabled people to make complex presentations, and any recipient, or anyone else who viewed the presentation, was able to copy the code that generated the final result. There was no encapsulation as happened in later Macromedia Director/Projector files. Innocence, naïveté, and good-natured leftover *kumbaya* feelings of the 1960s still pervaded the personal computer community. When I lectured, I sometimes wore Mickey Mouse ears and talked about the end of informal, less-than-professional graphics in a new age that valued quality visual communication. We were a minority among the enthusiasts who wanted to use every color and every font available in every display.

- I was in a place between professions, between worlds, as I often had been during my life. Unfortunately, that meant I was viewed a little suspiciously by members of each world. I did not fit in perfectly.
- For designers and artists, I was tainted by contact with the computer world and technology in general. I was perhaps a spy or a mole or a subversive agent intending to turn humanists, artists, and designers into automatons. I had to demonstrate my bona fides as an artist and designer. Fortunately, I had learned the language and references of artists and designers at Yale. I could wax enthusiastically about designers I favored: like the pioneers of the Bauhaus; my teacher Paul Rand; the Swiss-German school of graphic design; the minimalists and conceptualists like Carl Andre, Sol Lewitt, and Ed Ruscha; the theories of semiotics and semiology; and the experimenters in visible language, concrete poetry, and visual poetry.
- For computer scientists and other techies, I was tainted by contact with artists and designers. I was not a "true geek," with deep programming skills and only a limited amount of understanding of the underlying technologies. I had to demonstrate my depth of knowledge and understanding. Fortunately, I had learned the language and references of science, technology, and computer science. I could talk mathematics and a limited amount of programming language shop-talk; I was comfortable with technology and learning new systems, new applications, and new terminology.
- For the business world, I was tainted by being in contact with both artists/designers on the one hand and computer science geeks on the other. I wore a long beard and had wild hair. I looked somewhat like a stereotypical anarchist or terrorist (see Figs. 7.6–7.8).

Fortunately, I had learned enough of the language of strategy, tactics, contracts, and marketing to seem credible; I was comfortable wearing three-piece banker suits, white shirts, and ties. I had learned the sartorial language of elite executives at Princeton and Yale: blue blazers, gray slacks or jeans sometimes, ties, white oxford shirts, and black leather shoes or athletic shoes, as the occasion might require.

During the next nearly four decades, I was constantly doing a balancing act on a tight-rope stretched across different professions, different cultures, different signs/symbols, and different languages, even if we were all speaking English. For the next nearly four decades, I had to enter a room, size up the group therein, and quickly learn how best to speak, behave, and emote, to convince the group of people that I was "one of them" and trustworthy. Perhaps my mid-Western background and long experience living on the East Coast, in Germany, in Israel, in Hawaii, and finally in California helped me to morph into something acceptable and believable.

Among unusual circumstances, I was invited by the Canadian government to teach a short course (two weeks) in February 1982 about visual design with Teletext and Videotex at the University of Alberta in Edmonton. The technology was an early form of visual telecommunication that stirred much of the computer industry

Figs. 7.6–7.8 Photos of Aaron Marcus at the start of AM+A in the early 1980s. (Source: AM+A photo archive used with permission of the author)

for some years. Canada had favored Telidon, a Canadian version of the technology, developed by the Canadian Communications Research Centre (CRC) during the late 1970s and supported by commercial enterprises led by Infomart in the early 1980s. The Ministry of Telecommunications saw an opportunity to foster good design. In Edmonton, I had the unusual opportunity to experience the coldest weather of my entire life (−40 °C = exactly −40 °F!).

After I had had my epiphany in November 1979, regarding how to combine my decade of professional experience of graphic design with that of computer graphics, I had invented some terminology to explain what I thought we were doing. I remember making one-page leaflets that explained our services. I showed one of my latest to a well-known San Francisco industrial designer. He commented that my explanation was impressive, but he had no idea what we did after reading the document!

My Executive Assistant, Ms. June Simonsen (RIP) had joined us in the late 1980s and stayed for many years. She was an authentic British eccentric. Blonde, tall, speaking with a pronounced London accent, and powerful in voice and stature, with a background in public relations, and given to smoking small dark-brown cigarettes (which she discreetly smoked outside and left under the front-porch mailbox). She trained herself to use our Macintosh computer and did reasonably well. She was an unforgettable presence to those who spoke with her across America. It was she who told me I did not know how to write for business communication. I was initially affronted by her remarks. After all, I had published many articles and was intending to write at least one book. I lectured worldwide. How could she think I could not write properly? She maintained that everything must be "crrrrrystal cleeeeer." We argued heatedly, and I stomped off, but later I had to admit she was right, and I apologized. We still maintained our friendship because we each respected each other. Did I forget to mention? She was about 5–10 years older than me!

US Defense Department Advanced Research Projects Agency (DARPA) Project in Program Visualization, 1982–1985

Our first major AM+A project began in 1982. We worked closely with Ron Baecker, and his team of computer scientists at Human Computing Resources, Toronto, to research program visualization. This topic was the broad mission of the approximately 12–20 research projects that the DARPA Program Visualization Group had funded under the leadership of Dr. Craig Fields. Our parallel-project colleagues were leading computer scientists from around the USA.

One of them became a friend, colleague, client, and adviser: Dr. Andries van Dam, head of Computer Science at Brown University. Prof. van Dam educated many future leaders of the computer world and helped pioneer the use of hypertext. I later wrote an important paper about the future of user-interface design with him (Marcus and Van Dam 1991).

For two years, we all would meet occasionally with DARPA Program Visualization leadership to present our progress reports and to receive adjustment requests from DARPA as their representatives deemed necessary. I remember at one early meeting, I was pleased to have an opportunity to show to my esteemed colleagues, a page of the Jewish Talmud, which features "hypertext-like" text blocks in fixed positions (well-known to Talmudic scholars) on a single page "dialoguing" with other text contributors across centuries of time, and from different geographic locations (Fig. 7.9).

At the meetings, I explained how AM+A looks across centuries and across cultures to find innovative solutions to human-computer interaction and information visualization design. All funded projects would share their progress. We succeeded in completing the development of a "super-PrettyPrint" program that would produce decent page layouts based on inputted code, complete with commentary, headers, footers, and complex differentiations of code components. Here is how we described our work in an ACM SIGCHI 1983 conference paper (Baecker and Marcus 1983).

> Our overall research program consists of six topics:
>   The first research topic deals with the appropriate use of typography to reveal formal syntactic, semantic, and pragmatic properties of programs and program elements. A second concern is with the design and layout of program elements on the page using systems of grids, overlays, and windows. A third area for research is the possibility of substituting a set of well-designed icons or symbols (pictograms or ideograms) for certain combinations of alphanumerics that occur repetitively in program code. A fourth set of questions arise out of the possibilities that interactive computer graphics offer in the inclusion of movement, blinking, and other kinds of change into program documentation. More fundamentally, we must explore the relationship between static paper and dynamic screen representations of computer programs. A fifth problem area is in the depiction of large directed graphs of great complexity, networks in which nodes are not single points but entire frames (combinations of signs) and in which links are explicitly stated or implied connections between nodes. The final sixth research topic concerns the ability of a program visualization to facilitate the integration of the various conceptual levels at which a program may be described. Our work

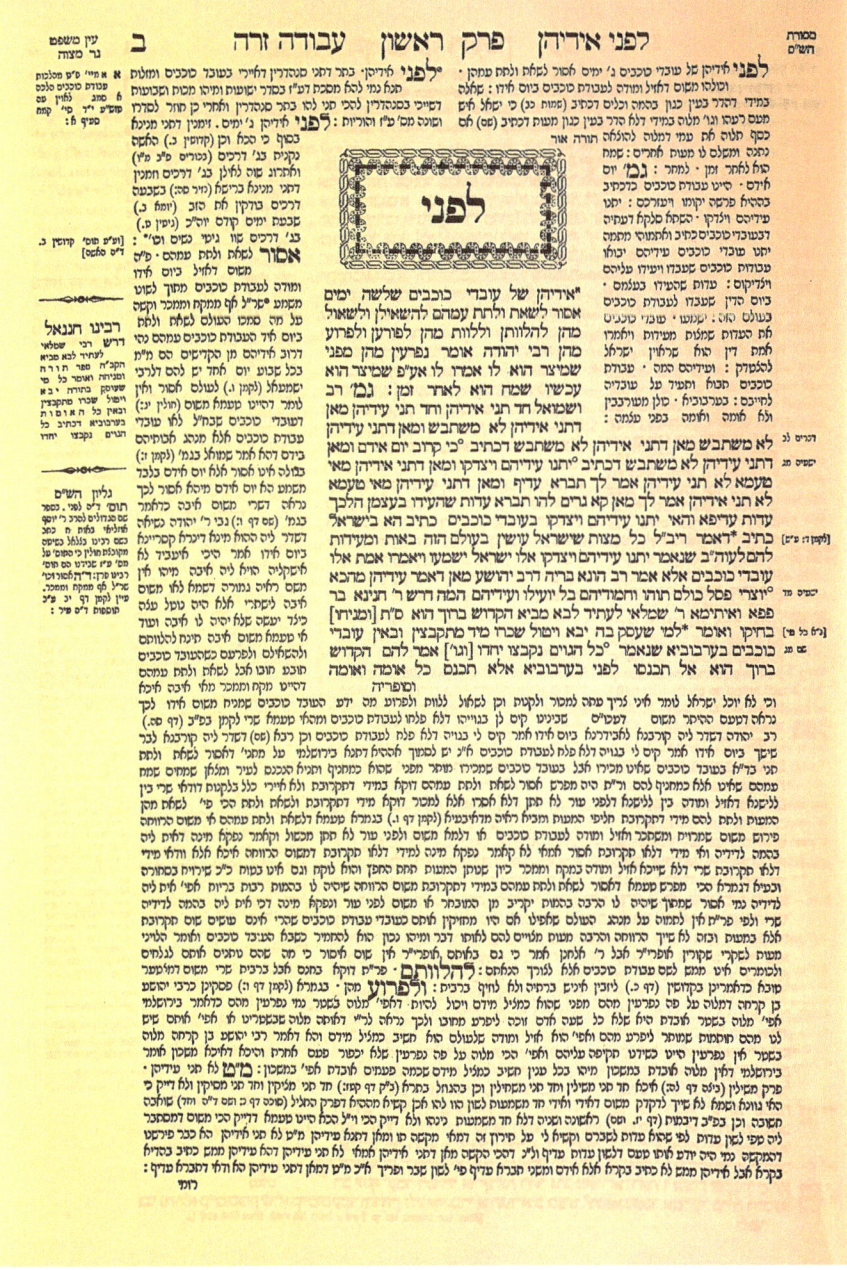

Fig. 7.9 Sample of a Talmud page similar to one used to explain the hypertext quality of "Torah documentation." (Source: Soncino Press, London; used with permission)

to date has centered on the first two of the above topics. We have adopted the following methodology:

1. We first developed a graphic design taxonomy for computer-based documents and publications. This was intended to be a checklist for approaches to the presentation of source code documentation.
2. We simultaneously developed a taxonomy of C constructs, a systematic classification of the language. This taxonomy was intended to be a companion checklist for insuring completeness in the representation of C source text.
3. We collected and systematized typical mappings from C constructs to typographic constructs. These examples were abstracted from real C programs prepared by typical experienced C programmers. We call such examples "folk designs."
4. We developed a systematic approach to the design of mappings from C constructs to typographic constructs, an approach which forms the basis for detailed visual research into effective presentations of C source code.
5. Finally, we constructed a first version of a visual C compiler, a program that maps arbitrary C programs into effective typeset representations of the source code. We are now producing numerous examples using this automated tool.

A Taxonomy of Typographic Constructs

In order to understand how source code might be displayed effectively in typeset form, it is necessary to analyze the graphic design possibilities of typography, the visual media of language expression. At a minimum this involves a systematic characterization of font selection, layout, and page sequencing. Many graphic design textbooks (Gerstner 1978) suggest a taxonomy of typographic form. Most large type display books show selections from the theoretical matrix of font, size, and line spacing possibilities. Graphic design manuals, e.g., (Chaparos 1981), display selections from the possibilities of page layout as well, while manuals on book design (Marshall 1965) prescribe formulations for annotation and page sequencing.

The authors are not aware of a complete, generic taxonomy of graphic design together with examples of each entity in the hierarchy. Consequently, we formulated a taxonomy suitable for our project. It seeks to organize the ways in which visible language can be presented. The taxonomy is not exhaustive, nor is it rigorously systematic; however, it does provide visual examples for as many entries as possible. The subjects include treatments of individual elements (characters, words, lines), groups (paragraphs, pages), segments, zones, even entire documents. Particular attention is given to the treatment of character specification (including font family, size, spacing, weight, width, texture, and style) and line specification (orientation, spacing, justification, and function in the page).

By presenting typical variations of the visual elements of programs, it was easier for computer scientists and graphic designers to carry on a dialogue about the means and results of different strategies for visualization. This taxonomy was necessary because the typical computer scientist is unaware of the varieties of display and is ignorant of the technical terms for referring to these differences. A visually oriented taxonomy of visible language is an indispensable research tool for our research in computer graphics.

Later in the article, we wrote (*op cit.,* p. 254):

Summary and Conclusions

"Our research at this point is a modest inquiry into the manner in which graphic design specifications for visible language may clarify the structure and function of source code and comments. We have made progress in constructing an automatic means of realizing improved conventions for the display of source code and of facilitating experimentation with approaches to these conventions. Even within this limited scope, many interesting and valuable areas of further investigation have revealed themselves. Their exploration will require careful analysis, testing, and evaluation, as well as creative imagination in formulating new categories and concepts of program symbology and metadata. Among issues that seem worthy of further study are these:

What are relevant initial program metadata, and how should these be displayed?

What would a taxonomy of program comments reveal about the length, position, reference relationship, linguistic style, and literary style of these comments? What implication does this have for typographic presentation of these comments?

How can the visual C compiler easily be used to construct significant visual metrics of program structure? What kinds of visual indexes would be useful to see?

"Is our schema for presentation general enough to account for varying views of program structure such as modules vs. files? Is the presentation equally suitable for the novice as well as the expert? Is the format appropriate for languages other than C? Is our design for a vertical page also adaptable to horizontal screen layouts?"

"During the course of the project, we were conducting user-centered design, although the phrase had not yet entered the general lexicon of HCI and computer technology. The term 'user-centered design' was developed by Donald Norman and his colleagues in his research laboratory at the University of California/San Diego and became widely popular after the publication of his book *User-Centered System Design: New Perspectives on Human-Computer Interaction*" in 1986. The concept gained further attention and acceptance in his book *The Design of Everyday Things* (originally titled *The Psychology of Everyday Things*)."

"In fact, we were 'embedded' with programmers, as we talked with them frequently and visited them frequently in Toronto. We called their attempts "folk designs" and defined them this way in our 1983 paper: 'By folk designs of C programs we mean attempts by programmers with little or no background in typography and graphic design to improve the appearance of their programs/ (*op. cit.*, p. 253)."

I am not sure how many versions of our designs we developed. Perhaps 100. This iterative design process was also fundamental to our work and our progress over a period of two years. This approach, also, became essential to our basic design process.

Another aspect of our design process was our desire to test our designs to make sure we were achieving desired outcomes. To our surprise, the head of DARPA's Program Visualization group, himself a psychologist with experience of research and testing, was not requiring us to test our designs. If I understood correctly, he felt that simply publishing and promoting our designs would have such an impact on programmers that they would respond positively and help to further improvements in the industry. Nevertheless, we felt we should engage independent human factors specialists to test our designs, which we did. We were satisfied to learn that novice programmers improved their understanding of code by approximately 20%, without any significant change in the programming language structure. This improvement was achieved simply by more legible, readable typography and layout (see Figs. 7.10 and 7.11).

Some of the changes in typography were innovative and subtle, like changing the sizes of embedded sets of parentheses, or spacing groups of constants and variables so that the semantics of the statements were more evident. We even added possible symbol extensions, e.g., for the likely comprehendability of code, an eight-rectangle gray-value indicator (see Fig. 7.12) that represented metrics such as how often the code text was accompanied by comments. (*Source: AM+A archive; used with permission*)

Later in the project funding period, my co-principal investigator Ron Baecker and I were amused and grateful that only our project was not cancelled when others seemed to show mostly plans and little progress, while we were able to get an initial text compiler to work.

Because of the relative success of achieving a typesetting and page-layout compiler for C-code, our project was, to my knowledge, the only one of about two dozen projects in its Program Visualization activities of DARPA that was not cancelled at the close of two years. We eventually reduced our (approximately) 1000-page report about our activities to a 300-page book, *Human Factors and Typography for More Readable Programs,* which we published through Addison-Wesley (Fig. 7.13).

We were never able to find a sponsor for a commercial version of our research-based version of the compiler, but over the next 5–10 years, we saw that many companies, whose representatives had seen our lectures or read our publications about our project, improved their code documentation. Through this means, we felt we had made a significant improvement to the typography of code publications, the largest publishing effort on earth.

Original C code example.

```
4                          Chapter 1: Visualizing Programs

Apr 20 12:59 1989   phone.c Page 1


/*
 * phone.c - Prints all potential words corresponding to a given phone number
 *
 * Only words containing vowels are printed.
 * Acceptable phone numbers range from 1 to 10 digits.
 */

#include <string.h>
#include <stdio.h>

typedef int      bool;
#define FALSE    0
#define TRUE     1

char    *label[] = { /* labels on each digit of dial */
    "0",
    "1",      "abc",  "def",
    "ghi",    "jkl",  "mno",
    "prs",    "tuv",  "xxy"
};

#define PNMAX    10      /* max digits in phone number */

int      digits; /* actual number of digits */
int      pn[PNMAX];        /* phone number */
char     *label_ptr[PNMAX];     /* current position in label, per digit */

main(argc, argv)
    int argc;
    char      *argv[];
{
    register int      i;
    bool              foundvowel = FALSE;

    /* For each phone argument ... */
    while (*++argv != NULL) {
        if (!getpn(*argv))
            fprintf(stderr, "PhoneName:  %s is not a phone number\n", *argv);
        else {
            /* For beginnings of label sequences */
            for (i = 0; i < PNMAX; ++i)   /* Reset label_ptr (pointers).*/
                label_ptr[i] = label[pn[i]];
            /* For each combination of characters ... */
            do {
                for (i = 0; i < digits; ++i) {
                    if (strchr("aeiou", *label_ptr[i]) != NULL)
                        foundvowel = TRUE;
                }
                if (foundvowel)  /* Only print things with vowels! */
                {
                    for (i=0; i!=digits; i++)
                        printf("%c",*label_ptr[i]);
                    printf("\n");
                }
                foundvowel = FALSE;
            } while (incr());
```

Figs. 7.10 and 7.11 Examples of original and improved pages of C-code as designed by AM+A during 1982–1985. (Source: AM+A documents archive. Used with permission of the author

Revised C code example:

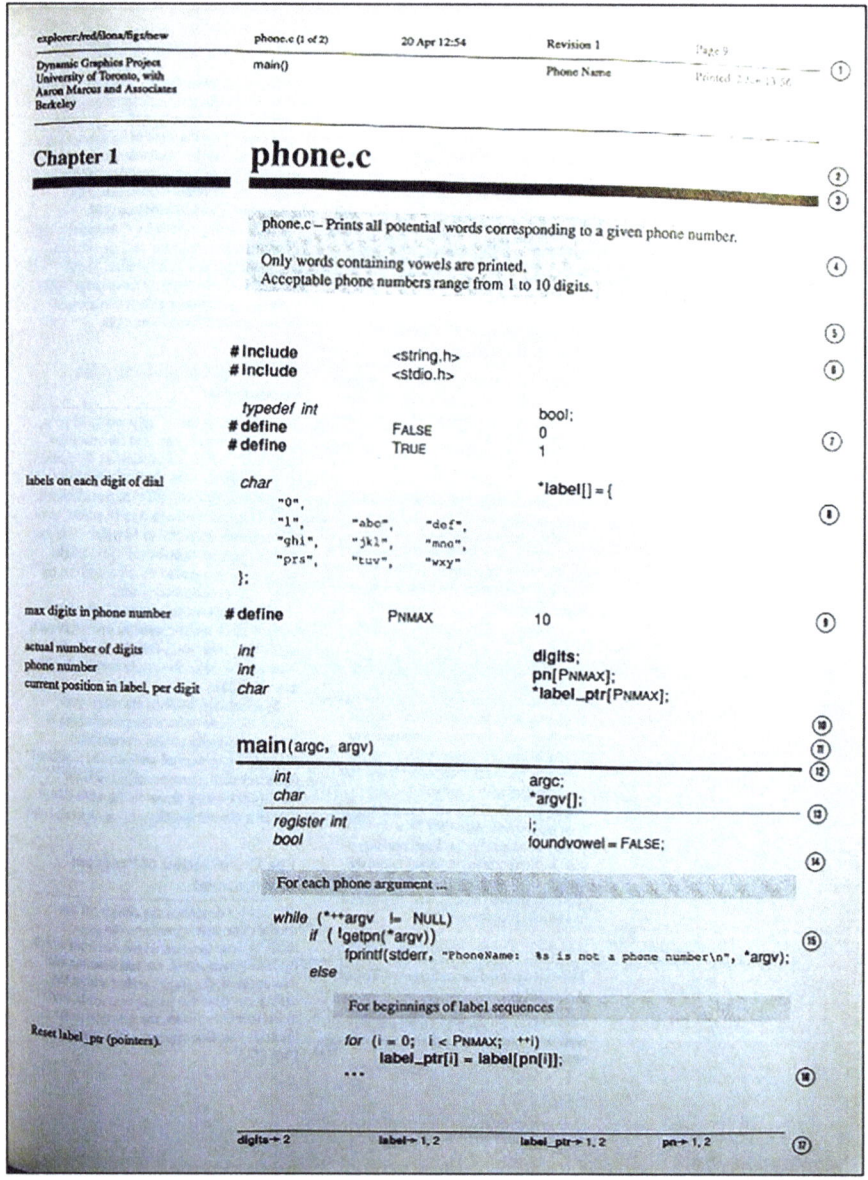

Figs. **7.10 and 7.11**   (continued)

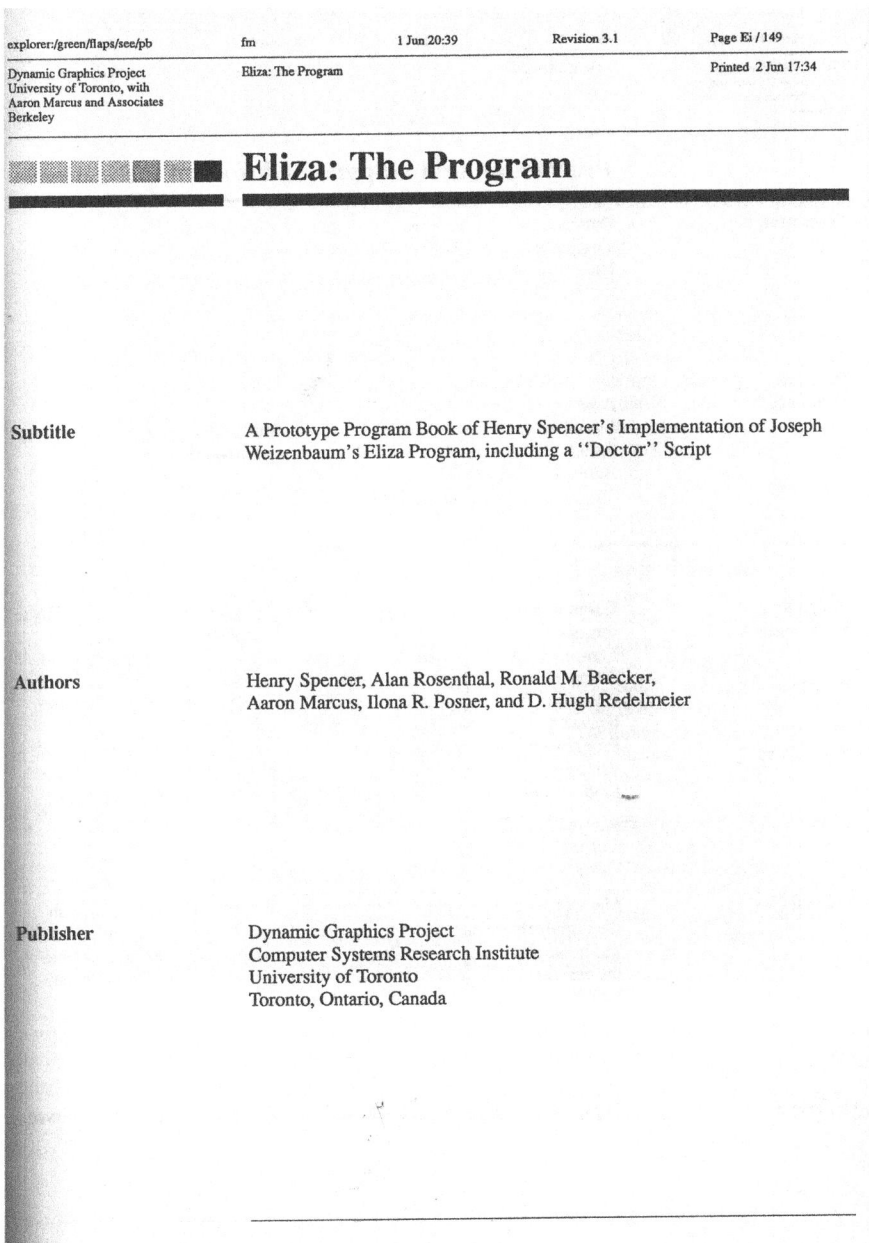

| explorer:/green/flaps/see/pb | fm | 1 Jun 20:39 | Revision 3.1 | Page Ei / 149 |
| Dynamic Graphics Project University of Toronto, with Aaron Marcus and Associates Berkeley | Eliza: The Program | | | Printed 2 Jun 17:34 |

Eliza: The Program

Subtitle

A Prototype Program Book of Henry Spencer's Implementation of Joseph Weizenbaum's Eliza Program, including a "Doctor" Script

Authors

Henry Spencer, Alan Rosenthal, Ronald M. Baecker, Aaron Marcus, Ilona R. Posner, and D. Hugh Redelmeier

Publisher

Dynamic Graphics Project
Computer Systems Research Institute
University of Toronto
Toronto, Ontario, Canada

Fig. 7.12 Example depiction of a code document for the Eliza program (which simulates a human therapy interviewer of the user of the code). The gray-value indicator at the top-left shows an eight-point symbolic indicator of the overall comprehendability of the code. One metric is related to the relative amount of comments embedded in the code; the more comments, the more likely the reader will be able to understand the code. (Source: AM+A documents archive. Used with permission of the author)

Fig. 7.13 Cover of the publication *Human Factors and Typography for More Readable Programs*, 1990, co-authored by Ronald Baecker and Aaron Marcus, produced from our DARPA-funded research project to improve the appearance of the C programming language. (Source: Addison-- Wesley Publishing Co.; used with permission of Pearson/Addison-Wesley)

Intran Metaform Project and Its Legacy, 1982–1983

In 1982, Peter Preksto, a lead software developer at Intran in Edina, Minneapolis, had heard about AM+A and decided we were the right group to help his company improve their graphical user interface (GUI) for a forms-design front end to the Xerox 9700, an industrial-strength laser printer used by large companies to print very large runs of forms and reports, e.g., insurance forms/reports, financial forms/reports, and government forms/reports. Because of my background in working on the 1980 Census Reports projects at Lawrence Berkeley Laboratory, and our current DARPA project, which we were simultaneously starting, I felt confident we could help them.

As we began our DARPA work, we had already begun negotiations and business agreements with Intran to design the graphical user interface for its Metaform software. Intran years later was sold to Xerox, and later, in about 1992–1994, we worked for Xerox to write/design a marketing diskette for the Intran software, the user interface for which was unchanged since we had first designed the user interface in 1982!

Our designs may today appear primitive, but they were beyond almost all computer technology at the time. One month before the Apple Lisa was announced, our GUI was announced and shown at the Xerox Xplor conference of February 1983, and several years before the Macintosh, but received less PR-renown due to Apple's much greater funds for and focus on marketing. Figures 7.14–7.18 show some typical scenes of the user interface, which featured iconic buttons and complex graphical layout.

In fact, all through the 1980s, and into the early 1990s, we worked with several different companies to improve the design of their documents. For example, we worked with Equitable Life Insurance to improve the design of quarterly reports produced with Xerox 9700 equipment, and I lectured several times at the Xerox-originated Xplor conferences, which brought together Xerox's customers and other vendors and their customers from across the USA and elsewhere.

Other forms-design projects followed. In 1982–1983, AM+A designed Xerox 9700-oriented forms for Datacopi, San Francisco, which were used by its clients Syntex and Davis Skaggs (see Figs. 7.19, 7.20, 7.21, and 7.22).

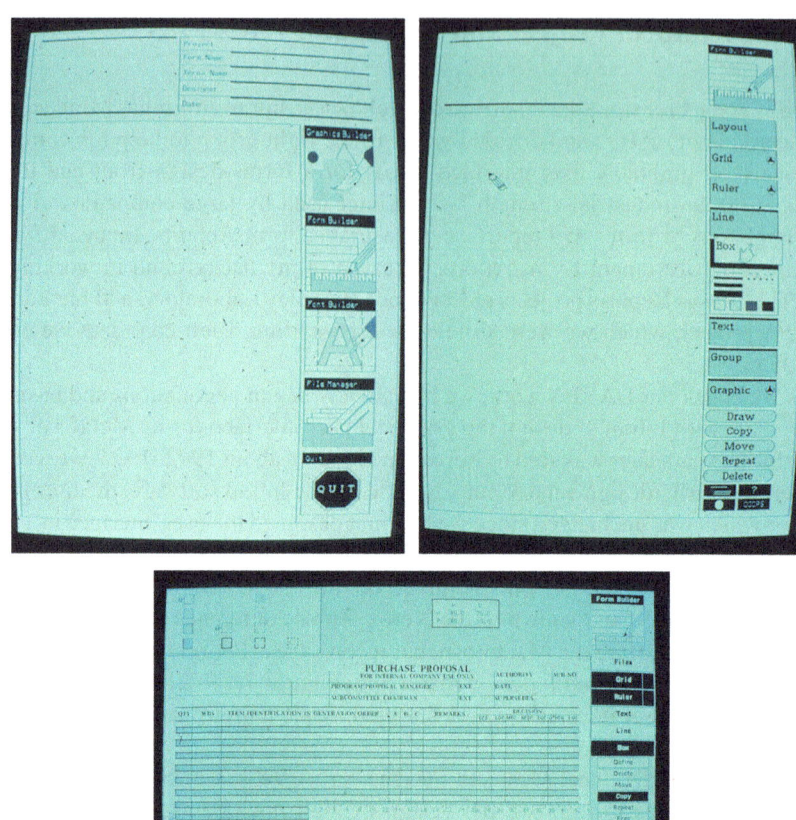

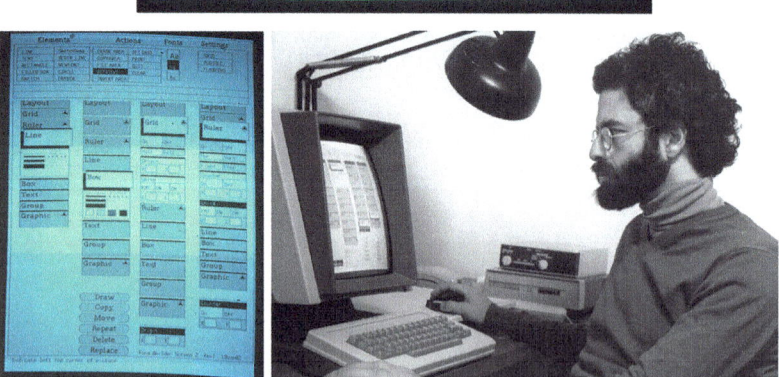

Figs. 7.14–7.18 Exemplary images from the Intran Metaform software's graphical user interface designed by AM+A and photo of Aaron Marcus with equipment. (Source: AM+A archives; used with permission of the author)

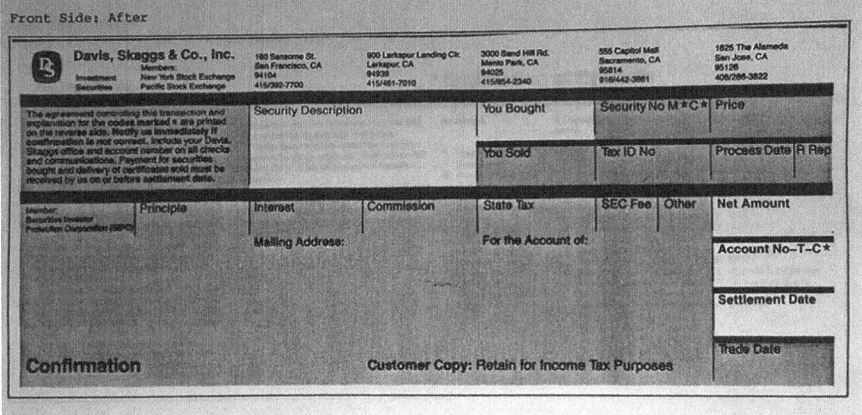

Figs. 7.19 and 7.20 Before and after designs of forms for Davis, Skaggs and Co. (Source: AM+A archives. Photos by AM+A, used with permission of AM+A)

SYNTEX U.S. EMPLOYEES INVESTMENT SAVINGS PLAN

Statement of Account for the 3 Months Ending December 31, 1982

123-45-6789 · Comp
A.N. Employee

Investment Funds

Your Voluntary Account:	GTD	TIA	VWF	ICA	SSF	TOTAL
Market Value on 9/30/82 ($)	1000.00	1000.00	1000.00	1000.00	1000.00	5000.00
Your Contributions	0.00	500.00	0.00	100.00	200.00	800.00
Withdrawals	0.00	0.00	-100.00	0.00	0.00	-100.00
Transfers	-500.00	500.00	0.00	-220.00	0.00	0.00
Interest/Dividends	15.00	N/A	20.00	100.00	100.00	35.00
Change in Market Value	0.00	10.00	0.00	-15.00	50.00	45.00
Market Value on 12/31/82 ($)	515.00	2010.00	720.00	1185.00	1350.00	5780.00
# of Shares on 9/30/82	N/A	200.000	50.000	100.000	20.000	N/A
# of Shares on 12/31/82	N/A	398.000	42.000	150.000	26.000	N/A

Your Regular Account (Pre 10/82)

	GTD	TIA	VWF	ICA	SSF	TOTAL
Market Value on 9/30/82	1000.00	1000.00	1000.00	1000.00	1000.00	5000.00
Withdrawals	0.00	0.00	-100.00	0.00	0.00	-100.00
Transfers	-500.00	500.00	-200.00	100.00	100.00	0.00
Interest/Dividends	15.00	N/A	20.00	0.00	0.00	35.00
Change in Market Value	0.00	10.00	0.00	-15.00	50.00	45.00
Market Value on 12/31/82	515.00	2010.00	720.00	1185.00	1350.00	5780.00
# of Shares on 9/30/82	N/A	200.000	50.000	100.000	20.000	N/A
# of Shares on 12/31/82	N/A	398.000	42.000	150.000	26.000	N/A

Your Tax Deferred Regular Account

	GTD	TIA	VWF	ICA	SSF	TOTAL
Market Value on 9/30/82	872.85	4178.46	0.00	0.00	764.75	5816.06
Your Contributions	0.00	499.98	102.00	0.00	123.00	724.98
Withdrawals	0.00	0.00	0.00	0.00	0.00	0.00
Transfers	-415.20	0.00	415.20	0.00	0.00	0.00
Interest/Dividends	10.77	52.04	8.20	0.00	44.39	26.62
Change in Market Value	0.00	0.00	0.00	0.00	0.00	0.00
Market Value on 12/31/82	468.42	4730.48	525.40	0.00	932.14	6567.66
# of Shares on 9/30/82	N/A	143.572	0.000	0.000	51.125	N/A
# of Shares on 12/31/82	N/A	162.324	8.425	0.000	52.987	N/A

Company Matching Account (XXX% Matched)

	GTD	TIA	VWF	ICA	SSF	TOTAL
Market Value on 9/30/82	1246.89	4270.02	0.00	000.00	457.89	5974.80
Company Contributions	0.00	499.98	102.00	00.00	123.00	724.98
Withdrawals	0.00	0.00	0.00	0.00	0.00	0.00
Transfers	-602.00	0.00	602.00	0.00	0.00	XXXXXX
Interest/Dividends	41.41	48.33	10.20	00.00	22.89	122.83
Change in Market Value	0.00	0.00	0.00	0.00	0.00	0.00
Market Value on 12/31/82	1059.30	4818.33	714.20	00.00	603.78	7195.61
# of Shares on 9/30/82	N/A	124.017	0.000	00.000	00.000	N/A
# of Shares on 12/31/82	N/A	170.198	10.082	00.000	43.242	N/A

Summary of Accounts as of 12/31/82

	GTD	TIA	ICA	VWF	SSF	TOTAL
Total Closing Market Value ($) All Accounts 12/31/82	2557.72	13568.81	2679.60	2370.00	4235.92	25412.05
Total Share Balance 12/31/82	N/A	1128.522	102.507	300.00	148.229	N/A
Share Price as of 12/31/81 ($)	N/A	12.023	26.140	7.900	28.576	N/A

Your Total Contributions to the Plan as of 12/31/82 . . . . $XXXXXXXXXXXX
(Less any withdrawals)

Total Vested Value (XXX% Vested in Company Account) . . . . $XXXXXXXXXXXX

If there are any errors on this statement, notify your Human Resource Department immediately.

SYNTEX

U.S. Employees Investment Savings Plan

Statement of Account for the Quarter Ending December 31, 1982

123-45-6789 Comp
A.N. Employee

INVESTMENT FUNDS

(Same account data as above, "after" design.)

If there are any errors on this statement, notify your Human Resources Department immediately.

Figs. 7.21 and 7.22 Before and after designs of Syntex forms. (Source: AM+A archives. Photos by AM+A, used with permission of AM+A)

NCGA Proceedings, 1984–1992

During 1982–1992, at the National Computer Graphics Association (NCGA) conferences, I organized many sessions about electronic publishing. I also gave tutorials and lectures about user interface design. The conferences were more commercially
and practically oriented in comparison to ACM SIGCHI conferences, which I also
started to attend in 1982.

In the NCGA *Proceedings* from the 1980s, I published many tutorial notes and
articles about color, icon design, and screen design. In one article, I published some
of the first images showing the possibilities for non-rectangular windows, including
those shaped like speech and thought balloons from the world of comic books. Such
speech balloons became ubiquitous in mobile phone messaging applications after
the 1980s (Fig. 7.23).

Figure 9B: Window Shapes

Fig. 7.23 Example of non-rectangular windows for graphical user interfaces, perhaps the first ever published, 1984. Imagine: windows thinking about something or speaking something. Published in the Proceedings of the National Computer Graphics Association (NCGA). (Source: AM+A archives; used with permission of author)

Hewlett-Packard Projects, 1984–2004

Beginning in about 1984, I first made contact with staff and professionals at Hewlett-Packard (HP), one of the founding companies of Silicon Valley. I lectured about user-interface design, color design, and typography to members of the Human Factors Department under Wanda Smith at the time. Separately, we later came to be selected for two unusual projects.

One of them, under the direction of James Aguilar, enabled us to digitize for the first time a clip-art library of 1000 images of HP equipment (see project description below). HP invited AM+A to complete this project without charging HP a fee, using HP equipment (including HP Vectra desktop computers) and their original documents, and then enabling AM+A to sell the library directly through HP to their customers. I asked what data they had from marketing to show how many copies we might sell. They said they had no such data. In those days, as one HP manager told me, they just developed products they thought were right and threw them out into the marketplace to see if customers would buy them! Since I was not independently wealthy, I politely declined their offer, and we were paid a fee. We were the first group ever to digitize the HP logo as part of our work with them!

The second project related to that experience. We established an agreement with HP to act as an HP-recommended provider of digitizing service of corporate logos and other symbols or imagery for HP's corporate customers worldwide. HP even distributed a leaflet advertising our services that was carried by HP sales force members (see Figs. 7.24 and 7.25). We digitized the logos and symbols of many companies in Europe, the Far East, and throughout the USA. For example, we were, I believe, the first to digitize the GE logo.

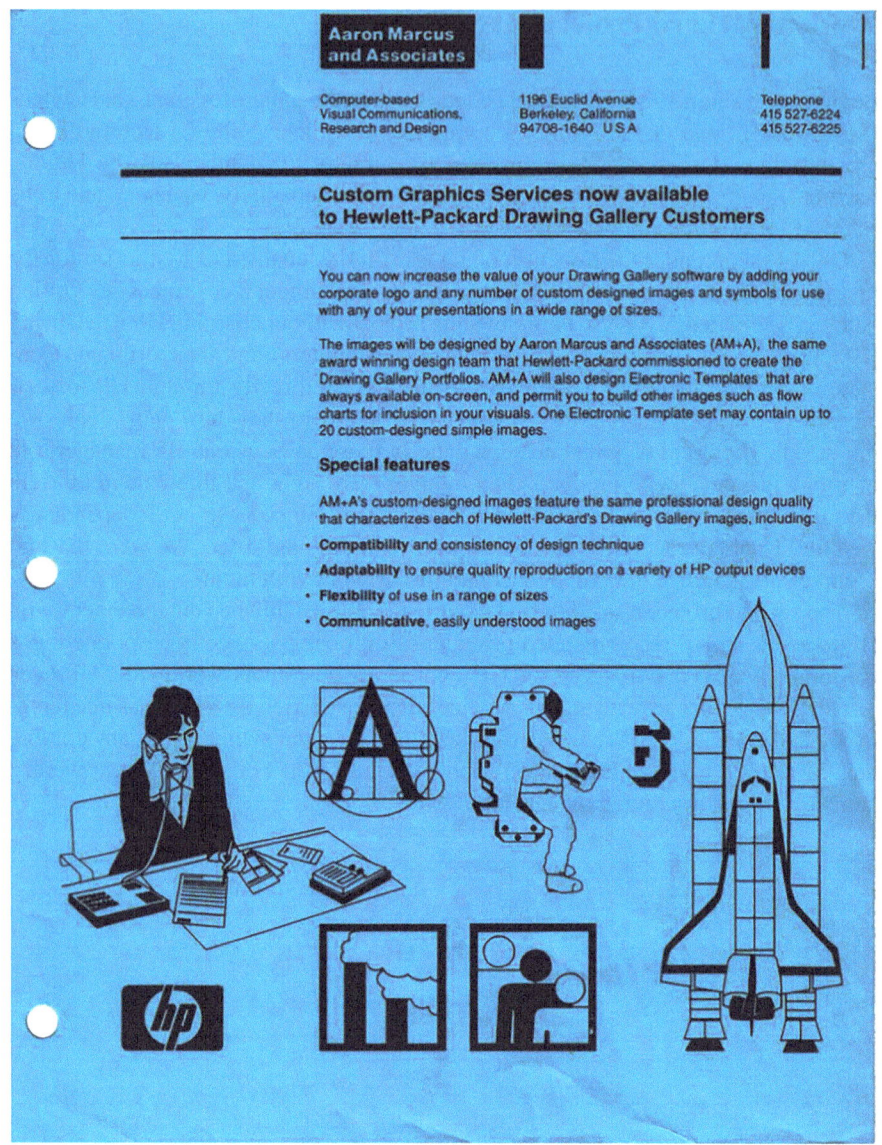

Figs. 7.24 and 7.25 HP leaflet advertising AM+A's digitizing services, about 1988. (Source: AM+A archives; used with permission of the author)

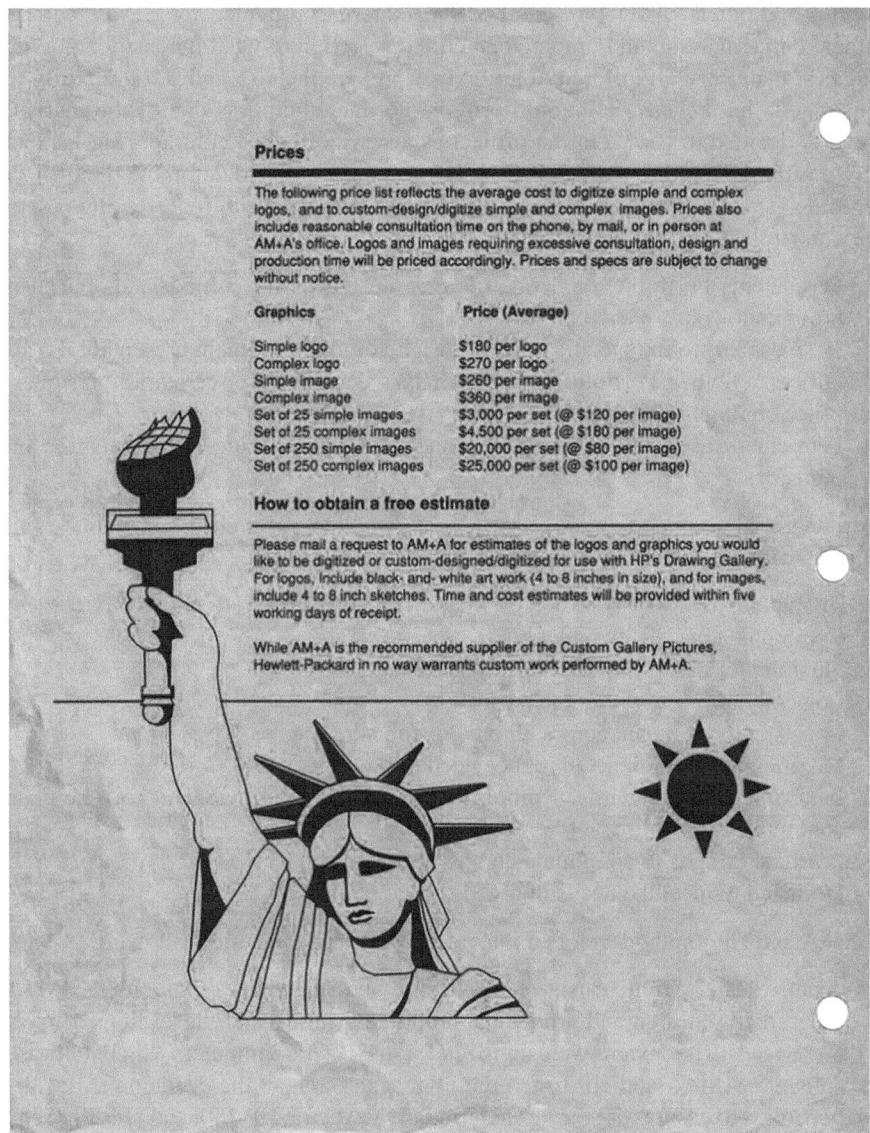

Prices

The following price list reflects the average cost to digitize simple and complex logos, and to custom-design/digitize simple and complex images. Prices also include reasonable consultation time on the phone, by mail, or in person at AM+A's office. Logos and images requiring excessive consultation, design and production time will be priced accordingly. Prices and specs are subject to change without notice.

Graphics	Price (Average)
Simple logo	$180 per logo
Complex logo	$270 per logo
Simple image	$260 per image
Complex image	$360 per image
Set of 25 simple images	$3,000 per set (@ $120 per image)
Set of 25 complex images	$4,500 per set (@ $180 per image)
Set of 250 simple images	$20,000 per set (@ $80 per image)
Set of 250 complex images	$25,000 per set (@ $100 per image)

How to obtain a free estimate

Please mail a request to AM+A for estimates of the logos and graphics you would like to be digitized or custom-designed/digitized for use with HP's Drawing Gallery. For logos, include black- and- white art work (4 to 8 inches in size), and for images, include 4 to 8 inch sketches. Time and cost estimates will be provided within five working days of receipt.

While AM+A is the recommended supplier of the Custom Gallery Pictures, Hewlett-Packard in no way warrants custom work performed by AM+A.

Figs. 7.24 and 7.25 (continued)

HP Graphics Gallery, 1986

HP commissioned AM+A to prepare 1000 images of clip art on a CD-ROM in 1986. The imagery included general themes as well as specific images of HP equipment, which could be used by HP employees, partners, and customers to enhance the appearance of documents prepared with HP equipment, especially its

Vectra computers. AM+A researched the materials provided by HP as well as other source material and prepared an edited selection of what it considered to be the best materials. HP offered to let AM+A prepare the disk and sell it directly to customers, but because HP could provide no data about the size of the market, AM+A decided to carry out the project as a service-for-fee contract. AM+A had to hire three people to work full-time for several months to complete the project on time. The images were divided into four categories, each representing a specific portfolio:

1. Permanent Portfolio (general images designed for office and business presentations)
2. Business Portfolio (specific images designed for management presentations)
3. Office Activities Portfolio (specific images designed for secretarial and inter-office communications)
4. Petrochemical Portfolio (chemical, math, and engineering images for the oil industry)

AM+A's goal was to produce a consistent, compatible, and well-designed library of images with the following characteristics:

• Adaptable, to ensure quality reproduction on a variety of HP output devices
• Communicative, easily understood
• Flexible, for use in a wide range of sizes
• Logically grouped within the portfolios
• Consistently designed across all the portfolios
• Maximum visual impact to reduce need for editing
• Inclusion of standard symbols from DOT and OSHA to facilitate communication
• Practical designs to communicate business concepts
• Designed to meet the needs of a wide range of users

AM+A and HP jointly developed image and portfolio categories following

In-depth research within business, academic, and scientific communities. AM+A proceeded to design and produce appropriate symbols and illustrations to meet these needs. The designs were digitized using HP 2700 computers with Paintbrush software. AM+A and HP tested the images throughout the development of the portfolios to ensure that they transferred to the Vectra, HP 150, and HP-3000 and reproduced well on HP plotter media.

Users of the Graphics Gallery software could special-order additional custom-designed, digitized images, including logos from AM+A to add to their 1000 image library. The custom-designed images were consistent and compatible with the original images (Figs. 7.26 and 7.27).

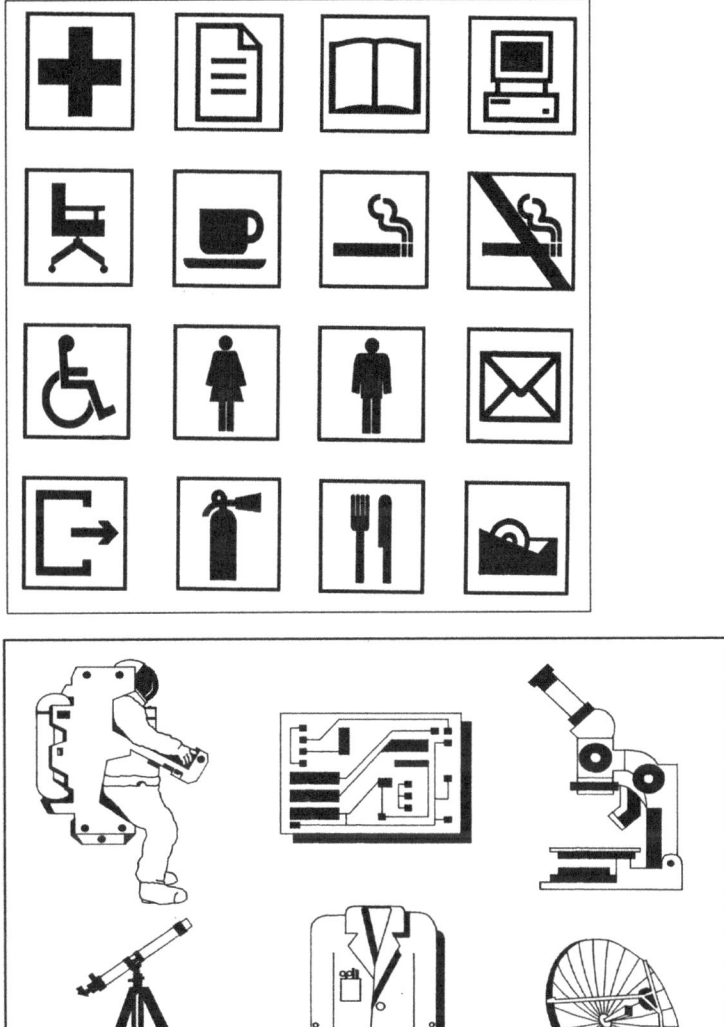

Figs. 7.26 and 7.27 Examples of the HP Graphics Gallery portfolio of imagery prepared by AM+A for HP, 1986. (Source: AM+A archive; used with permission of Hewlett-Packard)

HP Slide Standards, 1992

HP's Marketing Department commissioned AM+A to design company-wide standards for all marketing slides worldwide, to be produced with the four widely used applications, including one of HP's own products. After months of research and design, AM+A delivered the standards to HP, which distributed them with booklets written and designed by AM+A explaining the standards and with templates provided on diskettes (Fig. 7.28).

Fig. 7.28 Example of one of AM+A's booklets and diskette presenting HP's new slide standards. (Source: AM+A archives; used with permission of Hewlett-Packard)

HP Halo System, 2007

In 2003–2004, Dr. Fred Kitson, head of HP's Multimedia and Systems Lab (MMSL), part of HP Labs, saw AM+A Associate Eugene Chen and two others of AM+A make a presentation about our company, mission, and track record. He hired us almost immediately to work with him on several projects.

The most challenging HP project was working with HP's MMSL team on commercializing its virtual corporate meeting, high-resolution video, and telecommunication facilities called Halo, which it rolled out in about 2007. We had consulted about the user-interface design of the earlier version of this product when it was a confidential advanced research project. Now, HP was attempting to make the first commercial version using its MMSL staff. Halo used the highest quality video and fastest telecommunication systems available. The rooms in which participants sat during meetings featured a wall of three giant video screens facing a desk at which about six people could sit in a room that had very carefully designed lighting and furniture to match. The participants would see images of another similar room with people sitting at their desk, which might be thousands of miles away. From personal experience, I had realized that the images were so compelling that within about three minutes, one forgot that the people were not there and accepted the alternate reality of being together in a room with the other set of people. The system was to be used by the highest levels of corporate management. The system was expensive: about $500,000 per room when it was introduced (see Fig. 7.29).

The Halo system was intended specifically to foster human-human communication and *not* to feel high-tech and "computerish." Our role was to design the one computer-based system-management screen's user interface that was used to set up,

Fig. 7.29 Typical scene of the HP Halo virtual corporate meeting room product/service. (Source: HP Web site; used with permission of Hewlett-Packard)

conduct, and conclude meetings. To understand the users and to guide HP in its design, we interviewed about six different executive assistants who were usually charged with setting up and maintaining meetings.

From these interviews, we gained a better understanding of the user personas, the idealized descriptions of typical users, their preferences, objectives, work environments, and the subsequent likely impact on the design of the product. We also acquired a better understanding of the use scenarios, the typical broad interactions of the participants with the system. Based on our research, we recommended many detailed improvements in the design of the product's metaphors, mental models, navigation, interaction, and appearance of the screens used to communicate between computer systems and Halo participants and executive assistants who coordinated the meetings.

We had just completed this phase of the work when we were confronted with one of the most amazing events of the project: HP fired us in the middle of the project! Although our project manager liked us personally and professionally, she called one day, with some embarrassment, to say that she had to let us go, because we were not on HP's newly identified and announced list of qualified, recommended professional service vendors. Considering that we had worked with about four different HP departments on about six to eight projects over a period of 20 years, this seemed astounding and frankly unbelievable. The situation, I believe, was the result of a new high-level director of design coming into HP who favored a particular group of people to assist HP. Alas, we had to close down our project before the project was released, and all of our work was turned over to another external design team.

One year later, a Halo product team manager (from outside the research lab) contacted us from another HP corporate location. He was now responsible for revising the first commercial version of Halo. He had seen our reports from earlier, was impressed, and wanted to hire us to do usability studies of the commercial product! I hesitated to mention to him that, according to my understanding, our company was not an authorized vendor to HP. This matter never came up in our discussions! Apparently, as sometimes happens in large corporations, the left hand does not know what the right hand is doing.

Thus began our final major project for HP, one of the most challenging usability tests in our entire experience, because it involved our tracking about 24 people in 4 cities communicating with each other during a meeting. Our results showed many minor and some major errors in the design as implemented. It was astonishing to us that the vendor selected, while accomplished in industrial design, had relatively less experience and skill with the systematic, complex design needed for user interfaces, which needed to be implemented over hundreds of detailed screens. We lamented this state of affairs at HP, which had seen us removed from the project, with a new team inserted into the development process, but nothing could be done to change the past, only to protect the future quality of the product. We did the best we could.

Our experience with HP went downhill from there. We complained to the design executive who had organized the qualified vendor list, and he promised that we would be interviewed to become (possibly) a recommended vendor. Eventually, three of us at AM+A arrived at the appointed time for a one-hour credentials interview. Astonishingly, no video projector had been prepared in advance (usually a standard host logistics matter for meetings), and half the available time was spent trying to locate one. We now had half the time available to present our credentials and to answer questions. Again, to our astonishment, at least one, possibly two members of HP's staff appeared to have their eyes closed during the presentation, perhaps having dozed off. After we left the presentation, the three of us at AM+A agreed that we had never witnessed such a sham interview. We were never called upon subsequently to join the recommended list of vendors.

At a later time, we were informed that HP had begun a new worldwide system for hiring vendors for projects that involved a reverse-auction bidding for positions, projects, and locations. I discovered that in such an auction, all bidders could see the latest (anonymously posted) figures for bids of hourly rates and decide if they could go lower. This system was designed to drive down the rates of all bidders on all projects. We tried but failed to win any positions. I tried a few more times, and on the last cycle, even bid at enormously reduced rates, just to see if I could win one or more of the competitions. I actually did, but then HP never called us. When I contacted the bid organizers, they mentioned that "other factors" were included to decide about who would be selected. I had never in my professional life encountered such a seemingly idiosyncratic and erratic approach to selecting vendors, who would most likely be the least experienced and the least qualified. During those years, HP suffered greatly in the marketplace and experienced high-level corporate shake-ups. It all seemed to go hand in hand with the decline of what had been a good client relationship, to what had been previously a respected client in decades past.

Commodore Amiga, 1984–1985

In 1984, user-interface designs for most computers were simple and flat, that is, two-dimensional. Commodore Amiga, considered by industry experts to be the leading game machine of the time, invited us to consult with their software developers and to prepare an approximately 50-page visual design analysis with recommended redesigns for a new user interface of the Commodore Amiga.

AM+A wanted to design something innovative, even within the restrictions of current technology. We were fortunate to have this opportunity. One feature of the design was simple, but novel. The software could move pixels around the screen in a two-dimensional array, but we realized three-dimensions could be conveyed by depicting realistic-looking but simple visual imagery in isometric views. A rectangular box shape could be viewed with a front face and two of its sides receding back in space along a fixed angle of 30 or 45°. This means of depiction was familiar to me from my years of teaching in architecture schools/departments. We decided to use this approach to depict a *work desk* and *drawers* that could be opened to access *tools*. These objects are all visual metaphors for functions and data stored in the computer. At the time, there was nothing like it in the industry, only the two-dimensional imagery familiar to those who remember Pac-Man's flat imagery and action.

We were delighted to learn that Mr. Martin Przybylski, Assistant General Manager, and others of the development staff were pleased with our designs. However, the project was not to be realized. At the last moment, the programmers ran out of time to install the new bit-mapped imagery of our designs. Instead, they released a major new version with the old user-interface imagery in place. Our designs were confined to the dustbin of history. Sigh. So it has been sometimes, when erratic, unforeseen events have thwarted our attempts to innovate and to achieve the quality for which we strived. I am sure other design firms encountered similar exasperating and frustrating moments. Well, at least we had the satisfaction of knowing we were among the first to envision three-dimensional user interfaces for computer systems (Figs. 7.30 and 7.31).

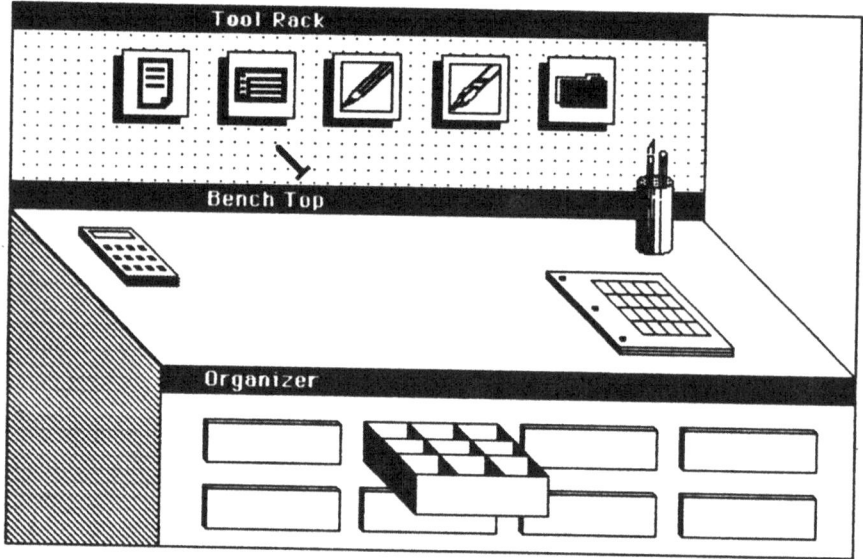

Figs. 7.30 and 7.31 View of AM+A's isometric depictions of the Commodore Amiga desktop imagery, 1984–1985. (Source: AM+A archives. Used with permission of author)

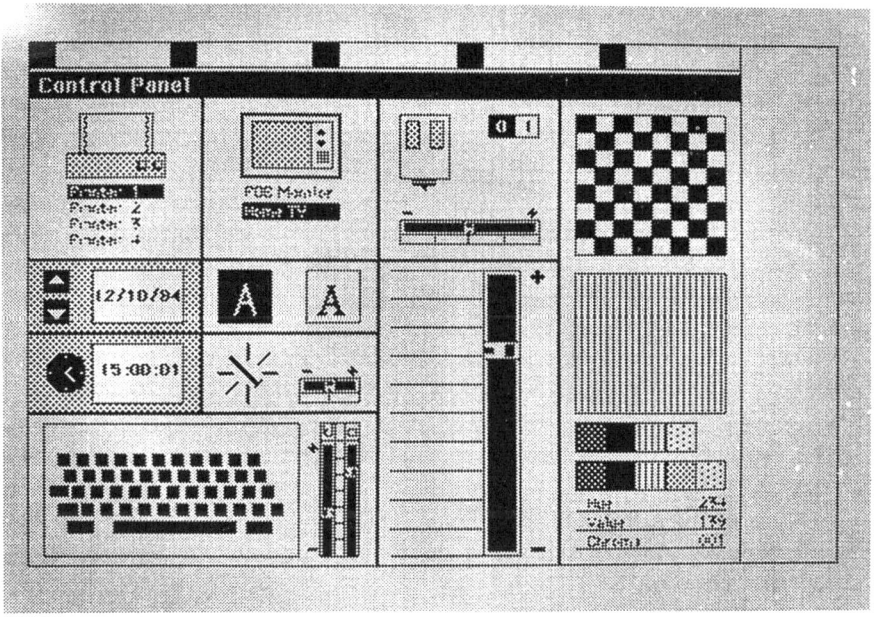

Figs. 7.30 and 7.31   (continued)

Summary Statement About the Early 1980s

Those were wild and crazy days, full of hope, promise, and fast progress. Doors seemed to open wherever I pushed.

I met many people who were friendly, interested, and engaging, and I spent many hours talking about philosophy, design, and technology.

Among others whom I met was Jaron Lanier, who now lives about seven minutes from my house in Berkeley, California, where he keeps about 1000 musical instruments that he claims to be able to play. He gained sudden fame by preparing for the May 1984 cover of *Scientific American* a depiction of a visual programming language. He became a pioneer of virtual reality. He proclaimed at some point when I spoke with him on the streets of Berkeley in the 1980s or 1990s that he envisioned virtual reality (VR) user interfaces that would not need any symbols or icons. Everything would be direct manipulation and/or maybe voice commands (like Nicholas Negroponte's and Bolt's MIT Architecture Machine Group Project: "Move that there." I voiced my dissenting opinion at the time that all human civilization had been based on communication with abstract signs, with metaphors, and that they would not be going away in future VR worlds. In fact, Verner Vinge's (RIP) significant science-fiction novel *True Names* proposed many such images being used to represent data, people, concepts, etc.

Another person I was fortunate to meet in the 1980s was Ted Nelson, the inventor of hypertext. In 1960, he founded Project Xanadu with the objective of creating a computer network with a simple user interface. Project Xanadu was to be a world-wide electronic publishing system that would use hypertext linking to create a universal library. In 1963 he coined the terms "hypertext" and "hypermedia." In 1974 he wrote and published two books in one, *Computer Lib/Dream Machines*, a copy of which I had in my library. They were considered "the most important book in the history of new media." Sadly, his grand ideas from the 1960s and 1970s never became completed projects. I met him at a SIGGRAPH conference, I think, in Texas. At that time, we talked long and hard, and I loved every minute. A few years later, I was able to convince Xerox PARC's SIGCHI Bay Area group meeting to feature Ted and me for an evening's debate on most everything. It was a lively exchange…but we were never asked back as far as I know.

Another person I met in those years was the late Jack Stoufacher, a noted San Francisco traditional typographer, graphic designer, and printer, featured in a Letterform Archive monograph edited by another friend, Chuck Byrne. Jack and I decided to gather at the Stanford Design conference for an evening to discuss the past, present, and future of typography, printing, and graphic design. Jack and I had a grand time. He represented the past. I represented the future. We discussed matters sipping glasses of wine on stage. Again, we thought the evening went well, but we were never invited back!

1985–1990

Microelectronics and Computer Technology Consortium (MCC), 1985–1990

During 1985–1990, AM+A was privileged to work with extremely smart software and hardware engineers at the Microelectronics and Computer Technology Consortium (MCC), in Austin, Texas, a long-term research group set up by Admiral Bobby Inman, with the objective of beating Japanese researchers in developing next-generation computer systems. US software researchers were very worried that Japan would jump ahead of the USA. MCC was the first, and for a time, one of the largest computer-industry research-and-development consortia in the USA. Large corporations paid many millions of dollars to support MCC and sent their advanced research staff (who typically worked 3–5 years ahead of commercial development) to work with the MCC staff on projects even further out (5–15 years ahead). Supporters included NCR, Digital Equipment Corporation (DEC), and Motorola.

The multiple sources of funding and levels of corporate secrecy/intellectual property protection produced the odd result that two workers in adjacent cubicles might not be able to talk about and share information about their respective projects because of separate nondisclosure agreements (NDAs).

We worked with all of MCC's five departments: Human Interface (HI), Database Systems, CAD/CAM (computer-aided design and manufacturing), Knowledge

Engineering, and Artificial Intelligence. I was so excited to be in MCC's new, white, high-tech building, that I was ready to leave Berkeley. Fortunately, I didn't. MCC came to an end in about 2000. At the time, many people were leaving San Francisco and Silicon Valley because of the traffic and high cost of living. They emigrated to Austin and brought, eventually, heavy traffic and a higher cost of living to Austin.

Among some of our projects, I mention a few:

Knowledge Engineering

We worked with researchers in knowledge engineering to visualize cognitive spaces more effectively and to visualize knowledge links of entities and relationships, including forward and backward chains of reasoning.

A famous computer science researcher Doug Lenat headed one of the groups in knowledge engineering. He and his co-workers were busy for many years on the CYC project, for which they attempted to create a computer system with all the knowledge of a newborn baby. Again, we helped their team by visualizing the user interfaces more effectively, particularly special tasks of knowledge visualization.

Human Interface Group

For the HI Group, we helped with a number of their projects in similar ways, consulting with them and advising them about how they could improve their user interfaces and information visualizations.

One project we worked on was making initial designs of multimedia workstations before there were ever such workstations. We designed sketches for hardware setups as well as user-interface designs. We commissioned from the composer David Gray short original musical compositions for what we thought would be useful: musical themes associated with specific applications, tools, states of operation, advancing the ideas of Bill Gaver who created sounds for the Apple Macintosh user interface (1989) and Meera Blattner, who invented the concept of earcons.

We also introduced the ideas of iconic faces to indicate data in large date depictions, using faces-in-the-crowd recognition abilities of the human visual system. This was somewhat related to Chernoff's research in using faces to depict data.

One unusual opportunity to assist, probably late in 1989, arose when the director of the Human Interface group had to make a major presentation to their corporate backers, members of advanced research groups at major companies. Just before the presentation week, I was asked to review all the slides of the presentations to these funders. The overhead slides seemed messy, cluttered, too dense, and potentially confusing. I had the rare opportunity to suggest/draw improvements for all the slides, even renaming projects so that they made better sense. The presentations went well, and the director thanked me for my efforts.

CAD/CAM Group

For the CAD/CAM group, we were assigned to attend major CAD/CAM conferences in the USA as observers and to gather information about what seemed to be the latest trends, what were the problems on which major developers focused, and what end-customers seemed to want. We reported our findings to the advanced R&D group at MCC and assisted them with tasks of best depicting user interfaces and complex information visualizations.

Unfortunately, almost all our work was classified as confidential, and we were not allowed to publish articles or images of what we had done. Consequently, other researchers, for example, at Xerox PARC, were able to publish and take credit for ideas that we had already explored in our projects with MCC. Such is life with advanced R&D projects (Figs. 7.32–7.34).

Figs. 7.32–7.34 Example images of advanced multimedia workstation ideas sketched by AM+A in 1989. (Source: AM+A Archives. Used with permission of the author)

Figure 7A: Sketch Idea for the Layout of an Encyclopedia Page

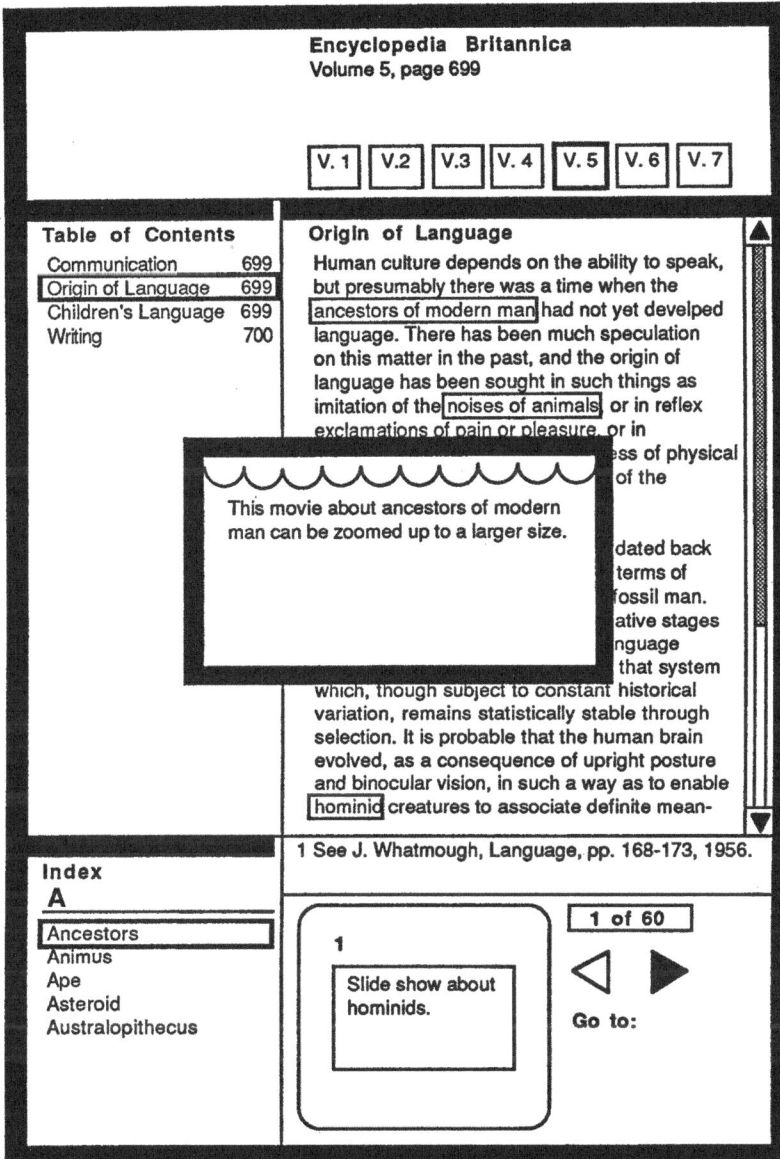

This electronic, multi-media encyclopedia page has a movie and a slide show that can be activated by selecting a text object (outlined text, which could actually be a color coded box to indicate the media type). Both the movie and the slide show can be zoomed up to a larger viewing size if desired. The heavy outline boxes around text serve as visual reinforcement of a verbal request.

Figs. 7.32–7.34 (continued)

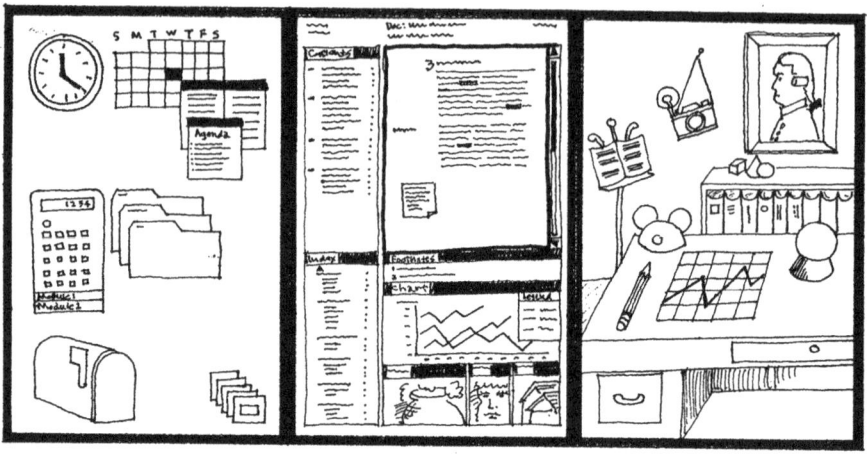

Figs. 7.32–7.34 (continued)

Scitex, 1986

In 1986, I learned about a new Israeli company called Scitex created by a very smart, very self-confident former military man, Effi Arazi. His graphic-arts editing and production product was superior to then leading products coming out of Germany and elsewhere. Many people in the printing professions were very impressed. I heard amazing stories about him: like the one about how he finished his military service in Israel and decided he wanted to study at MIT. He simply flew from Israel to Cambridge, Massachusetts, and walked into the administration offices and announced that he was here now and would like to begin studying. People were astonished at his *chutzpah* (cheeky bravado). Because of his military/engineering record and the force of his personality, I was told that he broke down administrators' complaints about not following protocol, and he was admitted without going through the regular admissions process.

I discovered in 1986 that he was in San Francisco, and I called him and told him I thought we should meet to discuss our improving his products' user interface design (being a little *chutzpadik*, also). He agreed! Nervously, I dressed in a business suit, brought along our work portfolio, and drove to his San Francisco hotel. When his hotel room door opened, he was dressed only in a towel around his waist. He had just stepped out of the shower. Astonished, and amused, I sat down to talk with him and show him some of our work. Amazingly, within about an hour, he agreed that we should work for him, and he wanted to fly me to Israel. I could not have been happier.

That meeting began a relationship for about a year in which we worked with his key software and UI developers to improve the screen layouts of his software. His offices in Herzeliyah were modern, clean, and elegant. They looked exactly like what the best of Silicon Valley (Cupertino) or Route 128 (Boston) high-tech offices would be like, and better than most. It was a privilege and an honor to be able to work with him and his staff for a period of time (Figs. 7.35–7.37).

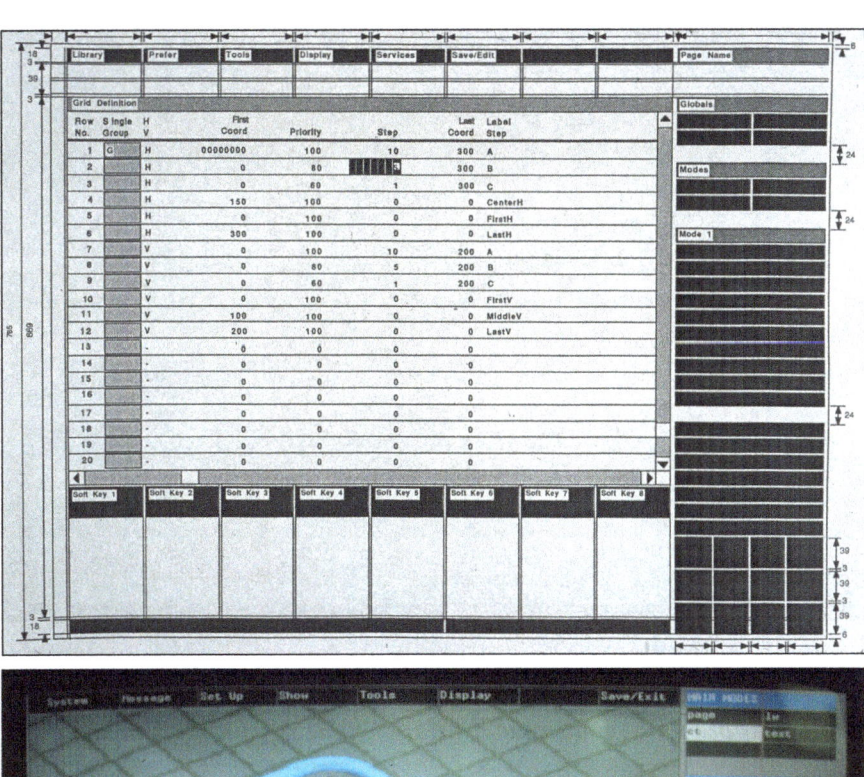

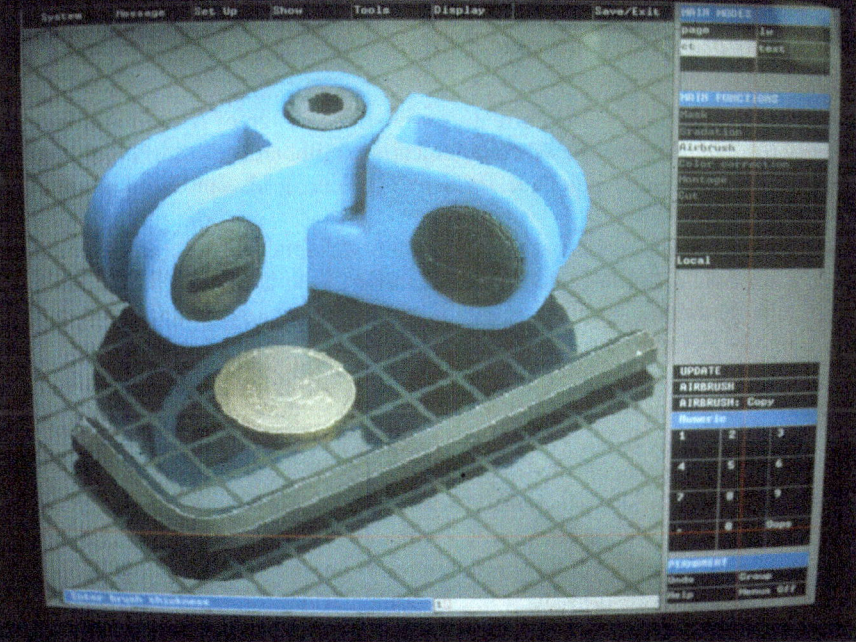

Figs. 7.35–7.37 Screen layout images in Fig. 7.35 for an improved Scitex workstation user interface. We had to calculate very clearly, completely, and carefully how many pixels the deep menus would require at a maximum of depth to make sure the grid had room for all menus across and down. (Source: AM+A archive; used with permission of author)

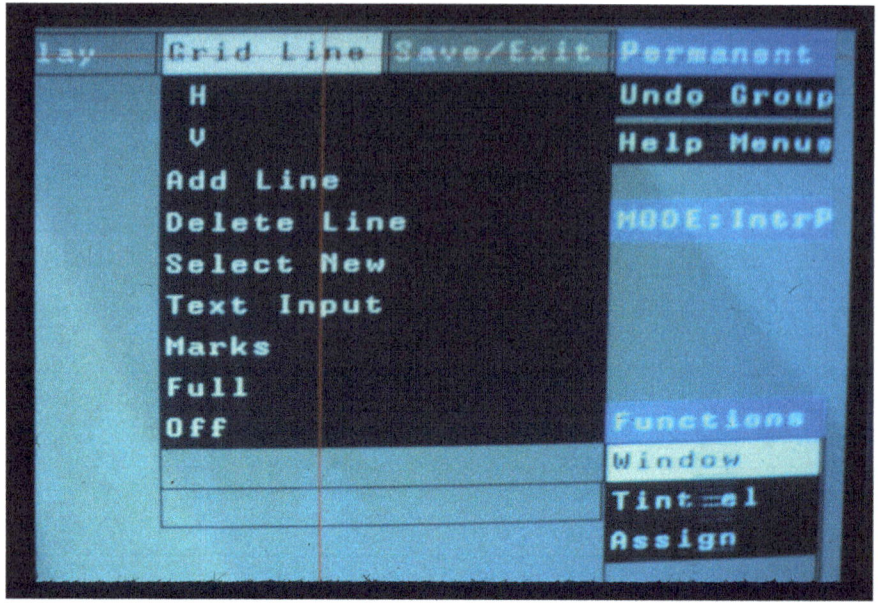

Figs. 7.35–7.37   (continued)

Apple's Apple-Link Personal Edition, 1988, Which Became AOL

In 1988, AM+A critiqued the current user-interface design of Apple's Apple-Link, an early form of computer-based communication (billboards, messages, etc.) among users. AM+A provided guidance for screen layout, grids, and icon design (see Figs. 7.38 and 7.39).

Based on the success of that review, AM+A was retained to serve as the design guide for Apple's Apple-Link Personal Edition, a unique joint venture between Apple and Quantum Computer Services, based in Vienna, Virginia. It was Apple's first joint development project with another company. AM+A was thought of as "design police" (and were so-named in an article published around that time), because we had to provide quick prototype design solutions to software developers under the leadership of Mr. Trevor Griffiths, Manager, Apple Engineering.

After the project was finished, Apple decided to abandon the project and released the software to Quantum, which in 1991 was renamed America Online (AOL). This company became a major entry in US technology history. AM+A's icon designs were used in the earliest editions of AOL until its own designers eventually replaced them with their own designs (see Figs. 7.40 and 7.41).

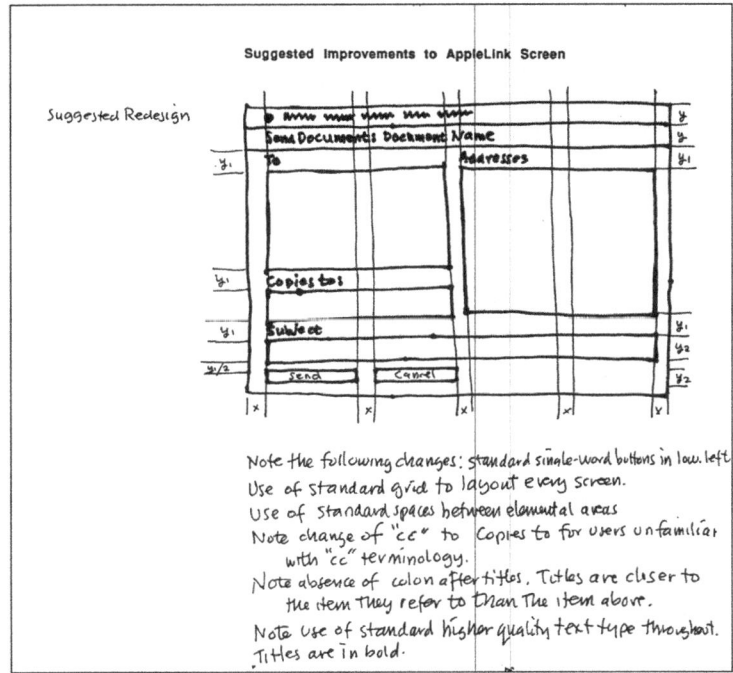

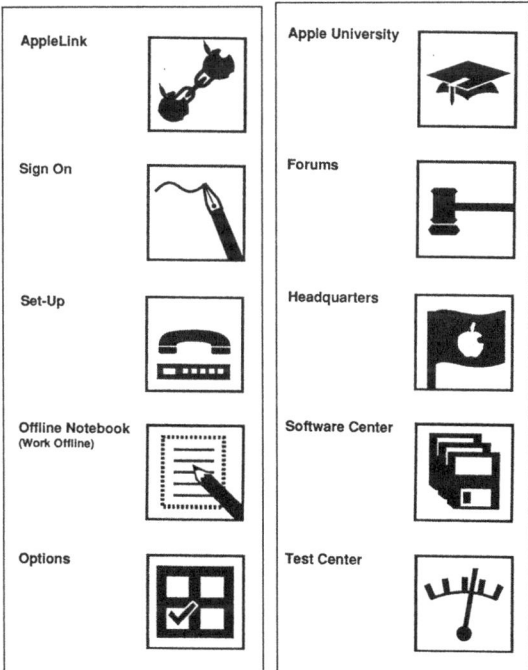

Figs. 7.38 and 7.39 Examples from AM+A's report to Apple, 1988. (Source: AM+A archive; used with permission of Apple)

Example of AM+A-recommended stacked, organized windows to be depicted on the screen, instead of more disorganized layouts:

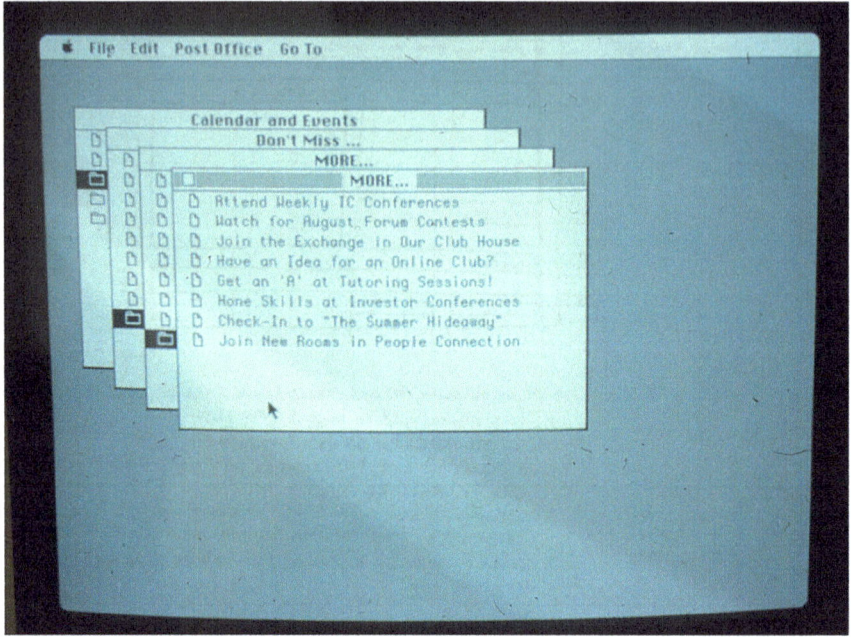

AM+A-designed improved icons for Apple Link screens:

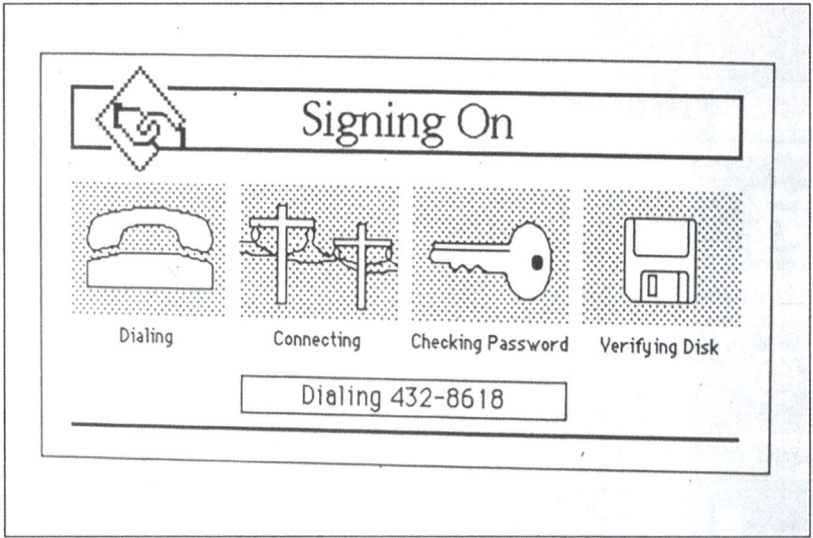

Figs. 7.40 and 7.41 AM+A icons and screen layout of Apple-Link Personal Edition that were adopted into the earliest versions of AOL. (Source: AM+A archive; Images designed by AM+A; used with permission of Apple)

Eastman Kodak Company: Design of a Common User-Interface Design (CUID) for KIMS, KEEPS, Atex, and Eikonix, 1987–1988

In 1987–1988, Dr. Daniel Rosenberg, Project Manager, Human Factors Department of Eastman Kodak, hired AM+A to assist in preparing a report showing the advantages of a common user-interface design for four document editing and management products, some of which had been developed in-house at Kodak, while others had been purchased from other companies: KIMS, KEEPS, Atex, and Eikonix.

The New York Times reported in 1985 that Eastman Kodak Company said that it would acquire "the Eikonix Corporation for $16.12 a share, or a total of about $56.3 million." Eikonix, which made digital image-processing equipment and optical systems, would be operated as a Kodak subsidiary, retaining its name and management, the company said. Analysts said the acquisition was part of Kodak's campaign to reduce its dependence on its traditional photography business, which has been stagnant in recent years. They said that Kodak's strengths had been in chemical-based imaging systems and that the Eikonix purchase would enable the company to enhance its expertise in electronic imaging. In the last year Kodak had expanded its production of floppy disks for computers and had entered the long-distance telephone business on a limited basis. (Source: https://www.nytimes.com/1985/03/21/business/eastman-kodak-getting-eikonix.html).

In 1986, *"The New York Times* reported that the Eastman Kodak Company said it would combine Atex Inc. and Eikonix Inc. to form a new unit, Electronic Pre-Press Systems, that would focus on high-volume electronic publishing applications. Atex made computer terminals and word-processing systems for newspapers and magazines, and Eikonix designed and made digital-image process equipment and computer-aided electro-optical systems. Both companies were based in Bedford, Mass., and would continue to operate as independent subsidiaries, Kodak said." (Source: https://www.nytimes.com/1986/12/02/business/company-news-kodak-to-merge-atex-and-eikonix.html).

In order to get the budget and the go-ahead for our project, Dr. Rosenberg had to gather information about the "true" cost of developing software, including the user interface. Such information was hard to acquire from corporate groups who wanted to protect the information about their costs. Nevertheless, Dr. Rosenberg was able to show that user-interface designs were becoming increasingly complex and that the cost of developing user interfaces was dramatically increasing. By re-using about 20% of the code (and UI parts), it appeared that the development costs could be recovered in about five products.

For this project, AM+A designed the complete look-and-feel for the products and wrote (together with an editor at Kodak) a window-management user-interface design document of about 300 pages. The design standards covered screen layout, typography, symbolism, and color. Kodak was so pleased with the project that they printed a four-page brochure about the project, which Kodak and AM+A co-presented at an informal presentation at SIGCHI's CHI-1988. The gathering attracted approximately 150 professionals from across the industry. The interim CUID schema was to be incorporated into an interactive prototype to be built with the Kodak rapid prototyping system in use at the Human Factors Department of Kodak.

One interesting footnote is that the legal department of Kodak would not allow the familiar red Kodak K sign, part of their corporate identity at the time, to appear on screens, because attorneys felt the screen resolution was so "poor" that it would diminish the quality of the Kodak corporate design standards (even though the screens were state-of-the-art and highest resolution at the time, about 100 dpi). We were disappointed. At a CHI conference shortly after this decision was handed down, I encountered Kodak equipment displays on the exhibit floor of the conference. There I beheld the Kodak K being used on screens. I asked the Kodak exhibit representatives (who were Kodak engineers) how they were able to get permission to use the Kodak K. They laughed and said they never asked; as software programmers, they felt they could do whatever they wanted and whatever they thought was best!

For the CUID, Dan Rosenberg (Kodak), Joy Underhill (Underhill Associates), and I (AM+A) co-wrote and AM+A illustrated a 300-page user-interface document that described the complete windowing system. This publication appeared just before the computer industry settled on some stable windowing systems like OpenLook and Motif after considering the X1 windowing system from MIT. It was a dramatic time with major revolutionary changes in the computer industry regarding how software information was going to be displayed.

1990

Apple Computer, Inc.: Market Activities Database User-Interface Design, May 1990

In May 1990, AM+A recommended redesigns for Apple's Market Activities Database (MAD) and provided assistance in the development and implementation of screen displays and page displays, assisted in the development of effective user documentation, and assisted in promoting future development and extensions of the MAD project. AM+A produced a Compendium of Figures to be used in conjunction with the MAD Human Interface Design Report. The compendium provided Before and After versions of the revised screen and page displays for easy reference. The accompanying figures of the revised screen and page displays show how AM+A used a familiar newspaper metaphor (headlines, sections, articles, etc.) to display different sections of content to assist users in navigating the content (Figs. 7.42–7.45).

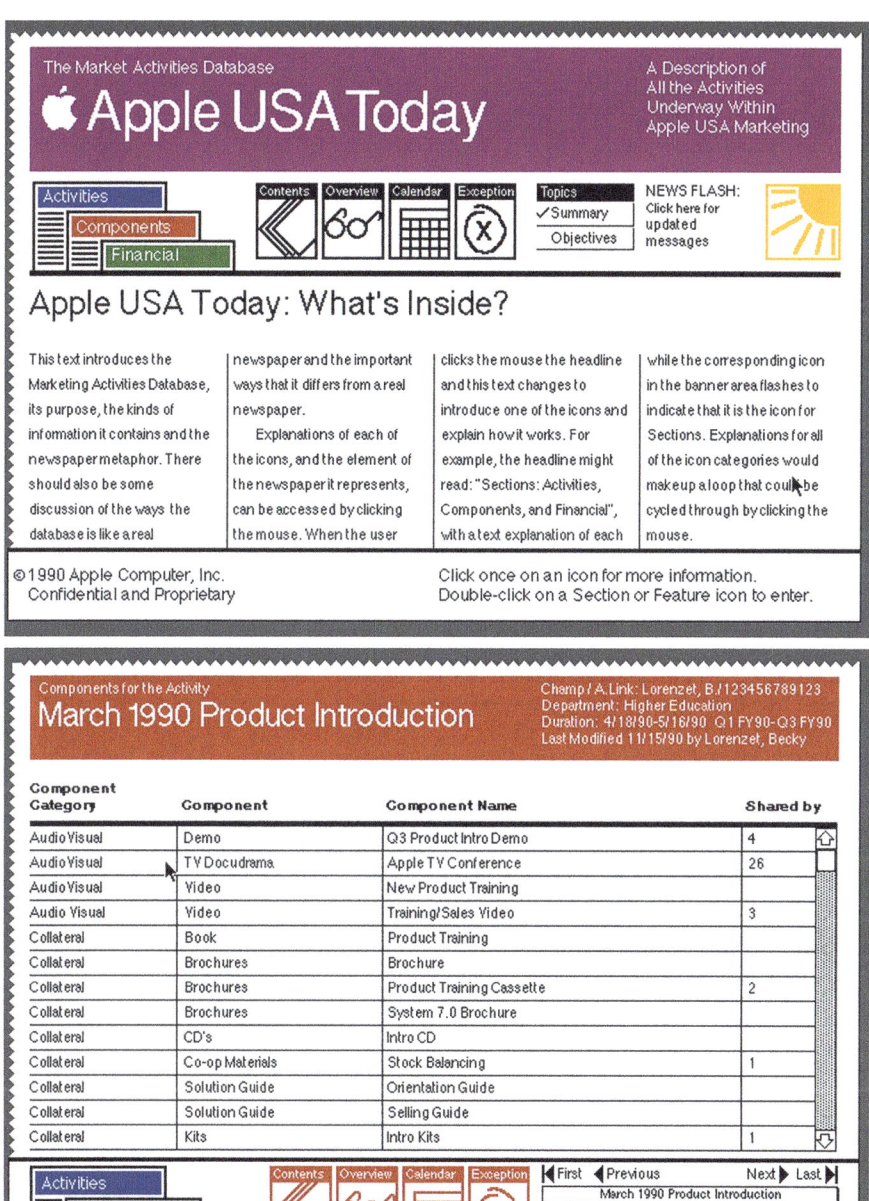

Figs. 7.42–7.45 Examples of AM+A's designs for Apple's Market Activities Database screens, 1990. (Source: AM+A archives. Images designed by AM+A; used with permission of Apple)

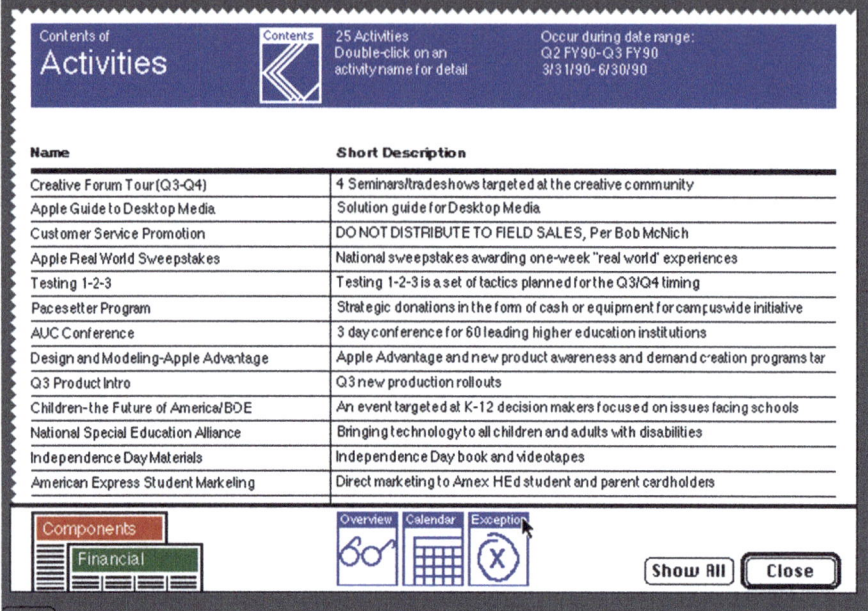

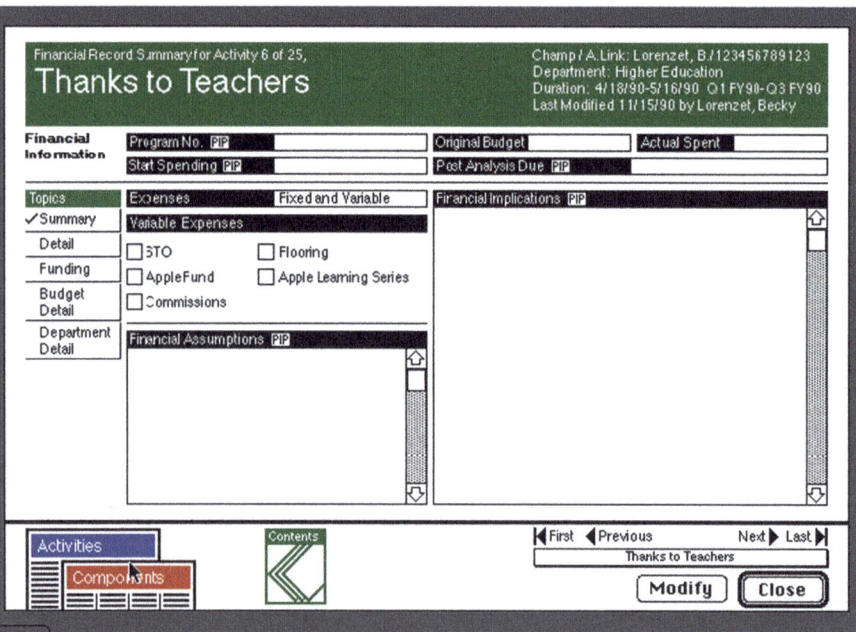

Figs. 7.42–7.45 (continued)

In October 1990, a neighbor had discovered that I was running a business out of my home and threatened to report me to the city. I decided it was time to move to an official business location, and I researched opportunities in Berkeley, Oakland, and nearby Emeryville. The story continues in the next chapter....

Bibliography

Baecker, Ron, and Marcus, Aaron (1983). "On enhancing the interface to the source code of computer programs," *CHI '83: Proceedings of the SIGCHI Conference on Human Factors in Computing Systems, December 1983*, pp. 251–255, https://doi.org/10.1145/800045.801621.

Bertin, Jacques (1967). *Semiology of Graphics*. Madison, WI, University of Wisconsin Press.

Chaparos, Ann, "Notes for a Federal Design Manual," Chaparos Productions, Washington, DC, 1981.

Eco, Umberto (1976). *A Theory of Semiotics*. Bloomington, IN: Indiana University Press.

Fertig, Scott; Freeman, Eric; and Gelernter David (1995). *"Lifestreams: An Alternative to the Desktop Metaphor."* CiteSeerXciteseerx.ist.psu.edu.

Gerstner, Carl, *Compendium for Literates*, MIT Press, Cambridge, 1978.

Hooper, James (2014). *Peirce on Signs: Writings on Semiotic by Charles Sanders Peirce*. Raleigh, NC: University of North Carolina Press. This anthology, the first one-volume work about Peirce's writings on semiotics, provides a basic introduction to the subject.

Innis, Robert E. (1985). *Semiotics: An Introductory Anthology*. Bloomington, IN: Indiana University Press.

Lakoff, George, and Johnson, Mark (1980). *Metaphors We Live By*. Chicago, IL: University of Chicago Press.

Levi-Strauss, Claude (1969). *The Raw and the Cooked*. Introduction to a Science of Mythology. Vol. 1. New York, NY: Harper and Row.

Marcus, Aaron (2002). "User-Interface Design and Culture Dimensions." *Proceedings of Internationalization Workshop, ACM SIGCHI CHI-2002*. Annual conference series, Minneapolis, MN.

Marcus, Aaron (2009). "Integrated Information Systems: A Professional Field for Information Designers." *Information Design Journal*, Vol. 17:1 (2009), pp. 4–21.

Marcus, Aaron (2015). *Mobile Persuasion Design*. London, Springer, pp. 1–11.

Marcus, Aaron, and Van Dam, Andries (1991). "User Interface Developments for the Nineties," *IEEE Computer*, Vol. 24, No. 9, September 1991, pp. 49–57.

Marcus, Aaron, and Ziegler, Juergen (1999). "Toward and Information Society for all: HCI Challenges and R&D Recommendations," *International Journal of HCI*, 11 (1).

Marshall, Lee, *Bookmaking: The Illustrated Guide to Design and Production*, R.R. Bowker, New York, 1965.

Pierce, Charles Sanders (1933–35). *Collected Papers of Charles Sanders Peirce*, Vol. I–VI, ed. By Harthorne and Weiss, Cambridge, MA: Harvard University Press.

Ruder, Emil, *Typographie*, Hastings House, Visual Communication Books, New York, 1973.

Chapter 8
Surviving the Recessions

Takeaways

AM+A moved out of my home into an office in 1990. We completed major projects for Hell Graphic Systems, Charles Schwab, Motorola, Apple, and Sabre. We were at the height of our strength and number of Associates.

1990–2003

In October 1990, I moved out of my home office, where AM+A had started in 1982, to our first official office in Emeryville, California, even then a growing high-tech center. Emeryville touted itself as a city that had the highest per-capita population of designer/artist studios of any city in the USA. Actually, the city had very little residential area, consisting of mostly warehouses, factories, businesses, etc. This "urblet" had carved itself out of land between Oakland and Berkeley.

I was thrilled at the prospect of two floors of space and 3000 square feet of floor area. I finally could design work areas that matched my design style: international, minimal, white surfaces, chromed steel, and professional. There was also much wall space for what became a collection of hundreds of masks in the reception area and my professional library which eventually housed about 15,000 publications, which I had been collecting all my life. We eventually had 18 employees, including myself, working there. In 1999, I opened a second office in lower Manhattan. For me, the era was one of growth and optimism.

In a sense, the creation of AM+A was my primary design and art project from 1982 and continuing for decades! The previous chapter and the ones following read somewhat like a list of project summaries. That is a necessary outcome of my work during this time. Each major client relationship, which usually lasted one month to seven years, required our absorbing enormous amounts of technical, customer, marketing, and logistics data from our clients. We sometimes knew more about a current project than the client's own staff! They knew they could trust us with much proprietary, secret data, with corporate ups and downs, and changes in their entire business organization.

Hell Graphic Systems (HGS), 1990

In 1990, Joel Friedman of Hell Graphic Systems (HGS) US office asked AM+A to assist in several ways to promote its products. Projects included the following:

- Marketing communications: AM+A prepared a Hell Color Service Bureau program and information kit for Hell Graphic Systems, Inc., including a poster overview kit, HCSB Seal for authorized service bureaus, color product identity, handouts, and a book cover for a customer-oriented book about HGS products for color printing.
- A large poster showing a comparison of traditional, desktop publishing, and HGS-based preparation of color documents. The objective was to show the superior characteristics of the HGS-based method.
- An interactive diskette-based display showing the contents of the large poster.
- Color leaflets showing key information about HGS Color Service Bureaus, which featured a focus on AM+A and its staff.

Unfortunately, just after all these materials were prepared and printed, HGS was bought by another company. The branding had to change, and distribution of all the materials was cancelled. We were dismayed at the outcome of all our work. Greg Galle, Designer/Analyst of AM+A, acted as senior designer and project manager for the project (Figs. 8.1–8.3, 8.4, 8.5, and 8.6).

Charles Schwab and Company, Inc.: Review of SAMS and Client Interface Architecture Documents, 1991–1993

During 1991–1993, at the invitation of Charles Schwab and Company, San Francisco, a noted investment firm, AM+A was asked by two key management staff to review a number of client applications and many Schwab Architecture Migration Strategy (SAMS) documents and to design a common user interface for all of Schwab's internal and some client-facing applications. This was an enormous and impressive assignment for which we were humbly grateful. Most of Schwab's computers were Microsoft Windows devices. AM+A reviewed many documents including: "Welcome to SAMS," "Guide to Developing Workbenches," "SAMS Implementation Strategy," and "Workbenches."

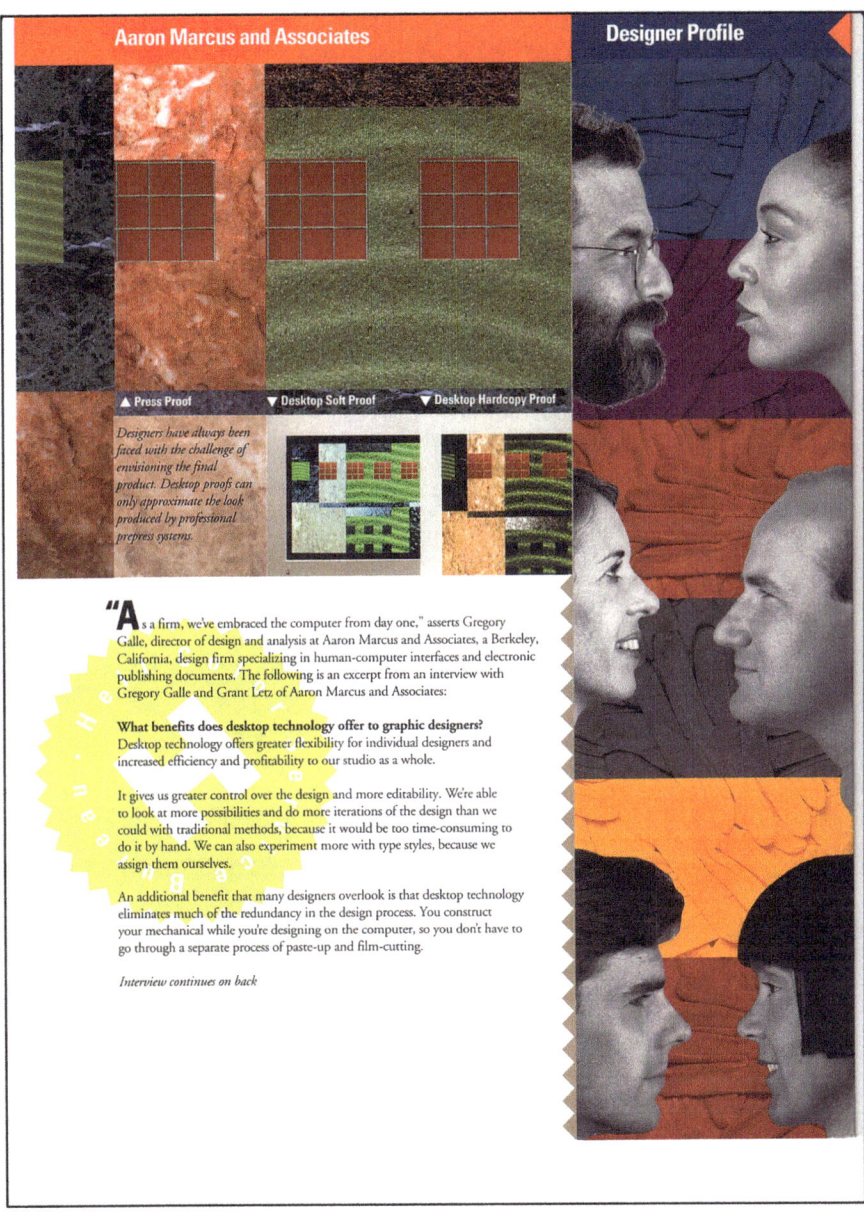

Aaron Marcus and Associates

Designer Profile

▲ Press Proof   ▼ Desktop Soft Proof   ▼ Desktop Hardcopy Proof

Designers have always been faced with the challenge of envisioning the final product. Desktop proofs can only approximate the look produced by professional prepress systems.

"As a firm, we've embraced the computer from day one," asserts Gregory Galle, director of design and analysis at Aaron Marcus and Associates, a Berkeley, California, design firm specializing in human-computer interfaces and electronic publishing documents. The following is an excerpt from an interview with Gregory Galle and Grant Letz of Aaron Marcus and Associates:

What benefits does desktop technology offer to graphic designers?
Desktop technology offers greater flexibility for individual designers and increased efficiency and profitability to our studio as a whole.

It gives us greater control over the design and more editability. We're able to look at more possibilities and do more iterations of the design than we could with traditional methods, because it would be too time-consuming to do it by hand. We can also experiment more with type styles, because we assign them ourselves.

An additional benefit that many designers overlook is that desktop technology eliminates much of the redundancy in the design process. You construct your mechanical while you're designing on the computer, so you don't have to go through a separate process of paste-up and film-cutting.

Interview continues on back

Figs. 8.1–8.3 Brochure and leaflets written and designed by AM+A for Hell Graphic Systems, c. 1992. (Source: AM+A archives; used with permission of the author)

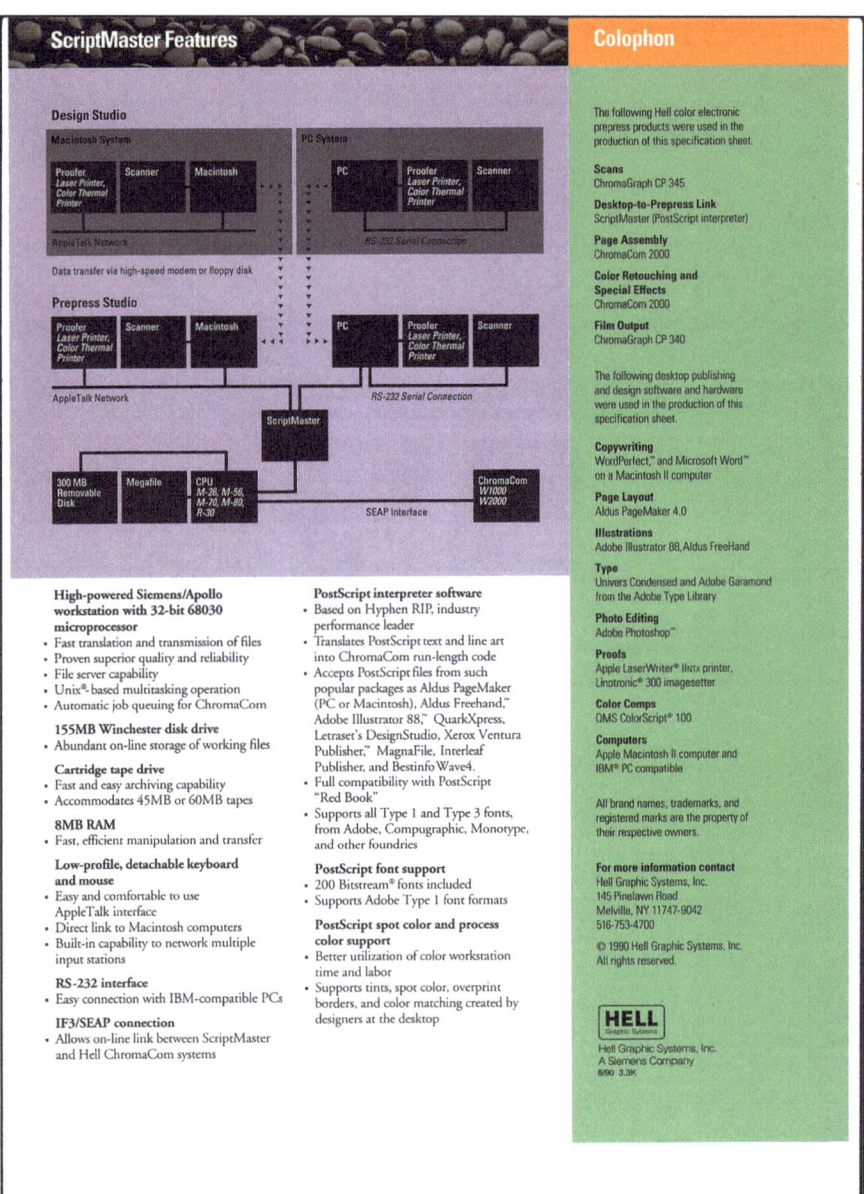

ScriptMaster Features

Design Studio

High-powered Siemens/Apollo workstation with 32-bit 68030 microprocessor
- Fast translation and transmission of files
- Proven superior quality and reliability
- File server capability
- Unix®-based multitasking operation
- Automatic job queuing for ChromaCom

155MB Winchester disk drive
- Abundant on-line storage of working files

Cartridge tape drive
- Fast and easy archiving capability
- Accommodates 45MB or 60MB tapes

8MB RAM
- Fast, efficient manipulation and transfer

Low-profile, detachable keyboard and mouse
- Easy and comfortable to use AppleTalk interface
- Direct link to Macintosh computers
- Built-in capability to network multiple input stations

RS-232 interface
- Easy connection with IBM-compatible PCs

IF3/SEAP connection
- Allows on-line link between ScriptMaster and Hell ChromaCom systems

PostScript interpreter software
- Based on Hyphen RIP, industry performance leader
- Translates PostScript text and line art into ChromaCom run-length code
- Accepts PostScript files from such popular packages as Aldus PageMaker (PC or Macintosh), Aldus Freehand," Adobe Illustrator 88," QuarkXpress, Letraset's DesignStudio, Xerox Ventura Publisher," MagnaFile, Interleaf Publisher, and Bestinfo Wave4.
- Full compatibility with PostScript "Red Book"
- Supports all Type 1 and Type 3 fonts, from Adobe, Compugraphic, Monotype, and other foundries

PostScript font support
- 200 Bitstream® fonts included
- Supports Adobe Type 1 font formats

PostScript spot color and process color support
- Better utilization of color workstation time and labor
- Supports tints, spot color, overprint borders, and color matching created by designers at the desktop

Colophon

The following Hell color electronic prepress products were used in the production of this specification sheet.

Scans
ChromaGraph CP 345

Desktop-to-Prepress Link
ScriptMaster (PostScript interpreter)

Page Assembly
ChromaCom 2000

Color Retouching and Special Effects
ChromaCom 2000

Film Output
ChromaGraph CP 340

The following desktop publishing and design software and hardware were used in the production of this specification sheet.

Copywriting
WordPerfect," and Microsoft Word" on a Macintosh II computer

Page Layout
Aldus PageMaker 4.0

Illustrations
Adobe Illustrator 88, Aldus FreeHand

Type
Univers Condensed and Adobe Garamond from the Adobe Type Library

Photo Editing
Adobe Photoshop"

Proofs
Apple LaserWriter® IInrx printer, Linotronic® 300 imagesetter

Color Comps
QMS ColorScript® 100

Computers
Apple Macintosh II computer and IBM® PC compatible

All brand names, trademarks, and registered marks are the property of their respective owners.

For more information contact
Hell Graphic Systems, Inc.
145 Pinelawn Road
Melville, NY 11747-9042
516-753-4700

© 1990 Hell Graphic Systems, Inc.
All rights reserved.

HELL
Graphic Systems

Hell Graphic Systems, Inc.
A Siemens Company
8/90 3.3K

Figs. 8.1–8.3 (continued)

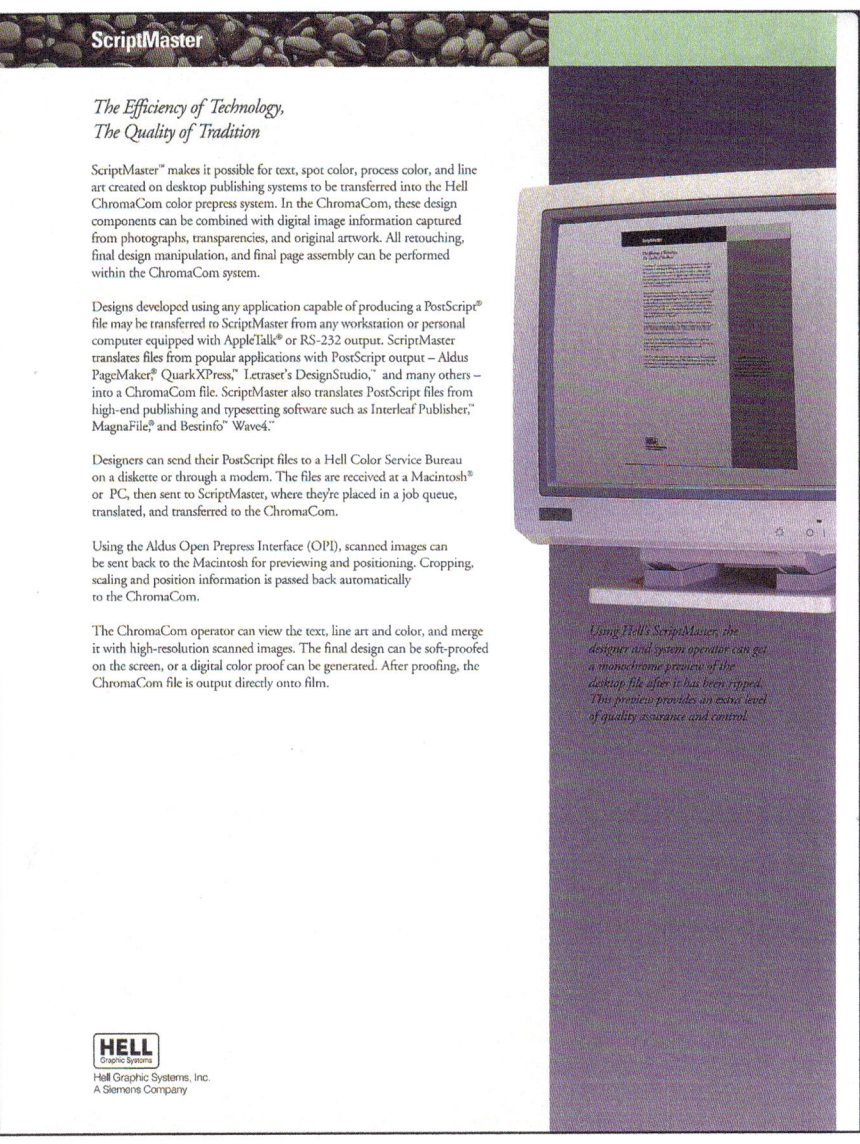

ScriptMaster

The Efficiency of Technology,
The Quality of Tradition

ScriptMaster™ makes it possible for text, spot color, process color, and line art created on desktop publishing systems to be transferred into the Hell ChromaCom color prepress system. In the ChromaCom, these design components can be combined with digital image information captured from photographs, transparencies, and original artwork. All retouching, final design manipulation, and final page assembly can be performed within the ChromaCom system.

Designs developed using any application capable of producing a PostScript® file may be transferred to ScriptMaster from any workstation or personal computer equipped with AppleTalk® or RS-232 output. ScriptMaster translates files from popular applications with PostScript output – Aldus PageMaker,® QuarkXPress,™ Letraset's DesignStudio,™ and many others – into a ChromaCom file. ScriptMaster also translates PostScript files from high-end publishing and typesetting software such as Interleaf Publisher,™ MagnaFile,® and Bestinfo™ Wave4.™

Designers can send their PostScript files to a Hell Color Service Bureau on a diskette or through a modem. The files are received at a Macintosh® or PC, then sent to ScriptMaster, where they're placed in a job queue, translated, and transferred to the ChromaCom.

Using the Aldus Open Prepress Interface (OPI), scanned images can be sent back to the Macintosh for previewing and positioning. Cropping, scaling and position information is passed back automatically to the ChromaCom.

The ChromaCom operator can view the text, line art and color, and merge it with high-resolution scanned images. The final design can be soft-proofed on the screen, or a digital color proof can be generated. After proofing, the ChromaCom file is output directly onto film.

Using Hell's ScriptMaster, the
designer and system operator can get
a monochrome preview of the
desktop file after it has been ripped.
This preview provides an exact level
of quality assurance and control.

HELL
Graphic Systems

Hell Graphic Systems, Inc.
A Siemens Company

Figs. 8.1–8.3 (continued)

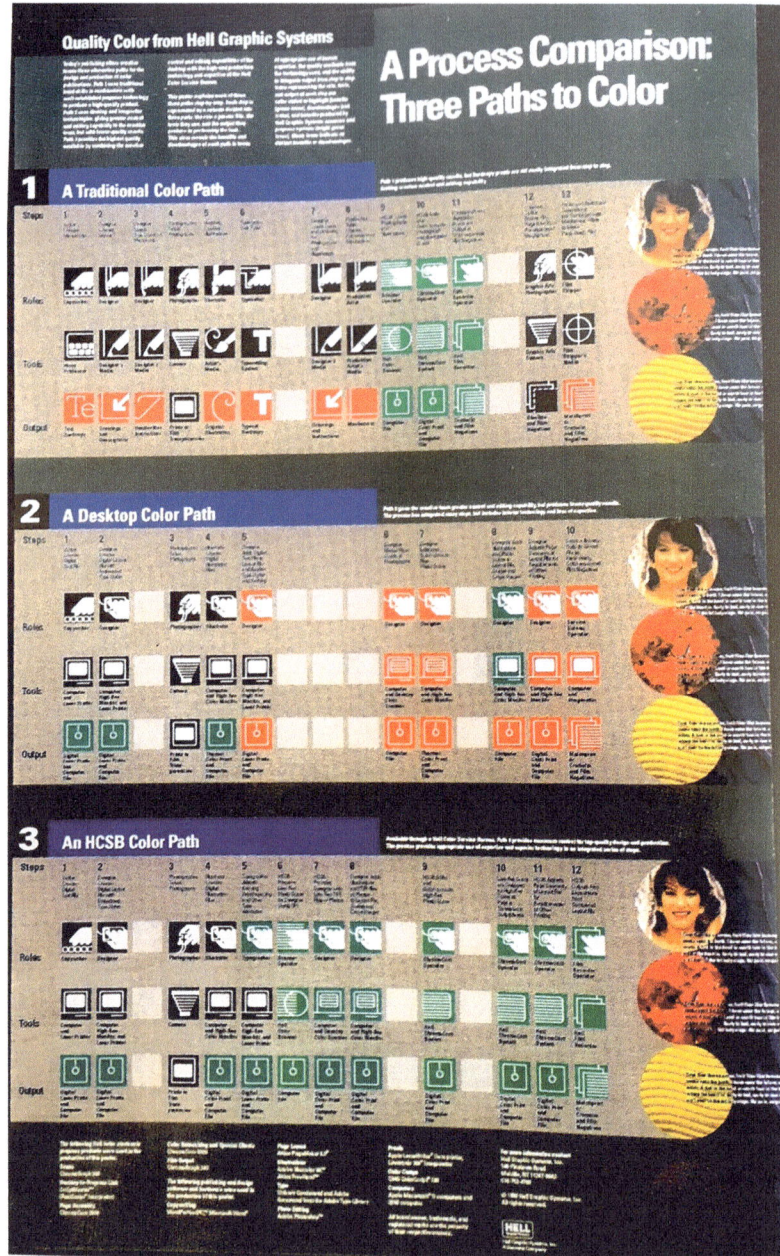

Fig. 8.4 Poster explaining and comparing three different means to achieve printed color documents, researched, written, and designed by AM+A for HGS, c. 1992. This project was very satisfying to work on. I had never seen a comparison of printing processes quite like the one we designed, and it was especially gratifying to enable viewers/readers to cross-compare the three processes; I was personally familiar with all three. I was glad we could use simple, clear forceful icons, which were designed for AM+A by one of our contractors. The following figure shows the screen adaptation of the poster as an interactive file. (Source: AM+A archives; used with permission of AM+A)

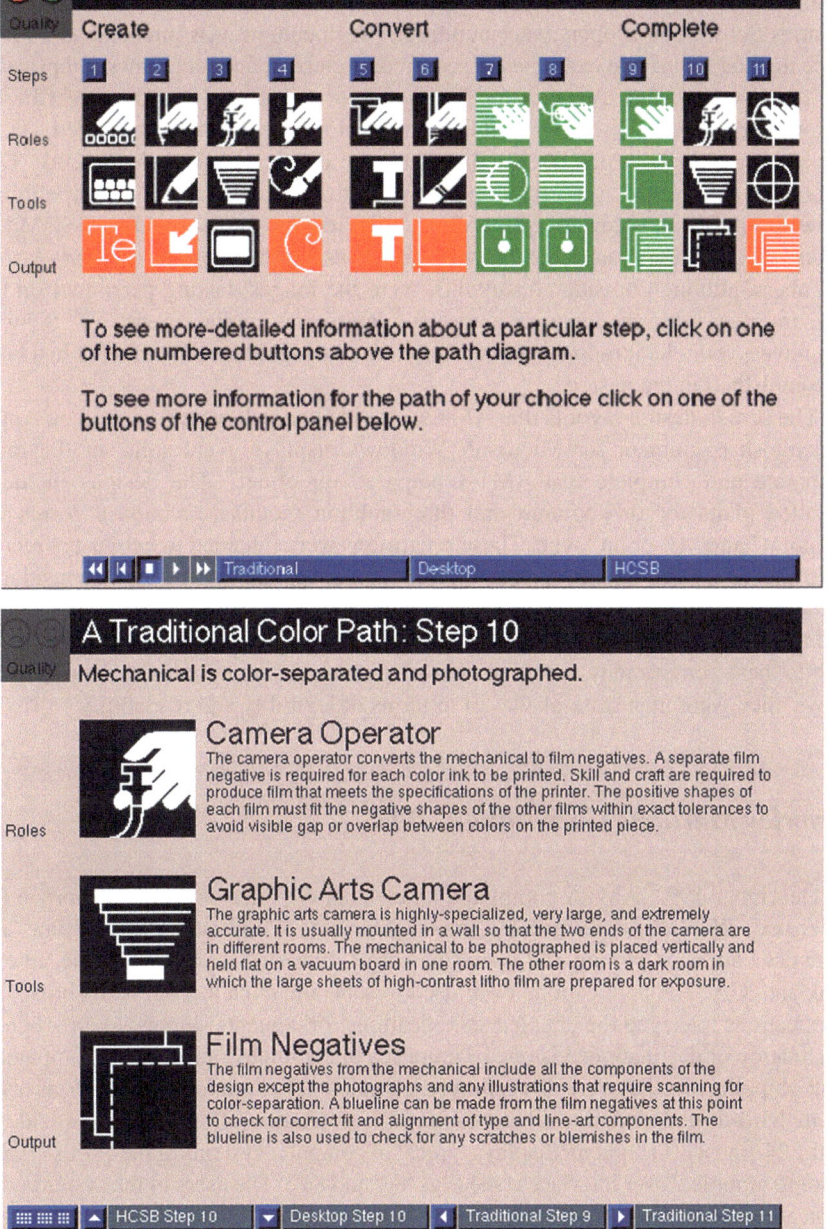

Figs. 8.5 and 8.6 Screen images from the interactive version of the poster explaining and comparing three different means to achieve printed color documents, written, designed, and scripted by AM+A for HGS, c. 1992. The icons looked good on the screen at this scale as well as on the printed high-resolution poster. The interactive controls made it easy to step through the processes and to compare the different solutions offered by each of the three technologies. (Source: AM+A archive; used with permission of the author)

AM+A then developed detailed rules and recommendations for the SAMS graphical user interface (GUI) for Microsoft Windows-based applications that Charles Schwab developers were building. The document was intended as a reference manual to provide examples of required, preferred, and recommended practice for the User Interface Architecture Team, a core group, and members of Charles Schwab development (software engineering) teams. The document provided a basis for shorter guidelines for developers that were quick, practical documents. This document also served as a transition document that would encourage compatibility between applications developed for Microsoft Windows and, eventually, OSF Motif, another windowing system, which was being considered. At one point, AM+A staff members, although outside consultants, were the longest-lasting personnel on the user-interface design team. Because of numerous replacements of Schwab employees, our client representatives turned to us for guidance about what had been accomplished in the past!

The screen design layouts that AM+A provided, which were designed on Apple Macintosh equipment for Microsoft Windows displays, were some of the most elaborate and complete that AM+A prepared for clients. The designs included detailed plans for two-column and three-column modular layouts of forms for "9-point" and "10-point" type. These repetitions were intended to help users recognize and keep track of similar and different content groups. AM+A also considered the depiction of data and data labels to promote legibility and readability. Numerical fields were usually flush-right text; alphanumeric fields were usually flush-left. While these screens may seem "primitive" in comparison to today's computer displays, they were then state-of-the-art in terms of legibility and readability.

Crowley Maritime Corporation, 1992

In December 1992, AM+A completed an unusual GUI design task: to improve the Microsoft Windows screens for Crowley Maritime Corporation, a maritime and logistics company owning and operating cargo ships that was based at the time in Oakland, CA. The applications were used to schedule containers aboard ships. The applications managed the detailed specifications for contents shipped to a particular destination or destinations via one or more sea liners run by one or more companies. The shipping details were exceedingly complex. The original applications used many hard-to-understand and hard-to-read text screens in all capital letters laid out in the 24-line × 80-character displays typical of computer systems of the 1960s–1980s prior to graphical user interfaces (see Figs. 8.7 and 8.8). The users of the system were typically women in their 20s through 40s who seemed comfortable handling the complexity but who would welcome more legible and readable displays. The number of containers, the number of ships, and the number of routes, so that containers would arrive at the same place at the same time, made for a formidable software design task. The GUI reflecting all the data to allow telephone operators to respond to changing conditions and to check the progress of shipments was also formidable. The layering of partial windows was more complex than anything we had ever seen in detail, although I had briefly seen advanced software for loading and unloading ships being developed in Singapore, when I was an invited consultant and tutor through the Singapore National Computer Board at the time, in the late 1980s.

We designed a graphical user-interface design style guide for Crowley Maritime's applications. The text explained the scope of Crowley Maritime applications and the organization of the GUI design style guide, GUI design objectives, issues, metaphors, mental model, and navigation. AM+A also prepared detailed screens that showed the client's developers exactly how to lay out their screens. The gridded design, the location of titling for data fields, and layering of partial components of screens to reveal and hide layers of information were all carefully depicted. The screens needed to be simple, clear, and consistent for (usually) women without formal advanced education who were nevertheless involved with very complex data and scheduling requirements. The style guide also covered details of screen layout, grids, and labeling conventions. Some of the Microsoft Windows 3.1 screens were some of the more complex that AM+A designed, with multiple interaction sections within one widow and multiple sub-panes within one of the sections.

Sample Before screens showing how Crowley Maritime data were displayed on 24-line by 80-character text displays typical of computer displays in the 1960s - 1980s.

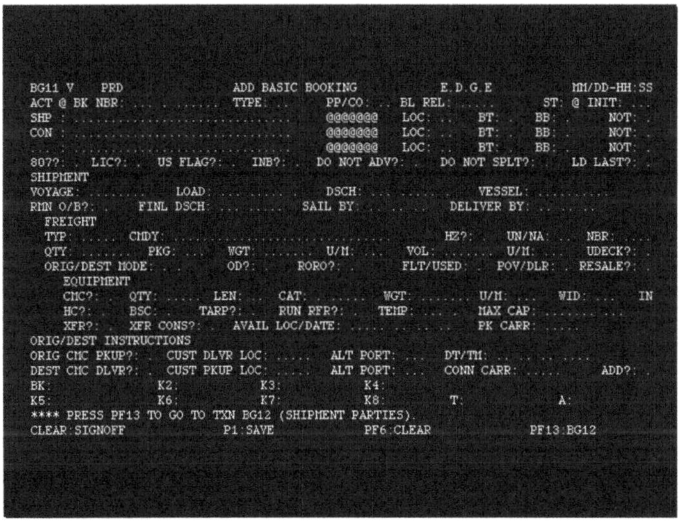

AM+A's revised design:

The design uses the relatively greater power of graphical user-interface design with Microsoft Windows. Note that the Shipment section of the screen in the middle can be changed to show one of three areas of data, and that the Freight details subsection has 18 different components that can be changed for each Shipment section. This layering of information was the most complex sets of screen layouts that AM+A had ever designed.

Figs. 8.7 and 8.8 Crowley Maritime container shipping screens, Before and After. Note the gridded layout, the specific labeling conventions and the accounting for multiple sections and multiple panes with sections in one window. (Source: AM+A archive; used with permission of Crowley Maritime)

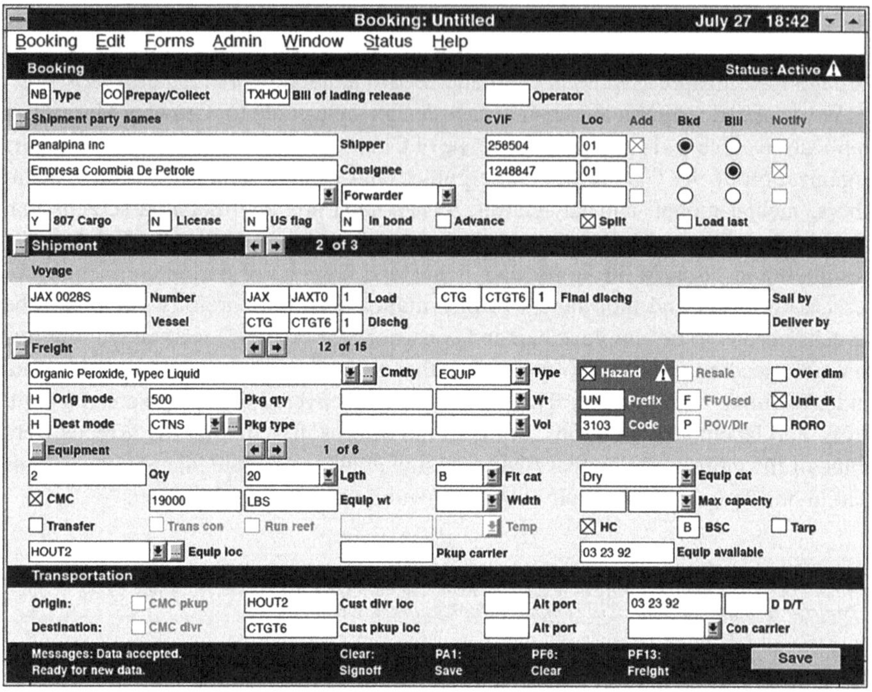

Booking: Untitled   July 27 18:42

Booking   Edit   Forms   Admin   Window   Status   Help

Booking   Status: Activo

NB Type   CO Prepay/Collect   TXHOU Bill of lading release   Operator

Shipment party names   CVIF   Loc Add Bkd Bill Notify

Panalpina inc   Shipper   258504   01   ⦿   ○   □

Empresa Colombia De Petrole   Consignee   1248847   01   ○   ⦿   ⊠

                                       Forwarder   ○   ○   □

Y 807 Cargo   N License   N US flag   N In bond   □ Advance   ⊠ Split   □ Load last

Shipment   ← →   2 of 3

Voyage

JAX 0028S   Number   JAX JAXT0 1 Load   CTG CTGT6 1 Final dischg   Sail by

              Vessel   CTG CTGT6 1 Dischg   Deliver by

Freight   ← →   12 of 15

Organic Peroxide, Typec Liquid   Cmdty EQUIP   Type ⊠ Hazard   □ Resale   □ Over dim

H Orig mode   500   Pkg qty   Wt   UN   Prefix   F Flt/Used   ⊠ Undr dk

H Dest mode   CTNS   Pkg type   Vol 3103 Code   P POV/Dir   □ RORO

Equipment   ← →   1 of 6

2   Qty   20   Lgth   B   Flt cat Dry   Equip cat

⊠ CMC   19000   LBS   Equip wt   Width   Max capacity

□ Transfer   □ Trans con □ Run reef   Temp   ⊠ HC   B BSC   □ Tarp

HOUT2   Equip loc   Pkup carrier   03 23 92 Equip available

Transportation

Origin: □ CMC pkup   HOUT2   Cust divr loc   Alt port   03 23 92   D D/T

Destination: □ CMC divr   CTGT6   Cust pkup loc   Alt port   Con carrier

Messages: Data accepted.   Clear: PA1:   PF6:   PF13:   Save
Ready for new data.   Signoff   Save   Clear   Freight

Figs. 8.7 and 8.8   (continued)

Lawrence Berkeley Laboratory, Human Genome Project, 1992

For over a decade after I left Lawrence Berkeley Laboratory's (LBL's) Computer Science and Mathematics Department as a Staff Scientist, my friends at LBL continued to call on AM+A for consulting assistance, especially John McCarthy (RIP), a database and statistics expert. In 1992, LBL hired AM+A to provide UI-design assistance for its Human Genome project. LBL was one of several centers attempting to develop tools to assist scientists in unraveling the human genome. It was, needless to say, very exciting and a great honor to be working on depictions of the human genome (Figs. 8.9 and 8.10).

Motorola

During a period of about 20 years (about 1987–2007). AM+A served several groups at different development sites within Motorola to design prototypes of advanced products by improving the user interface of their products, including smart-car navigation systems, personal digital assistants, television electronic program guides, other applications, and even keyboard designs.

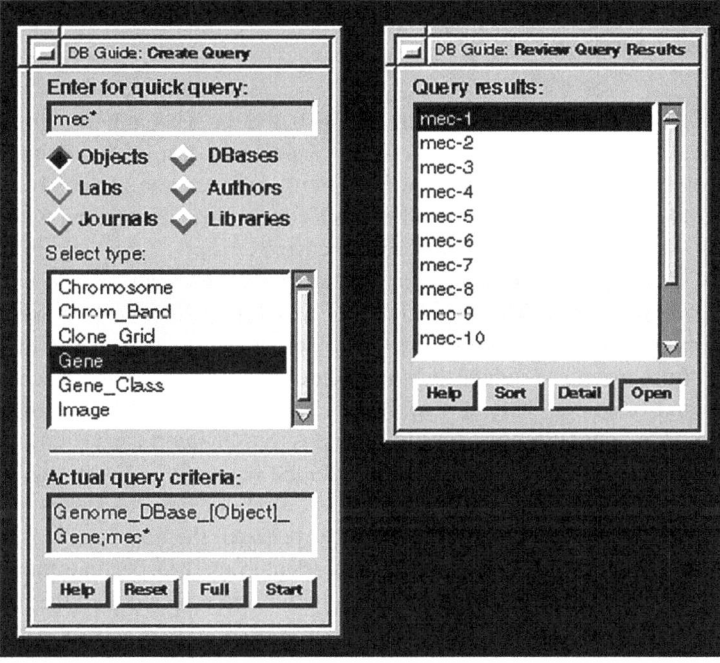

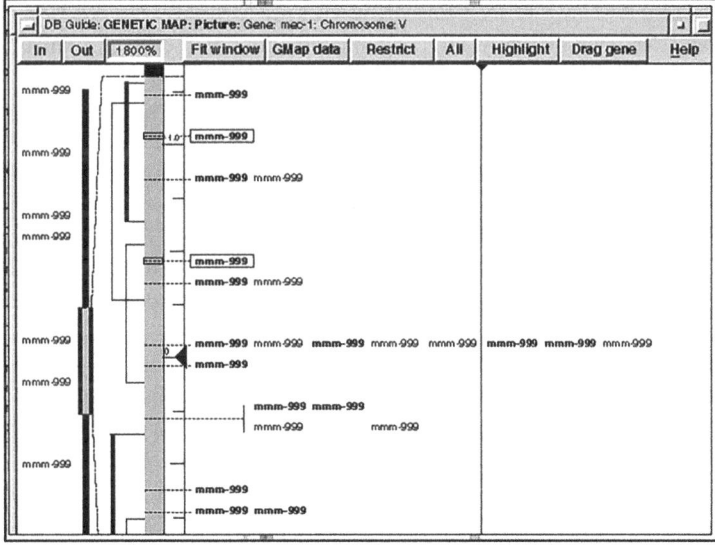

Figs. 8.9 and 8.10 Screen designs by AM+A that improved legibility and readability of query and retrieval dialogue boxes and the human gene mapping itself, 1992. At that point in time, software developers used the Motif window-management system pictured. (Illustrations by AM+A; used with permission of Lawrence Berkeley National Laboratory)

Motorola, 1989–1992: Advance GPS Smart-Car Navigation System

During 1989–1992, a Motorola R&D group based in Schaumberg, Illinois, and headed by Alan Kirson, invited AM+A to research and design the complete look-and-feel of a new "smart-car" navigation system, and example of GPS-based navigation. AM+A was invited based on the client's experience of working with AM+A on several other projects over several previous years.

AM+A developed the user interface for a prototype in-car vehicle-navigation system developed for the Motorola ADVANCE project, which was a combined private enterprise and US government project, somewhat unusual at the time. User interfaces for consumer products beyond the desktop enabled users to access complex data and functions without significant display complexity and without extensive novice documentation. Successful solutions to user-interface design consist, as always, of partially universal and partially unique solutions to the design of metaphors, mental models, navigation, appearance, and interaction. By managing the user's experience of familiar structures and processes, the user-interface designer can achieve more compelling forms. The user interface can become more usable and acceptable. Users can become more productive and satisfied with the product in achieving their personal and professional objectives.

AM+A did tests of the "half-VGA resolution" (VGA resolution for screens is 640 × 480 pixels with a refresh rate of 60 Hz) for legibility and readability of the displays and designed hundreds of icons, map displays, and screen displays. We were asked to do a design that did not seem "computer-like"; thus, a *minimum* of dialogue boxes was used. We were successful, also, in convincing the software and hardware development team to simplify the initial screen shown to users. The original design showed 2 screens with 9 choices each, or 18 choices. We felt this amount of choice was daunting and inappropriate for general consumer use. There was no online help; the system had to be self-revealing. We were able to convince the development team to stop development momentarily and simplify the mental model. The revised initial screen was simply four choices: Trips, Maps, Traffic and Weather, and Directory.

A complete case study appears in Bergman (See Bibliography: Bergman, 2000) and Marcus (2000). The system was one of the more advanced in the USA at the time. I lectured about the project internationally and later published the case study. Unfortunately, because the project then was a joint commercial/government-sponsored effort, Motorola decided, as far as I understood, to cancel the project just before the system went into a final 1000-auto street-test phase in Chicago, because of the zooming costs of user-testing required for government regulations. Consequently, one year later, all our work, all our deliverables, and the entire project reverted to public domain and was stored in a theoretically public location but known only to a few people at the University of Michigan Transportation Research Center. Motorola contacted us about a year later and asked us for our project materials because they had misplaced theirs in their voluminous folders! We were paid a small consulting fee to find, organize, and send all our project materials to Motorola. Perhaps the project information is still being stored somewhere in public locations to this day. Alas, this kind of snafu happens with some commercial and government-sponsored projects (Figs. 8.11–8.20).

Main Menu screen showing novice icon buttons on the right.

Map screen at mid-level zoom with "Button button" that brings back control buttons.

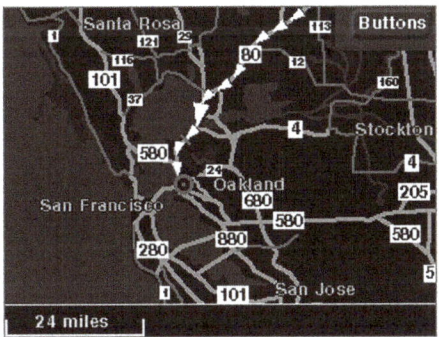

Map screen with simulated hand controlling movement of the Zoom Box. Notice the off-center cross-hairs so that the finger does not obscure the target.

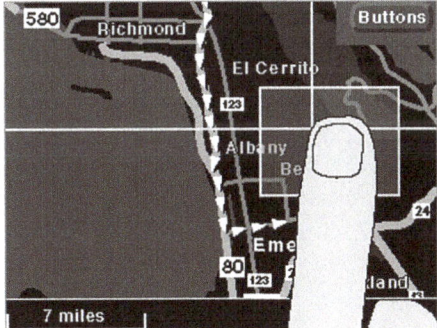

Scene from visual design tool that enables designers and client representatives to experiment with different appearance characteristics.

Figs. 8.11–8.20 Images of the Motorola Smart Car navigation system project. (Source: AM+A archive, used with permission of author. Designs by AM+A; images are in the public domain)

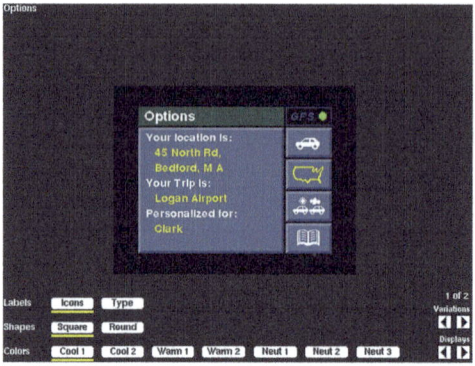

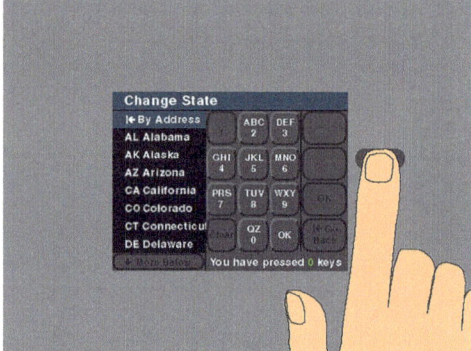

Selecting a trip. The additional "expert" buttons in the left column appear when an external hard button is selected.

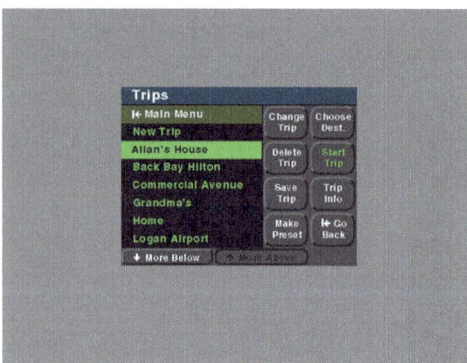

Figs. 8.11–8.20   (continued)

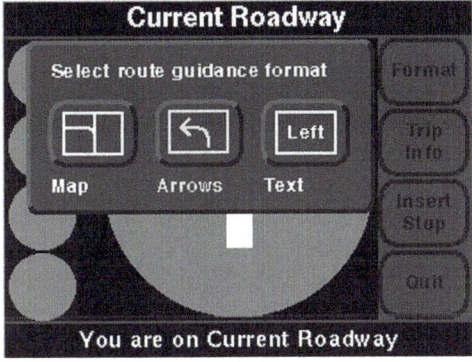

Example of single-maneuver arrow sign to guide user during driving, with urgency indicator at left.

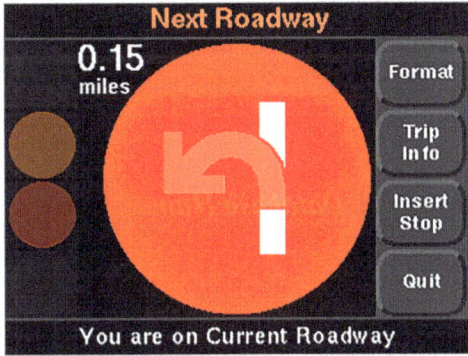

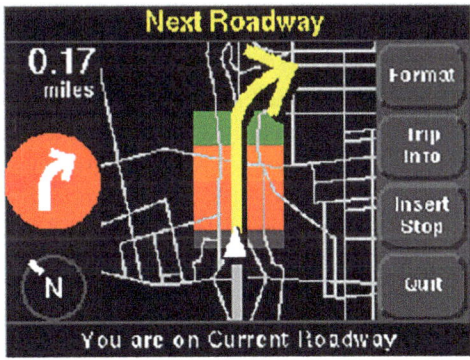

Simulated use of touch-sensitive keyboard with location guides displayed.

Figs. 8.11–8.20 (continued)

Figs. 8.11–8.20 (continued)

Apple Computer, Inc.: Market Activities Database Human Interface Design Report, May 1990

In 1990, AM+A presented to Apple Computer's Marketing Department design revisions we made to Apple's Market Activities Database (MAD) and provided assistance in the development and implementation of screen displays and page displays, the development of effective user documentation, and promoted future development and extensions of the MAD product.

   AM+A produced a Compendium of Figures to be used in conjunction with the MAD Human Interface Design Report. The compendium provided Before and After versions of the revised screen and page displays for easy reference. Of significance was the concept of designing the user interface to appear like a newspaper front page, with different sections defined by color, typography, and titles (Figs. 8.21–8.24).

ACM Communications *Article: "Human Communication Issues in Advanced User Interfaces," April 1993*

In early 1993, I was privileged to co-write with Prof. Andries Van Dam, Brown University, a major article about the future of user-interface design (Marcus and Van Dam 1993). Writing the article was one of the most challenging writing tasks I ever had. Andy was demanding. Even more so, he admitted, was his personal editor, who critiqued our joint writing. By carefully organizing our thoughts into an article

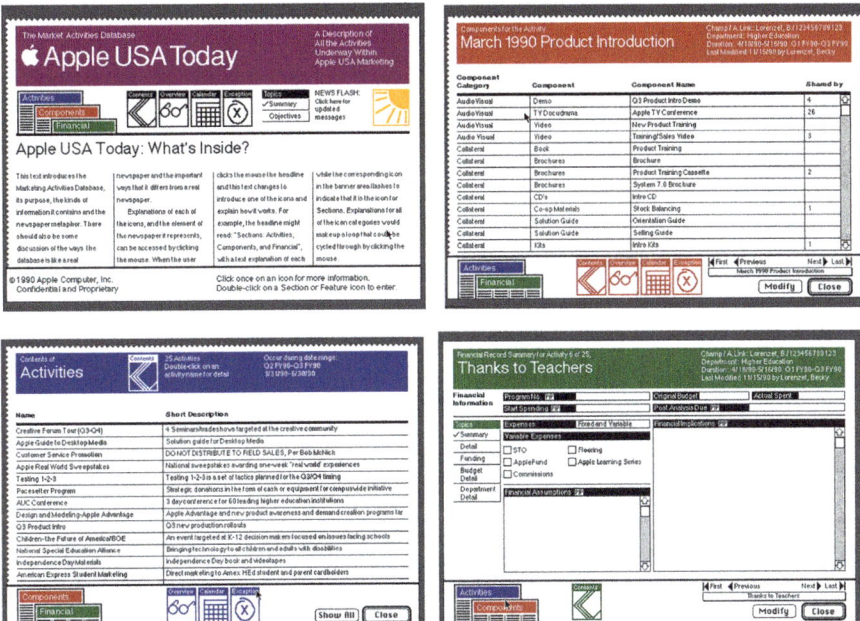

Figs. 8.21–8.24 Example images of the Apple MAD human interface design by AM+A. (Source: AM+A archive; Illustrations by AM+A; used with the permission of Apple)

outline and rewriting the text about ten times, we were finally able to get her OK. The results, I had to admit, were excellent. What made this writing opportunity unusual for me was that I could illustrate a future design challenge: culturally diverse user interfaces. I illustrated the concept by taking an ordinary Print dialogue box and showed how it might appear for sophisticated European tastes, for women, for children, and others. At that time, no one had considered such a concept. These were some of the first-ever typographically "sophisticated" examples of user interfaces ever to be published. Over the next 20 years, it became a more acknowledged and practiced skill as designers customized user interfaces in many different ways for specific groups.

What was amusing is that at the time, one research group (comprised mostly of women) took the concept design intended to represent something for women and "tested" them with users and found them wanting. Our designs might have been criticized (we ourselves had not carefully designed or tested these throw-away concepts), but we felt the concept could not be argued away (Figs. 8.25–8.28).

In 1993, we felt that future industrial products would possess human-computer interfaces incorporating innovative input and display technologies, including gestural input, multimedia, three-dimensional displays, and agents. These technology advances offered challenges and opportunities to designers of human-computer communication and interaction. In particular, developers would need to analyze and

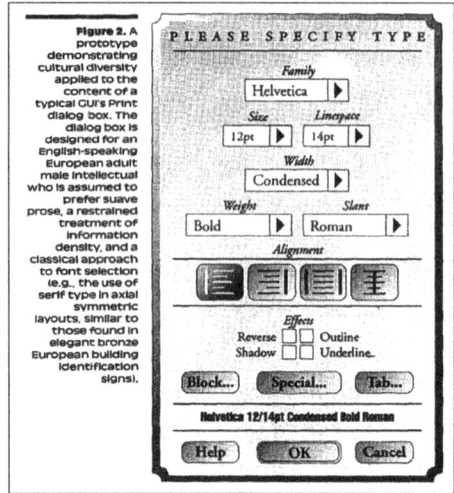

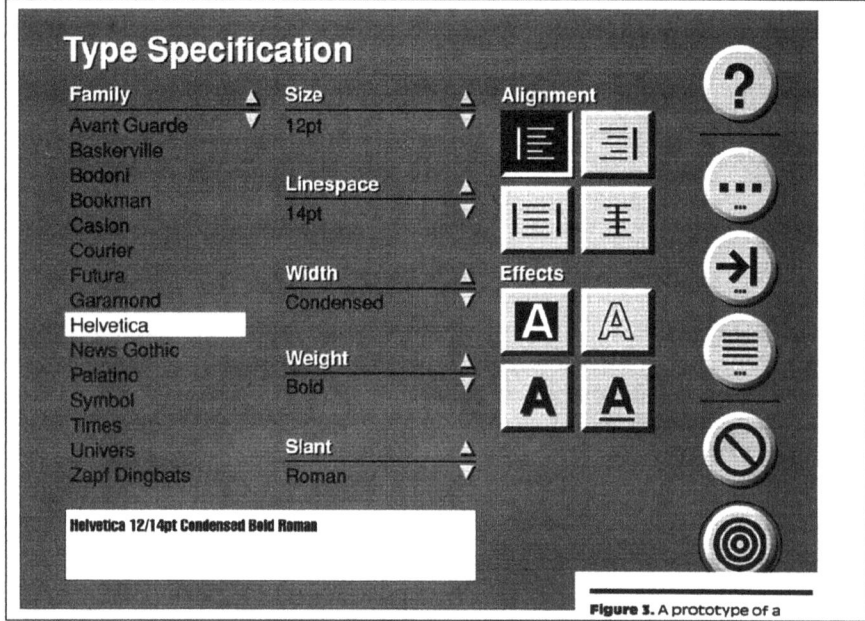

Figs. 8.25–8.28 Examples of different dialogue box designs as published in the article cited. Design concept by Aaron Marcus; design production by AM+A staff. (Source: AM+A archive; illustrations by AM+A; Aaron Marcus. 1993. Human communications issues in advanced UIs. Commun. ACM 36, 4 (April 1993), 100–109.Used with permission of AM+A)

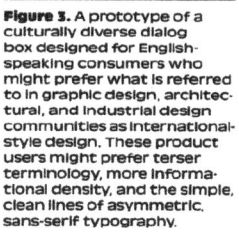

Figure 3. A prototype of a culturally diverse dialog box designed for English-speaking consumers who might prefer what is referred to in graphic design, architectural, and industrial design communities as international-style design. These product users might prefer terser terminology, more informational density, and the simple, clean lines of asymmetric, sans-serif typography.

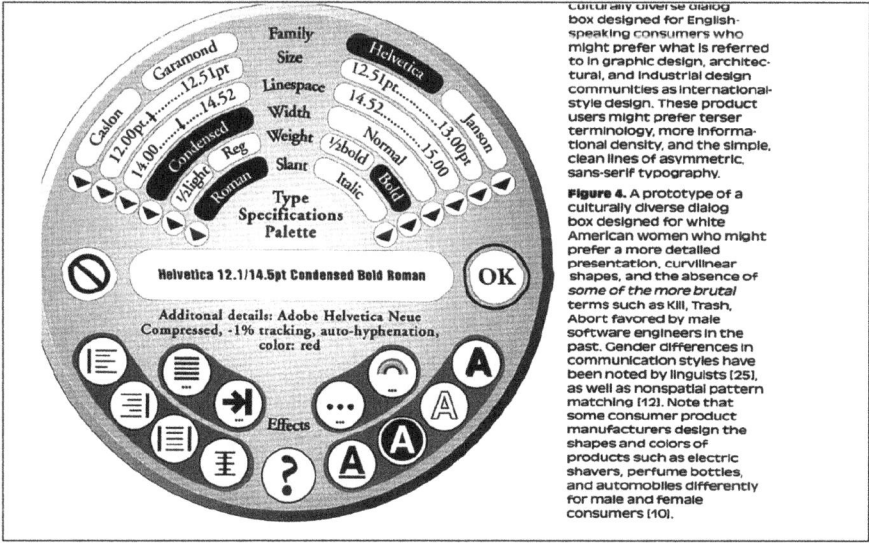

Culturally diverse dialog box designed for English-speaking consumers who might prefer what is referred to in graphic design, architectural, and industrial design communities as international-style design. These product users might prefer terser terminology, more informational density, and the simple, clean lines of asymmetric, sans-serif typography.

Figure 4. A prototype of a culturally diverse dialog box designed for white American women who might prefer a more detailed presentation, curvilinear shapes, and the absence of *some of the more brutal* terms such as Kill, Trash, Abort favored by male software engineers in the past. Gender differences in communication styles have been noted by linguists [25], as well as nonspatial pattern matching [12]. Note that some consumer product manufacturers design the shapes and colors of products such as electric shavers, perfume bottles, and automobiles differently for male and female consumers [10].

Figs. 8.25–8.28 (continued)

design new metaphors that embody fundamental terms, images, or concepts that make products more immediately comprehensible as well as appealing to a wide variety of users. To clarify the communication challenges, I discussed in the article metaphors, rhetoric, and semiotics, the science of signs, as well cultural diversity in user interface design. These were all new topics for the user-interface design community. In fact, I organized a semiotics-oriented "Birds of a Feather Group" and a session at the CHI conference that were, to my knowledge, the first to introduce semiotics into the discussion of user-interface development.

ShareData, 1993

In 1993, ShareData, a Silicon Valley software company that enabled its client companies to manage their portfolio of stocks, approached us to incorporate their corporate identity into the screen designs of the software. We welcomed the challenge.

Working with their enlightened and cooperative staff, we were able to add large--scale type, corporate colors, and a sophisticated typographic design to the layout of screens. These were some of the first adaptations of corporate identity standards to screen designs (Figs. 8.29 and 8.30).

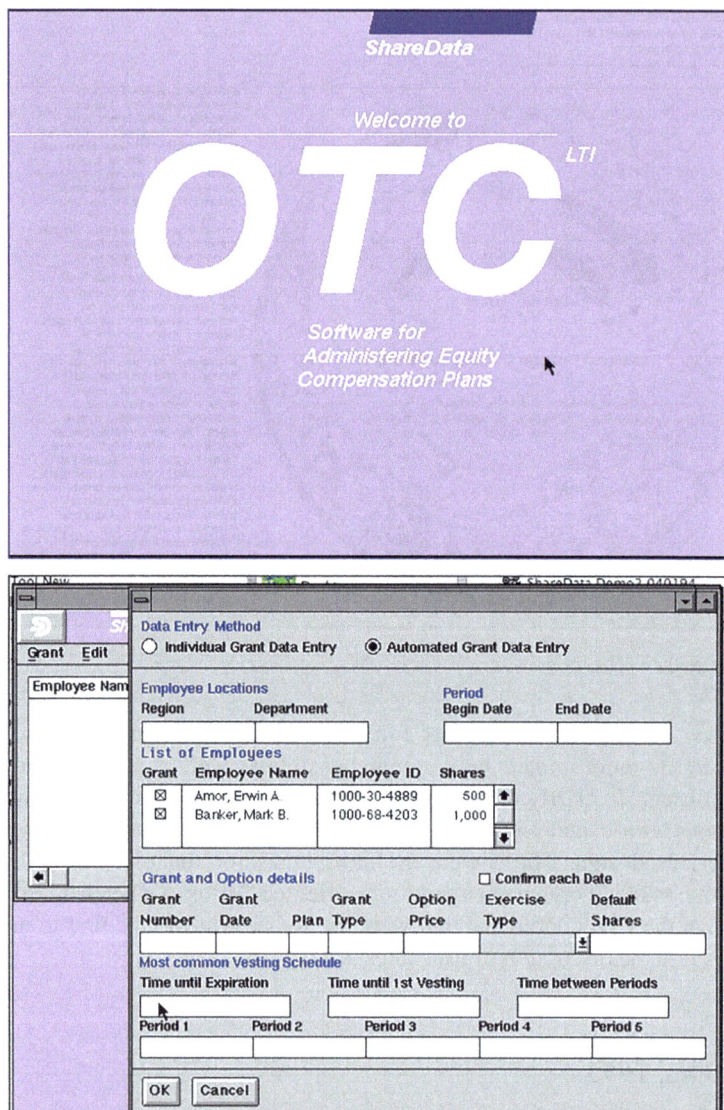

Figs. 8.29 and 8.30 Sample screens showing the incorporation of sophisticated corporate identity (typefonts, colors, layout) into screen designs of ShareData software. (Source: AM+A archive; used with permission of the author. Images designed by AM+A)

Kaiser Clinical Information System (CIS) User Interface, 1996

In 1996, for Timothy Anspaugh, Design team leader, for Kaiser Permanente, the nation's largest healthcare provider, with headquarters in Oakland, California, AM+A prepared a report analyzing the current Clinical Information System's (CIS) (i.e., hospital information system's) graphical user interface (GUI) and recommended design improvements. AM+A also prepared a draft document to serve as a user-interface guidelines document. AM+A was able to prepare its designs with a modest input of information from the Kaiser team and based the design details on AM+A's knowledge of typography, grid-based layout, color, and symbolism. The report emphasized multiple document-interface (MDI) window management and its impact on users with differing levels of computer experience, task needs, and educational levels. The report offered guidance in possible areas of improving the GUI, and an overall navigational model to accommodate the needs of both the novice and experienced users. The actual implementation of the new system took many years after AM+A's involvement and the contributions of several rounds of software providers. The actual system was not finished for approximately 20 years!

Sabre Travel Information Network, 1994–2002

In 1994, at a CHI conference, Janice James, manager of the usability/testing staff of Sabre's Travel Information Network (STIN), came up to me and asked me an unusual question: What did I know about metaphor design? I was startled because this was the first time a CHI-community member had ever uttered the word "metaphor" to me. I had written about the importance of metaphors for several years and felt they were a fundamental user-interface design component. We discussed their importance briefly, and she said she would get back to me about a project on which she felt we could help.

That brief meeting led to a team of three people from AM+A, including myself, going to the headquarters of STIN, or Sabre, then a part of American Airlines, located at the Dallas-Fort Worth Airport. Sabre was preparing a major innovation in its travel-booking system, used by one-third of the world's travel agents. The system contained about 42 terabytes of data, which was a lot in those days. Sabre originated in about 1973 as a then-innovative computer data system that linked airlines with travel agents and could put the latest flight data (as well as data about rental cars and hotels) into the hands of travel agents worldwide. There were even sensors on airplanes that sent data when the aircraft landing gear had been raised or lowered, so Sabre often knew first when planes had departed or landed.

That first meeting involved Sabre marketing department staff (where the project had originated), travel agents, and others gathering to imagine how a new approach to understanding and presenting travel data could be envisioned. Many schemes were discussed and illustrated by a visualizer, an illustrator hired to depict the ideas.

We served as user-interface design consultants. Among AM+A staff who assisted on the sequence of Sabre tasks were John Armitage, Wolfgang Heidrich, Karl Wieser, and Ed Guttman.

From that original set of meetings and revised drawings, Sabre team members decided to base the new system on a depiction of a planet, Planet Sabre, whose surface depicted all the primary functions of the system (air, car, and hotel booking; weather conditions, etc.).

Over the next seven years of working with Sabre, AM+A's task was to design the detailed screens of all the functions of the system, the detailed windows, dialogue boxes, icons, and other elements that constituted the hundreds of individual displays that enabled users to interact with the data. The project was enormous in scope and unprecedented in detail for AM+A, but we rose to the challenge. There were several other aspects of the client relationship that were notable.

Sabre's Marketing Department leaders, led by Michael Sites, our patron and good friend, wanted an out-of-the-box solution, so they wanted us to have minimal contact with the software engineers. This seemed odd because we normally relied on close contact, collaboration, and communication with the software engineering groups of our clients. When we finally met with the software engineers after two years of design-development, they were naturally skeptical. Fortunately, we had done our homework, and they could find only two significant "bugs" in our designs, which we could easily solve through adding some additional buttons.

In the beginning, Sabre had its own user-testing lab, which tested each of our design versions. In all, they conducted about 40 tests, the most of any client in AM+A's career. For reasons unknown to me, perhaps for corporate cost-cutting, this lab was completely dismantled during the latter years of our engagement.

One of our staff, Wolfgang Heidrich, was lured by our client to join Sabre. He had the most interaction with the Sabre team. At first we were shocked, but then we realized that, as the new project manager, at Sabre, for our team, he knew us very well, and communication was facilitated! This was an unexpected benefit to the change.

Because travel agents in 1994 did not have much experience with Microsoft Windows, in which Planet Sabre was based, we also had to help train them in the Windows operating system. For that reason, Sabre commissioned us to develop an interactive game or simulation of Planet Sabre called Wayfinder, which was loosely based on the movie *Casablanca*. By moving icons around and clicking on the screen components, travel agents could become familiar with this new graphical user interface. In the first training sessions, when travel agents were asked to use the mouse to move the icon depiction of a person, being unfamiliar with mice and graphical screens, some travel agents picked up the mouse and placed it over the icon *on the screen*, trying to move the icon! Of course, with today's touch-screens, they might have succeeded. Then, it was an innocent error.

At one point in our work with Sabre we were working with three different business units: the travel agents version of Sabre, a related corporate booking business, and Travelocity, a new "start-up" within Sabre intended to enable end-users to book

flights. We designed prototypes for the first version of Travelocity, including different versions intended to appeal to different age groups. That was ahead of its time
but was not carried forward.

Our work with Sabre ended when the three principal leaders of Sabre left to form
Orbitz, a competitor booking system. For a short time, we ceased working with
Sabre and began working with Orbitz, designing some of its first branding screens.
However, because Orbitz and Sabre were involved with legal battles about the use
of proprietary information, I decided to end all of our working relations with both
companies in order, in my opinion, to be less likely to be drawn into litigation activities between the two companies. Sadly, that ended our multiyear engagement with
Sabre. It was a good run while it lasted, and I was very grateful for the opportunity
to assist with a major revolution in graphical air reservation systems (Figs. 8.31–8.61).

*Examples of the earlier version of Sabre, which used 24-line x 80-character displays of text-only
data, which was good for its time in the early 1970s, but was now 20 years out of date in display
capabilities:*

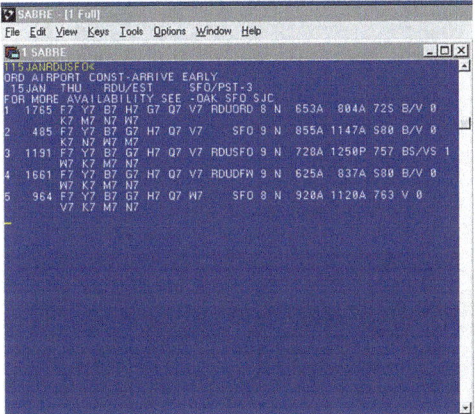

Figs. 8.31–8.55 Planet Sabre home screen and Graphical Air project images, 1994–2002. (Source:
AM+A archive; used with permission of the author)

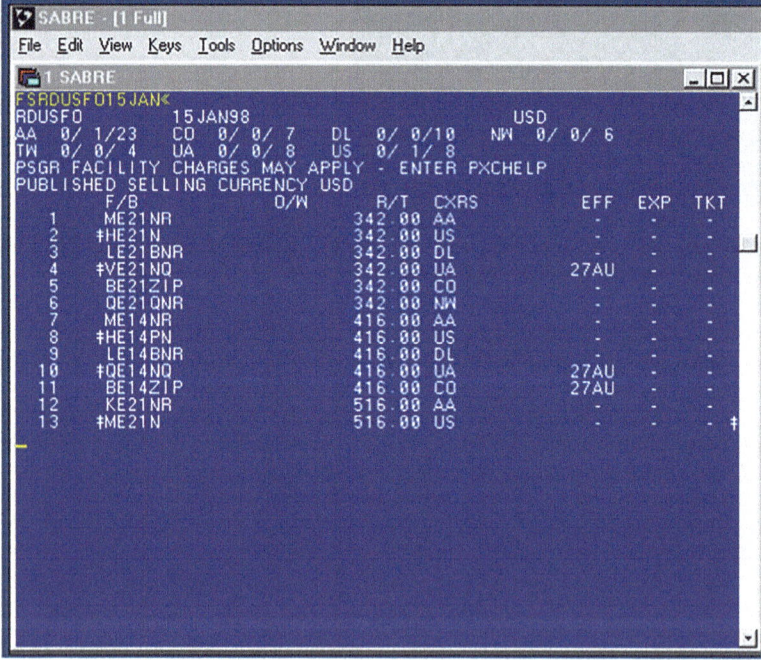

Earliest imagery of Planet Sabre tool bar before AM+A involvement:

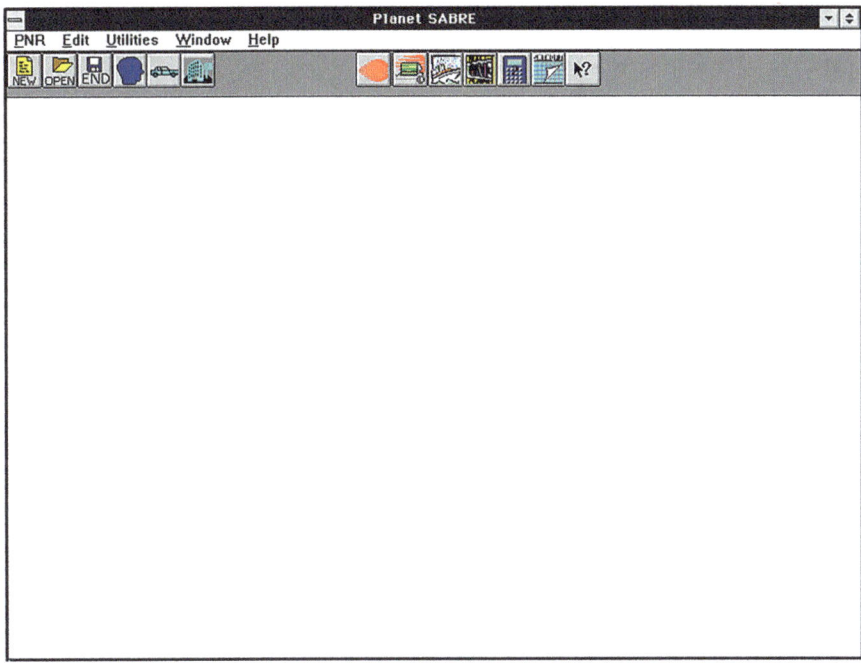

Examples of the Planet Sabre metaphor image selected for further development by AM+A:

Early Planet Sabre image:

Early Tool Bar image:

Example of Tool bar with parts of graphics overlapping into an active window. At the time, the Microsoft Windows operating system could not allow such overlaps. AM+A felt such overlaps added dramatic visual imagery and valuable brand identity to the design. We had to accept the limitations of current technology in the later designs:

Revised Planet Sabre design. Sabre requested that we make the Traveler and the colors "happier." This request was the first time any client asked us to redesign the emotional mood of a user-interface design, in about 1997. The Customizer dialogue box allowed users to choose a representative Traveler, changing gender and race to be more appropriate.

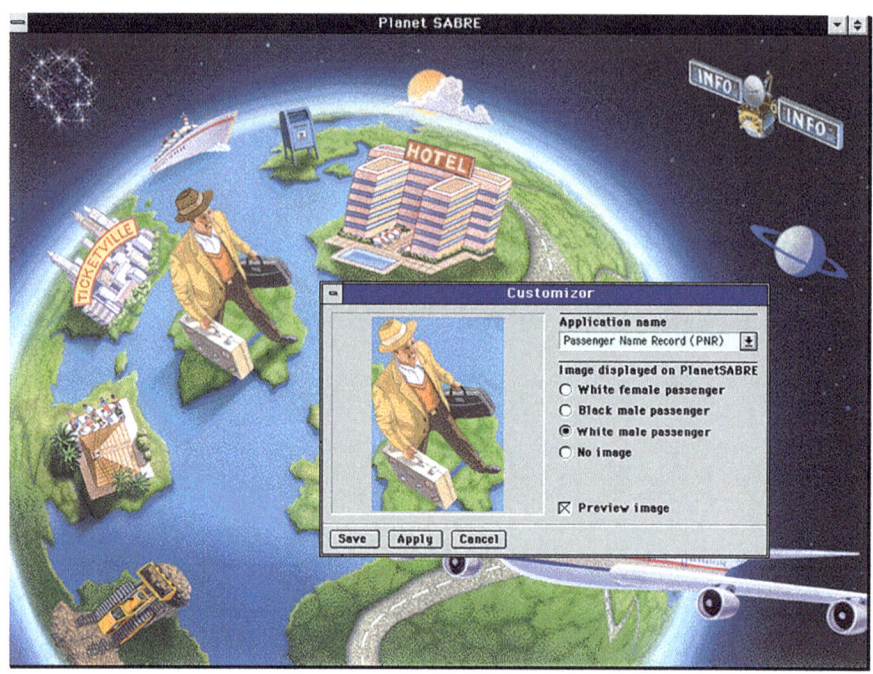

Example of dialogue box to choose the type of car representing car rentals:

Planet Sabre 1.0 prototype image showing the ability to change Passenger Name Record data:

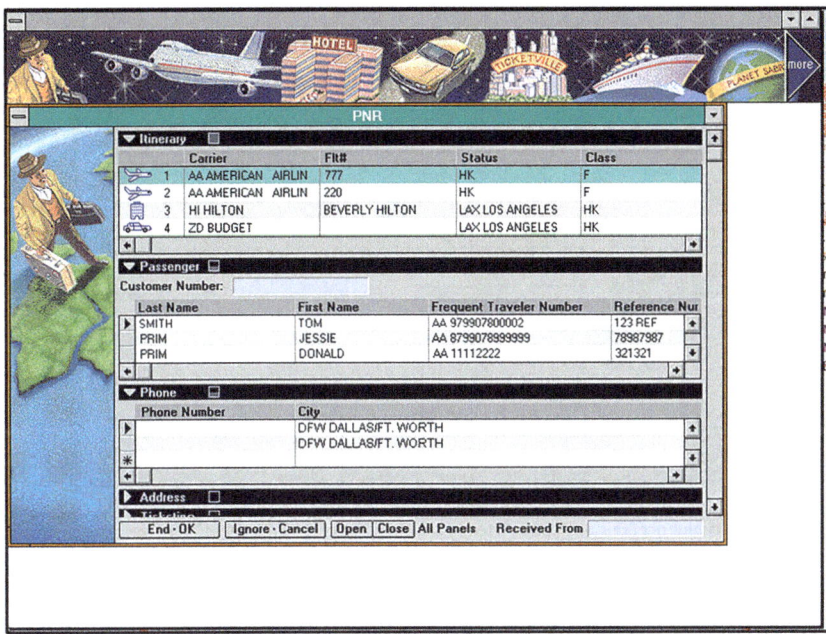

Seat Map application to enable seat selection using a graphic image of a plane's seating chart:

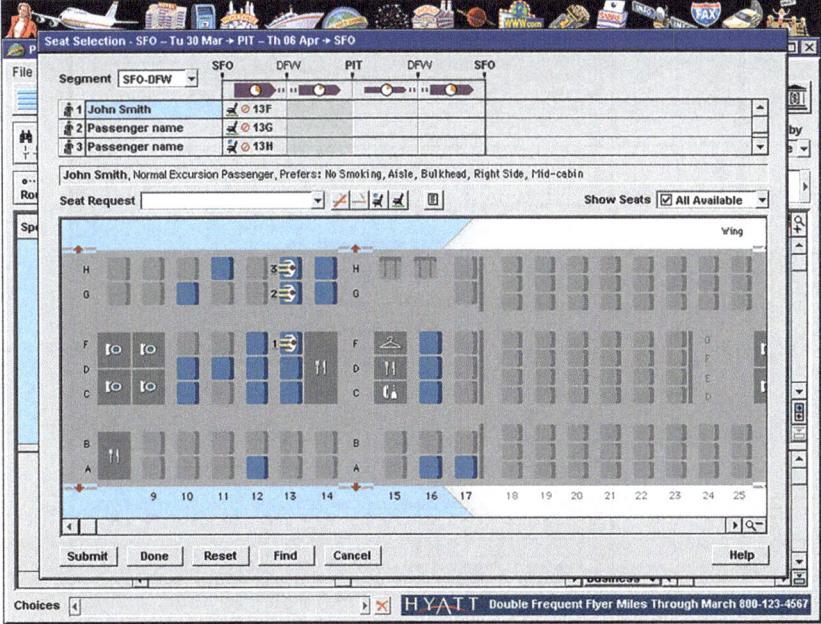

Graphical Air sketches, from the beginning to the final version.

The initial rapid prototype served to propose and demonstrate basic methods of data visualization, flight itinerary creation, and intra-itinerary navigation:

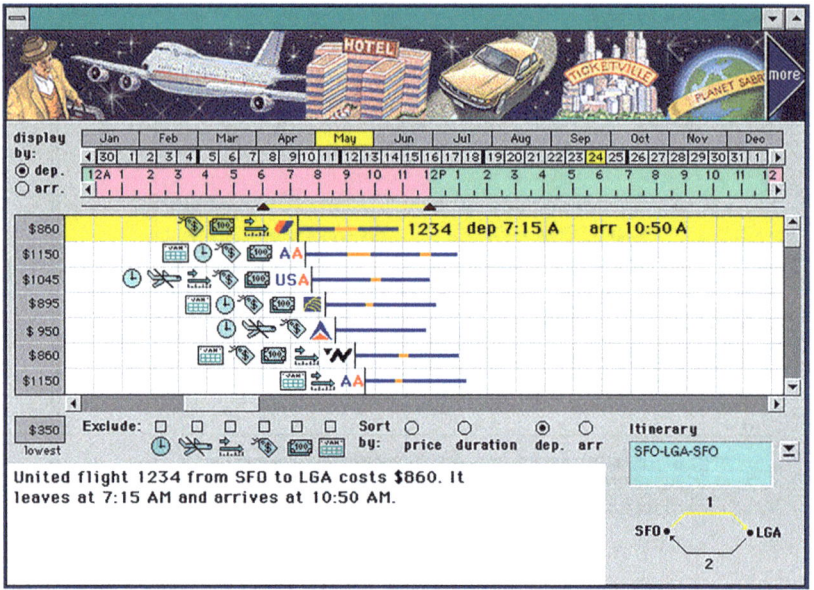

Alpha 0 noninteractive prototype included more product features and adopted the full-screen size of the target platform. Its primary objective was to act as a vehicle to communicate intended functionality to users as a way of stimulating feedback:

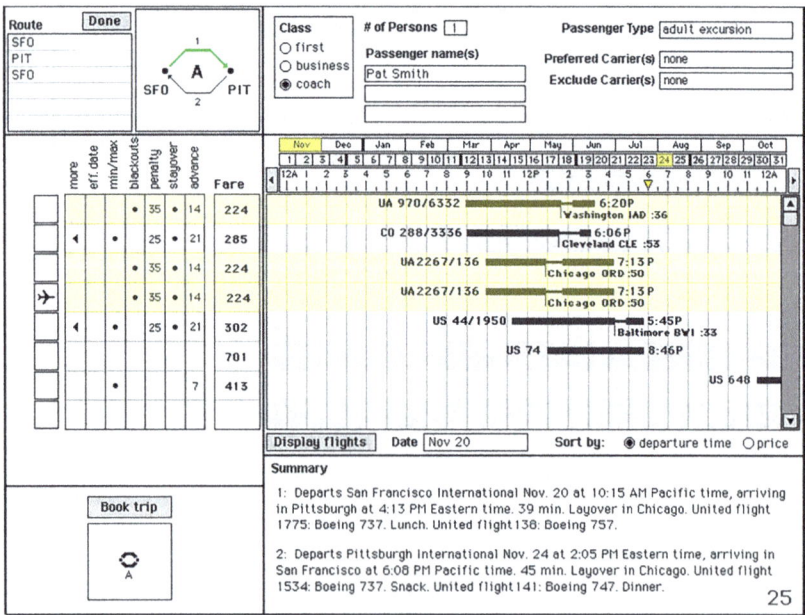

AM+A designed two overall mental models, one presented in three distinct appearance systems (Vanilla, Spice, and Grape) and one presented in one appearance system (Lite). Vanilla, Spice, and Grape each have two variations that convey alternative structural designs of key functionality, such as the Calendar and Route Map.

A focus group confirmed users' understanding of the design's underlying structure. Based on user feedback, AM+A began work on Alpha 1.0, which included an interactive prototype and static design alternatives for important elements. In Alpha 1 interactive prototype, AM+A designed an easy-to-implement, standard-looking user interface. AM+A built a miniature flight database to demonstrate interactive work simulations for three predetermined travel-booking scenarios:

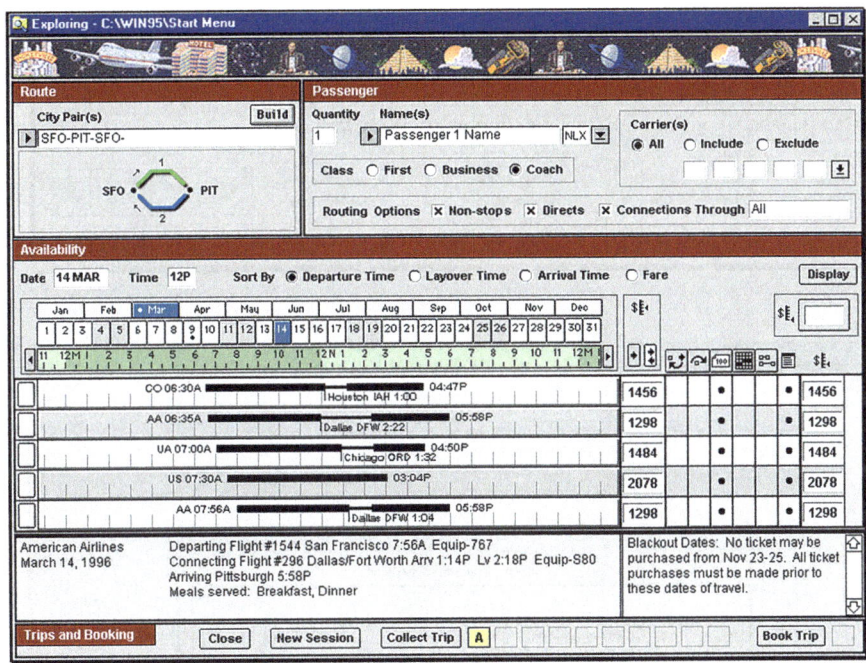

Vanilla's color palette and style suggest a standard GUI. The metaphor of the windshield and control panel depicts flight bars as buttons that are viewed in the windshield. There is a distinct separation between the flight segment bars and the fare rule matrix:

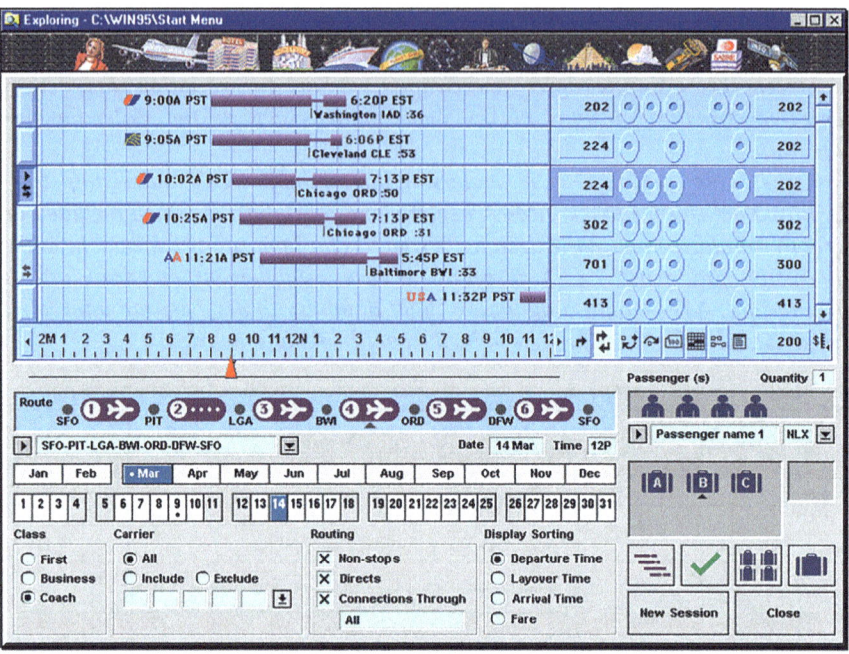

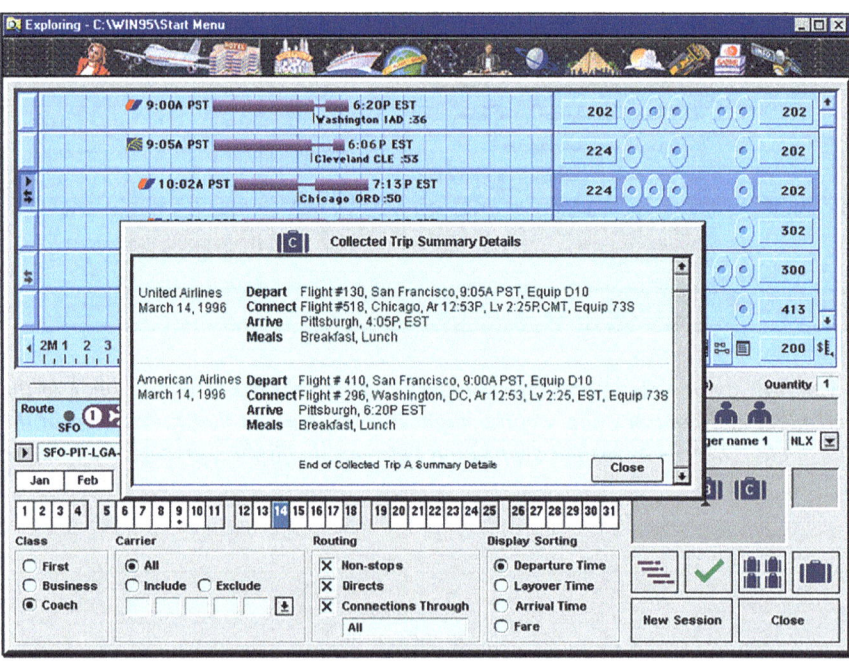

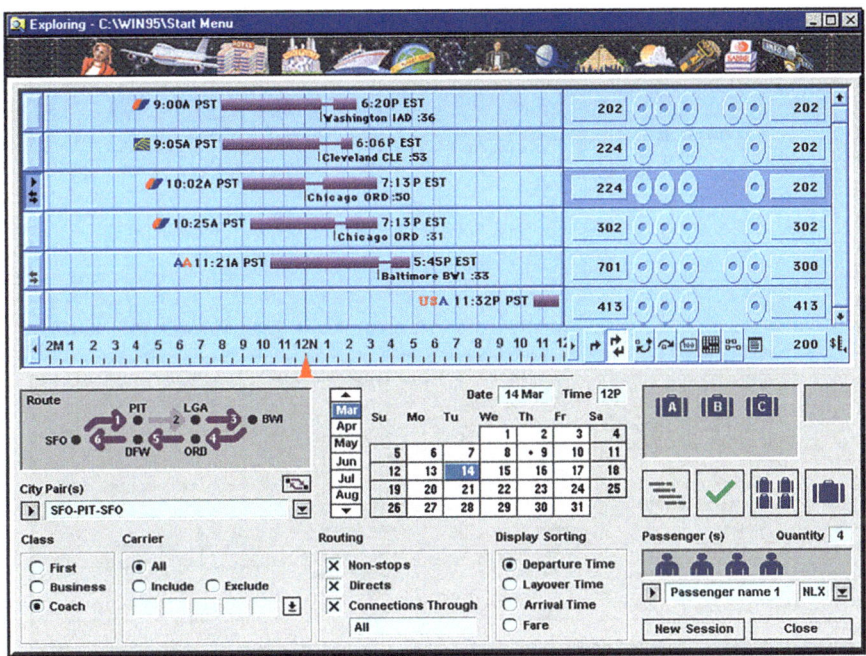

Spice's metaphor is a textured surface made up of two major tiles. Active elements float over this surface. Flight-bar data are minimized to show only carrier logos and connecting cities:

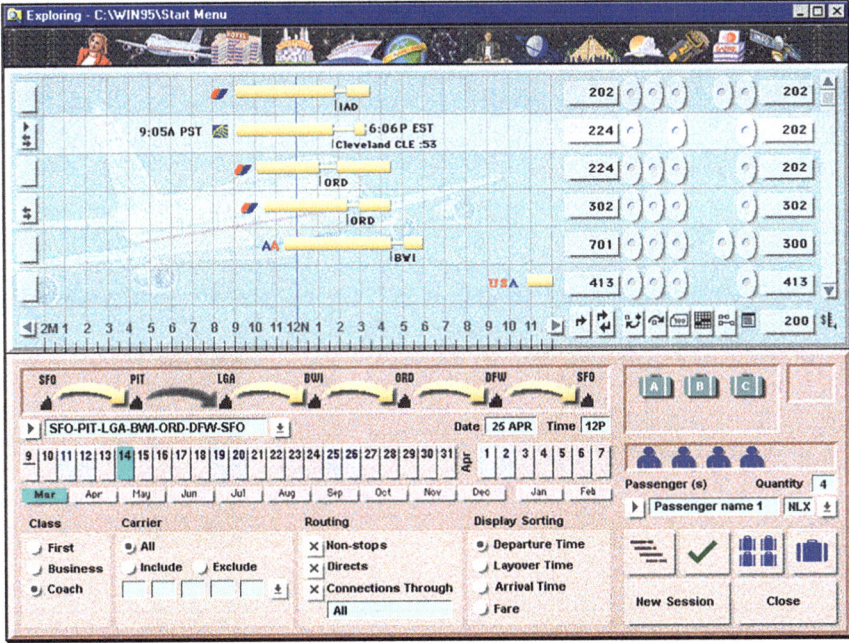

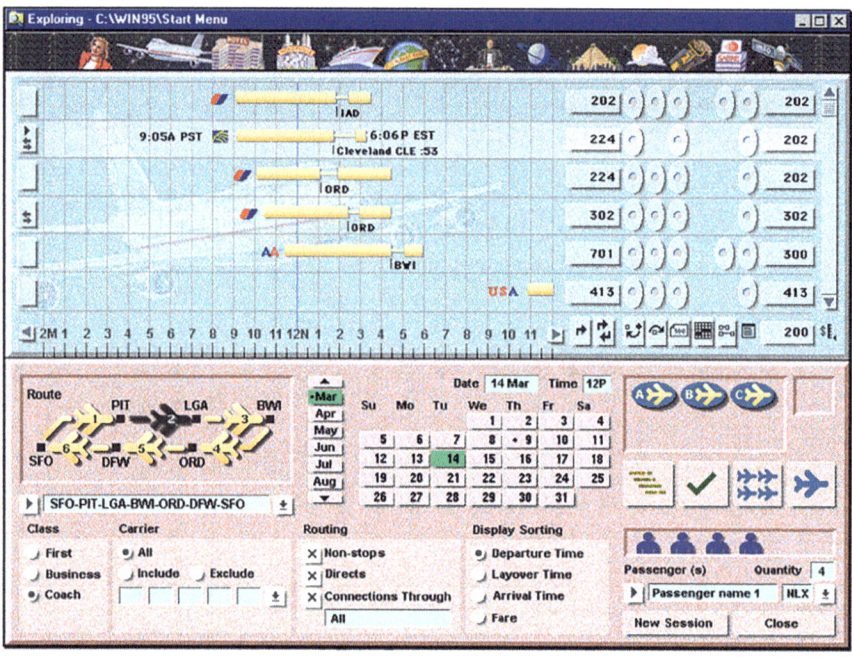

Grape's style uses alternative colors, curvilinear shapes, and rounded buttons to create a playful, friendly, easy-to-use appearance:

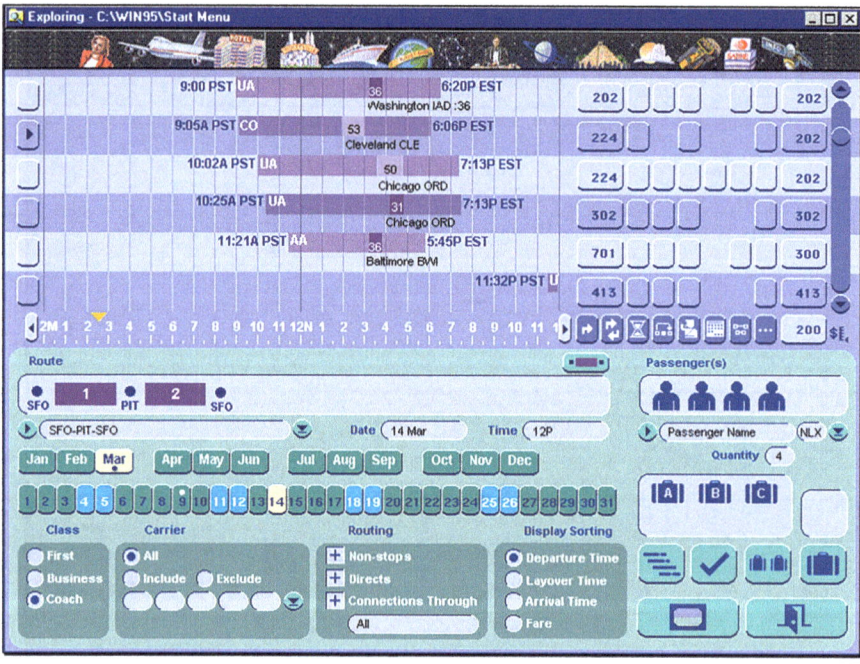

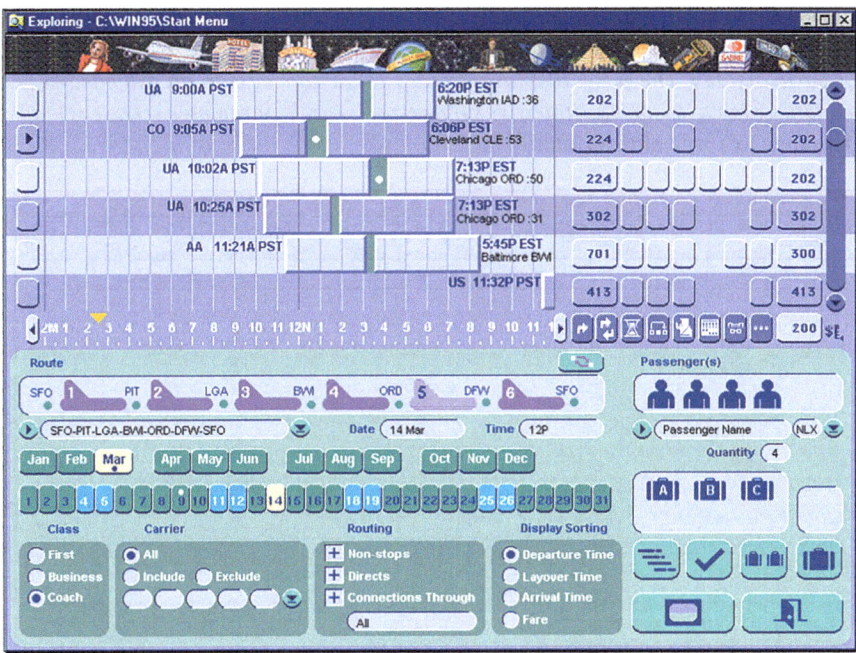

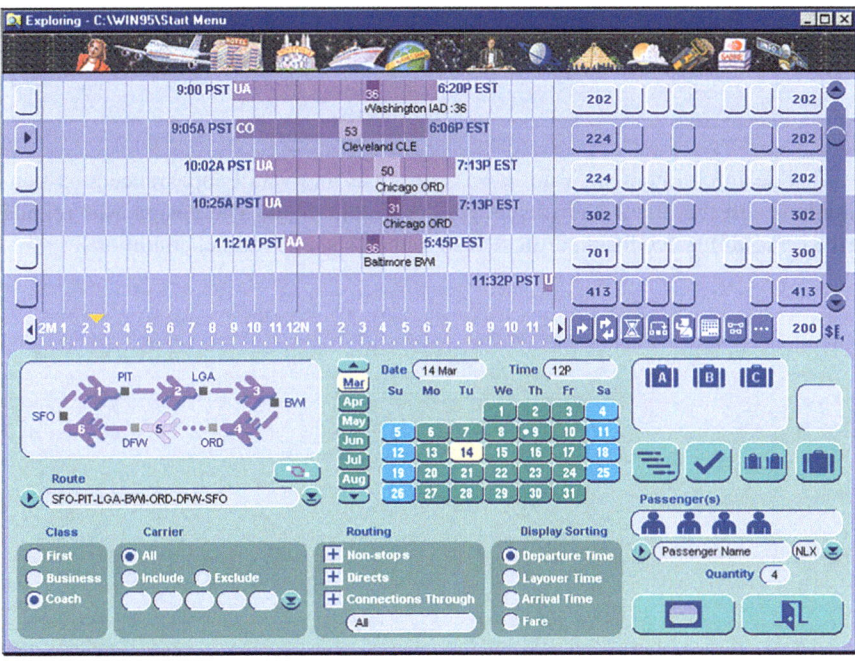

The Lite version addresses issues of customizability and future expansions of functionality. Lite provides permanent access to main functions with a very simplified basic display. The basic display provides random access to an extended set of secondary displays, such as itinerary summaries, search-parameter sets, seat maps, comprehensive rule outlays, etc.:

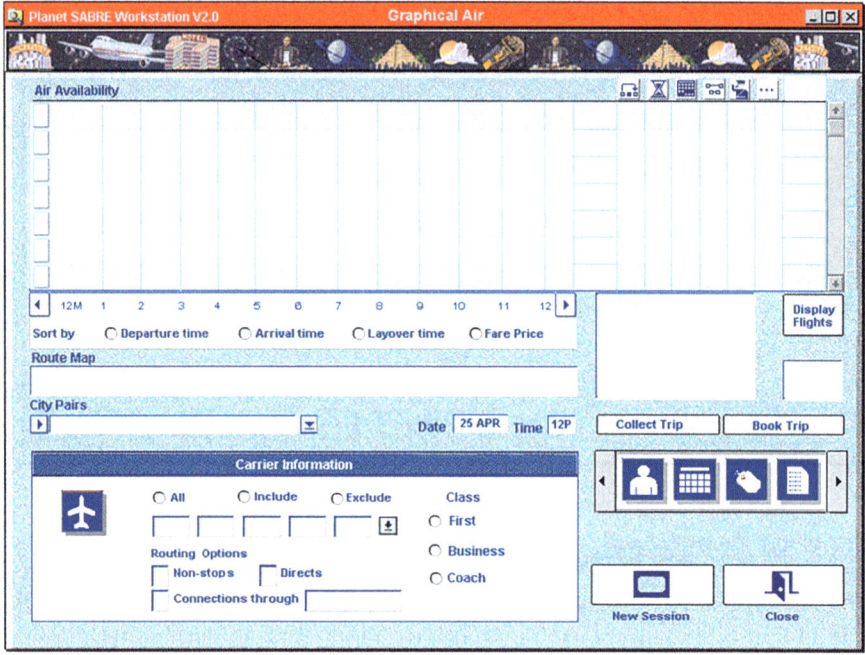

Final design refinement: Vanilla was chosen as an overall appearance after consultation with the client and travel-agent representatives. The design was refined based on usability feedback, critical design analysis, and market conditions:

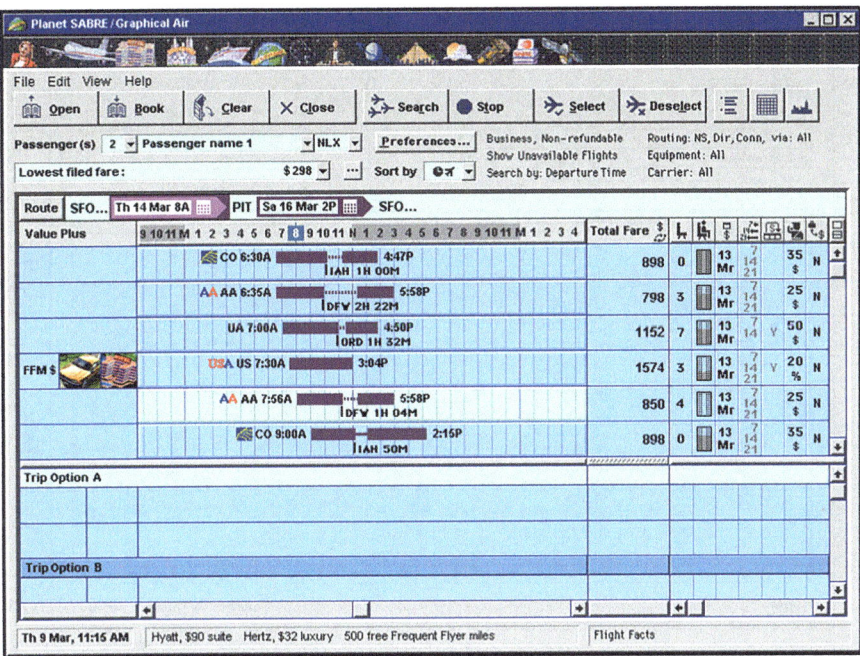

The image below was similar to the near-final version that was implemented. Note the appearance of ads or special offers by airlines, hotels, and car-rental companies that appeared for the first time with the air-booking data:

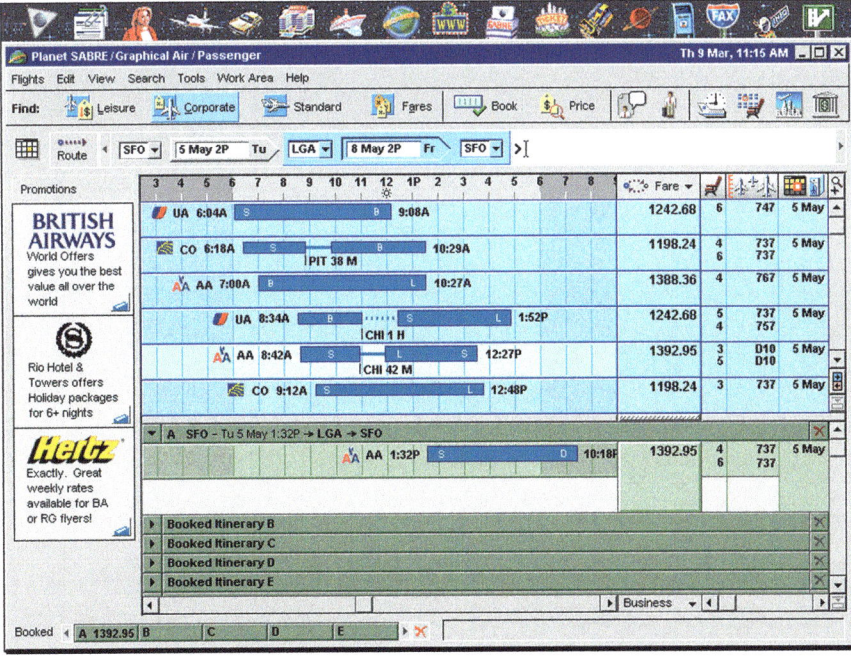

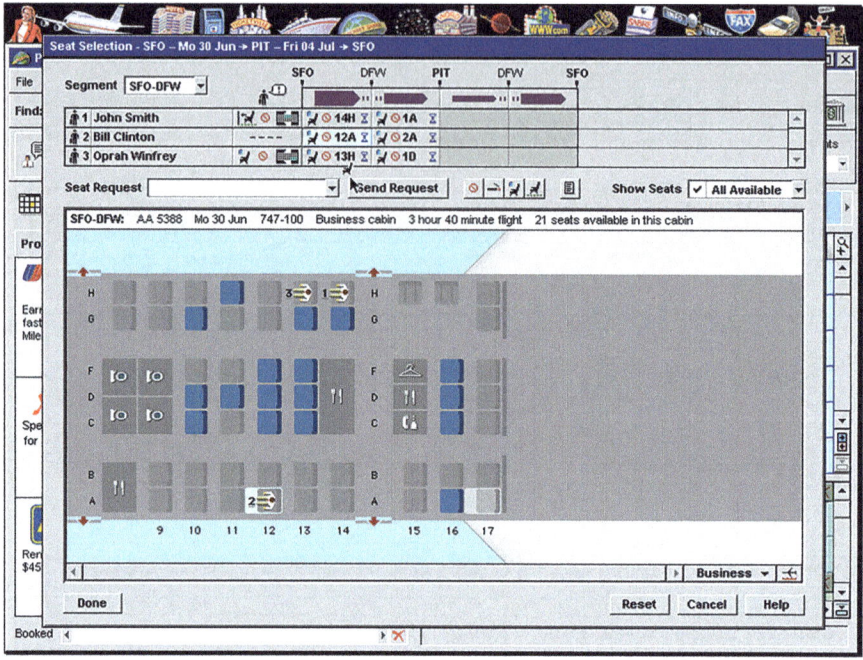

Fig. 8.56 Planet Sabre Seating diagram and other functions, 1994–2000. Depiction of Planet Sabre's airplane seating and seat reservations, one of the first such depictions, about 1997. (Source: AM+A archive; used with permission of AM+A)

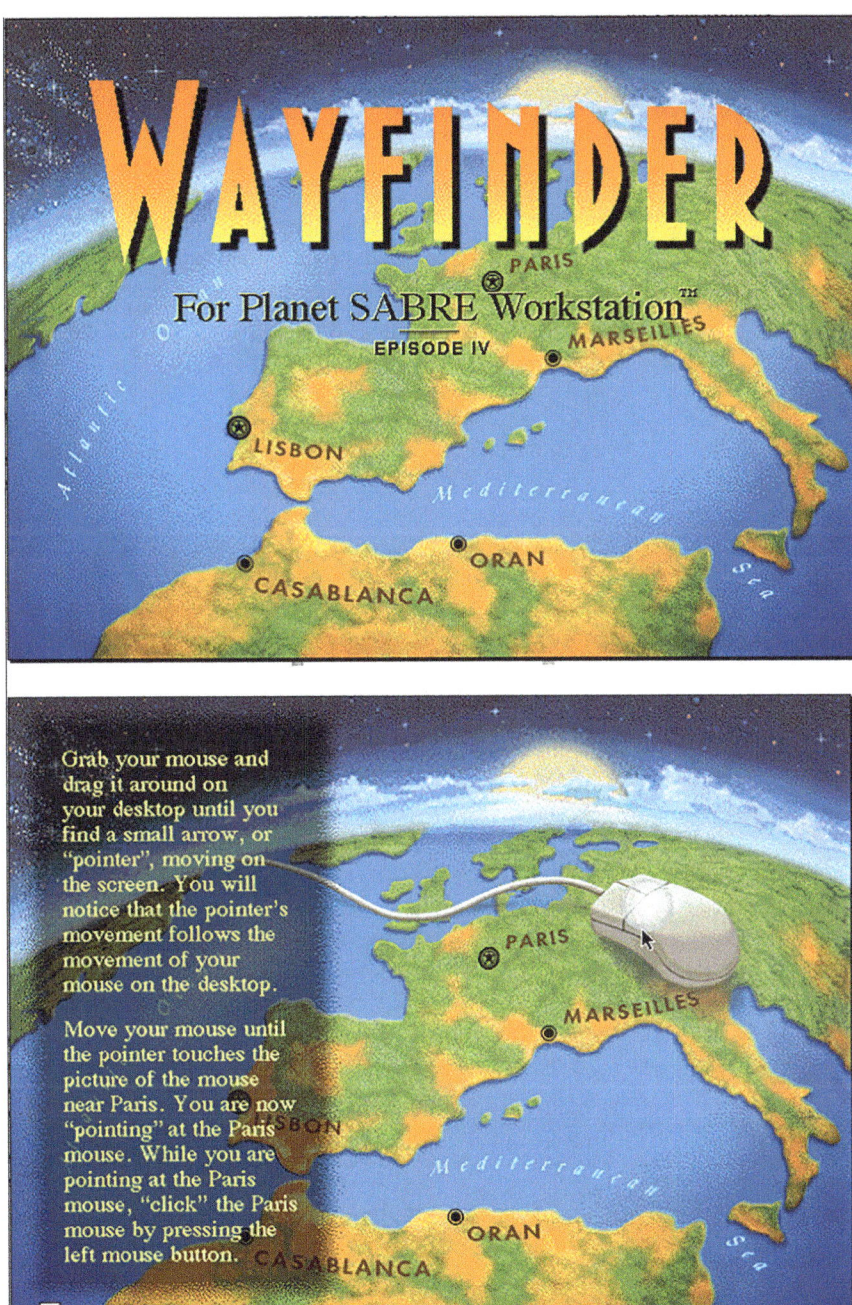

Figs. 8.57–8.61 Scenes from "Wayfinder," the interactive training game AM+A developed to enable travel agents to learn about Microsoft Windows and Planet, 1997–2000. (Source: AM+A archive; image designs by AM+A; used with permission of the author)

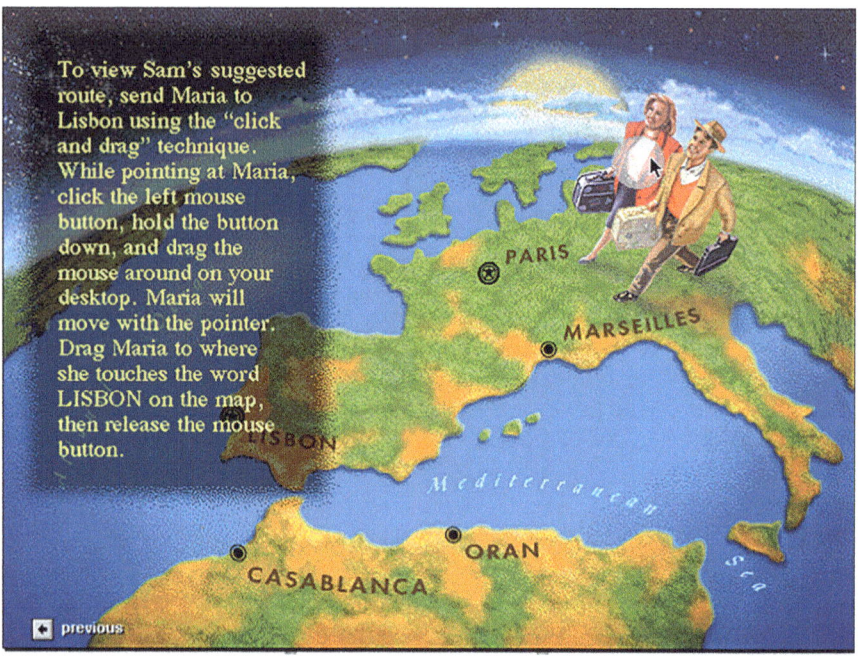

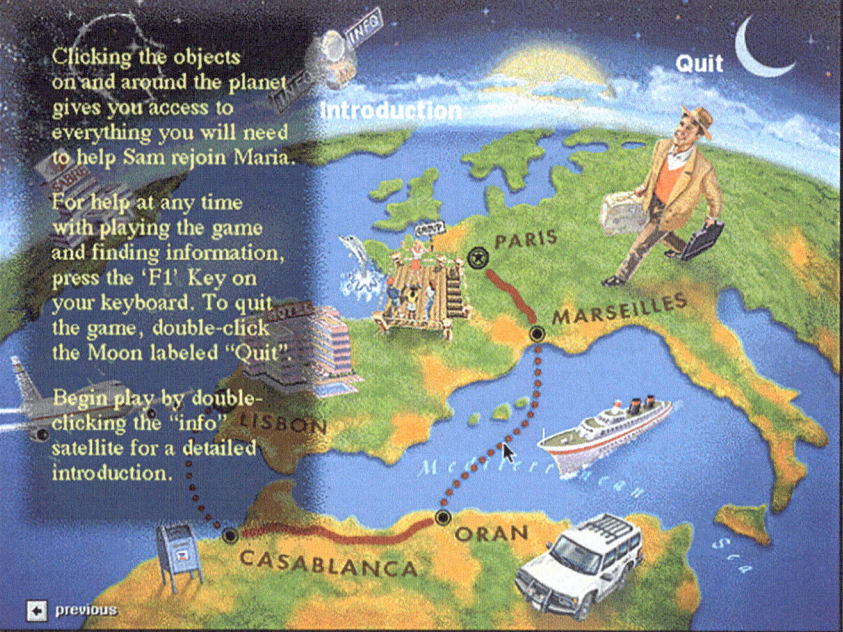

Figs. 8.57–8.61   (continued)

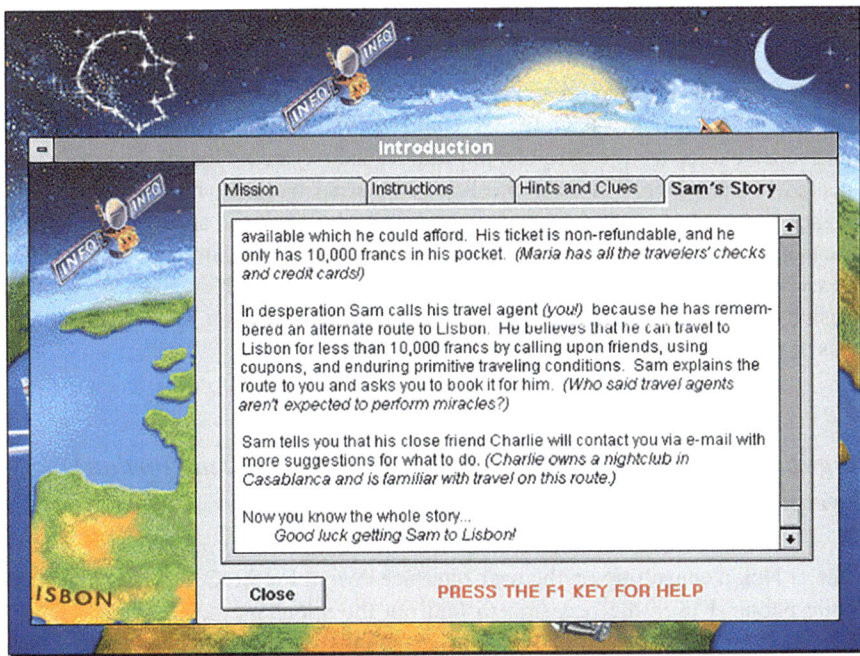

Figs. 8.57–8.61 (continued)

1994–2000

Computer-Animated Film, About Mid-1990s

Sometime in the mid-1990s, AM+A discussed the idea of creating a full-length feature computer-animated movie with Glen Hoptman, who had secured rights to Ben
Shahn's illustrated book *Alphabet of Creation*. The book told of the letters of the
Hebrew alphabet competing for beginning the Torah's text. Judson Rosebush was to
be the technical lead to make the computer animation work. I was to be the creative
lead in charge of the visual design. Glen sought funding while I tried to visit the
home/studio of Bob Dylan near Minneapolis/St. Paul. I had suggested to the team
that he might be willing to write the musical score and lyrics for the work. I stayed
with Rabbi Manes Friedman in St. Paul, who at that time was Bob Dylan's spiritual
guide as he reconnected with Judaism. Alas, I did not succeed in arranging a meeting
with Bob Dylan, and Glen did not succeed in finding the funds for the project. This
was just one of many potential projects that never got off the ground during the 40+
years of AM+A, but it was an exciting, motivating aspiration for a while.

Random House Interactive Book Design, 1994

In 1994, Random House approached us with an unusual offer: to design a template for an interactive "book" on a CD that would be used for multiple publications. We would receive a fee for the template plus additional payments for all the books that appeared in the series. This was the first time that I had ever heard of a graphic designer receiving a design fee addendum each time a book appeared using the same design. We had hoped for about ten books in the series, but unfortunately, the series was cancelled after only three books were published. Nevertheless, we had occasion to think out and design the standards for all navigation and content in this series of publications (Figs. 8.62–8.67).

Kingdom of Jordan, GUI-Design Workshop (Amman, Jordan), November 1996

While at Nokia consulting on the user-interface design for the Communicator 9000 mobile phone, I used the occasion to find out the telephone number of the royal palace in Amman, Jordan. It had occurred to me that within a month or two, I was scheduled to give a lecture at a conference in Israel, and I thought of providing a complimentary workshop about user-interface design to the software engineers of Jordan in celebration of the good relations among Jordan, Israel, and the USA at the time. I realized that my former Princeton student Lisa Hallaby, now Queen Noor of Jordan, might be interested. I was informed of an unusual telephone service in Finland that could find the phone of anyone in the world, so I asked for the royal palace in Jordan's telephone number and called Queen Noor! The phone was answered by a man who sounded like he was speaking from an underwater telephone booth, but I could understand his English well enough to learn that he thought I should fax my proposal to the number he gave me. I typed out a two-page proposal and faxed it from my Apple computer. Within a few days, I was back in California and received a reply. She had accepted my proposal!

Queen Noor had arranged a driver for me in Jordan. I made my way by taxi to the Allenby Gate connecting Jordan and Israel, walked across, and found a chauffeured Mercedes limousine waiting for me that whisked me to Petra five hours' drive south of Amman, where *Indiana Jones: The Last Crusade* film was shot. Petra is a gorgeous Nabataean ruin of an ancient trading city of 20,000 people carved into the solid sandstone rock 2000 years ago. As I walked around the ruins, ruminating on history, the Middle East, time, and beauty, I suddenly realized that I was having a strong pain radiating from the region of my heart down my left arm. I recognized the pain.

Twenty years earlier as a graduate student in graphic design at Yale, I had had a similar excruciating pain. I thought then in 1967 in the Medical Pavilion of the Toronto World Expo, a world's fair, that I was having a heart attack and would soon die. When I could no longer stand, I lay down, then thought to crawl behind a display cabinet to discreetly die. Fortunately, my feet were sticking out, and a passing

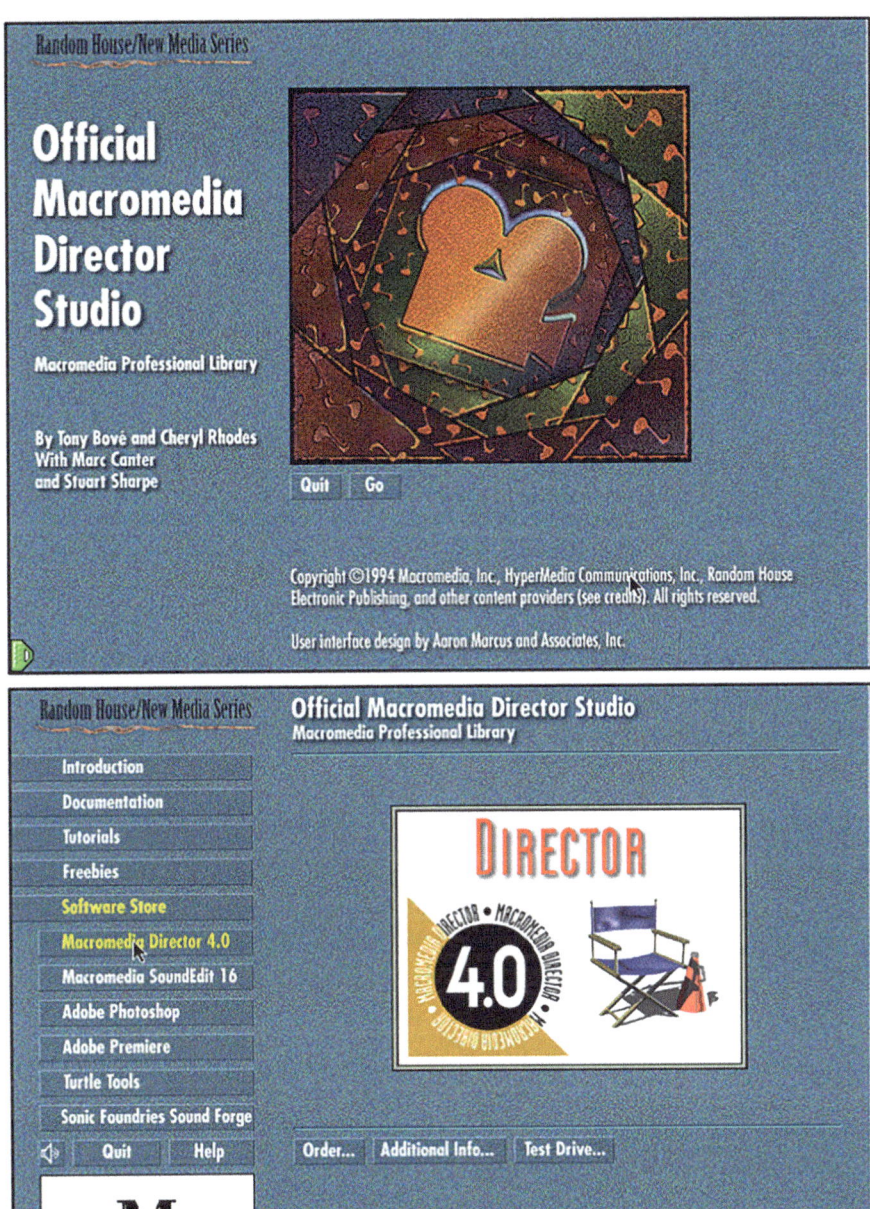

Figs. 8.62–8.67 Screen designs from the Random House publication series designed by AM+A. (Source: AM+A archive; images by AM+A; used with permission of Penguin Random House)

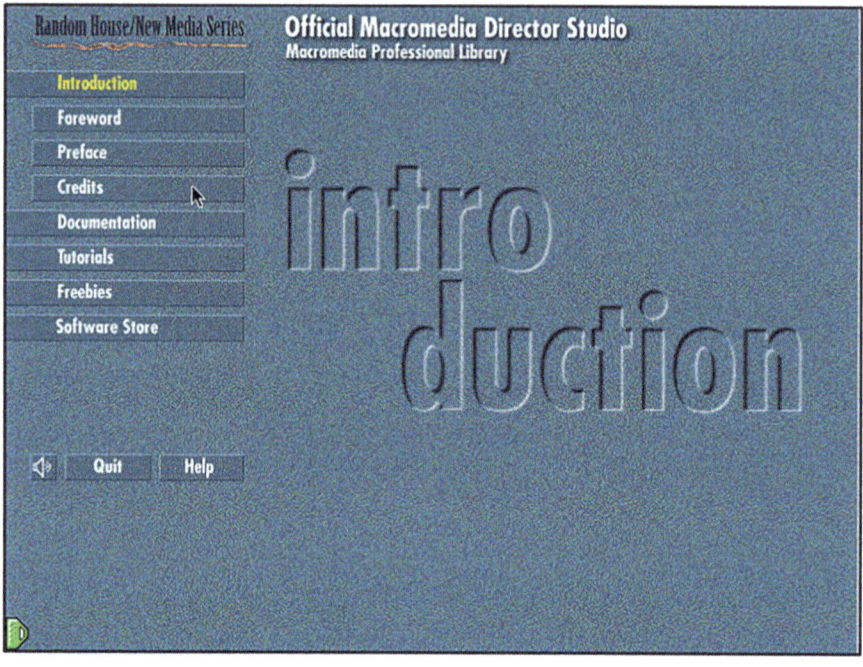

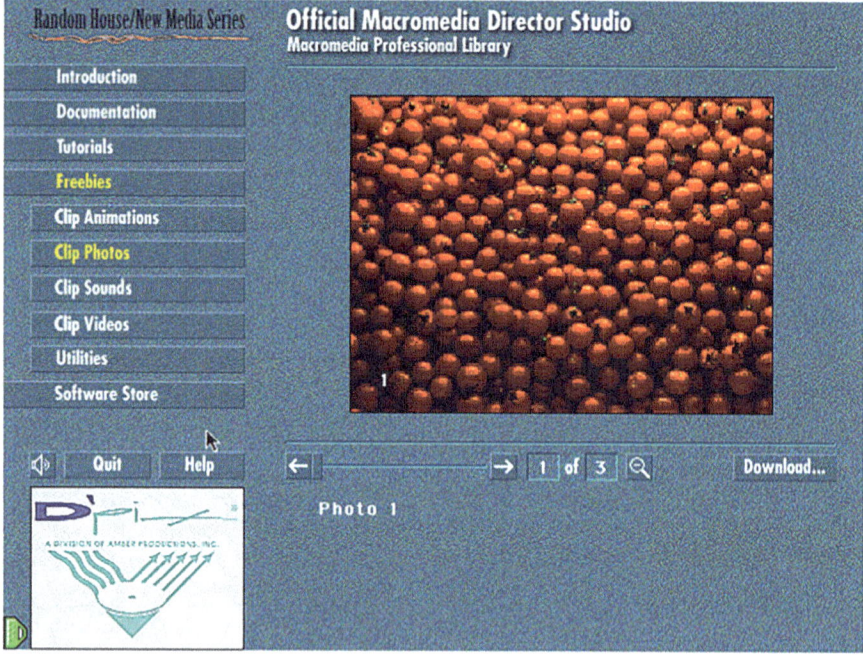

Figs. 8.62–8.67   (continued)

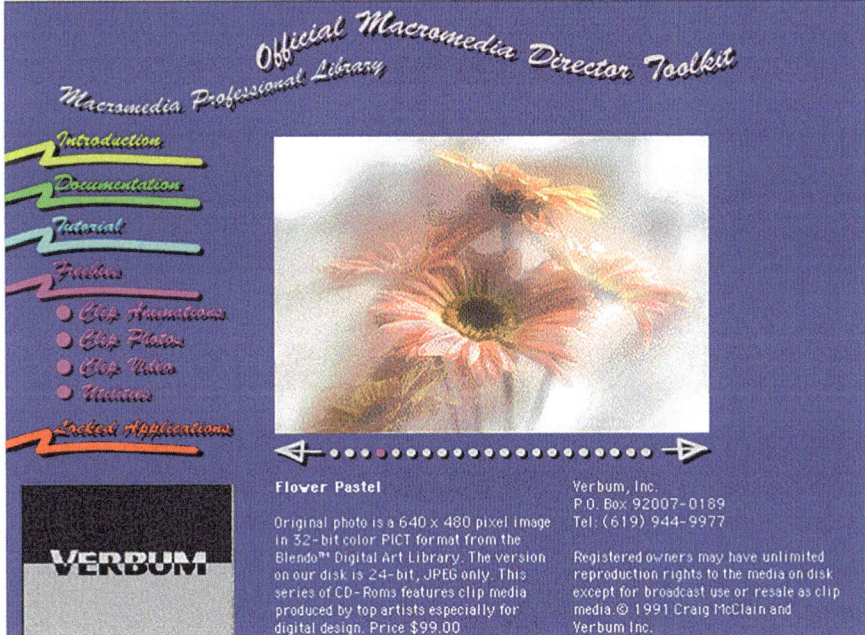

Figs. 8.62–8.67 (continued)

tourist noticed me and called an ambulance. In the hospital, I was diagnosed as having a partially (15%) collapsed left lung and was merely required to have bed rest until my lung re-inflated, which took about two weeks in Toronto and back in New Haven.

Now in 1996, I confidently assumed I was having the same problem, unaware that this time it really was a heart attack, and I was suffering angina. I did not want to check into a hospital five hours from Amman, so I continued the tour, visited the site of the Madaba mosaic map of Jerusalem, one of the earliest maps of this holy city, and visited Gerasa, one of the largest and best-preserved Roman ruins outside of Italy. Then I returned to Jerusalem for the weekend (Sabbath) and came back into Jordan a second time to have an audience with the Queen and to present my workshop. My audience with Her Majesty lasted 40 minutes. Her assistants were surprised it went on so long. We talked about our children, she told me stories, she told about His Majesty King Hussein, and what words of advice she had for Israeli software developers whom I would be addressing soon. She mentioned that one of her daughters was then an undergraduate in an East Coast university and lived without bodyguards. I expressed my surprise and asked her why. She said she wanted her daughter to know what freedom was like; once she graduated, she would live with bodyguards for the rest of her life. She told a story about the King visiting the USA (for medical treatments) and wanting to visit their daughter. Rather than drive in a chauffeured limousine, he rented a car, just like "any American or tourist" and drove up to visit their daughter. On the way, he became hungry and stopped at a diner to order a hamburger. When the astonished proprietor learned who his customer was, he immediately put up a sign in his restaurant: "Our Hamburgers are Fit for a King!" In regard to a message to Israeli software developers, she said that it would be good to establish business relations between Israeli and Jordanian developers. Such business relationships cannot bring about peace between the two countries, but when established, help to maintain peace, she added. I mentioned that comment when I spoke in Israel later that week.

As for the workshop, about 70 participants from all around the Arab world attended. I was surprised to see participants from Saudi Arabia, Egypt, as well as Jordan. It was the first UI workshop ever held in Jordan as far as I knew. My host was Mr. Karim Kawar, President, Kawar Group and Former Jordanian Ambassador to the USA, who was head of the Jordanian Computer Society. He was very kind and gracious to me during the visit. At the start of my lectures, before I came out to the large lecture room, he suggested that I might want to remove my *kippah* from on my head. He explained that there was no use needlessly antagonizing or alienating my audience. I agreed and removed my head-covering. The workshop proceeded without incident.

Samsung (South Korea), 1997

In 1997, my contacts with members of Samsung's UI development team, in particular Ms. Amy Chung, led to our being invited to give three one-week workshops in Seoul about UI development. Each visit would be separated by 1 month, so that participants could work on "homework" and have an opportunity to think about challenges we gave to them. Who attended the workshop? People working on the user-interface designs of mobile phones, cameras, microwave ovens, refrigerators, and even nuclear-reactor control panels.

During the first visit, I was asked, also, to give a high-level executive briefing about the value of UI design. This was an unusual opportunity to affect top management across many lines of business. I like to think that this lecture helped to catalyze Samsung's future world-renown corporate commitment to good user-interface design, especially for mobile phones.

One special feature of our workshop was that we gave participants the challenge of designing improved versions of a graphical airline booking reservation system. This challenge/opportunity was in fact the subject of our work for American Airlines/Sabre. We contacted our Sabre client managers, who, to my delight, were accepting of this unusual situation. At no time in our previous experience and at no time since did a client ever give permission for another company (in a noncompetitive industrial sector) permission to assist on solving a client's design challenges. It all worked out well in the end. The participants enjoyed working on a "real-life" project in our sessions and during the month break. Our other client received good design thinking and sketch solutions to detailed aspects of our own current design challenges.

Our Workshops End Abruptly

We returned for the second workshop, and all went well. We were enjoying our visits and learning much about Korean culture, history, work styles, and personalities. It was interesting to note that many managers were females, quite unlike in Japan, where most of the staff was male. These women were very smart and worked very hard. I was impressed.

Alas, after our second workshop, while we were waiting to schedule the third and final installment, the Korean economy suffered a tremendous blow, and the Korean Won was devalued by 50% in about October 1997. That meant our costs to Samsung were doubled. They decided to cancel the third workshop, and that event ended our first engagement with Samsung.

AM+A 15-Year Commemorative CD, 1997

In 1997, AM+A issued a 15-year commemorative CD that featured the history of AM+A, its projects, and some of its Associates. AM+A wrote and designed the content. Designer/Analyst Luke Ball was responsible for managing and developing much of the content. We were pleased with the content, and some of the imagery was used in exhibit posters we used for marketing our services (Figs. 8.68–8.72).

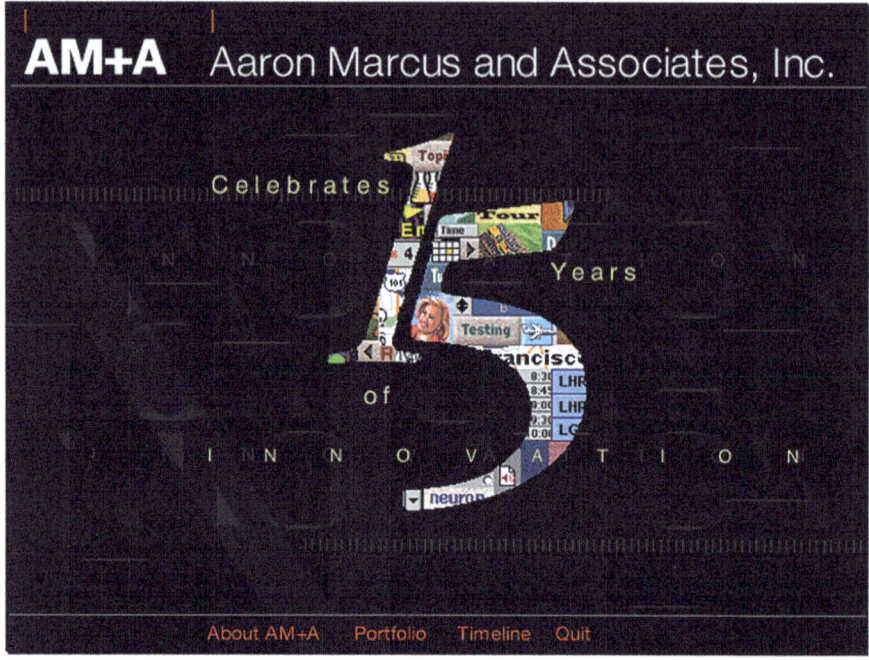

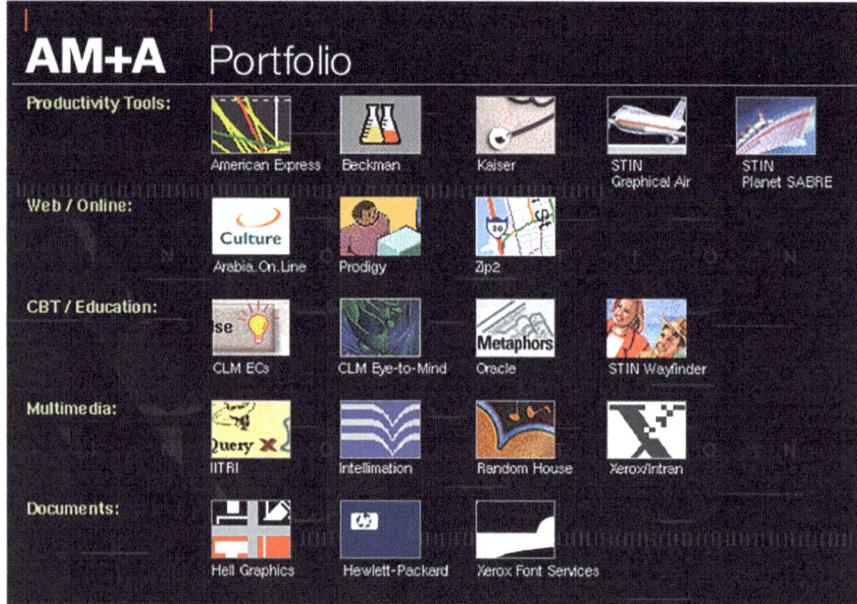

Figs. 8.68–8.72 Scenes from AM+A's commemorative CD. (Source: AM+A archive; Images by AM+A; used with permission of the author)

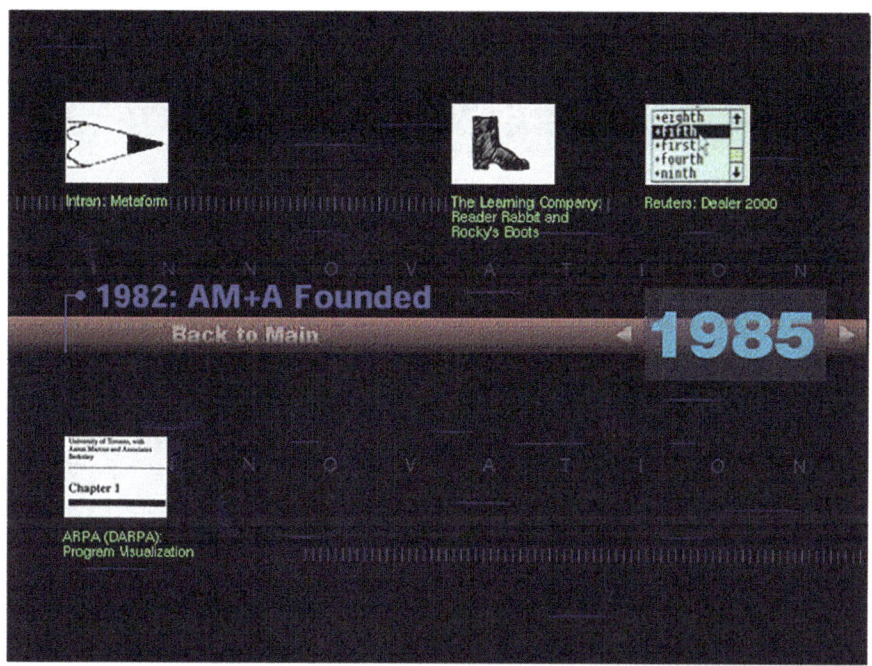

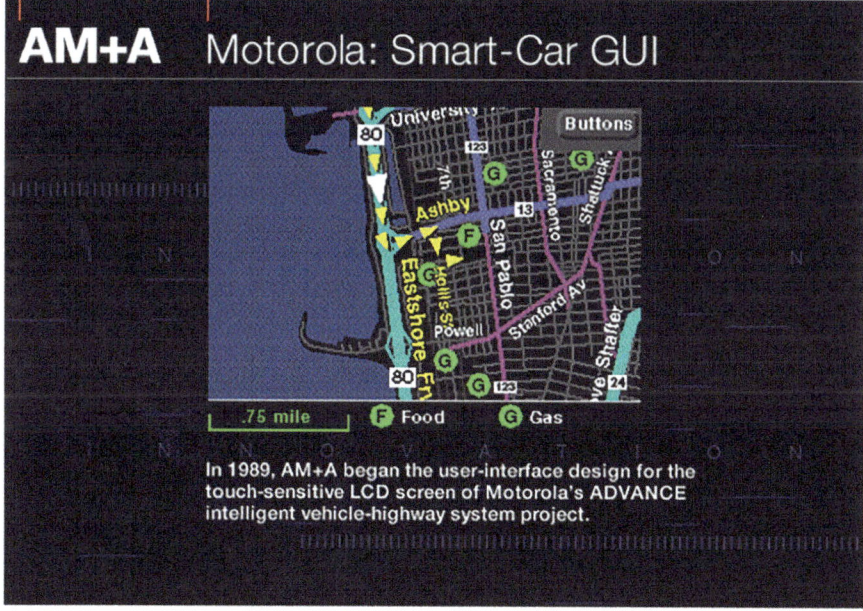

In 1989, AM+A began the user-interface design for the touch-sensitive LCD screen of Motorola's ADVANCE intelligent vehicle-highway system project.

Figs. 8.68–8.72 (continued)

In 1994-5, AM+A designed an innovative Planet SABRE Workstation™ user interface for SABRE Travel Information Network, Inc., the world's largest private online system.

Figs. 8.68–8.72   (continued)

Samsung Mobile Research, 2000

Despite the late cancellation of our third workshop, we continued to have good relations with Samsung (I would see Amy Chung and other South Korean Samsung staff members at the CHI conferences). In 2000, Amy Chung, now managing about nine projects simultaneously (it seemed amazing to me that she could do this, even with many assistants), engaged us to research the needs for advanced mobile phones in North America and to develop 100 design concepts for such phones, that is, suites of functions.

We carried out user research by giving tape recorders to potential users to understand their needs. They had no experience with smart-phone functionality, so we had to encourage them to be aware of needs and wants, and to record them whenever they realized they needed some kind of functionality or data. After working with our team, headed by Eugene Chen, a Senior Designer/Analyst at AM+A, we prepared 100 new ideas and presented them in a report in which each was described and visualized, and in an interactive multimedia demo using Macromedia Director. We even sent two of our staff to South Korea to present our findings.

Samsung was kind enough to give us permission to publish a case study of our project in CHI's magazine *Interactions*, to sponsor and help organize an informal gathering at CHI 2001 in Seattle (which attracted about 150 attendees), and to include us in their exhibition booth with demos of our work for them. In general, the project was one of the most successful of our client relations and produced excellent results.

We lost access to all future development news once we turned over our ideas to the Samsung UI designers, who had to work with software and hardware staff to

Fig. 8.73 Example image of smart-phone UI concept for Samsung. The design was similar to an iPhone but appeared 7 years before iPhones were introduced. (Source: AM+A archive; Image designed by AM+A; used with permission of the author)

bring out products for the intended target of North America in 2003. One of our ideas was turned into a product by Samsung, a device that one could affix to a car door or home door, that would tell a phone to change settings automatically for the correct use environment. During the intervening years, from 2000 to 2003, Samsung rose in the mobile world to second behind Motorola thanks to its devotion to good UI design. We like to think we played a role in that success (Fig. 8.73).

Oracle, Worldwide Education, GUI Design CD-ROM, 1997

In 1997, AM+A was asked to prepare an interactive training CD-ROM for Oracle Worldwide Education (WWE). AM+A used Authorware to produce the CD and hired a third party to assist. The subject matter was Oracle's Forms front-end to its database-management software, which was itself so complicated that an entire supplementary and lucrative business line was necessary to provide training to end-users. To supplement the in-person courses and other training documents, CD-ROMs were considered a valuable medium. WWE had just begun to develop authoring guidelines, but these were minimal. Preparing the necessary deliverables for our client was tedious and time-consuming, and our budget was almost entirely used up on our third-party software developer. The Oracle manager recognized the faults of his management and the limited documentation he had provided, and he gave AM+A a second project (which we partially feared). However, by this time, Oracle had benefited from our previous bad experience with them and had commissioned detailed product specifications. Although daunting, by carefully following the requirements (which had been missing in our first project), we were able to quickly and efficiently deliver user-interface guidelines for their software, even using our own classic AM+A GUI-design training content, which was an added benefit for our fixed-fee project, in addition to earning back some of the money lost on the first fixed-fee project (Figs. 8.74 and 8.75).

Screen from Developer 2000 ™ Forms (v4.5) Online Mentor, designed by AM+A, 1997:

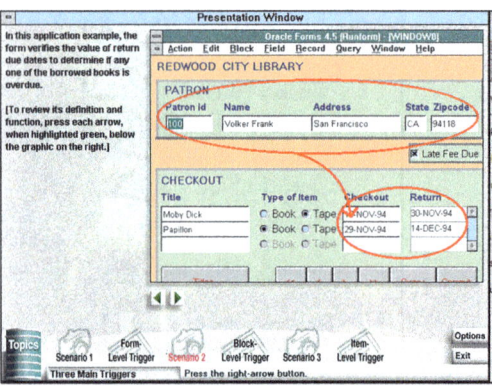

Screen from CD-ROM that uses some AM+A GUI-design content:

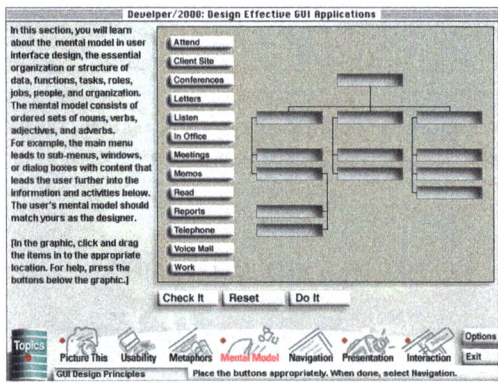

Figs. 8.74 and 8.75 Screens from the Oracle Developer 2000™ Forms (v4.5) Online Mentor including GUI-design training, which used some AM+A GUI-design content. (Source: AM+A archive; images by AM+A. All Oracle images are copyrighted by Oracle and are used with permission of Oracle)

Visa, 1997–2003

AM+A developed another successful relationship with Visa, Inc., based in Foster City, CA. We began working with them because Sara Garrison and Michael Lloyd Davies had moved to that company from the US Federal Reserve Bank, San Francisco Chapter. They had both been our client representatives and patrons of AM+A and wanted to continue their relationships with us. Sara became a Vice-President of engineering and was proposing a more Internet-based framework in which Visa would operate. We helped to write and design a PowerPoint presentation that helped to convince the two top levels of bank committees that oversaw Visa and led to the successful deployment of her approach. At one point we prepared a document to review the many projects we did. Most of these projects were managed at AM+A by Sam Ackerman, our Marketing and Development Manager (Fig. 8.76).

Fig. 8.76 Table of AM+A projects for Visa from about 1997–2003. (Source: AM+A archive; used with permission of the author)

Through our multiyear engagement, we worked on more than 33 projects at Visa, helping to train their staff and to improve the design of their software applications' user interfaces.

We also provided multiple days of training in UI design to their staff. Visa's Manager of Corporate Training, Larry Aiken, provided this letter of commendation about our tutorials:

From: "Aiken, Larry" laiken@inovant.com
 To: 'Aaron Marcus' Aaron@AMandA.com
 Subject: UI Design Class
 Date: Fri, 11 Jul 2003 09:09:10 -0700
 Aaron –
 I would also like to take the opportunity to thank you for the excellent job AM+A has done in preparing and delivering an effective, useful, and enjoyable Advanced User Interface Design class for Visa and Inovant staff.
 The class participant comments were highly favorable, which leads me to believe that we achieved our goals of level-setting the User Interface Designers in the organization, raising the bar for consistent and usable interfaces, and providing a forum for our staff to network and meet with others who have complementary experiences to round-out design efforts. I appreciate the time taken in the class to provide the class members with time to discuss and begin forming a center of excellence in user interface design. This group, under your guidance, coalesced into a unified group that will be a critical component in project management within the Inovant and Visa organizations.
 Thanks to you and your staff for using our comments and suggestions to customize the class agenda and contents to ensure that the materials were applicable to our circumstances, organized according to RUP best practices, and included sufficient hands-on experience for the group to expand their understanding of the concepts.
 And finally, thank you for the candid comments regarding the class participants. This information will enable us to ensure that staff participants receive the support and assistance necessary in their future efforts.
 As we move forward in institutionalizing the User Interface Center of Excellence, I look forward to your comments and feedback.
 Thanks—Larry

Projects for Visa and its sub-company Inovant (which consisted of software developers) became the largest and most complex of our history. Many of them were based in financial applications and focused on usability issues. Most were not informal and customer-facing projects. However, we also consulted on Visa's customer-facing Web site, helping them to improve the appearance and appeal of their screens (Figs. 8.77–8.82).

Visa Card detailed screen list for banks:

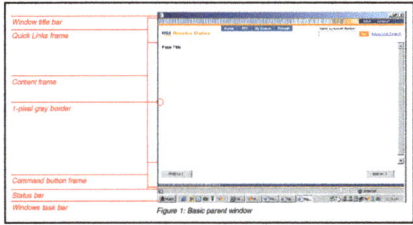

VISA Visa Information Source   **BigBank**

Umsatzabrechnung
Ackerman (045634)

Conhuge Corp. Marketing
18. März 2002 bis 29. April 2002

Buchungsnummer	Transaktionsdatum	Buchungsdatum	Name	Ort	Buchungsbetrag (EUR)	Umsatzsteuer
2469216207700066242320	18.03.2002	19.03.2002	OnStar/Mobile Services	888-864-2801 USA	18,00	0,00
2429910208106103952100	21.03.2002	25.03.2002	Citgo #6690 Sekulski Auto Shop	Lewisburg PA USA	28,39	0,00
2490604208889600261030	29.03.2002	01.04.2002	swissotel	New York NY USA	389,79	0,00
2432301209224842601011	02.04.2002	03.04.2002	Homestead Resort	Hot Springs VA USA	250,00	0,00
2412151209200038520421	02.04.2002	03.04.2002	American Surgical Assoiation	Manchester MA USA	250,00	0,00
2429910209706103981200	05.04.2002	08.04.2002	Citgo #6690 Sekulski Auto Shop	Lewisburg PA USA	27,67	0,00
2445501209720985725221	07.04.2002	09.04.2002	Sunoco	Lewisburg PA USA	30,60	0,00
1425810210900103811100	07.04.2002	10.04.2002	Citgo #6690 Sekulski Auto Shop	Lewisburg PA USA	30,22	0,00
2469216210800002894255	18.04.2002	19.04.2002	OnStar/Mobile Services	888-864-2801 USA	18,00	0,00
2469216210900000154395	18.04.2002	19.04.2002	OnStar/Personal Call	888-4ONSTAR USA	104,52	0,00
2445501211121125718995	18.04.2002	19.04.2002	Sunoco	Montandon PA USA	30,74	0,00
2424651211420634972405	18.04.2002	22.04.2002	APCDA: Wilkes-Barre Airport	Avoca PA USA	13,25	0,00
2416405211537800001977	18.04.2002	22.04.2002	Exxon-Mobil #04694147	Harrison PA USA	12,70	0,00
2445501211421831514789	18.04.2002	22.04.2002	SHEETZ #078	Chambersburg PA USA	20,37	0,00
2445501211162117315587	19.04.2002	22.04.2002	SHEETZ #197	Stephens City PA USA	24,95	0,00
2445501211821185705724	19.04.2002	22.04.2002	Sunoco	Lewisburg PA USA	33,21	0,00
2410838212020782038903	21.04.2002	23.04.2002	Powerhouse Eatery	White Haven PA USA	58,31	0,00
2445501209720985725221	21.04.2002	23.04.2002	Sunoco	Lewisburg PA USA	30,60	0,00
2429910210906103911100	23.04.2002	25.04.2002	Citgo #6690 Sekulski Auto Shop	Lewisburg PA USA	30,22	0,00
2469216210800002894255	23.04.2002	25.04.2002	OnStar/Mobile Services	888-864-2801 USA	18,00	0,00
2429910210906103911100	24.04.2002	25.04.2002	Citgo #6690 Sekulski Auto Shop	Lewisburg PA USA	30,22	0,00
2469216210800002894255	24.04.2002	25.04.2002	OnStar/Mobile Services	888-864-2801 USA	18,00	0,00

(weiter)

Zahlen Sie im Juni bei Pabst Computer mit Ihrer Visa Commercial Card und sichern Sie sich 10% Rabatt!

Dieser Auszug wurde von Hans Augsburger am 07.07.2002 um 14:23 Uhr erstellt.   Seite 1 von 84

Resolve Online UI Style Guide, written and designed by AM+A, showing a sample basic parent window layout, 2002.

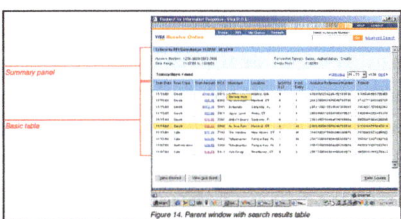

Resolve Online UI Style Guide, written and designed by AM+A, showing search results table layout, 2002:

Figs. 8.77–8.81 Screen images from different Visa applications that were improved by AM+A. (Source: AM+A archive; images by AM+A; used with permission of the author)

UI Pattern Analysis for UI Guide Document, explanatory diagram written and designed by AM+A, 2002

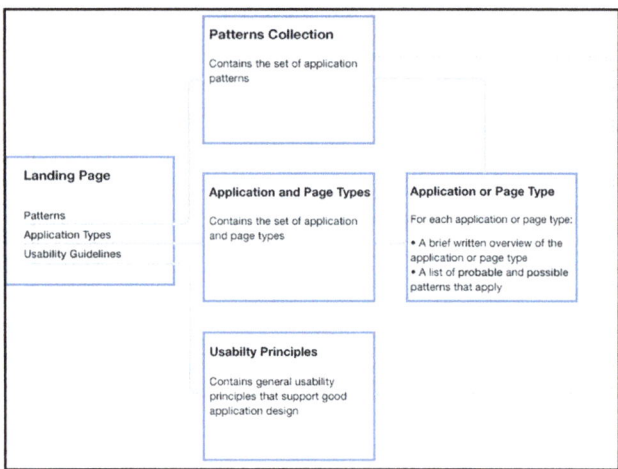

Figs. 8.77–8.81   (continued)

Federal Reserve Bank of the USA (FRB), 1997–2002, and FRB/ SF, AMI Advanced App Design, c.1997

For about 5 years, 1997–2002, AM+A worked with three branches of the US Federal Reserve Bank: San Francisco, New York City, and Chicago. AM+A provided training to their developers in San Francisco and New York City, designed an improved Intranet for the Chicago branch, and developed a guiding prototype of an integrated system for managing all the banks of the USA for San Francisco's branch.

In 1997, AM+A designed a fairly complete set of screens for AMI, an advanced application under development that would enable the FRB for the first time to review the status of all 8000 US banks to determine if any were at risk. Prior to this time, the FRB relied on a mixture of media and techniques: faxed reports, electronic communication, paper documents, etc. AM+A had to guess at the capabilities of Internet application development tools about 3 years in advance of reality. AM+A worked closely with FRB technical experts during this time. The application was subsequently completed approximately in agreement with AM+A's designs (Fig. 8.82).

Commentary

The FRB was very satisfied with AM+A's work. In 2004, one of their Senior Vice-Presidents wrote this letter of commendation:

This letter of recommendation sets forth the key experiences and benefits of employing AM+ A while I was Senior Vice-President and Product Manager of the Support Function Office of the Federal Reserve System. In this role, I was in charge

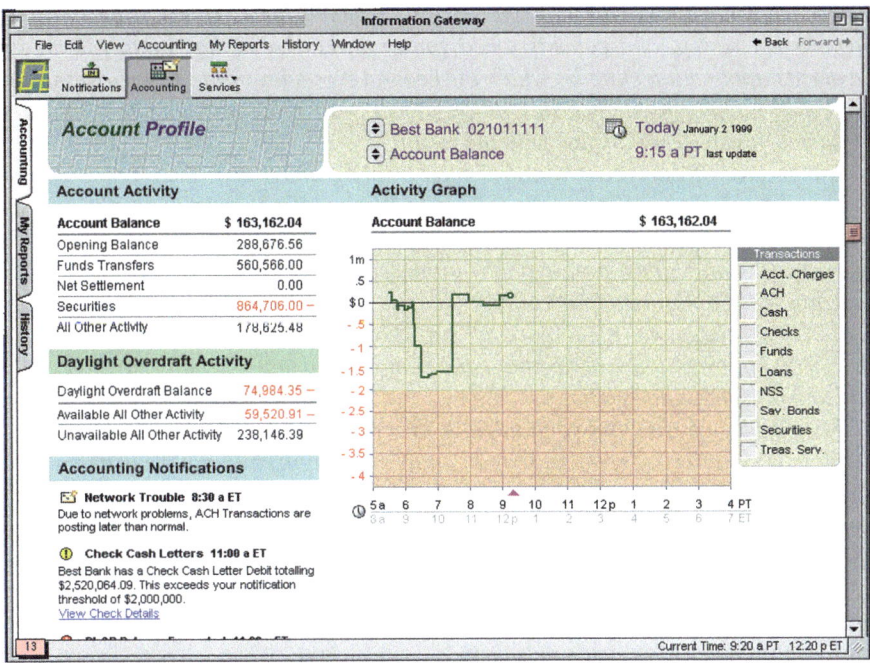

Fig. 8.82 Screen from the FRB AMI demo prepared by AM+A, c.1997. (Source: AM+A archive; image by AM+A; used with permission of AM+A)

of engineering and software development for the Fed's web-based financial ser-vices. My understanding is that, in addition to the work you provided to the Support Function Office, you also served a number of Federal Reserve Banks (e.g., San Francisco, New York, and Chicago, among others) during the period 1997–2002. I personally monitored and managed your work during the 1999–2001 timeframe.

Your firm had already come highly recommended by Ms. Sara Garrison, the previous Senior Vice President and Support Function Office Manager, and Mr. Michael Lloyd Davies, who worked for her.

AM+A helped develop improved versions of client-server and Web-based user interfaces by analyzing existing applications, designing new standards, working with our development teams to implement them, and participating in the Fed's nationwide planning meetings. Your over-all role was to help establish organization-wide standards. In all circumstances, AM+A delivered high-quality services, documents, and presentations. In fact, on one or more occasions, your deliverables were key instruments of getting executive management acceptance and in leading the way to new initiatives and key improvements in the applications we were then rolling out. One especially important project was the Accounting Management Information (AMI) prototype, which showed extensive simulations of Web-based integrated applications planned for about 3 years out. This prototype was widely circulated to groups throughout the FRB and helped guide our future developments. The application suite was later implemented and deployed success-fully. Your work was crucial to its beginning and middle stages.

In fact, your demo was so impressive that management of the U.S. Treasury Department saw it, and commissioned you to develop a similar prototype for its payments application suite by which all Federal Agencies of the U.S. Government are paid. I understand that this project went very well, and that the Treasury Department was very satisfied with the results.

It is my recollection that you presented training about user-interface design to software developers at the New York Federal Reserve Bank, in 1999 or 2000, which was also well received, and provided the base for the web design of the System's most secure and highest profile application-Fedwire. It is through this application that billions of dollars are transacted on a daily basis between financial institutions. I also appreciated your guidance in strategic matters related to user-interface design and information visualization, and I am pleased that you and your staff could sit in on our planning meetings.

My experience was that you and your firm delivered high quality products and services in a variety of roles (research, analysis, design, training, envisioning, and strategic design planning), using extremely professional practices, and a very pleasant staff derived from the corporate culture and standards that you inculcated. In short, you exceeded our expectations greatly, and did it on a timely basis. The success in the Federal Reserve System is a tribute to your leadership and industry accomplishments. I am pleased to be able to recommend your company to any and all potential clients for similar projects.

Sincerely,

Kerry Webb

Kerry Webb,
Professor, Department of Economics
107 Smith Building
Brigham Young University
Provo, UT 84602

Cogito Learning Media, 1997–2002

In 1997, through a friend, Jim Maurer, I was introduced to Ms. Linda Chaput, who had been associated with *Scientific American* magazine, a publication to which I have subscribed since I was about 10 years old. She had started Cogito Learning Media (CLM), a learning company that produced multimedia educational products, which was based in San Francisco and New York City.

By the time we finished working with CLM, we had helped to design more than 30 CD-ROM products and to script them using Authorware. CLM had developed a large body of scientific and technical imagery for its products. Keeping track of all the product assets was itself a tremendous catalogue- and database-maintenance project.

We did so much work with CLM that in 1999, we decided to open an office in New York City using space in their New York office. They were very generous to our needs and comfortable with our doing projects for other clients. This interim office gave us time to find a second AM+A location at 5 Desbrosses Street, near Canal and Varick in Manhattan. It was very exciting, and challenging, to run two offices. I had to travel often to New York City, and we arranged for joint company meetings via telephone and the video connection each week to keep track of new staff and new clients/projects. Ed Guttman became the Director of our New York office. Karen Brown headed our Emeryville office.

Among other CLM product series, AM+A designed and produced the user interfaces for the Knowledge Now video educational products.

Eye-to-Mind Knowledge Summaries, 1999

In 1997, CLM posed for us our most challenging project: to design a new form of product, intended to be very inclusive of text, imagery, video, and sound, and very inexpensive (about $10, then very low-cost) because CLM already owned rights to most of the imagery. CLM hired subject-matter experts to write the text of knowledge summaries, each of which was called "Eye-to-Mind." They were unlike anything on the market. The CD-ROM products were a kind of knowledge advertisement, which made the subject matter unusually appealing for college-level students and above (and to their faculty), introductions that would provide incentives to learn more about an entire topic.

At first, we had to develop metaphors for how to understand the content sections and the controls to access it. We decided to adopt a nonlinear approach to the content and a UI that was a little mysterious, unlike many of the UIs we usually designed to be extremely self-revealing. Ed Guttman served as Senior Designer for the CLM products. Our first project was a CD-ROM discussing HIV and Aids (Figs. 8.83, 8.84, and 8.85).

At first, Linda Chaput did not know for certain what kind of illustration style she wanted. We used a thick paper catalogue of US illustrators' portfolios, through which she could quickly flip, to help her decide which styles seemed most appropriate and appealing. This technique enabled us to quickly find styles that were right, even if she could not verbalize which styles she sought. We had used this technique earlier with Sabre management.

The results of our work were considered successful by the client and by critics. One design award judge said that Eye-to-Mind represented what multimedia products could become at their best.

Sadly, CLM could not make the transition quickly enough to Web-based products and seemed to disappear from the marketplace shortly after our "tour of duty" with them ended. The CLM team was one of the finer groups of people with whom we worked.

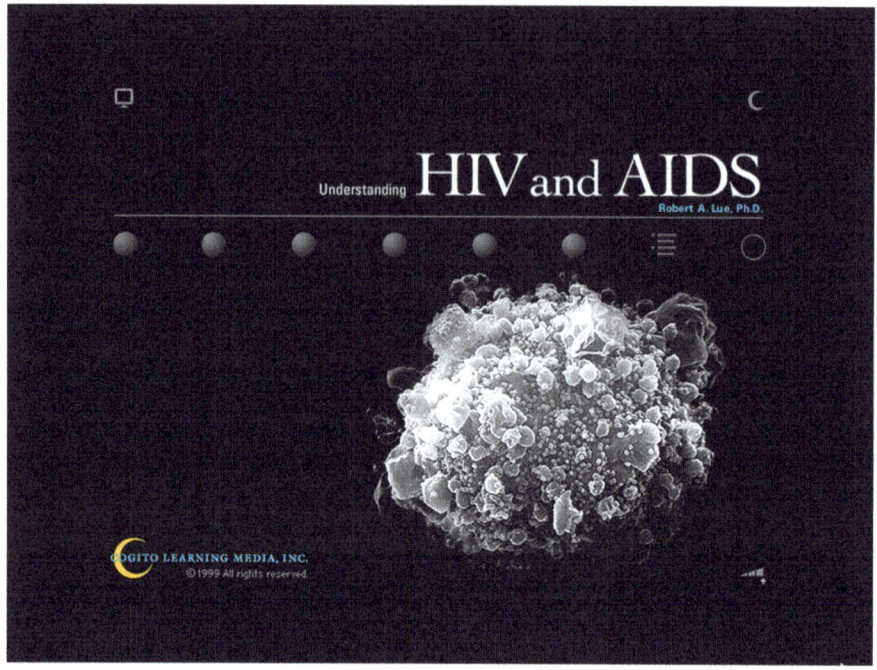

Fig. 8.83 Eye-to-Mind "HIV/AIDS" product images designed by AM+A. (Source: Images from AM+A archives, used with permission of Cogito Learning Media)

Getty Museum Web Site Design, 2000

The J. Paul Getty Trust is an international cultural and philanthropic institution devoted to the visual arts made up of the J. Paul Getty Museum in Los Angeles, the Getty Research Institute, the Getty Conservation Institute, and the Getty Grant Program. Besides hosting more than 3000 works of art, the Getty Web site presents event information, professional reports in conservation and art history, job listings, grant information, research tools, videos, and more. During March to September 2000, the Getty Trust came to AM+A to help design their first-ever unified Web site. The project was a challenging exercise in large-scale information architecture. Prior to the launch of the redesigned getty.edu, several different groups had developed their own sites with no standards or centralized efforts.

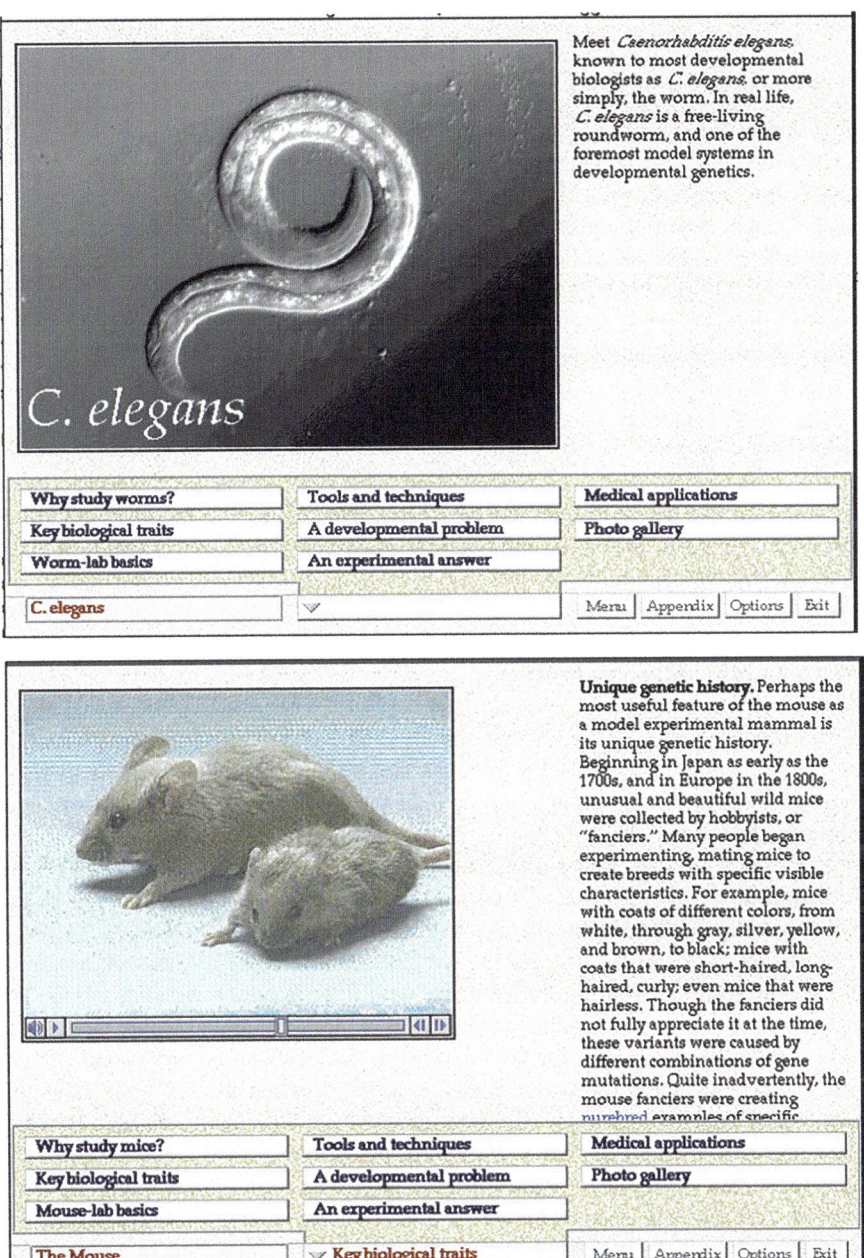

Figs. 8.84 and 8.85 Images from Knowledge Now video educational CD-ROMs. Screen layouts designed by AM+A. (Source: AM+A archive; used with permission of Cogito Learning Media)

Participants

Project participants included the following:

Vicki Porter, Project Lead, J. Paul Getty Trust
Aaron Marcus, Principal Designer, AM+A
Samuel Ackerman, Project Manager, AM+A
Eugene Chen, Design Lead, AM+A
Kent Miller, Visual Design Lead, AM+A
Larry Guan, Designer/Analyst, AM+A
Junghwa Lee, Designer/Analyst, AM+A
Alison Martin, Designer/Analyst, AM+A

Objectives

The objectives of the redesign were to present one coherent brand and navigation for all Getty content, bring the most interesting and compelling content to the top level, and encourage exploration and discovery.

Design and Development Process

Integrating all of this legacy content and creating a coherent information architecture was no small task. AM+A's first task was to meet with representatives from many Getty stakeholder groups to reconcile their differing needs. Many strategic decisions that could have become political were grounded by a user-centered approach. In particular, user portraits helped to clarify the design strategy. With the Getty, AM+A created a set of target user portraits (personas). These portraits encouraged lively discussions that drove many key design decisions.

For instance, the target user for the Art Collections, "Chris," was seen as someone who would be exploring the Web site with little intent or direction. Thus, the design was focused on offering many paths of exploration and avoiding dead ends. AM+A capitalized on cross-indexed data from the Getty about artists and subject matter to provide users a means of easily traveling between areas of interest. Detail views allow users to see many different perspectives on a single piece. "Thelma" was a professional art historian with need to access many of the Getty's more technical resources. Through detailed discussions, it became apparent that Thelma would be an unlikely user of the Art Collection—as we had initially assumed— since as a professional, her needs would be very specific and technical. "Brian," the user portrait for the Visitor's Guide sub-site was defined as someone who might visit the Getty one day and Disneyland the next. Hence, this section was given a very pragmatic focus and filled with logistical aids such as wheelchair access and parking information. With this basis, we were able to move on to designing a navigation system that would accommodate the full breadth and depth of content. Schematic designs such as those shown in Figs. 8.7 and 8.8 were created, focusing primarily on details of the browse and search navigation systems.

Solution Details

After analyzing the various information structures that were inherent in the content, we defined a robust "toolkit" of page types and navigation devices (such as sub-sites, sections, subsections, breadcrumbs, see-also links, etc.) that could handle any kind of content situation. To handle content of this scale, it was necessary to divide the entire site into eight sub-sites. These sub-sites were each given their own color identity to help the users maintain a sense of place. Figure 9.0 shows several pages of the new design system.

After organizing the major content groups, AM+A focused on enabling useful and engaging interactions. The Web site includes more than 3255 works of art from the J. Paul Getty Museum in Los Angeles. To port images of these works successfully to the Web, AM+A had to ensure an easy, pleasurable, and educational browsing experience for even the most casual of users. In the "Explore Art" section of getty.edu, shown in Figs. 9.1 and 9.3, AM+A capitalized on cross-indexed data from the Getty about artists and subject matter to provide users a means of easily traveling between areas of interest. Detail views allow users to see many different perspectives on a single piece.

The Getty also has an impressive, rich, and dense calendar of events. The new calendar, which AM+A developed for the Getty, allowed users to find events in an intuitive way: either by date or event type. We created a way for users to find information that is most pertinent to them. Finally, after developing the site's architecture, navigation, and interaction, AM+A was still faced with the challenge of creating a visual design worthy of presenting the works of art—the challenge of designing a digital museum. The architect Richard Meier had created a highly modernist world-class museum to physically house the Getty's collection of classical works and antiquities. Our clients wanted to retain that juxtaposition, but avoid a growing perception of the Getty as austere. We were chartered with introducing a sense of whimsy that would be warm and welcoming to the local Los Angeles population. AM+A designers explored many different visual directions. Some of these are shown in Fig. 8.92.

In the final design, friendly and saturated colors provide the backdrop for clear, crisp, legible type, while some elements, such as the Getty logo, were tilted to express a light sense of playfulness.

Post-launch Result

The site was launched in February of 2001. Post-launch usability tests were conducted. Positive results included that users appreciated and were able to use the site's cross-linking features. One negative finding was that many users did not think the large type links on the home page (e.g., Visitor Guide) were clickable. The Web site developers at the Getty have continued to find new possibilities within the design. For instance, Fig. 8.93 shows a follow-on snapshot of Getty.edu's home page featuring a whimsical insect that crawls across the Getty logo via dHTML animation to promote a then-current exhibition (Figs. 8.86, 8.87, 8.88, 8.89, 8.90, 8.91, 8.92, and 8.93).

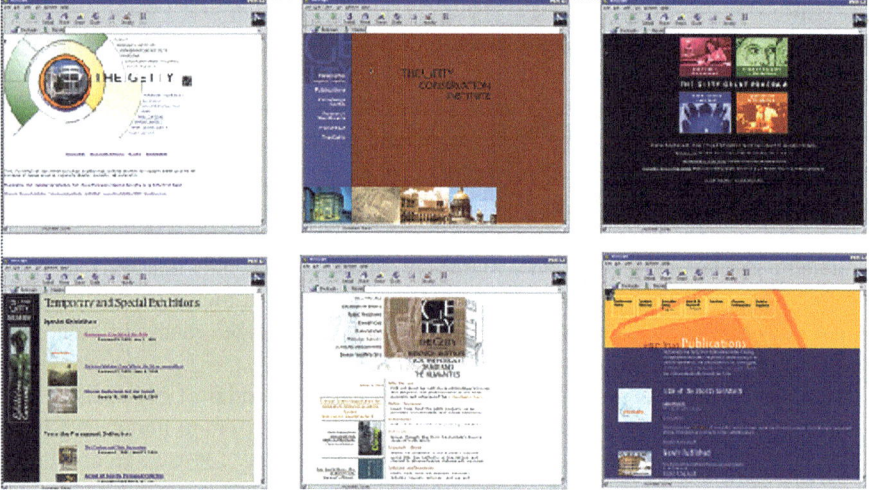

Fig. 8.86 Images of several Getty Web sites before AM+A's design integration. (Source: Images from Getty Web site; used with permission of Getty Museum)

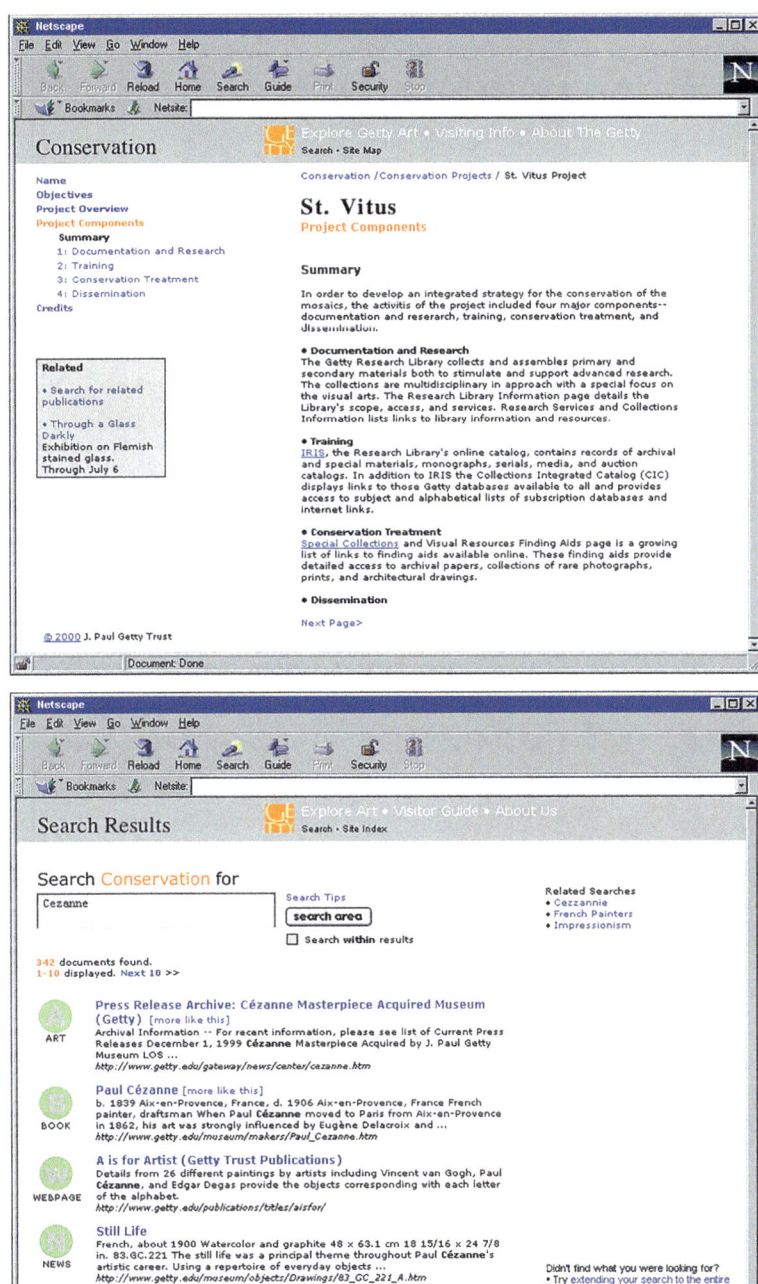

Figs. 8.87 and 8.88 Navigation study schematic and search results study schematic. (Source: AM+A archive; images by AM+A; used with permission of Getty Museum)

Figs. 8.89 and 8.90 Color-coding and organization of J. Paul Getty Trust sub-sites. (Source: AM+A archive; images designed by AM+A; used with permission of Getty Museum)

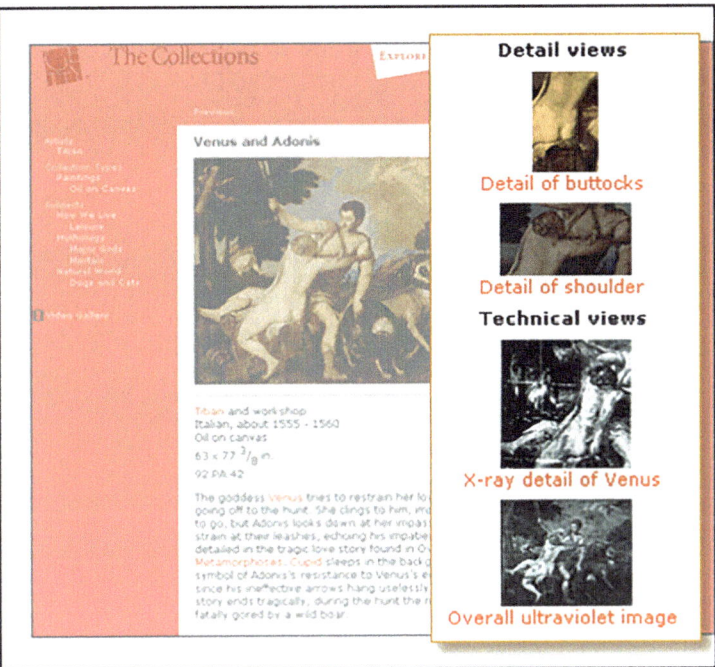

Fig. 8.91 On many pages, users are exposed to detail or alternate views of a piece. (Source: AM+A archive; images designed by AM+A; used with permission of Getty Museum)

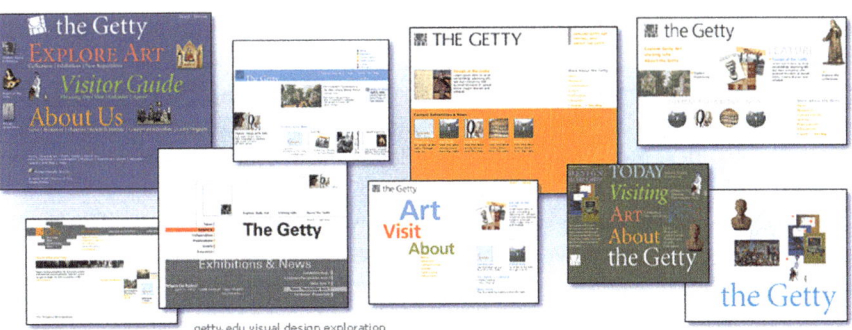

Fig. 8.92 Home page variations created during visual exploration. (Source: AM+A archive; images designed by AM+A; used with permission of the Getty Museum)

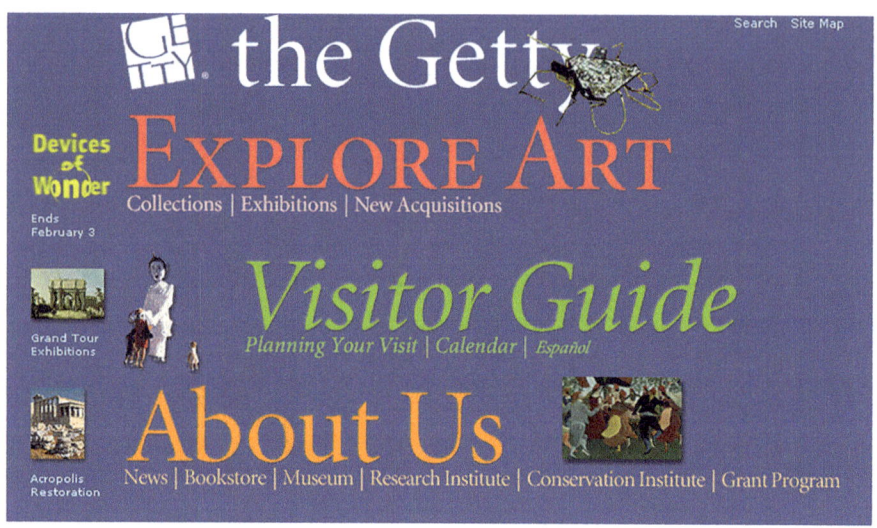

Fig. 8.93   A dHTML insect crawls across the Getty logo on the home page to promote Devices of Wonder exhibition. (Source: AM+A archive; image designed by AM+A; used with permission of the Getty Museum)

Microsoft NetGen's Three Degrees Software, 2001

In 2001, Microsoft's NetGen development group hired AM+A to design concept screens for its Three Degrees proposed product, an application suite that emphasized file sharing and messaging for teenagers. We were told by Microsoft staff that this was the first time that teenagers were sequestered by Microsoft in a house (with parental permission) to observe their social/computing behavior. We studied Microsoft reports prepared by a third party that showed the current week's (and rapidly changing) favorites among teenagers in the USA, for colors, images, fashions, personalities, etc. We based our sketches on this information and our own intuition and memories from childhood.

We were told our sketch designs were shown to Bill Gates himself to get his approval for going ahead with the product development. According to news we received, the functionality was later absorbed into a Microsoft general product line rather than a stand-alone product. Nevertheless, AM+A had an unusually free set of conditions for designing sketches for a specialized user interface; the prototype screens reflected this freedom. Larry Guan and Claudia Dallendoerfer, AM+A Designer/Analysts, were primarily in charge of the detailed visual designs (Figs. 8.94–8.97).

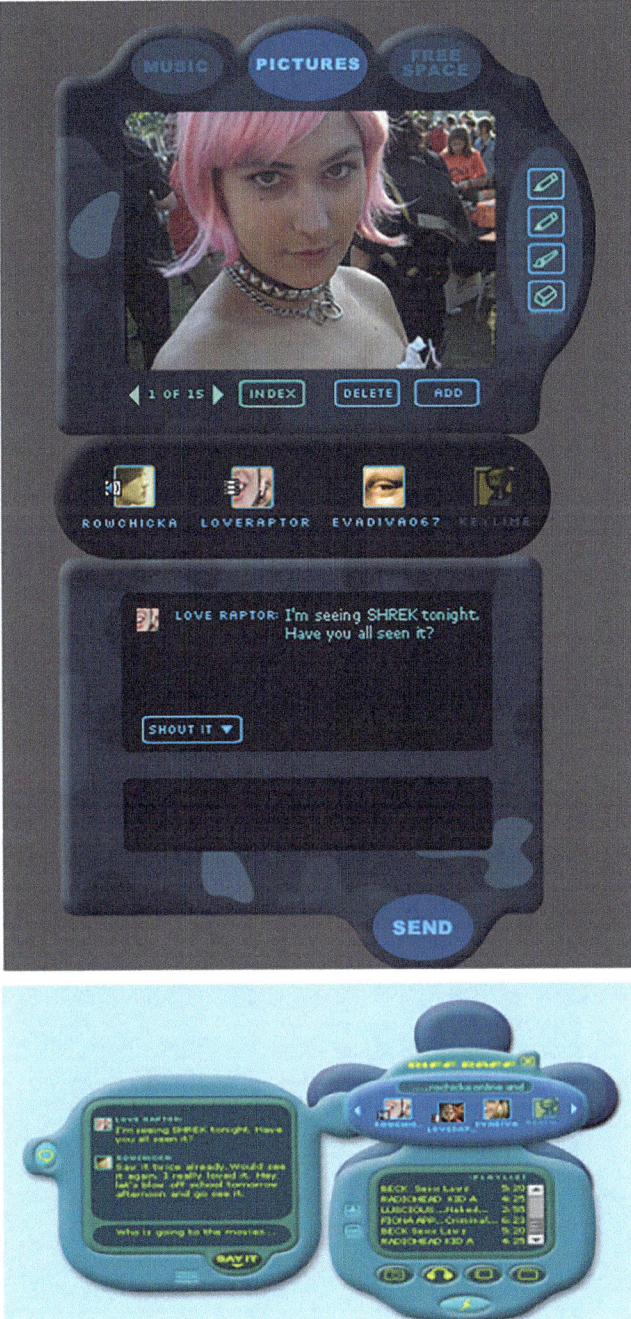

Figs. 8.94–8.97 Screen sketches from AM+A's initial designs for the NetGen Three-Degrees product, 2001. (Source: AM+A archive; images designed by AM+A; used with permission of Microsoft)

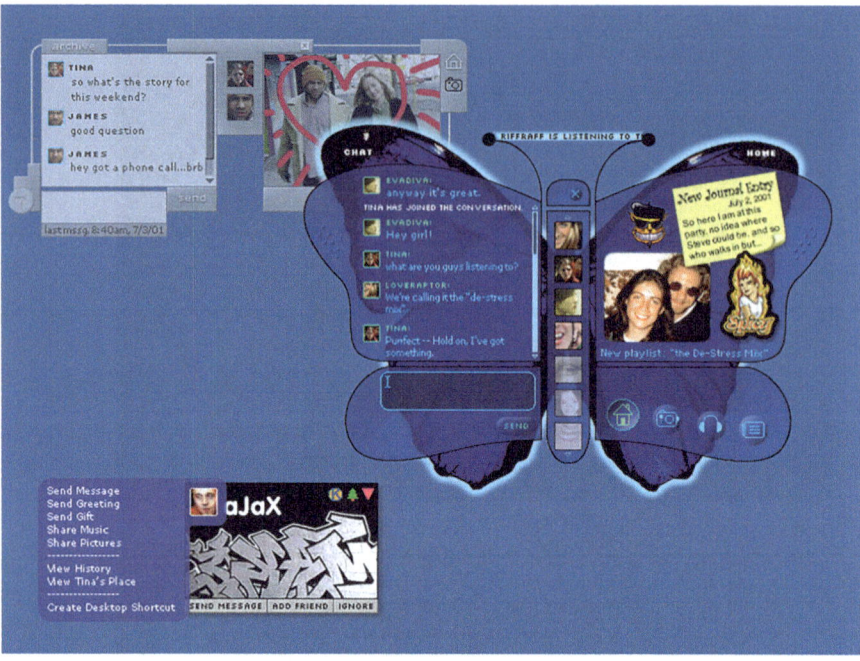

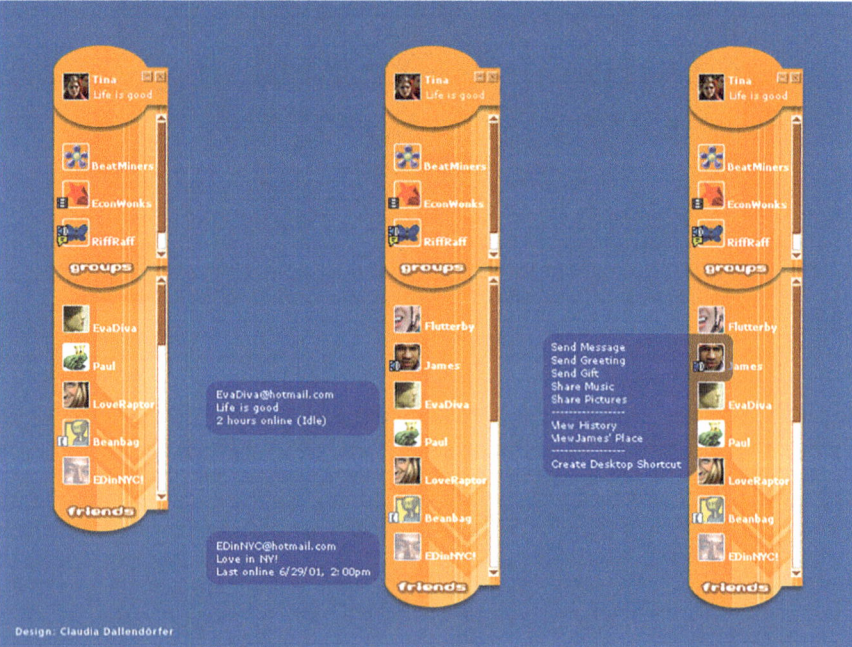

Figs. 8.94–8.97 (continued)

Acknowledgments I am indebted to many fine people who assisted AM+A during these years, especially my Associates, whom I have listed in an Appendix. In addition, I would like specifically to mention these people:

Arazi, Efraim, formerly, Scitex, Israel

Baecker, Ron, University of Toronto

Chaput, Linda, formerly founder and CEO, Cogito Learning Media

Fields, Craig, formerly, DARPA

Kirson, Allan, formerly, Motorola

Kunitomo, Kyoji, formerly, Ricoh, Japan

Lanier, Jaron, then independent researcher for VR

McCormick, Ann Piestrup, formerly founder, The Learning Company

Nelson, Ted, Xanadu

Noor, Her Majesty Queen, formerly Kingdom of Jordan

Rosenberg, Dan, formerly, Eastman Kodak

Sites, Michael, formerly SABRE

Van Dam, Andries, Brown University

Bibliography[1]

Baecker, Ronald M., and Marcus, Aaron. *Human Factors and Typography for More Readable Programs.* Addison-Wesley, Reading, Mass, 1990, 348 pp, 141 refs.

Baecker, Ronald M., and Marcus, Aaron. "On Enhancing the Interface to the Source Code of Computer Programs. *Proc.* SIGCHI Conference, ACM, December 1983, pp. 251–255.

Bergman, Eric, Editor (2000). *Information Appliances and Beyond: Interaction Design for Consumer Products (Interactive Technologies.* San Francisco: Morgan Kaufmann, ISBN: 1-55860-600-9.

Marcus, Aaron (2000), "User Interface Design for a Vehicle Navigation System." In Bergman, Eric (2000), Editor, *Information Appliances and Beyond: Interaction Design for Consumer Products.* San Francisco: Morgan Kaufmann, pp. 205–255. ISBN: 1-55860-600-9.

Marcus, Aaron and Baecker, Ronald M. (1982). "On the Graphic Design of Program Text", *Proceedings*, Graphics Interface 82, 1982, pp. 302–311.

Marcus, Aaron, and Van Dam, Andries (1993) "Human Communication Issues in Advanced User Interfaces." *Communications of the ACM.* April 1993, 36:4, pp. 101–109.

---

[1]The following references contain substantial information as case studies of some of the projects mentioned above.

Chapter 9
Learning to Run a Virtual Office

Takeaways

After traveling to China, I returned and realized I had to close both offices of AM+A in 2003 and continue as a virtual company, which I did successfully. We continued with successful projects for major clients such as Kaiser and Siemens.

2003–2008

In 2002, I traveled to China with my second wife Leslie Becker on a two-week self-guided tour of that country to get a feel for this once isolated or slumbering, but now awakening, giant. The trip was memorable. In October 2002, I had asked the Directors of my two offices in Emeryville and lower Manhattan if all seemed well as I dared to take the time off. Oh, yes, they said. Everything was going fine. Only it wasn't. The USA was entering the financial storm of the 2003 recession following the Dot-Com Bust. After I returned from China, I realized most of our client work was stalling. There were no renewals. We had lost key corporate clients in the NYC office. Problems were also evident in cash flow for the Emeryville office.

By early March 2003, I realized that we were headed for a cliff. I reluctantly decided I needed to close the New York City office, which I had started in 1999. I was shocked, terrified, sad, distraught, and tense. I flew with my Systems Administrator Joe Dobrowolski on a red-eye, showed up unexpectedly, and let go everyone, then began the clean-up of the inevitable mess. Within that day, everyone was gone, within a few weeks, all the equipment, clients, prospects, and other threads had been wrapped up. I was stunned by it all and walked around in shock.

Over the next few months, things continued to progress downhill. We had shrunk to about 11–12 people total from a former 25 people. Two of my competitors, Metadesign and Maus Haus in San Francisco, had similarly shrunk from larger numbers than our former maximum to our current size. This transition number 12

A. Marcus, *Bridging Art, Design and Technology: My Lifetime Work*, https://doi.org/10.1007/978-3-032-04342-9_9

seemed like a magical status. Perhaps only in the San Francisco Bay Area could the following happen: We three competitors, Metadesign, headed by Bill Hill, President of Metadesign SF, Maus Haus, headed by Malcolm Guthrie, President of Maus Haus, and I, who knew and liked each other, agreed to establish a conference call every Friday at 12 noon for about an hour just to lament together and to share challenges, issues, and solutions that might help the others. The telephone conversations were also something like group therapy. This ritual continued for some months. I felt blessed by such companions to share our communal misery.

We noted at one point that half the graphic design and user-interface design companies listed in the San Francisco telephone book seemed no longer to have working numbers.

By 31 July 2003, with the recession rolling throughout the nation, our Emeryville office faced the same dilemmas. We had not been dependent on dot-com companies, but our corporate clients had stopped hiring us, saying they liked us, but had no budgets for outsiders. By 31 August, my office rent agreement had conveniently run out.

I decided to close my office then and move back into my house's home office, in which my company had begun in 1982. I was again stunned and dismayed by this state of affairs and nervous about what the future held for AM+A and myself. In tears, I gathered my remaining staff and told them the bad news. They were helpful to organize and conduct a clearing out of all equipment, library holdings, software, etc. Again Joe Dobrowolski was instrumental in my maintaining my sanity through this transition. My library of 15,000 books, journals, and magazines, which I had gathered over a 40-year period of time, was rapidly reduced to 5000 precious items moved to my house and set up in the former AM+A bookcases. We transferred, also, all basic equipment and software to my home office.

By 1 September 2003, AM+A was completely relocated back to my home office in Berkeley, California. I decided to explore how to use former staff members as contractors, along with new contractors, to continue some small projects and to wait out the storm. Instead of declaring bankruptcy, we simply contracted and economized. To my surprise, I discovered by the end of 2004 that I had a very good year in terms of net income, because I no longer had to support a staff of 25 and two offices with duplicated equipment! I had managed to turn lemons into lemonade!

Indeed, AM+A continued as a virtual design office, one of the first of its kinds. I even wrote an article for a professional journal about how to run a virtual design office. Necessity is the mother of invention, and we had discovered we were again on the cutting edge of innovation of business structures. We continued to grow stronger and had solid projects during 2004–2008.

Throughout all this turmoil, we continued to complete interesting, challenging, pioneering projects. In fact, as happened before, some of our competitors gave us (i.e., turned over to us) projects that were too complex and challenging for them. What a glorious situation!

2003–2008

California Cancer Registry, CCR

For the California Cancer Registry (CCR), AM+A consulted with its staff to improve the user-interface design of software that its office had developed to encourage doctors to report cases of cancer in California. This software and the context were innovative. Cancer cases were rising, and the government wanted to study how cancer evolved in different circumstances around the USA, because it was not uniform. It was crucial to get doctors to report their cases, but filling out the forms required was time-consuming and daunting for the office assistants who had to complete the work. How could the situation be improved? By better user-interface design, especially data visualization.

The screens were too detailed and complex, and we had to reconfigure them to make them easier for the office staff to fill out the forms and submit them. Also, we wrote/designed PowerPoint presentations to explain to CCR's own team, and to prospective clients for their software, CCR's approach, the process, and its competitors. We also designed printed collateral used for marketing the software at medical and government conventions. CCR wanted to sell its software to other state government cancer registries throughout the USA. Mr. Stephen Fuchslin, Information Systems Chief, was our patron and guiding light. AM+A Associates assisting on the project included Laurie Wigham, Gabe Atiya, and Rebecca Thomas.

San Jose Police Department, 2004

In 2004, AM+A started one of its more unusual projects. The clients were attorneys for the San Jose, California, Policemen's Union. The end-users were heavily armed! We were hired to research the usability issues of a new vehicle communication system intended to improve the lives of one of the more advanced police departments in the nation: Silicon Valley's. Jim Gasperini, a Senior AM+A Designer/Analyst, conducted usability testing and interviews with the officers, which I reviewed afterwards, and we found more than 18 significant problems with the system that had been developed for them. Our report was waived by the mayor of San Jose at City Hall meetings that discussed the politically and financially sensitive situation, and an article appeared in *The New York Times* commenting on our report. Eventually, the software supplier changed its mind about cooperating with the police department in rectifying the errors, and all was solved without lawsuits. We published a case study in *Interactions* Magazine (Marcus and Gasperini 2004).

At that time, Police Departments around the nation were renovating or acquiring new software to help the police do their job. This project and the publication of its results helped to educate other police departments about how to avoid the problems encountered. The most serious one was that the police managers in charge did not know *that they did not know* about user-interface design and the necessity of including such activities in their project plans. They had not budgeted for it and did not realize there were professional experts who should have been called in from the beginning. What a loss of money, time, and improved products! We were glad we could help this one group in the ways we did (Fig. 9.1).

Fig. 9.1 Opening illustration for the *Interactions* magazine article about the San Jose Police Department's project (Marcus and Gasperini 2004). (Source: AM+A archive; used with permission of the author)

Siemens TTB, 2005–2014

During 2005 to 2014, Siemens' Technology-to-Business office, Berkeley, California, an advanced R&D group linked to two other such offices in Germany and China, hired AM+A as UI-design experts to assist their advanced development researchers. This was unusual at the time for such researchers to rely on outside user-interface design experts to work closely with advanced research groups, even from the beginning, to visualize concepts and to help team members to "be on the same page" in regard to development strategy and tactics. Although we had helped to pioneer this kind of work in 1982, we still encountered companies and groups that were not familiar with the process and the professionals who could assist.

Stu Goose, one of TTB's lead researchers, usually managed our projects. One project in 2005–2006 was to design the user interface for a media controller in vehicles that would send sound from a variety of sources (Music CDs, voice-output from a navigation system, games, DVDs, etc.) to various seat positions. The technology innovation was the use of special speakers in the roof of the car over all seat positions that could send stereo sound to each driver/passenger, which focused the sound downward in a non-spreading column, so that one person could not hear the sound being directed to the person sitting adjacent. No earphones were required. The front-seat passenger could act as a "media jockey" to assign sound from many sources to each seat position, e.g., children in the back seats could enjoy their desired media, without bothering parents in the front seats. The system was showcased at the Consumer Electronics Show (CES) of January 2007 in Las Vegas, and Stu Goose included me in a technology report paper as a co-author published years later (Goose et al. 2016).

During 2008, AM+A provided GUI guidance for a virtual-meeting system. Such systems were just being introduced around the world. We helped to improve the design of screen layout, icons, and general appearance of images. What made this system different from HP's Halo system mentioned earlier, for example, was the ability to make a virtual meeting system work on a regular PC, not requiring extremely complex and expensive equipment and meeting rooms. Today, such low-cost meeting systems are taken for granted; then, they were rare, sometimes unique, and innovative (Fig. 9.2).

In 2012–2013, AM+A devoted much of one year to interviewing Siemens TTB staff (specifically "technology visionaries") about the unique Siemens TTB Innovation Process in order to write/design a large poster that summarized and explained the complete, thorough, and innovative process. This process had been developed over a decade under the TTB Program Manager, Dr. Chenyang Xu, Ph.D. The process enabled an internal fast-track start-up process for new products and services designed to meet specific Siemens corporate needs. Ms. Laurie Wigham and Ms. Rebecca Thomas of AM+A helped to complete this project successfully (Fig. 9.3).

During this period of time in 2007, AM+A also provided to Siemens Corporate Research office in Princeton, New Jersey, a two-day workshop about user-interface design and helped to analyze staff and document needs in order to grow their User-Interface Design group quickly.

Fig. 9.2 Screen display showing conceptual design of a virtual meeting system, 2008. (Images designed by AM+A; Source: AM+A archive; used with permission of the author)

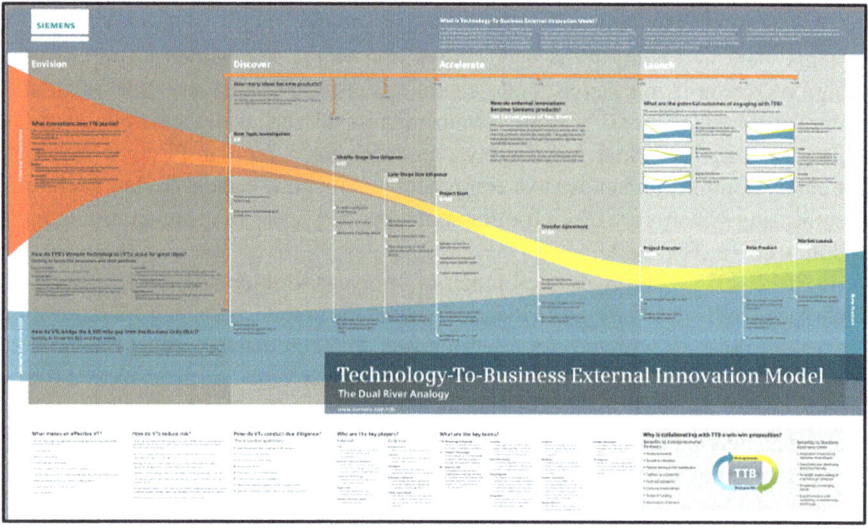

Fig. 9.3 Siemens TTB Innovation process diagram written and designed by AM+A, 2012–2013. (Image designed by AM+A; source: AM+A archive; used with permission of Chenyang Xu, former Director of Siemens TTB)

Ubitrotech, South Korea, GPS Car Navigation, 2007

By 2007, many companies worldwide were vying to introduce GPS navigation systems. In that year, Ubitrotech, a South Korean software development company, contracted with AM+A to provide the complete UI for their GPS vehicle navigation under development. AM+A Designer/Analyst Jean Benoit-Levy led the visual design team, AM+A proposed several visual treatments for all maps, tables, menus, etc. (Fig. 9.4).

Intel, Parallel Computing Editing Application, 2008

AM+A's projects have ranged across almost all vertical markets, platforms, contexts, and user groups. Our project for Intel was quite unusual. Most computers in the world are serial computers, doing one thing, then another. More of a rarity are parallel-processing computers, which have multiple cores of hardware that can handle separate threads of computing, and the threads can send/receive messages from other threads. Relatively fewer programmers in the world are familiar with this kind of computing, which some experts think is more like how the human brain works and represents the future of all computing.

Fig. 9.4 Icon design proposal for GPS navigation system showing an extremely refined, abstract approach to sign design, designed by Jean-Benoit Levy, an AM+A Associate, 2007. (Source: AM+A archive; used with permission of Jean-Benoit Levy)

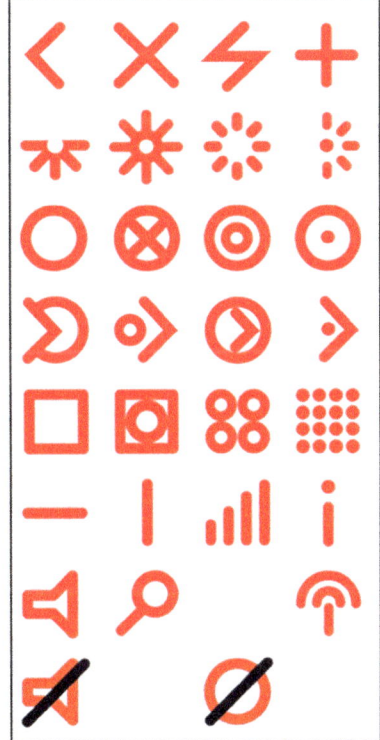

In April of 2008, Intel engaged AM+A to facilitate their development and testing of the user interface for its Threading Advisor product, a Microsoft Visual Studio 2005 Add-on, designed to assist C++ developers in improving program performance by providing targeted code analysis, advice, and instruction for implementing parallelism within a serial computing program environment. Target users of Threading Advisor were software developers and architects experienced in writing serial code, yet unaccustomed to coding that supported parallelism, and possibly even unfamiliar with core threading concepts.

Intel's Threading Advisor represented one of four tools within an integrated suite of products designed to address threading-specific needs at each stage of the development lifecycle; the release of these products represented Intel's bid for a leadership role in an emerging, mainstream market for software designed to boost performance by taking advantage of multi-core processors. Although the three other products were being developed concurrently and not within scope, a key project goal was that Threading Advisor UI be extensible to the rest of the suite. Jennifer Dumpert was a lead Designer/Analyst on the project, assisted by a contractor Astrid Javier. That our designer/analysts could learn the key concepts and provide specific guidance was an impressive statement of how diligent, smart, and capable our Associates were (Fig. 9.5).

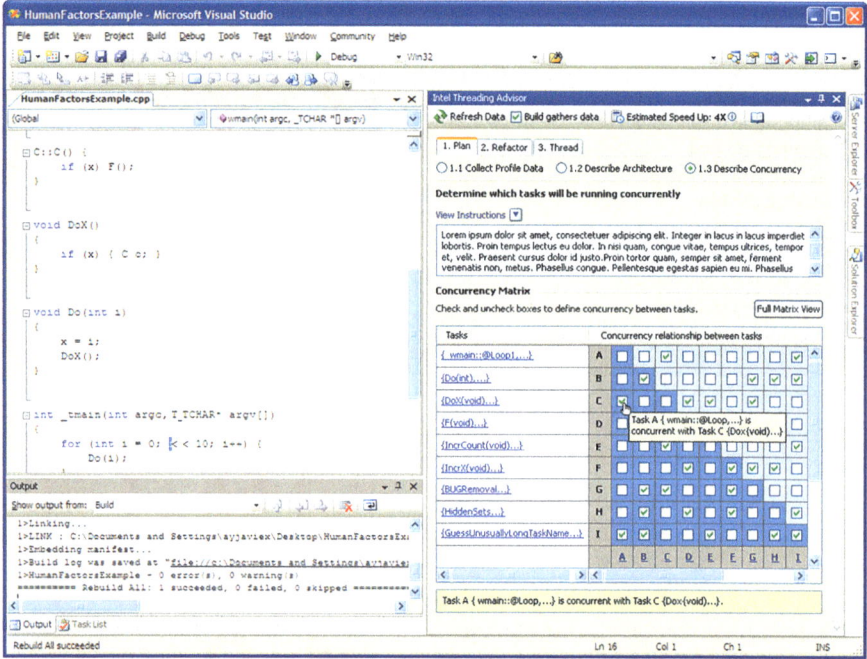

Fig. 9.5 Scenes from the UI improvements suggested by AM+A for a revolutionary type of software-editing application targeted to programmers. Most programmers are not familiar with parallel programming. AM+A had to study and learn key concepts to facilitate design improvements, 2008. (Source: AM+A archive; Image design by AM+A; used with permission of Intel)

Kaiser, Online Medical Library, 2008

Kaiser Permanente (KP) is an integrated managed care organization, based in Oakland, California, founded in 1945 by industrialist Henry J. Kaiser and physician Sidney R. Garfield. Operating in nine states and Washington, D.C., Kaiser Permanente is the largest managed care organization in the USA. In about 2007, Kaiser Permanente had 8.7 million health plan members, 156,000 employees, 13,729 physicians, 37 medical centers, 400 medical offices, and $34.4 billion in annual operating revenues and $1.3 billion in net income.

Kaiser Permanente's Care Management Institute (CMI) was an institution within the KP nonprofit health maintenance organization (HMO) with a mandate to drive, fund, and catalyze care management activities. CMI strove "to make the right thing easier to do."

Among other benefits for all Kaiser's doctors, nurses, and other medical professionals was its centralized information resource, an online medical library, which all could consult. Medical professionals *must* keep up with a wide range of changes, innovations, new medicines, new techniques, and new tools. It is an exhausting, time-consuming process. Kaiser's offering made it easier to check the latest and the best information....if it were presented in a usable and useful way! AM+A was offered an opportunity to make this happen. It was not the first time that AM+A has helped clients to improve access to large bodies of knowledge.

In 2007, AM+A won a major project to conduct usability studies of Kaiser Permanante's online medical library of documents and to design improvements. Physicians, nurses, and other medical professionals all consulted this library throughout the nationwide Kaiser system. The project required a year to complete and involved onsite visits at three Kaiser sites to interview users. The results were successful. AM+A was able to show increased usage and increased positive evaluations by users. Designer/Analyst Jim Gasperini was the primary AM+A staff person assigned to the project, with the assistance of AM+A Associates Larry Guan, William Wong, and Rebecca Thomas.

In June of 2006, Kaiser Permanente engaged AM+A to analyze and test the usability of the Clinical Library (CL), a Web-based internal information resource. The Clinical Library makes a wide variety of clinical information available to physicians, clinicians, and nurses, both during actual patient care and at times when they are engaged in research or study. Through the Clinical Library, KP clinicians and nurses can find internally produced guidelines for medical conditions and procedures, find and print out patient handouts, reach other Kaiser Web sites, access external resources such as journals and medical texts, and reach a wide variety of other resources of an operational or managerial nature.

Working with a team from CMI, AM+A drew up an interview script and interviewed 16 clinicians and nurses in their offices in four KP regions: Colorado, Northern California, Northwest, and Southern California. We gave subjects a series of mostly medical questions and asked them to find answers using the Clinical Library.

The Usability Analysis report resulting from this study detailed both the powerful potential of the CL to serve its target audiences and numerous severe usability issues currently limiting its effectiveness, particularly during time-critical periods of actual patient care.

The report detailed 31 major "observations" concerning usability issues, grouped in 4 general categories such as "Search Issues" and "Navigation Issues." A fifth category detailed observations of the effectiveness of "Clinical Tools," a partial restructuring of the CL UI that had been implemented in the Colorado region. We prepared a table of priorities based on comments by the interview subjects. AM+A made preliminary recommendations for how each issue could best be resolved.

In the fall of 2007, Kaiser asked AM+A to propose a usability analysis and design project to address some of the issues discovered in the 2006 report. The proposal divided work into two phases:

Phase 1 was a rapid, two-month project focused on a "proof of concept" redesign of the most time-critical parts of Clinical Library, with four rapid tasks including a paper user test conducted by phone.
Phase 2 was a six-month complete redesign, including the development of an interactive prototype and three user tests in the field.

AM+A's work for this client was well received and led to improved usage of and satisfaction with its online library. Those were the stated initial objectives. AM+A was able to help the client achieve them.

About This Period in AM+A's History

During the immediate years after the closing of AM+A's physical offices, we were able to present ourselves as a virtual design and usability-analysis company just as we had when we had operated from Emeryville and New York City. Our clients did not perceive that we were any different than before. We maintained our Web site, our client communication, and our deliverables as before. We were privileged to complete significant, challenging projects for major corporate clients. We were thankful for the opportunities offered to us. We worked with former AM+A Associates as well as a larger team of part-time contractors to complete the work. We had proven that there were good opportunities even with a virtual design firm.

Then a completely unexpected event occurred: a second recession of 2009–2012. AM+A had started in the recession of 1982. We survived the recession of about 1992. We had survived the recession of 2002. I was not expecting another major recession to begin until about 2012 to follow the decade cycle I had experienced before. Such was not the case. I discuss the next years in the next chapter.

Bibliography[1]

Goose, Stuart; Riddle, Larry; Fuller, Chris; Gupta, Tarun; and Marcus, Aaron (2016). "PAZ: In-Vehicle Personalized Audio Zones." *IEEE MultiMedia*, 23:4, Oct.-Dec. 2016, pp. 32–41

Marcus, Aaron, and Gasperini, Jim (2004). "ALMOST DEAD ON ARRIVAL: A Case Study of Non-User-Centered Design for a Police Emergency-Response System." 13:5, September/October 2006, pp. 12–18.

---

[1] These references discuss some of the projects described above.

Chapter 10
Developing Mobile Prototypes Using Persuasion Design

Takeaways
During this time, I was able to keep AM+A alive, focused on mobile persuasion design projects using interns, moved my professional library and archive of projects to several museums, and invented/designed a way to use US currency to make more money using "Facebucks."

2008–2018

In December 2008, I noticed that three major projects all wrapped up at about the same time, and I expected circumstances to require about 3 months to land significant new projects. Instead, clients and prospects seemed to disappear one after another…once again! I struggled mightily during 2009–2012 to keep us going, with only small success. To keep myself busy, I initiated a series of intern-based research projects in mobile persuasion design. Our interns (whom we first used beginning in 2002) came from all over the USA, Europe, India, China, and South America for a three-month period. I was blessed to have these young, eager, enthusiastic, and intelligent people around my conference table, sometime just one person, sometimes as many as six at a time, as we planned, researched, analyzed, designed, and documented our ten "Machine" projects. We were able to publish papers about all of them, to present them at conferences, and eventually to collect the documentation into a book published in 2015 (Marcus, 2015a). They are described in detail below.

While outside client projects gradually died away, I was able to develop these prototype mobile projects, book publications, lectures, and tutorials into the ongoing work of AM+A. I also pushed forward various plans to lecture more in China and had intended to open a kind of teaching/design center in Shanghai. However, negotiations faltered with that institution and later with the College of Design and

A. Marcus, *Bridging Art, Design and Technology: My Lifetime Work*,
https://doi.org/10.1007/978-3-032-04342-9_10

Innovation at Tongji University in Beijing. My one solid contact remained with the Dalian Maritime University in Dalian (Prof. Zhengjie Liu, whom I had known for many years) and more recently with the Beijing Normal University's Psychology Department. I was grateful for these China contacts, which allowed me the opportunity to keep tabs on UX developments in China.

By 2014–2015, the transition of AM+A to a sole proprietorship in a winding down state was complete. I decided it was time to plan my legacy and pushed forward negotiations with the San Francisco Museum of Modern Art (specifically with Joseph Becker, Associate Director of Design), the RIT Vignelli Design Center (Roger Remington, Director), the Victoria and Albert Museum in London (Douglas Dodds, Senior Curator, Word and Image Department), and the Letterform Archive (LFA) in San Francisco (Rob Saunders, Founder and Executive Director) to accept donations of most of my design and artwork of the past 68 years. I am grateful for their interest. Gradually, I also was able to place other works at the Computer History Museum in Mountain View (via Chris Garcia, Curator, and Dag Spicer) and the Berkeley Art Museum (Richard Linder, Director). I succeeded, also, in transferring my entire remaining professional library of about 5000 publications to the LFA/San Francisco archives collection in 2016.

I was somewhat in shock to see most of my professional library, what remained from the closure of my office in 2003, as well as about four four-drawer file cabinets full of documents and saved examples of my work, disappear in a truck to LFA. My home office seemed bare, and my life seemed "over" without these physical symbols of my interests and achievements. Who was I now? What was my legacy? What was I to do with the rest of my years on earth? All of these questions repeatedly swirled in my mind as I looked at the empty spaces where my books and files had been.

For these last years, 2017–2025, my primary task has been to organize text and images about the work of AM+A and my own art and design work since about the age of 10. The task has been daunting at times, but I prepared an agreement to write a monograph about my life's work to be published by LFA. I wrote the first draft of the complete monograph in 2017–2018, and spent about 4 years coping with LFA's slow progress to complete the publication. Eventually, LFA decided to cancel the book contract, but I was able to sign a follow-on contract with Springer UK to publish the book you are now reading. I am grateful to Ms. Helen Desmond, my editor, for shepherding the project to completion, Mr. Jacob Shmulewitz, Springer Publishing Assistant, and Ms. Charlotte Denton, Editorial Assistant, who assisted me with permissions. I am also grateful to my new (third) wife Sandra Speier, who helped me by reviewing chapters.

A summary of some key AM+A projects during 2008–2018 follows, similar to Chaps. 6–8. Readers can jump from project to project as their interests lead them.

2009–2018

Oracle, Forms and Reports, Built-In Online Help, 2009

In continuing work for Oracle under the leadership of Dan Rosenberg, then head of all UX development at Oracle, AM+A was tasked to write/design screens for short bursts of built-in online help (Quick Tours) for several products: Oracle Forms, Reports, and Procedure Builder, products of about 2009. What was special about this project is that online help was being built right into the software applications, instead of separate files or printed/online publications. This was an innovative approach at the time. As usual for many of our projects, the content was complex and technical in nature (Figs. 10.1–10.4).

Unnamed Silicon Valley Company, Cross-Cultural Analysis, 2010

In 2010, a Silicon Valley company, whom we are not permitted to name, wanted to develop tools that would assist its software developers to work better together by taking into account cultural differences among their dispersed, diverse staff. This was an innovative consideration for software development and brought into being what I had been lecturing about for more than 10 years: culture-centered UI development. They had many skilled programmers; they could code whatever they needed. What they lacked was a way to understand what metrics to consider among a limited number of office locations, including their headquarters. We were pleased to put into practice guidelines and recommendations we had published during the previous 10 years.

AM+A conducted a cross-cultural analysis of five cities in which the company had significant numbers of staff and to determine the best "orthogonal" collection of cities that demonstrated different, desirable dimensions of culture. The company was developing tools to better manage cooperation, communication, and collaboration among its Silicon Valley headquarters and sites abroad. It planned to use AM+A's analysis to help inform its decisions about which sites to use in its further tool development. Dr. Emily Gould, AM+A Cultural Analyst, and I served as the consultants to assist on the project. I had worked with her for some 10 years, including collaborating on workshops and publications at conferences.

We succeeded in helping our client to alter its plans for how many and what cities to consider and to give them new concepts to consider for each location: namely, the gender make-up, the relative numbers of digital natives (under 30 years of age) vs. older employees, and whether the locations were newer, high-growth cities vs. older, established cities. The client was pleased with the outcome of the project and went on to pursue its tool development objectives. These considerations became more frequent among high-tech development strategies in the coming decade. We were simply among the first to become involved, as far as I know (Fig. 10.5).

Oracle Forms screen:

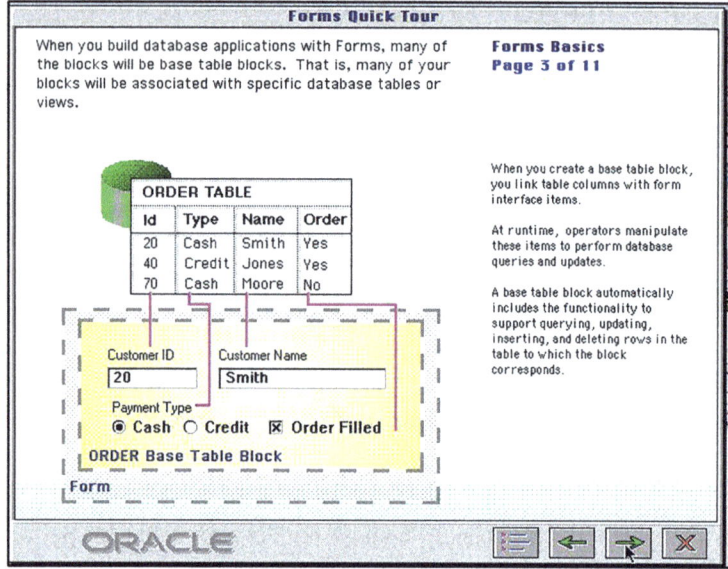

Oracle Reports screen:

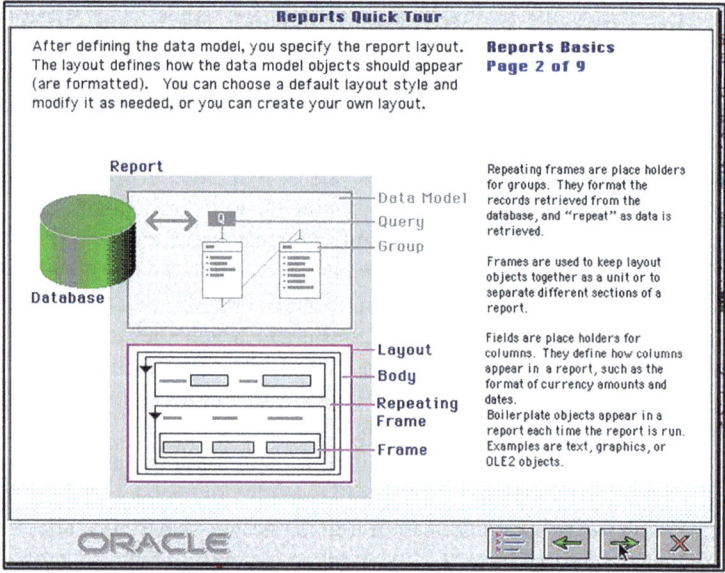

Oracle Procedure Builder screen:

Figs. 10.1–10.4 Screens from the built-in online help (Quick Tours) for Oracle Forms, Reports, Procedure Builder, and Graphics, 2009. (Source: AM+A archive; imagery designed by AM+A. All images are copyrighted by Oracle and used with permission of Oracle)

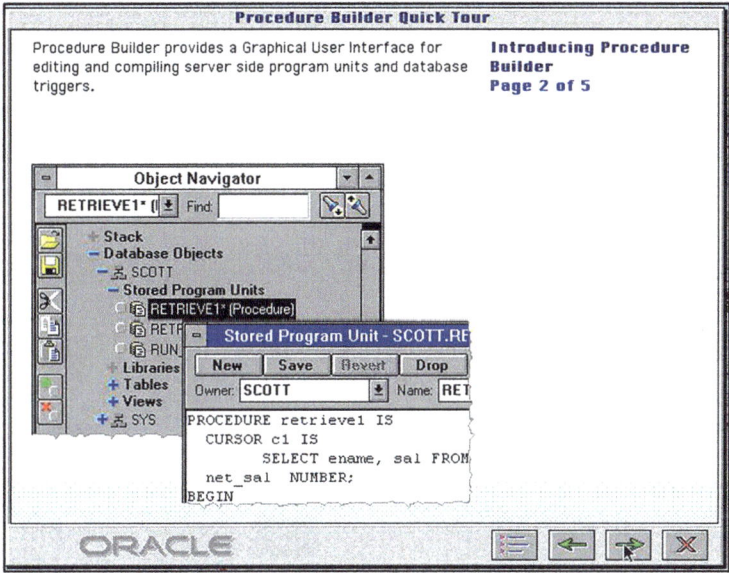

Oracle Graphics screen:

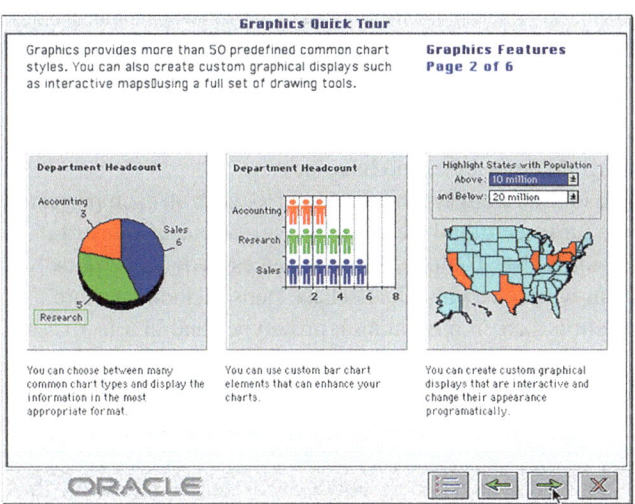

Figs. 10.1–10.4 (continued)

AM+A Machine Projects, 2009–2014

As mentioned earlier, beginning in 2009, AM+A began the development of ten prototype mobile applications (which we called Machines) that emphasized persuasion theory, based on the research of B.J. Fogg at Stanford University, and other researchers. For each machine a different base of subject matter was chosen, e.g., energy

Cross-Cultural Comparisons with CA City

	CA City USA	Amsterdam Netherlands	Bangalore India	Singapore	Toyko Japan	Dubai UAE	Shanghai China
Power Distance, Hierarchy	1.0	0.95	1.93	1.85	1.35	2.00	1.22
Individualism	1.0	0.88	0.53	0.22	0.51	0.42	0.94
Digital Natives, Under 30 Years Old	1.0	1.07	3.60	0.40	1.13	0.73	2.00
High Growth, Newer Cities	1.0	0.43	2.18	1.03	0.17	2.70	1.94
Female/Male Gender Ratio	1.0	0.90	0.58	1.10	0.61	0.42	0.81

Aaron Marcus and Associates. Inc.

Fig. 10.5 Presentation image showing the recommended and optional additional cities resulting from AM+A's analysis. (Source: AM+A archive; AM+A designed the image; used with permission of the author)

conservation, health maintenance, education, driving safety, retirement planning, storytelling, marriage maintenance, and happiness.

AM+A recruited interns from around the world to work on each project in groups of one to six people for three-month periods. We carried out as many of the standard steps of our profession's User-Centered Design Process, which we ourselves helped to pioneer and about which we published. These steps included research, planning, design, implementation (screen presentation prototypes and in a few cases interactive simulations with small databases), testing, documentation, and maintenance. These steps included creating personas (typical user descriptions) and use scenarios, competitive product analysis, designing key metaphors and mental models (information architecture), and limited user testing.

AM+A wrote detailed white papers about each project based on the interns' research, design, and testing reports, and we published articles about each project in professional journals and conference proceedings. Half of the projects won design awards for information design from the International Institute for Information Design based in Vienna, Austria.

These Machine projects influenced other designers and researchers around the world. We gave away the knowledge, rather than protecting it, because we believed in the value of these studies. We did not pursue each project to working prototypes, because there was not time enough, money, and personnel to carry out such real-world development. We merely wanted to seed the ideas in other development centers and let others carry on the concepts to completion. This is indeed what happened for several of the Machines, which was gratifying to observe. I describe and illustrate some of the Machine projects below in the following sections.

Note: I advised/warned people in my lectures, publications, and book during 2009–2015 about the possible dangers of using persuasion design in software. Our projects assumed that the concepts, motivations, and product objectives concerned only benign improvements in the world and assumed a benign ethical system underlying everything. This is not always the case; the success of malignant propaganda in the twentieth and twenty-first centuries has shown how easy it is to persuade people to undertake inhumane, evil behavior. These dangers enhanced by modern artificial intelligence, robotics, and connected social platforms are discussed extensively in Harari's book *21 Lessons for the 21st Century* (Harari, 2018) and in Orlowski's film, *The Social Connection* as reported by Girish (2020).

Since some of these developments seem inevitable, we thought it best to show how good intentions and good outcomes could promote beneficial improvements. Mobile applications seemed the most appropriate platform.

Green Machine, 2009

A twenty-first-century global challenge is finding a sustainable way of life. I had been interested in the subject since my involvement with the Visualizing Global Interdependencies project at the East-West Center in 1978 (discussed in Chap. 5).

The Green movement helped to increase people's awareness of sustainability issues and propelled development of innovative products to help decrease our ecological footprint. Smart Grid applications, which enable users to monitor household, vehicle, or business energy consumption, are one of these innovative products. Most products were at the time targeted to the PC and did not focus on innovative data visualization. Critical data visualization helps to build awareness, but does not result automatically in effecting behavioral changes, which is required to ensure the Earth's future and our survival. The question then shifts to how exactly to motivate, persuade, educate, and lead people to reduce their energy consumption. This project researched, analyzed, designed, and evaluated powerful ways to improve "green behavior" by persuading and motivating people to reduce their energy consumption through a mobile phone application we called the "Green Machine." AM+A designed and tested a prototype based on behavioral change-process issues-analysis to persuade people to "go green." Published articles and a book (Marcus, 2015a) explained the development of the Green Machine user interface, information design, and information visualization.

Although today there are many applications that offer some or all of the pictured functions and data, at the time, nothing like this application existed, as far as we knew (Figs. 10.6–10.11).

SAP, Adaption of Green Machine to Enterprise Software, 2010

One spinoff project based on our Machines occurred when SAP, a global enterprise software company, selected AM+A to assist their US development staff to adapt the Green Machine philosophy to enterprise software. This was a new development platform for our Machines. We had designed them for personal mobile phone use, not for corporate systems, which would be a new context and a new set of users. This project originated because of the leadership of the then Director of User-Interface Design, Dan Rosenberg. AM+A associates involved with the project were Jennifer Dumpert, Larry Guan, and Laurie Wigham.

AM+A did extensive analysis of SAP users worldwide in regard to their understanding of their ecological concepts, the terminology they used to describe environmental issues, and their commitment to different levels of engagement. We also

We attempted to visualize the data in an appealing way with measurements that could be easily grasped. The icons at the bottom of the screens revealed the key metaphors of the application:

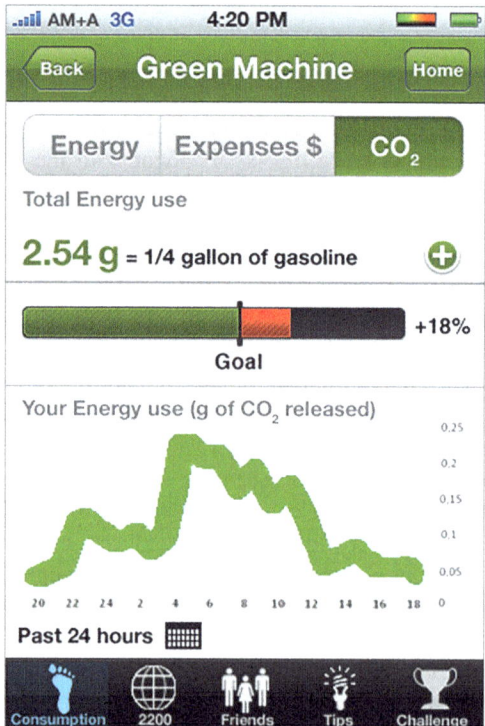

The depiction of data facilitated showing competitions with friends/family to increase energy conservations as an incentive to practice good habits:

Figs. 10.6–10.11 Exemplary screens of the Green Machines showing key content and functions. (Source: AM+A Archive; images designed AM+A; used with permission of the author)

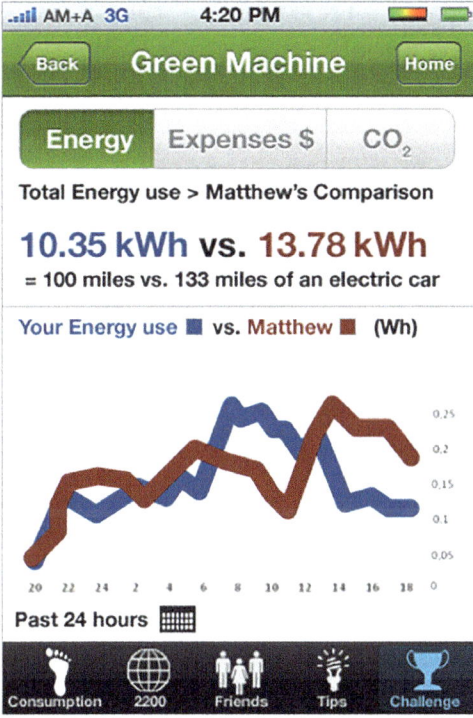

As a further incentive, we showed a prototype for a future
data reporting of dire consequences if the earth continued to practice
energy conservation as the current user practiced. Even though
this seemed somewhat negative, we found in limited testing that users
reacted favorably to this approach:

Figs. 10.6–10.11 (continued)

Connecting the user to a specific social network for news, ideas, techniques, could motivate some users:

Figs. 10.6–10.11 (continued)

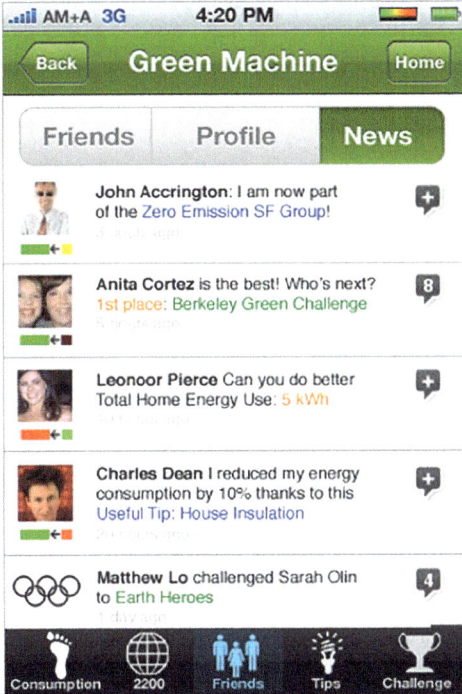

Showing comparative metrics for products/services,
could enhance the user's decision-making:

Figs. 10.6–10.11 (continued)

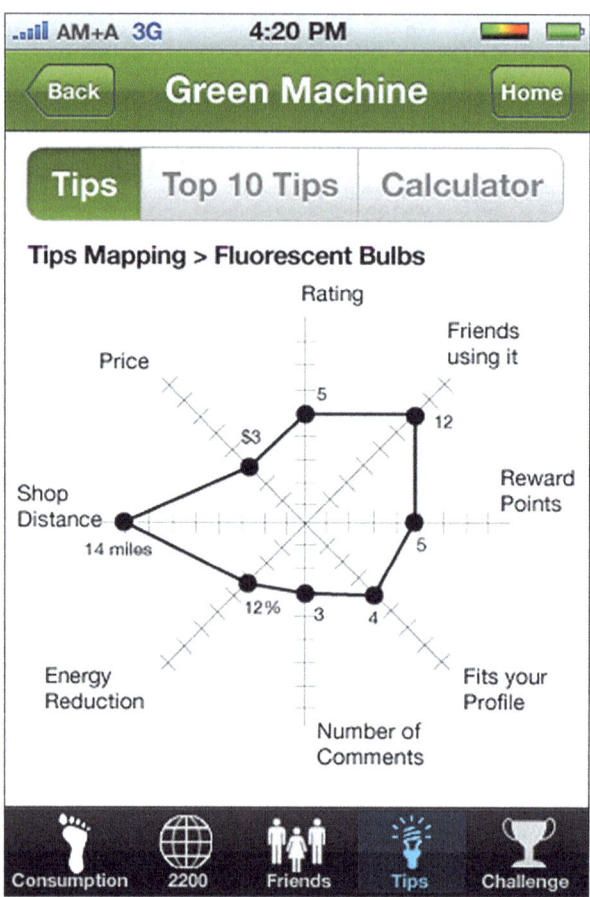

Figs. 10.6–10.11 (continued)

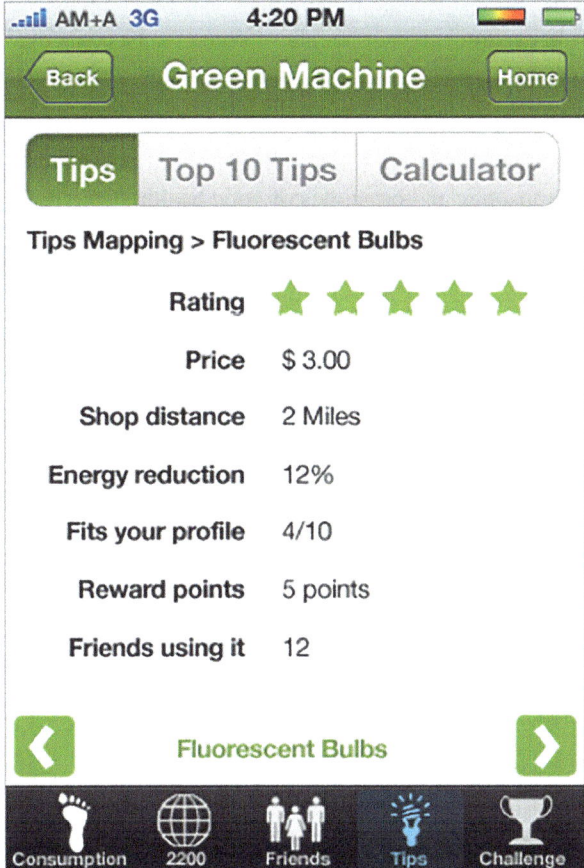

Figs. 10.6–10.11 (continued)

developed a number of innovative techniques for using available data and contexts to encourage ecological behavior. In fact, AM+A became a signer to three SAP patent applications based on this project.

AM+A's involvement was viewed as successful, and the presence of a corporate client showed that any of the Machines could be adapted to enterprise use-context, which was a significant advancement for the Machines in general.

Health Machine, 2010

A second area of development concerned health. Like all of the Machines, there was a personal connection to me. I had been diagnosed as pre-diabetic in 2009, which challenged my life habits and assumptions about my health. I had to change eating, exercise, and nutrition habits. These changes and the Kaiser classes I attended influenced my thinking about the Health Machine.

Information-design/visualization techniques can be combined with persuasion design to effect behavior change in people who need to be concerned about obesity and Type 2 Diabetes. Careful attention to exercise and nutrition is crucial. This project developed the conceptual design for a mobile application to persuade people to make these changes in their nutrition and exercise. Current applications in this market at the time were good but not based on a persuasion program. The project introduced the philosophy and principles of good health maintenance and also persuasion design, then combined them into the functions and content of a prototype design for smart-phones. The design concept included the idea of a virtual pet "living" in the phone whose health depended on the user's behavior (Figs. 10.12–10.20).

The basic depiction of metrics for nutrition was a primary location for users to monitor their behavior (My Condition). As with the Green Machine, the icons at the bottom displayed the key metaphors: My Condition, 2020 (a view into the future based on the user's current behavior), friends (a focused social network of people supporting the user's behavior), Tips (advice and recommendations), and Challenges (competitions, games, and other incentives to change behavior):

A review of one's most recent meal or snack to sensitize users to the impact of certain foods:

Figs. 10.12–10.20 Exemplary prototype screen designs showing functions and content of the application. (Source: AM+A archives; images designed by AM+A; used with permission of the author)

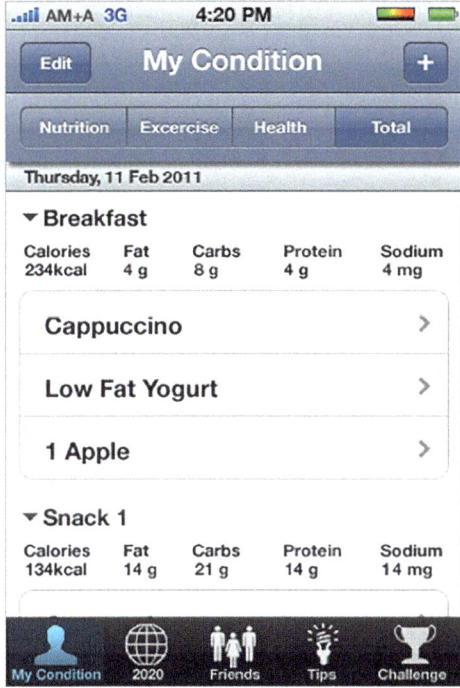

A competitive comparison screen, in this case showing the user's behavior compared withthat of some mentor or idol (in this case Lady Gaga, who might license her daily food consumption and exercise data to some company willing to pay for that information):

Figs. 10.12–10.20 (continued)

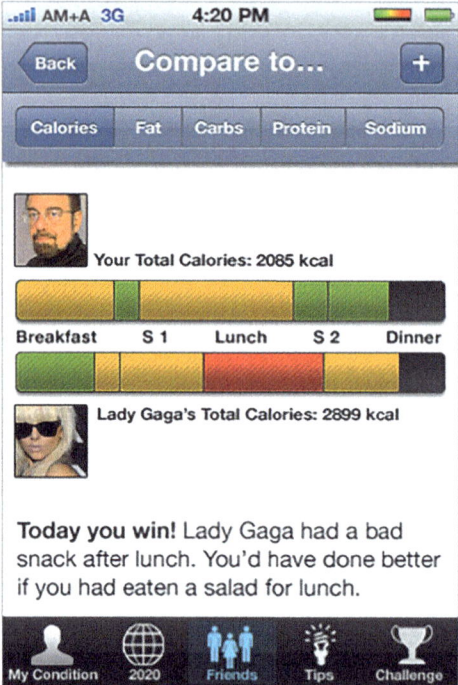

A sample game, which tests the user's understanding of the types of food he/she should eat and the amounts. Many people do not have a good understanding of this basic information:

Figs. 10.12–10.20 (continued)

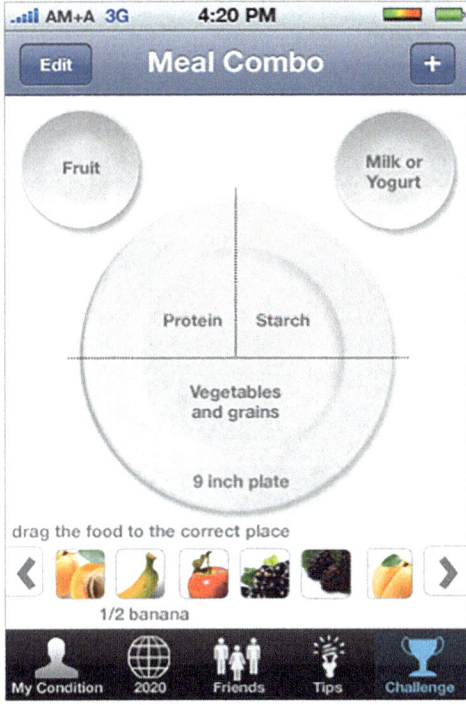

An example of gathering data for the app with a food bar code reader that can quickly determine the nutritional contents of foods of interest and convert that to data for the app:

Figs. 10.12–10.20 (continued)

Being able to see the impact of eating a junk-food snack on one's nutrition score for the day can provide a strong incentive to avoid un-needed calories and other nutrition components:

Figs. 10.12–10.20 (continued)

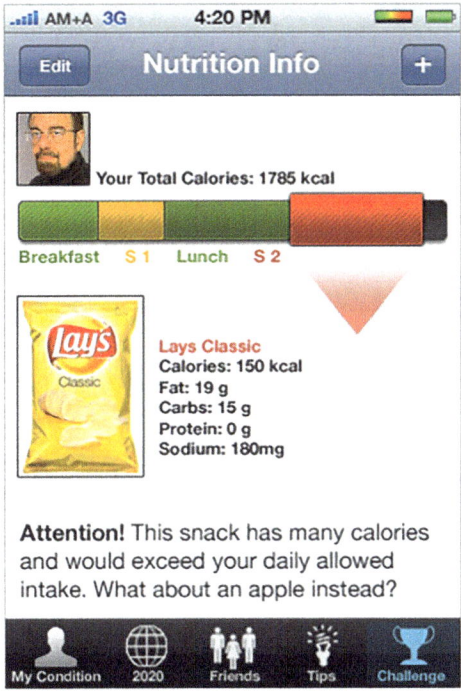

The presence of a cute animal "living" in the app, whose existence is dependent on the user's behavior, which can be a strong incentive for some users, who may care more for their pets than themselves:

Figs. 10.12–10.20 (continued)

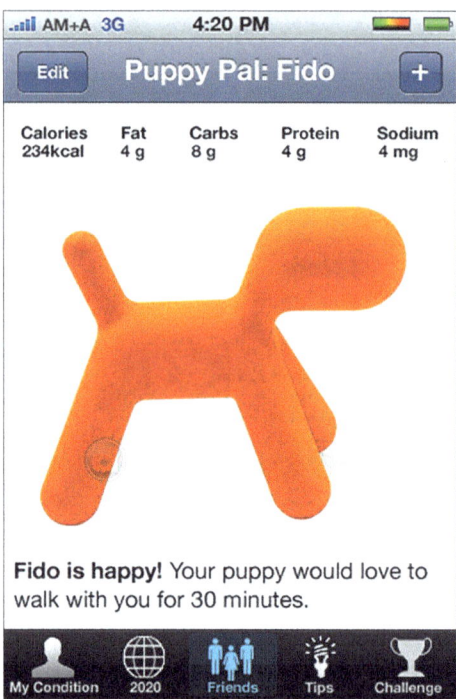

Sample challenges (daily, weekly, or monthly) for the user
to provide incentives to good behavior and rewards for
good behavior:

Figs. 10.12–10.20 (continued)

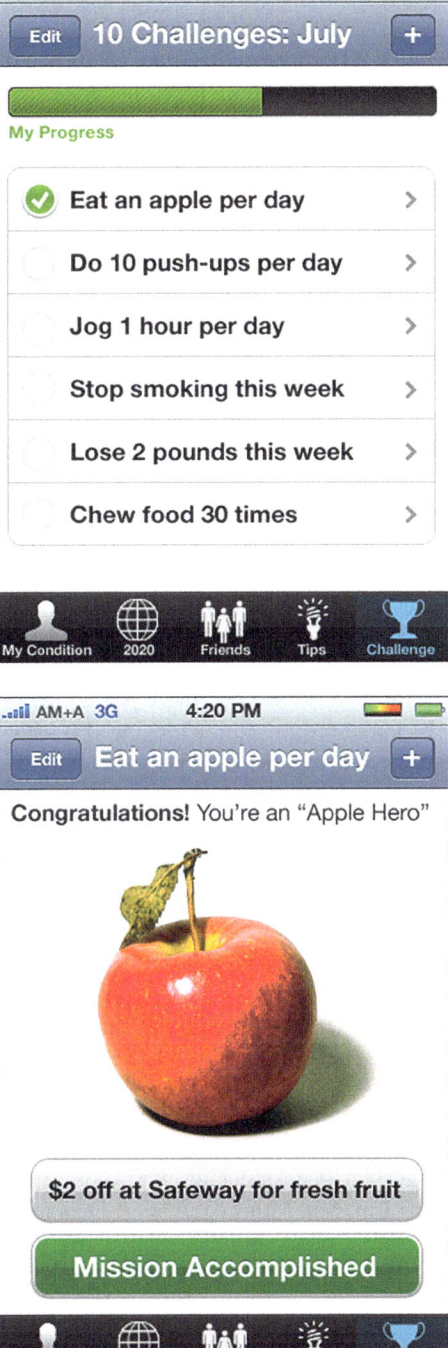

Figs. 10.12–10.20 (continued)

Happiness Machine, 2013

In a later Machine, called the Happiness Machine, we turned our attention to happiness, a topic that is of increasing attention to healthcare workers, government officials, the general public, and even design specialists.

Happiness is a fundamental key to success in the twenty-first century. During the last decades, many researchers and professionals investigating what happiness is and how to achieve it have proposed happiness principles to help people to live happier lives. Despite numerous proposed happiness theories and training sessions oriented to turning theory into practice, people often fail in following the principles to achieve happiness. In an era of increasing economic, social, and political pressures and consequent stress, it seems more and more people are in need of assistance. The practice of happiness-inducing behavior risks fading more and more into the background of daily personal and professional lives.

In the AM+A Happiness Machine project of 2013, we researched, analyzed, designed, and evaluated effective ways to foster a shift from unhappy or happy states to greater happiness by changing people's daily behavior in the short- and in the long term. We studied six major theories of achieving happiness (for details of the theories, see Marcus 2015a). The main objective of the Happiness Machine was to motivate and persuade people of all ages, all genders, all cultures, and all economic and educational levels to open themselves up more intensely toward techniques of daily practice and interaction with people, objects, and contexts, which can make their journey through life deeper, more personally enriching, and an educational experience. To make progress in achieving this objective, as in the other Machine projects described in Marcus (2015a), AM+A planned, researched, analyzed, designed, implemented (in the form of sample screens), evaluated, documented, and prepared training documents for several versions of a mobile phone application conceptual prototype, which combined happiness theory with information design/visualization and persuasion design, and embodied the results in a user-centered design process. The initial target market was North American young adults, i.e., likely early adaptors.

For this project, we used marketing students in a nearby educational institution to interview a variety of target users to determine key attributes that would make the product, its functions, and its data more desirable.

This project, like several others, won design awards from the International Institute of Information Design, Vienna, Austria, and inspired several research design groups in Europe and elsewhere to undertake similar projects.

AM+A Intern Designer/Analyst Associates who assisted on this project included: Mr. Yu-Hsien (Jonathan) Liu, Ms. Min Lee, AM+A Designer/Analyst, Ms. Megan McQuade, and also Prof. Robert Steiner, University of California/Berkeley/ Extension Program, International Diploma Program, and his students (Figs. 10.21–10.26).

Our research identified happiness components that we combined into a diagram of five key activities that promote happiness:

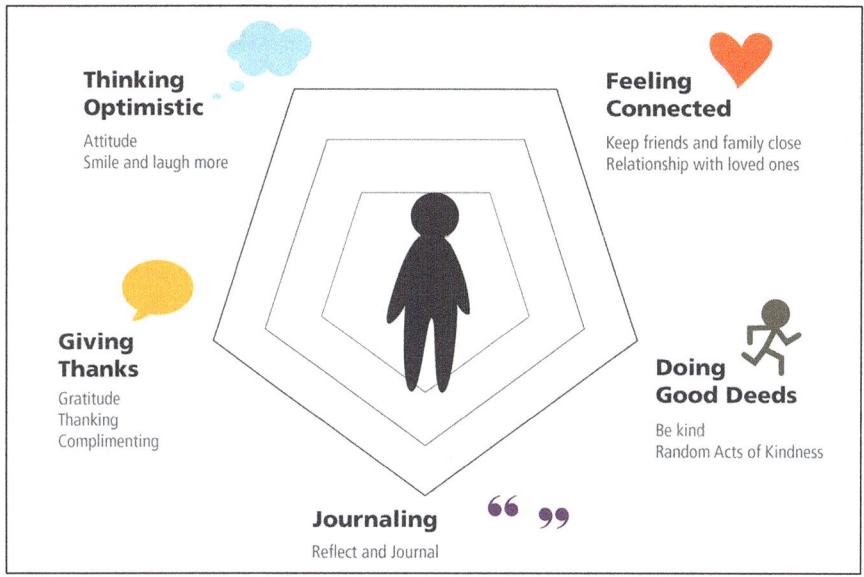

For each Machine, we designed a detailed Information architecture that showed all the structure of the machine. This diagram shows the information architecture of the Happiness Machine:

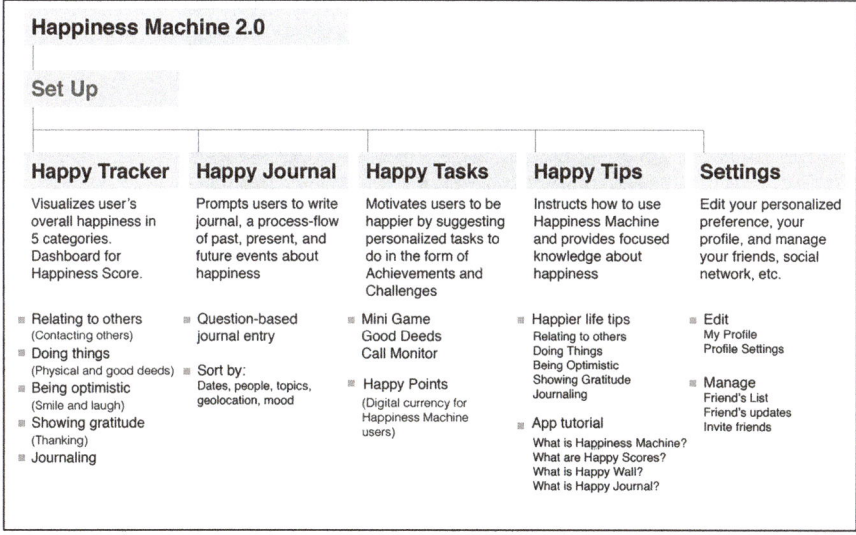

Example concept prototype opening screen that showed one's "happiness score" and the key action tasks (metaphors) of the application that can be explored individually further:

Figs. 10.21–10.26 Example images from the white paper about the Happiness Machine, 2013. (Source: AM+A archive; images designed by AM+A; used with permission of the author)

Depiction of key metrics for the five key functional areas, including relating to others, doing things (being active), Smile-o-Meter (smiling a lot), showing gratitude, and writing in journals. The user can easily see his/her weak spots needing improvement or extra attention.

Figs. 10.21–10.26 (continued)

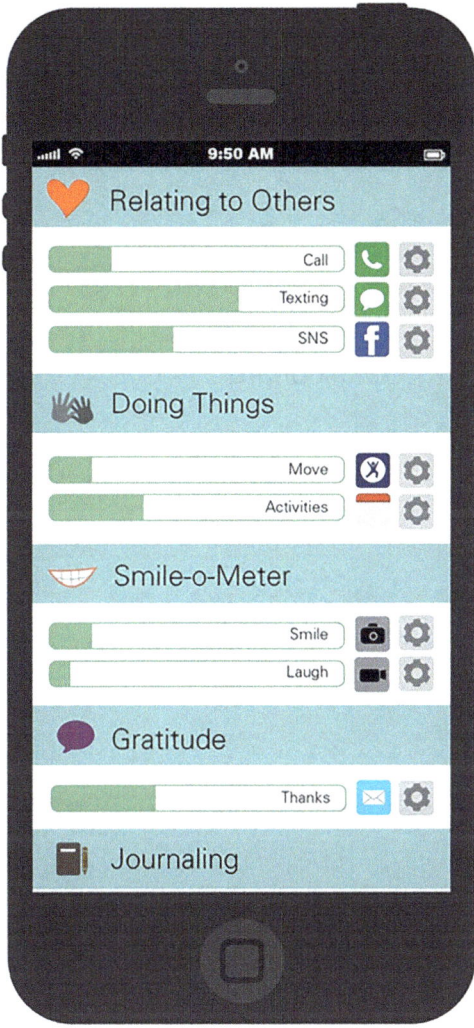

An example of an app oriented to a particular user typeor
persona.The contents are changed to be more useful to
the particular characteristics of the persona. An outgoing,
egotistical person might need different tasks, tips, and
journal suggestions than a shy, giving person:

Figs. 10.21–10.26 (continued)

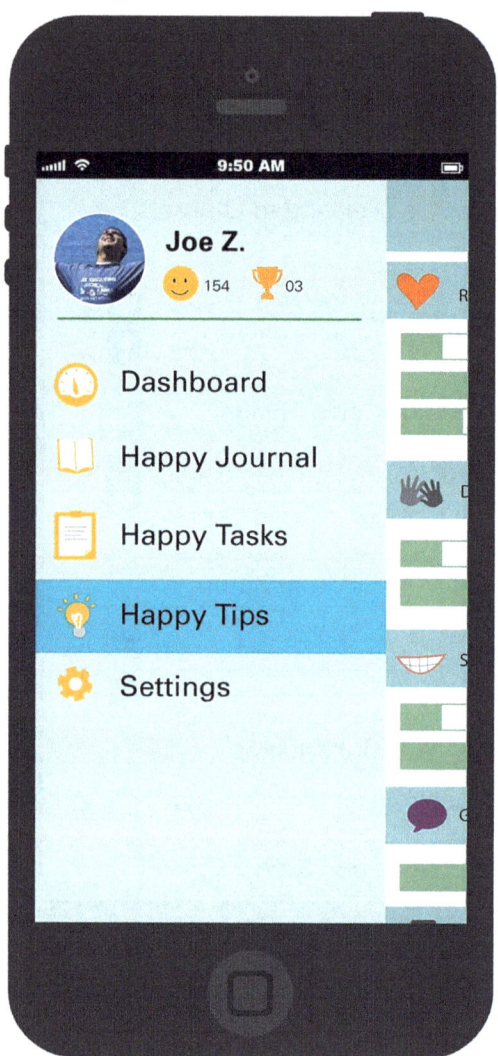

Sample journaling suggestions for the above persona,
which are tuned to the type of persona:

Figs. 10.21–10.26 (continued)

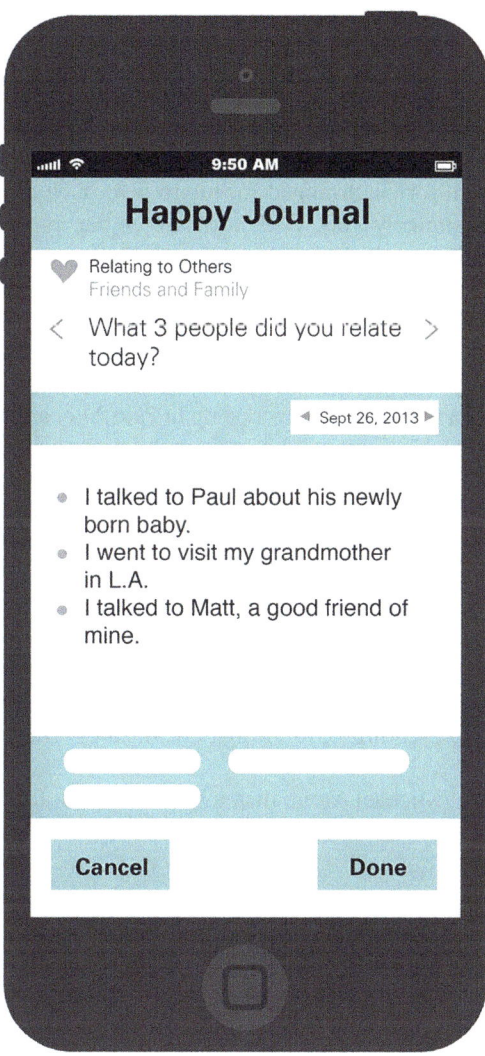

Figs. 10.21–10.26 (continued)

SAP Workshops in UX Design, 2012

In 2012, I had an opportunity to organize and present the most complex, wide-scale, international UX design workshop in my own history.

During 2011–early 2012, Dan Rosenberg, Director of User-Interface Design at SAP in Palo Alto, California, arranged for me to give three days of workshops in UX design to approximately 1000 SAP software engineers and UX designers in seven countries: USA, Canada, China, India, Israel, France, and Germany. Two days were for UX designers and 1 day was for software engineers. This was the largest training project I had ever undertaken. It took approximately one year of planning to finalize the course contents and to arrange business contracts in seven different countries with seven different sets of SAP corporate entities and governmental and corporate rules. I did a test run of the workshop in Palo Alto, and then adjusted some content to meet feedback comments. I had given the workshops successfully in five of the countries to about 500 people (they were often oversubscribed, and sometimes it was difficult to find rooms large enough in corporate buildings to contain audiences of more than 100 people). Suddenly, in late 2012, I learned the bad news: Dan had had a falling out with the head of the company over some corporate/philosophical matters and had been quickly let go. In a matter of weeks, as I was beginning to arrange for travel to France and Germany, my project was cancelled.

The cancellation was a great disappointment, but I was thankful for the opportunity thus far provided. My workshop was the culmination to approximately 20 years of preparing and presenting UX design workshops beginning in 1980 at SIGGRAPH 1980.

My first employee, Michael Arent, then a Vice-President for UX Design at SAP, served as the SAP project manager for this project (Fig. 10.27).

Dollar Redesign: FaceBucks, 2012

I conclude this section with a humorous (but serious) conceptual art project that I began in 2009 and continued even into 2020 during the first reign of President Donald J. Trump. The project combines my interest in semiotics, persuasion design, politics, and finance. A version of this description and images appear in Marcus (2015b).

The USA has been heading toward a fiscal crisis for years. Under the then current presidency (Barack Obama), the situation has only exacerbated the problem. Beginning in 2009 with variations since then, I proposed a solution by redesigning the US currency and changing the business model of our currency:

A simple change in our "money production policies" could increase significantly US Treasury revenues and help reduce our deficit.

The US Treasury could have decided before the beginning of the 2012 campaign that it was perfectly legal and fiscally advantageous to let all those who wished to

Fig. 10.27 Photo of Aaron Marcus and workshop participants from SAP/Palo Alto, 2012. (Source: AM+A archive; photo by Michael Arent, used with permission of Michael Arent and Aaron Marcus)

support the winner of the Elections for President to have the winning candidate's image appear on a limited number (say, one million) of $100 US currency bills…provided they paid $100 million for that "edition" with the image. If they wanted to buy more "FaceBucks" they could. Organizations would put in money and get some public relations value for their donations. They might even be able to distribute a certain number of them in desired locations, provided they actually paid for their face value; otherwise, they would be released randomly by the US Government at appropriate times and places.

If the sponsors preferred to have a more "populist" denomination, they could buy "FaceSpace" on $1 bills, which have less monetary value but greater circulation. $100 million per image might put the candidate's face on 100 million bills per set. The sponsors would be allowed to purchase some of the bills for communication purposes and give them away, sell them at higher cost as keepsakes, or trade them for "non-denominational" versions of currency.

For example, there are about three billion one-dollar bills in circulation, the most of any denomination, and these bills last about 21 months, well within the four-year period of a presidency. That means, if there were only 600 sponsors of images, the US Government could quickly raise $60 billion over a two-year typical circulation cycle and perhaps raise another round during the second two years of a presidency. This "Campaign to Fund Facebucks" could be the start of a movement to put new faces on our currency and to raise $600 billion if 6000 sponsors can be found worldwide over a four-year period. This large sum would do much to lessen the US deficit.

Had the US Treasury implemented this strategy then, these new designs would have allowed the first non-Caucasian to appear on our US currency. In the future, if a woman were elected, we would see the second occasion of a woman to appear on US currency (Martha Washington was the first in the nineteenth century). Even people and companies/organizations outside the US might contribute to the cost of Presidential FaceBucks, thereby enabling other wealthy individuals or groups to contribute officially to the celebration of the winner.

Over the past few years, our US currency has been undergoing graphic redesign, with new images of past Presidents, more colors, new typography, and additional anti-counterfeiting techniques. I thought then was the perfect time to make this historic change in "outside funding" of our currency. The cost of printing and detecting such bills would not be prohibitively expensive. These FaceBucks might become highly desirable outside the USA as well, much like our movie production, which might bring further sponsor contributions.

Taxing the wealthiest individuals and companies is always challenging. This simple suggestion gives sponsors with wealth a tangible benefit in return for their funds: something desirable, valuable, and noteworthy. Some people complain about money spent to buy elections. FaceBucks enables people to buy FaceSpace, but not necessarily to buy elections. FaceBucks also recognizes that our currency is one of our valuable remaining iconic worldwide communication "products." FaceBucks allows the US government to use money to make money.

It was too late for the Election of 2008, 2012, 2016, 2020, and 2024. It seems likely that the current 2024 President would be a great supporter of this "tremendous idea." This opportunity should not be ignored as we prepare for a next national election (Figs. 10.28–10.34).

Figs. 10.28–10.34 Examples of FaceBucks suitable at the time of the 2012 Presidential election, 2012. (Source: AM+A archive; AM+A designs; used with permission of AM+A)

The Election Campaign of 2012 between Democratic incumbent President Obama and Republican candidate Governor Mitt Romney was almost over. Meanwhile, Congress has been unable to pass sufficient legislation to curb the increasing US deficit (currently about $1.1 trillion) and the US debt (currently about $16.2 trillion). Obama image credit: Public Domain. Romney image credit: Gage Skidmore.

Additional Figures: Hello Kitty dollar, or Hello Kitty Kash, Buffet Bucks, Obama Bucks, BabyBucks, etc., designed by Aaron Marcus using public domain imagery wherever possible, or images for which the Author has permission, e.g., Lily Sonia Marcus, shortly after her birth, or Warren Buffet in a photo taken by a student visiting him. Author claims Fair Use of images for non-profit artworks. Hello Kitty image is copyright and trademarked by Sanrio, Inc., and appears under Fair-Use practice for educational and artistic/design usage.

10.28–10.34 (continued)

Concluding Remarks for This Chapter

The period of 2003–2018 was a remarkable change for me from 1990 to 2003. I had closed my two external offices in California and New York, I avoided bankruptcy and continued operations as a virtual company, I was blessed with three grandchildren from my son and daughter and their spouses, I was saddened by the divorce from my second wife, Leslie Becker. I was saddened by the eight arterial stents that had to be placed in my body to keep me alive.

However, I was blessed in many ways: finding a new life partner, Sandy Speier, with whom to enjoy my final days on earth, gaining the interest of the San Francisco Museum of Modern Art in my work, gaining the interest and publishing commission from the Letterform Archive, San Francisco, (later from Springer Publishing UK), and gradually absorbing the concept of my retirement from both the worlds of graphic design and HCI/UX/computer technology.

Acknowledgments I am indebted to many fine people who assisted AM+A during these years, especially my Associates, most of whom I have listed in an Appendix. In addition, I would like to mention these specific people:

Arent, Michael, Vice-President, SAP
Aye, Ms. Nancy, Manager, Kaiser
Kitson, Fred, Director, HP Mobile and Media Research Lab
Goose, Stuart, Siemens, Senior Researcher and Visionary Engineer, Technology-To-Business Research Lab
Lindholm, Christian, Nokia, Director, UX Department
Rosenberg, Dan, Director, UX Department, SAP

References

Girish, Devika (2020), "'The Social Dilemma' Review: Unplug and Run." New York Times, 2 September 2020, https://www.nytimes.com/2020/09/09/movies/the-social-dilemma-review.html.

Harari, Yuval Noah (2018), *21 Lessons for the 21st Century*. New York: Spiegel and Grau.

Marcus, Aaron (2015a). *Mobile Persuasion Design*. London: Springer. http://www.springer.com/gb/book/9781447143239.

Marcus, Aaron (2015b). *HCI/User-Experience Design: Fast Forward to the Future*. London: Springer. http://www.springer.com/gb/book/9781447167433

Chapter 11
Looking Backward, Looking Forward

Takeaways
*The monograph was unexpectedly delayed several years because the publisher can-
celled the contract for its own business reasons. I was able to finish the monograph
and find a new publisher, Springer. I expect to slow down, retire, and devote my life
to personal objectives.*

An Unexpected Digression

In early 2018, I had finished writing the first version of this monograph. I was happy
and excited to see progress toward publication. But then progress slowed down and
eventually came to a halt in 2020–2021. Many images were scanned in high definition for possible use in the book. I was told page proofs would soon be forthcoming.
But on a fateful day, the head of LFA, the publisher, asked for a meeting with me at
my home office. I suspected bad news. Actually, it was terrible news. LFA had
decided to pursue another publishing business model, had made agreements with a
publisher in Europe, and that publisher had looked over the candidates for forthcoming publication (mine was one of several), expressed its opinion that it was not
interested in *any* of them! Consequently, LFA was cancelling its contract with me,
and I now had to find another publisher.

It took me many months to recover from the shock and disappointment. I don't
know what the other authors who expected to be published thought of the situation.
After exploring several options over the next few years, I finally was able to arrange
with Springer UK (Ms. Helen Desmond) to publish my book. I was delighted that
we could begin again almost 6 years later, and since that time of contract signing in
early 2024, I have reviewed and edited each chapter several times, assisted by my
wife Sandy Speier, and Ron Baecker…

© The Author(s), under exclusive license to Springer Nature
Switzerland AG 2026
A. Marcus, *Bridging Art, Design and Technology: My Lifetime Work*,
https://doi.org/10.1007/978-3-032-04342-9_11

Beginning to Slow Down

All during the 1980s until recently, I had attended many, many conferences world-wide. At times, I would have one conference every month for a period of several months. I attended ACM's SIGGRAPH conference in 1980 and a string of SIGGRAPH conferences at which I gave user-interface design tutorials for seven years in a row. In 1982, I attended the first ACM SIGCHI conference and continued to give papers, tutorials, and other presentations there for about 20 years. I regularly attended the National Computer Graphics Association's conferences for about 10 years until it ceased operations in about 1992. I also was a member of the Human Factors and Ergonomics Society (HFES) for about 20 years and gave lectures and tutorials.

In 2011, the Human-Computer Interface International (HCII) Conference, which I had attended since about 1985, permitted me to start a new conference in their series of associated sub-conferences. I am grateful to the leaders of HCII, Dr. Gavriel Salvendy and Dr. Constantine Stephanidis. My conference was called Design, User Experience, and Usability (DUXU), and I became its Chair. The first year we had about 400 attendees, about one-fourth of the HCII attendance. Interest was strong for a new conference. We continued successfully for 13 years. In that time I was assisted by several co-chairs, the most important and enduring of which was Elizabeth Rosenzweig, Chair of World Usability Day. Finally, in 2024, I retired from the conference. It was a sad and sobering moment for me, the conference continues in the good hands of Dr. Martin Schrepp, UX Expert at SAP Research in Germany (Fig. 11.1).

Concluding Comments

What began as a fascination with the mysteries of the Earth, the universe, human signs, and human communication continued throughout my life.

During my earlier career in creating visual typographic/sign artworks, I was fascinated by what signs could become and enjoyed inventing new modes of communicating them.

During my early years of working with computers, I found them intriguing, but also challenging and frustrating. The more I demanded of them, the less satisfied I was with the results.

During my AM+A career, I loved best the challenging design problems in which I had no idea how to solve the client's needs/wants. Eventually, I would find a way, and this led to a sense of great satisfaction. As an example, I recall once finding a way to visualize 500 entities on a screen, each of which was accompanied by 7 ± 2 metrics in one of 7 ± 2 states, so that the viewer could make an executive decision in a few seconds about which entities met his/her needs. This solution harked back

Design, User Experience and Usability 2023 (DUXU 2023)

Call for Your Participation in a Conference for Designers

13th International Conference on Design, User Experience and Usability, an affiliated Conference of HCI International 2024 (HCII2024) which gathers about 2000 people from about 80 countries, Washington Hilton Hotel, Washington DC, USA
29 June - 4 July 2024
http://2024.hci.international/duxu

Proceedings published by:
🖄 Springer

Co-Chairs:
- *Aaron Marcus*, Principal
  Aaron Marcus and Associates, Berkeley, CA USA,
  aaron.marcus@bamanda.com
- *Prof. Elizabeth Rosenzweig*,
  Brandeis University, Waltham, MA, USA,
  eliz@bubblemtn.com
- *Prof. Marcelo M. Soares*, PhD, School of Design,
  Southern University of Science and Technology
  (SUSTech), P. R. China, soaresmm@gmail.com

Submit your work:
https://2024.hci.international/submissions.html
Presentation/panel sessions (with no papers) permitted.

User experience (UX): how a person thinks, feels, and acts with usable, useful, and appealing interactive products and services. The conference showcases how products/services are perceived, learned, and used; design knowledge, methods, and practices, with a focus on deeply human-centered design processes. Topics:

Accessibility, illiterate users, differently able
Aging
Anthropology, ethnography
Artificial Intelligence (AI), Human-Centered AI
Branding, marketing
Chart, map, wayfinding, diagram design
Color, image, signage, icon design
Creativity
Design thinking, philosophy, patterns
Design/evaluation
Diversity: women, children, elderly, gender, people of color
Emerging Technologies
DUXU in Africa, China, and Middle East
Education, training
Emotion, motivation, persuasion design
Ethics, politics, social, racial issues
Gamification, especially in enterprise applications
Globalization, localization, culture issues
Financial products/services
Health, Covid-19,
Heuristics, personas, use scenarios
History of HCI, UX
Information/knowledge design/visualization
Internet of Things (IoT)
Management of DUXU processes, maturity models
Metaphor, mental-model, navigation design
Mobile products/services
Personalities, psychology
Persuasive technology
Robots, AI agents
Sci-Fi, speculative fiction, future trends
Search design
Semiotics: sign/symbol/icon design
Service design

Fig. 11.1 Call for papers oriented to designers for DUXU23. (Source: AM+A archive; written and designed by AM+A; used with permission)

to what I had envisioned in the late 1970s as a universal way to present complex information visually: a pattern of colored pixels, discernable by the human eye, the semantics of which the viewer would know how to interpret easily, having learned the schema. This project was an example of what powered my "search for visual meaning" for decades.

Being inquisitive and wanting to learn more was a lifelong pre-occupation that sought and found many targets for my curiosity:

- Artificial intelligence and neural networks
- Astronomy
- Baroque music
- Cinema, especially 1930s–1950s, science fiction, historical dramas, comedies
- Computer technology: combining interactive computers with visual/acoustic display media
- Cosmology, origins of the universe, multiverses, etc.
- Earth's earlier epochs
- Egyptian culture and art, from the earliest dynasties to about 500 BCE
- Geneology, family histories
- Judaism and Israel
- Mathematics in general
- Music, especially classical, country, Middle-Eastern, and rock-and-roll
- Organizing people
- Persuasion theory
- Religion, especially Judaism
- Quantum physics
- Science in general, especially physics
- Science fiction
- Semiotics, the science of signs
- Solar system, its origins, characteristics, and future
- String theory
- Technology, especially robotics, and social networks
- Time systems
- Typography and graphic design history
- Visible language systems, in particular, world language-systems, icons/symbols, and cartoons
- Visual formalism, structuralism, synthesizing form, function, and technical requirements

Even today, solving challenging puzzles of visual design still thrills me. And I enjoy doing *The New York Times* Wordle puzzle each morning.

In my visible-language-oriented artwork, I always seemed to be pushing the limits of our understanding of signs in terms of space, time, technology, semiotics, psychology, culture, and history. My interest always seemed to guide me to search for meaning in the seemingly meaningless. On the other hand, in my design work, especially after 1978, I became committed to exploring how to make large amounts of information understandable, accessible to all, and to incorporate advanced computer-graphics technology to achieve successful solutions.

For all of my professional life, I enjoyed teaching and writing about what I knew or had learned. I am grateful that I could enjoy teaching at such institutions as the following:

- Bezalel Academy of Art and Design/Jerusalem Graphic Design Department and Industrial Design Department
- Hebrew University/Jerusalem, Communications Institute and Geography Department
- Princeton University School of Architecture and Urban Planning, and Visual Arts Program
- University of California/Berkeley, College of Environmental Design
- Yale University School of Art and Architecture, Graphic Design Department

Publishing books about my interests or achievements has also been intellectually enriching and gratifying. I am also grateful that I could publish with these institutions, among others:

- ACM Press/New York
- Addison-Wesley/Reading
- Letterform Archive/San Francisco
- Springer Publishing/United Kingdom
- West Coast Poetry Review Press

Serving on the Editorial Boards or on the Editorial Advisory Boards was also a way that I could contribute assistance to publications that I valued. Among others were these:

- *Information Design Journal*
- *Print Magazine*
- *User-Experience Magazine*
- *Visible Language*

Looking back, the road was rocky, thorny, erratic, zigzagging in unexpected directions, challenging, and frustrating…but my path also provided enormous amounts of pleasure, satisfaction, and delight. I am grateful for the opportunity and ability to make this particular journey and grateful to those who assisted me, encouraged me, and mentored me.

Challenges Ahead

A particular challenge lying ahead for me is determining what "retirement" will mean for me. I am looking forward to engaging in activities that are not tied to keeping supervisors, staff, and clients satisfied, as I did for 40 years. Instead, I hope to return to visual communication interests of decades ago and pursue self-generated challenges.

I am already enjoying more time to read: to read histories of nations and the continual emergence of political structures; mystery/detective novels; science-fiction novels; the design/artistic creations of other cultures and other times; and Jewish thought and history.

I also have been enjoying more time to review the movies of the last 40 years, many of which I missed while I was so busy working. I even enjoy some of the classics of the silent-movie era, an interest inspired by my wife Sandy. I am particularly intrigued when viewing the movies my parents might have seen in the 1920s–1940s. In a sense, I feel I am able to relive their lives through the background contexts of the movies of *their* lifetimes. In a way, I feel as if I am "going to the movies with them" and gaining insight into the challenges they faced decades ago.

Today and in the future, I am grateful for a loving partner with whom to enjoy life together in the final years of our lives and for four children and five grandchildren with whom we can spend time together.

While returning to drawing with ink, I have also returned to one of my earliest pleasures, drawing cartoons (in the style of R. Crumb) of weekly readings of the Torah in which I place my own grandchildren as participants and witnesses (see accompanying figures). It is a great formal distance from much of my work over the past 60 years, but my interest in drawing and cartooning has been a thread throughout my life and career since childhood. Drawing gives me a special pleasure, so I always look forward to the occasions of quiet reflection, meditation, and concentration.

As for what I have learned from life over the past seven decades, I mention these maxims, some of which I have been able to internalize better than others:

- In problem-solving, to "think outside the box," look to other times and other cultures for helpful hints leading to creative insights and solutions.
- If things seem bleak, go to sleep. In the morning, one will have a different, fresher, more optimistic perspective.
- It is wasteful to let anger simmer and burn; better to forgive, or at least to forget.
- It usually takes about three times to get something right, no matter what one's task or objective is.
- Patience and perseverance lead to success and satisfaction in the long term.
- Spend time with family and friends, one's most important assets in life.
- Wherever and whenever possible, find a way to do good deeds.
- Be demanding of one's self before being demanding of others.
- Learn to speak less and listen more.
- Speaking other languages introduces one to other, valuable ways of understanding the world and thinking about "reality."
- The fault, dear Brutus, is not in our stars, or in the failings of others; it is usually in our own failings, but it is challenging to blame one's self; it is, alas, easier, but unproductive, to blame others.

- One can learn from almost anyone (a specific lesson from the Jewish/Hebrew document *Pirke Avot*, Ethics of the Fathers).
- Enemies are usually just people like one's self, but with different views of life objectives. We're all human. Try to understand and forgive them.
- Being able to diagram what we are talking about is helpful to bring out into the open where we agree and where we disagree; diagramming also helps to illuminate different meanings we attach to the words we share.
- Be grateful for what one knows, and don't presume to be superior in general to others because of some specific achievement or skill.
- Be grateful for whatever good health and happiness each day brings.
- A reasonable life objective is to help others make smarter decisions faster; figuring out how to achieve this objective, then designing the right documents/systems, can accomplish much good.
- One can never achieve perfection, but it's worthwhile to strive, as long as the effort does not become obsessively compulsive and wind up hurting one's self or others.
- There is no end to learning; one should continue during one's lifetime for as long as possible.
- No one is so truly unique in how we think, act, and feel; we are all typical in some ways.

So, perhaps I have gone full circle and returned to my roots, just in time to become a helpless infant at the close of my life. Thanks for joining me on a reminiscence tour of the last three-quarters of a century (Figs. 11.2–11.7).

Figs. 11.2–11.7 Drawings by Aaron Marcus of grandchildren based on Torah parshiyot (weekly readings) in which he embeds his grandchildren. (Source: AM+A archive; Aaron Marcus' drawings; used with permission of the author)

Figs. 11.2–11.7 (continued)

Figs. 11.2–11.7 (continued)

Appendix A: AM+A Associates, Staff, Interns, and Contractors

The author thanks those approximately 180 people who have served in one or more capacities to assist AM+A to achieve its objectives during 1982–2025.

The following attempts to list those who served as Associates/Employees, other outside contractors, and/or interns at AM+A during 1982–2025. Names usually appear with an approximate date of beginning service expressed as month (two digits, followed by year (two digits). In the case of Interns coming from countries outside of the USA, the country of origin is usually indicated. In some cases, contractors became employees, and interns became contractors. They are listed under their highest level of service, but their starting dates usually indicate the date of any official connection to AM+A. The author apologizes for any inadvertent omissions or other errors.

AM+A began from a home office in Berkeley, CA, in 1982, with three people: Aaron Marcus, Michael Arent, and Bruce Browne. AM+A moved its offices in 1990 to Emeryville, CA. Employees were hired during the period of time that AM+A operated outside of home-office locations in Emeryville, CA, and New York City, NY, 1990–2003. The New York City office, in Lower Manhattan, for most of its time located about 15 blocks from the World Trade Center on Desbrosses Street, operated from 1999 to 2003. Because of the Great Recession in 2002–2003, AM+A closed both offices and moved back to a home office in 2003. AM+A was incorporated during 1994–2014.

Associates/Employees

Note: Associates/Employees primarily served as Designer/Analysts, Executive Assistants, Administrative Assistants, Systems Managers, Programmers, and Technical Writers. The dates given are their approximate first and final association with AM+A.

A. Marcus, *Bridging Art, Design and Technology: My Lifetime Work*, https://doi.org/10.1007/978-3-032-04342-9

Ackerman, Sam, 1996-06
Anderson, Jennifer, 1992-93
Ancheta, Jane, 1903-06
Armitage, John, 1995-00
Arent, Michael, 1982-85
Ball, Luke, 1999-2003
Blacker, Mallory, 2012
Brown, Karen, 2000-03
Browne, Bruce, 1982-85
Chen, Eugene, 1998-03
Ching, Lynne, 1994-97
Coleridge, Christina, 1998-2003
Dobrowolski, Joe, 1994-2018
Donahue, Kathleen, 2000-03
Frank, Volker, 1997-2002
Gallé, Nicholas Gregory, 1986-90
Gasperini, Jim, 2000-14
Gibson, Steve, 2006-07
Good, Alan, 2003
Gould, Emilie, 1999-2012
Gross, Angela, 2000-03
Guttman, Edward, 1999-2000
Ireland, Benedict, 2001-03
Kennedy, Darren, 1999-2002
Kim, Hyolin, 2001-02
Kochavi, Uri, 2000-03
Koulias, Jim, 2002-04
Krantz, Kevin, 2007-08
Lee, Ahree, 2006-07
Lee, Jung-Hwa, 2001-04
Letz, Grant, 1992-95
Leviner, Hadas, 2001
Marcus, Simon, 2001-03
Marquart, Sherry, 1988-90
Martin, Allison, 2000-02
McFarland, Amanda, 2012-14
Mele, Marisa, 1999-01
Miller, Kent, 1994-2003
Millican, Crissy, 2006-10
Mullet, Kevin, 1986-90
Older, Morris, 1997-2017
Ortiz, Antonio, 2000-03
Pacho, JoAnn, 1997-2000
Regan, Sandra, 1985-90
Reunala, Pia, 2001-03

Plotner, Brenda, 1995-97
Rosdil, Anna, 2011-12
Sanchez, Larilyn, 2001-03
Sato, Nonoko, 1997-2002
Simonsen, June, 1984-88
Thomas, Rebecca, 2008-14
Thompson, Andrew, 1996-99
Tien, Pamela, 1999-07
Wallace, Martha, 2012
Wigham, Laurie, 2005-07
Wieser, Karl, 1996-2000
Wymore, Melanie, 2000-03
Zimmerman, Beate, 2000-01

External Contractors

Note: Contractors were hired during 1982–2014. During the years that AM+A operated from the owner's home, only contractors were used, some of whom operated on a recurring basis.

Applova, Dominique, 2003
Atkins, Kris, 2006
Baumgartner, Mary, 1995-2005
Baxter, Angelia, 2007-08
Birbragher, Susanne, 1998-2000
Becker, Leslie, 2009
Black, T. Andrew, 2009
Blank, Todd, 1990-92
Bugental, Joe, 2008
Clarke, Stephanie. 2003
Cofrancesco, Paul, 2000-03
Constantinides, Tony, 2007
Cytrynowicz, Mike, 2010-2012
Dallendörfer, Claudia, 2000-05
Duderstadt, Hank, 1990-95
Dumpert, Jennifer, 2003-2010
Gabriel-Petit, Pabini, 2004-05
Gibson, Steve, 2006-07
Grunewald, Jessica, 2000
Guan, Larry, 1990-2003
Heidrich, Wolfgang, 1994-99
Javier, Astrid, 2008
Kanterovich, Dmitri, 2004-05

Kibble, Shane, 2005
Kim, Hyemin, 2009
Lasky, Sandra, 2007
Lee, Amy, 2009
Lee, Ari, 2006
Levy, Jean-Benoit, 2006-14
Lilien, Janice, 2005
Lin, Karen, 2013
Lutrell, Heather, 2003
Mohanrao, Neerajan, 2006
Marcus, Elisheva, 2005
Marcus, Joshua, 2005
Marx, Beth, 2005-06
Miller, Drue, 2003
Naramore, Tristan, 2006-10
Nies, Kim, 1009
Ota, Yukio, Japan, 2007
Park, Seeonghee, 2004
Perez, Angel, 2009-120906
Pickup, Kathy, 2012
Posner, Ilona, 2010
Rafferty, James, 2007
Reetz, Randall, 2006
Reynolds, Erika, 2008-10
Riehart, Dale, 2011
Rinzler, Peter, 2012
Robert, Dale, 2011
Roschuni, Celeste, 2014
Rosen, Emily Jane, 2016
Schaefer, Henning, 2007-10
Schultz, Eugene, 2011
Slade, Michael, 2007
Smith, Lois, 1984-85
Venkata, Levanya, 2006
Webb, Nancy, 1995-99
Wells, Gregory, 2013
Xiao, Shirley, 2014

Interns

Note: Beginning in 2000, AM+A contracted with students or professionals (who might be changing careers) to serve as paid or unpaid interns to assist in AM+A projects, especially its 10 Machine projects, on which interns worked almost exclusively during 2009–2014. Those interns usually worked for a period of about 3 months as Designer/Analysts. Primary sources for interns included California College of the Arts, San Francisco; Carnegie Mellon University; Institute of Design, IIT; and University of California, Berkeley.

Abromowitz, Scott, 2012
Ahn, JinYoung, 0107
Alexander, Chava, 2007
Anguiano, Sheila, 2013
Atiya, Gabriel, 2004
Baumgartner, Valentina-Johanna, Austria, 2002-03
Benker, Janine, Germany, 2006
Berger, Arne, Germany, 2009
Brejcha, J, Czech Republic, 2009
Chambers, Chris, 2011
Chambers, Kimberley, 2004
Chew, KiaHwee, Singapore, 2014
Chiou, Megan, 2012
Correia, Raul, Venezuela, 2007
Davis, Darold, 2009
Doerr, Carmen, 2003
Elliott, Drake, 2011
Goeck, Oliver, 2006-07
Griffiths, Neil, 2001-02
He, Phoebe Xuewei, China, 2010
Horowitz, Margo, 2009
Isaacs, Catherine, CCA, MFA, 2011
Ito, Takeshi, Japan, 2009
Jean, Jérémie, France, 2009
Kimura, Kaoru, Japan, 20508---> 2008
Krishnamurthi, Niranjan, India, 2009
Law, Caroline, 2007
Lecca, Nicola, Italy, 2012
Lee, Michael, 2008
Lee, Min, 2013
Lemes-Moreira, Vivian, Brazil, 2014
Lima, Lucas, Brazil, 2004
Liu, Yu-Hsien, Taiwan, 2013
Li, Yi, China, 2012
Li, Eileen, Philippines, 2009
McQuade, Megan, 2013
Micoogullari, Lina, Turkey 2008
Narula, Chirag, India, 2012
O'keefe, Carlene, 2011
Ota, Chika, 2004

Park, Seongee, 2004
Peng, Yuan, China, 2012
Perez, Angel, 2006
Princci, Bartu, Italy, 2010
Qu, Hong, 2004
Rosenthal, Jenna, 2012
Savvidis, Hélene, France, 2011
Schieder, Theresa Katrina, Germany, 2012
Senel, S, Turkey, 2004
Seo, Jung Eui, South Korea, 2007
Shick, Aubrey, 2015
So, Kenneth, China, 2013-14
Suh, Ethan, China, 2007
Thianthai, Tim, Thailand, 2011
Tse, David, 2000
Wang, Albert, Taiwan, 2007
Yankee, Tenzin, Nepal, 2012-13
Yu, Allan, China, 2012
Yuan, Rosa, China, 810--->2010
Yun, Ji-Young, South Korea, 2008

Appendix B: AM+A Clients

The author thanks approximately 500 companies, educational institutions, governmental agencies, and others who contracted with AM+A for planning, research, analysis, design, documentation, evaluation, training, and/or management services to achieve their business objectives during 1982–2025.

For some of the 242 project clients, AM+A provided multiple projects, sometimes over multiple years. For example, AM+A worked with Hewlett-Packard on several projects for more than 20 years, approximately 1982–2004. AM+A worked with Visa for approximately five years on approximately 33 projects. AM+A worked with three lines of business at American Airlines/Sabre for approximately seven years. AM+A worked with three branches of the US Federal Reserve Bank for five years.

A few clients contracted with AM+A for software development services.

Training clients contracted only for lectures, tutorials, and workshops, usually, but not always given by Aaron Marcus. These events served as training/education activities but also as marketing activities for AM+A.

The 196 entries contain conferences, on-site client presentations, and other locales. For many conferences, AM+A provided multiple tutorials, lectures, papers, and workshops. In many cases, AM+A published papers, exhibited posters, and led discussion groups at conferences.

Besides the master list of all project clients and training clients, lists appear for clients grouped under general technology or subject-matter categories. These will facilitate appreciating the broad experience AM+A acquired in diverse vertical markets during approximately 40 years.

A. Marcus, *Bridging Art, Design and Technology: My Lifetime Work*,
https://doi.org/10.1007/978-3-032-04342-9

Clients for Projects

3Com
Academy of Art University
Ablex Publishers
AC Nielsen
Activant
Addison Wesley Longman
Adobe
Amdahl
American Center for Design
American College of Physicians
American Institute of Graphic Arts (AIGA)
Anoto (later called LiveScribe)
Arabia On-Line (Jordan)
Arbor Software (earlier called Hyperion)
Association for Computing Machinery (ACM)
3Com
Aspect Telecommunications
AT+T
Austria
Autodesk
Avenue A (Razorfish)
Bank of America
BankInter (Spain)
Banter
Beckman Instruments
Billeo
BioScience Communications
BLOC
Blue Chip Expert
BMG Music
BMW (Germany)
Bose
Brandwynne, Lois, Pianist
Brobeck, Phleger, and Harrison, LLP
Brown and Bain, LLP
Communications of the ACM
Calico
California Cancer Registry
Camstar
Canada
CareAssured
CareFX

Celunite
Center for Research in Vocational Education (CRVE)
California College of Arts and Crafts
Charles Schwab
China
Cisco
Cogito Learning Media
Cohen, Millstein, LLP
Collabrx
Communication Arts
Compulink
Compuserve
Computer History Museum
Congregation Beth Israel
Consolidated Legal Concepts
Computer Graphics Pioneers
Computervision
ConsenSys
Country Bank
California Virtual University
Comergent Technologies
Commodore Amiga
Crowley Maritime
Cybercash
DaimlerChrysler (Germany)
Decision Point/SurfNotes (Israel)
Design Pacifica
DHS, Ltd. (Ireland)
Digital Equipment Corporation (DEC)
Digite
DLA Piper US, LLP
Done.com
Douglas Aircraft Corporation
Dragon Design Foundation (China)
DTS (Digital Theater Systems)
Dupont
E-Trade
Eastman Kodak
eBay
Elixir (Opus)
Elsevier
Embark
Emerson
Emtek
Enterprise Engines

Epocrates
ePrint
Epson (USA)
EPRI
Equilibrio
eWorld Learning
FedEx
Feinberg, Day, Alberti, and Thompson, LLP
Fidelity
Filemaker
Finkelstein, Alan
Fish and Richardson, PC
Fitzpatrick, Cella, Harper, and Scinto, Attorneys
Ford Foundation
Forrester Research
FORTH
FourTen
Foxboro
Franz LISP
Fujitsu (USA)
Fujitsu Open Systems Solutions, Inc. (FOSSI)
Fujitsu Japan (Japan)
General Electric
General Motors, Buick Division
Geoworks
Gerson Lehrman Group
Getty Trust
Gigabeat
Gloo
Goldberg, Lowenstein, and Weatherwax, LLP
Google (Adwords)
Golden Turtle Press
Gracenote
Harvard BioScience
Harvard BioVision
Health Design Network
Heald
Healinx
Hell Graphics Systems
Hewlett-Packard (HP) HP Halo Product Development Group
Hewlett-Packard (HP) Human Factors Department
Hewlett-Packard (HP) China (China)
HFI
Human Genome Project
I-Logix

IBM, Federal Systems Division/Air Traffic Controller Development Group
iEscrow.com
IIT Research Institute (IITRI)
InFocus Systems
Innovis (Weyerhauser)
Institute of Design, IIT
Intel (Dealys, Eastmill, Parallel Processing)
Intellimation (PreVue)
International Institute of Information Design (Austria)
IQ Financial
IRIS Software
International ThinkLink Corporation
Indiana Chapter of Usability Professionals' Association
ITC
Japan Patent Office (Japan)
JDA Software Group
JEITA (Japan)
Johnson Controls International
JustSystems (Japan)
Kaiser Permanente User-Interface Design Group
Kaiser Permanente Online Library Services
Kanisa
Keibi
Keker and Van Nest, LLP
King Abdul Aziz University (Saudi Arabia)
Lawrence Berkeley National Laboratory
Levanta
Letterform Archives/San Francisco
Liberty Mutual
Lifetech
Lionbridge
Live Process
LoCoS (Japan)
Los Alamos National Laboratory
Lovells Law Firm (United Kingdom)
MacWeek
ManageStar (RealClear)
Match21
McDonald Douglas
McGraw-Hill
McKesson.0604
Medtronics
Mentor Graphics
Microcomputer Technology Consortium (MCC)
Micropro

Microsoft
MindAlliance.com
Magnus Museum
Morgan Kaufman
Motorola
Motorola Israel (Israel)
N2K
NASA Johnson Space Center (TAE)
NASA Mountain View (Color consulting for US Space Station)
National Computer Graphics Association
National Institute of Health (NIH)
NCR
NDS Technologies Israel Ltd. (Israel)
National Expert Witness Network
National Library of Medicine (NLM)
NEC (Japan)
Nellcor
NetCentric
NetIQ=>Webtrends
New Alloy
New York City Transit Museum
News Datacom (Israel)
NLM.GrtflMed.2
NLM.GrtflMed.2.zip
Nokia (Finland)
Nokia (United Kingdom)
Noverus
NTT Data (Japan)
O'Brien-Kreitzberg Construction
Omaha Central High School, Hall of Fame
Omnibox
Optavia
Oracle
Orbitz
Pacific Bell
Pacific Power and Light
Paradux
Pascal
PeopleSoft
PIE/Logos Competition
Pinpoint Solutions
Plato
Point Forward
Predictor Systems
Princeton University, School of Architecture

Prodigy
PSDI
Q2Ware
Quintus
Qwest
Random House
Rapport (Israel)
ReDesign Research (RDR)
RealClear
Responsys.com
Resumix
Reuters
Ross Systems
Vignelli Center for Graphic Design, RIT
Sabre
San Francisco Museum of Modern Art
San Jose Police Officers Association
San Jose State University Art Museum
Sanofi Diagnostics Pasteur
SAP
Schwalb Consulting
Scitex (Israel)
SendMail
Servador
ShareData
ShowMeTV
Siemens, Corporate Technology
Siemens, Technology-to-Business
SIGGRAPPH (ACM)
Silicon Valley Expert Witness Group
Smart Advocate
Softbank (Japan)
StudioAsterisk
Surfnotes (Israel)
Symantec.0609
T. Rowe Price
Tamabi
Teamware (Finland)
Teklicon Expert Witness Agency
Tektronix
The Learning Company
Thomson Reuters Expert Witness Services
Tiscali (Italy)
TMA Resources
Tradiant (GTNexus)

Trading Dynamics
Twilio
Ubitrotech (South Korea)
United States Department of Defense/DARPA
United States Department of Energy
United States Department of Labor
United States Federal Reserve Bank (Chicago, New York, San Francisco)
United States Treasury Department
University of California System
University of California/Berkeley
University of California/Berkeley Extension
UIWizards
UMI (University of Michigan)
Un-Nameable Company
Unigraphics
Unisys
United States Federal Reserve Bank, San Francisco, New York, and Chicago
    Branches
Usability Consortium
Usenix
UXNet
Vantive
Verity
Vhayu
VirginAmerica
VIsa
Visual Engineering
Vitalcom
Web Of Culture
Wells Fargo Bank
Wells Fargo NIA (LIBRA Cognitive Modeling Specifications)
Wilson, Sonsini, Goodrich, Rosati, LLP
Xerox (Font Systems, Design Network)
Yahoo

Clients for Lectures, Tutorials, and Workshops

Advanced Visual Interfaces Bari, 1994; Trento, 2001 (Italy)
American Center for Design
American Express
American Institute of Graphic Arts, 2003, 2004, 2009, 2012
Applied Human Factors and Ergonomics 2010, 2012, 2014
Asia-Pacific CHI, 2002, 2004, 2006, 2008, 2012

Association for Computing Machinery (ACM), International Workshop on
    International Collaboration 2009
Association for Computing Machinery (ACM), Special Interest Group for
    Documentation (SIGCOC) 2001
Association for Computing Machinery (ACM), Special Interest Group for
    Computer-Human Interaction (SIGCHI) 1983, 1987, 1990, 1992, 1993, 1995,
    1996, 1997, 1999, 2000, 2001, 2002, 2003, 2004, 2005, 2007, 2009, 2010,
    2011, 2012
Association for Computing Machinery (ACM), Special Interest Group Graphics
    and Interaction (SIGGRAPH),1980, 1982, 1986, 1992–1997, 2003,
    2014–2015, 2023
AT+T Israel (Israel)
ATypI 2005
BAER 2005
Baidu (China)
BankInter (Spain)
Behavior, Energy, and Climate Change (BECC), 2010
Bezalel Academy of Art and Design (Israel)
Bolzano University, 2011 (Italy)
Brazilian Society of Information Design, Information Design International 2013
    (Brazil)
Business Forms Management Association 2010
Chinese Academy of Fine Arts (China)
Carnegie-Mellon University
Carnegie-Mellon University West
Charles Technical University (Czech Republic)
Checkpoint (Israel)
CHI South Africa 2000, 2005 (South Africa)
Cisco Collaborative Technologies and Systems 2006
Compulog (Israel)
Computer Graphics and Media Design 2014
CURE, Usecon 2009 (Austria)
DD4D (Austria)
Dalian Maritime University, Computer Science Department (China)
Das Büro (Germany)
De Tao Masters Academy (China)
Designing Integrated Systems 2002
Deutsche Telekom (Germany)
Diagrams 2006
Dobry Web, SRO (Czech Republic)
Design of User Experiences (DUX) 2003, 2005
Design Net/Spotlight (South Korea)
Design, User Experience, and Usability 2011, 2013–2024
East-West Center
Embassy of Finland

EUPA 2002

Fachhochschule Joanneum (Austria)

FORTH 1998/Crete (Greece)

French Ministry of Culture

Fujitsu-Ten (Japan)

Globalization San Francisco 2010

Going Green Silicon Valley 2010

HCD-Net (Japan)

HCI UK, 2003 (United Kingdom)

Human-Computer interface International (HCII), 1993, 1995, 1997, 2001, 2003, 2005, 2007, 2009, 2011–2024

Hewlett-Packard (HP)

Hewlett-Packard (HP) China (China)

Hochschule für Gestaltung/Basel (Switzerland)

Hochschule für Gestaltung/Schäbisch-Gemund (Germany)

Hochschule für Technik Rapperswil (Switzerland)

Hong Kong Design Institute/Vocational Training Center (China)

Hong Kong Polytechnic University, School of Design (China)

Hong Kong Productivity Center (China)

Human Factors and Ergonomics Society (HFES) 1998, 2004, 2010

Human Factors and the Web 1998, 1999, 2000, 2001

IBM/Federal Systems Division

IBM New Paradigms in Using Computers, 1999, 2005

ICOGRADA 2000, 2005

Illinois Institute of Technology/Institute of Design, UX/HCI Course, 2004–2014

Illinois Institute of Design, Institute of Design, On/Off Workshop 2002, Pathfinder Lecture 2006

Incheon Design Conference 2008 (South Korea)

Information Visualization (United Kingdom)

IndiaCHI/South India (India)

IsraelCHI

Interact 2001 (Japan)

International Institute for Information Design/Data Designed for Decisions (DD4D)/ Paris 2009 (Austria)

International Institute for Information Design/Financial Forum, 2002 (Austria)

International Institute for Information Design/Financial Information Design 2005

International Institute for Information Design/Mobile Plus Chennai 2011 (India)

International Institute for Information Design/Healthcare 2005

International Institute for Information Design/Vision Plus, 2002, 2005, 2009 (Austria)

International Symposium on Interaction Design and Human Factors ((IIDHF)) 2014 (Japan)

International Workshop on Internationalization of Products and Services 1999–2005, Rochester, Baltimore, London (UK), Austin, Berlin (Germany), Vancouver (Canada), Amsterdam (Netherlands)

Internet Publishing Expo New York, 2001
Internet World 2002/New York, 2003/San Jose
Intracom 2008 (Canada)
Intuit
Ireland HCI Cork, 2011 (Ireland)
IsraCHI (Israel)
IXDA Bangalore, 2004 (India)
IXDA New York, 2017
IT-Online (Russia)
KyotoCHI (Japan)
LG Electronics (South Korea)
Liberty Mutual
LogTel (Israel)
Localization Industry Standards Association (LISA) (Switzerland)
Localization World (LocWorld) 2010 (Seattle), 2011 (Berlin, Germany)
Los Alamos National Laboratory
Lugano University (Switzerland)
Macromedia Users Conference 1997
MagnaSteyr (Austria)
Medeanalytics
Microsoft
MobileHCI 2005, 2011, 2013 (Munich)
Mobile Phones and Car Navigation 2000 (Tokyo)
MX 2007 Design Conference (Mexico)
National Institute of Design (India)
NordiCHI 2004 (Finland)
North Carolina State University
Parsons School of Design
Persuasive Technologies 2007
Princeton University, School of Architecture
Program for the Future
QAI Bangalore (India)
QualcommWorkshop.080310
SAAS
Samsung (South Korea)
Samsung Israel (Israel)
San Jose State University, Human Factors and Ergonomics Society
SAP US
SAP Canada (Canada)
SAP China (China)
SAP India (India)
SAP Israel (Israel)
School of Design, Mobile, Technology, and Communication/Rio de Janeiro (Brazil)
SeeingKnowing/University of California/Berkeley

SIGGRAPH Asia 2010 (South Korea), 2011 (Hong Kong), 2014 (China), 2015 (Japan)
Smart Energy 2010
Society for Scholarly Publishing
Society for Technical Documentation
Software Development Conference
SonicRim
Siemens Germany (Germany)
Stanford, Computer Science Department
Stanford Design Conference
Studio 2000
South-by-Southwest 2008 (SXSW)
Summit: The Future of CAD/CAM 1999
T-Systems (Germany)
Technical University of Vienna, Institute of Software Technology and Integrated Systems (Austria)
Tekla (Finland)
Tama Art University (Japan)
Tiscali (Italy)
TechComm 1999
Training and Documentation Solutions (TDS), Ltd. (Israel)
U-Lab (Russia)
United Kingdom Embassy in San Francisco
United Nations, Graphic Design Department
United Nations Organization, IAADS (Austria)
Universidade de Estado do Rio de Janeiro, Centro de Tecnologia e Ciéncias, Escola Superior de Desenho Industrial (Brazil)
Universidade Federal de São Carlos (Brazil)
University of the Arts/Helsinki (Finland)University of Bauru (Brazil)
University of Bolzano (Italy)
University of California/Berkeley/Extension
University of California/Berkeley, Mobile/Vehicle Studies
University of California/Berkeley, HCC 2000
University of California, Human-Interface Design/EECS
University of California, Information School
University of California/Santa Cruz/Extension
University of Hawaii, Computer Science Department
University of Helsinki (Finland)
University of Illinois, School of Art and Design
University of Nebraska/Omaha, IAADS
University of Oulu (Finland)
University of Salzburg (Austria)
University of Science and Technology (China)
University of Texas/Austin, School of Information
University of the Americas/Pueblo (Mexico)

University of Toronto, Computer Science Department and Knowledge Media
    Design Institute
University of Washington
Universal Design Yokohama 2002 (Japan)
UXPA India
UPA Israel (Israel)
User Experience Professionals Association (UXPA, formerly UPA), 1992, 1998,
    1999–2010, 2012, 2013, 2015
US Federal Reserve Bank (New York, San Francisco)
Usability Professionals Association (previously UPA)
User Friendly/UPA China 2007, 2012–16 (China)
Victoria and Albert Museum (United Kingdom)
Visual Media Alliance
Web2.0
Web Design and Development, 1997, 1999, 2000, 2001
Wireless Systems
World Meter Design
World Usability Day 2005, 2006
Xconomy

IT, CAD, Office Productivity, Hardware

Anoto, later Livescribe: Smart Pen
Arborware, later Hyperion, later Oracle
Computervision
Digital Equipment Corporation (DEC)
eCAD
Electric Power Research Institute
Embark
Epson
Foxboro
Fujitsu Corporation (Japan)
Fujitsu/ELM
HP
HP Laboratories, Mobile and Media Systems Lab
Honeywell
IBM, Government Systems (Air Traffic Control)
Indigo, later part of HP
Intel
Lawrence Berkeley Laboratory, Human Genome Project
Levanta
Motorola (Israel)
NetIQ

NTT (Japan)
Oracle
Pacific Power and Light
Peoplesoft, later Oracle
Teamware (Finland)

Clients.Education+Training

AIGA (American Institute of Graphic Arts) Conferences
CHI (ACM Special Interest Group on Computer-Human Interaction) Conferences
Cogito Learning Media
Eastman Kodak Corporate Training
HCII (Human-Computer Interaction International) Conferences
Hebrew University, Jerusalem (Israel)
HFES (Human Factors and Ergonomics) Conferences
Institute of Design, IIT
Intel Learning Web site
Lionbridge Globalization
McGraw-Hill Library, School Systems Software
Oracle Worldwide Training
Random House
Samsung Research and Development Center (Israel)
SIGGRAPH (ACM Special Interest Group on Graphics) Conferences
STC (Society for Technical Communication) Conferences
The Learning Company
University of California/Berkeley
University of California/Santa Cruz
University of Toronto
UPA (Usability Professionals Association) Conferences
Visa Corporate Training
Clients.Education+Training, 0309

Finance, Insurance, Banks

American Express
Bank of America
BankInter (Spain)
Billeo
Charles Schwab
Citicorp TTI
Country Bank

eBay
Equitable Life Assurance
Fidelity
IQ Financial
Iris Financial Software (developing for Merrill Lynch)
NCR
Noverus Financial Planning Systems
Reuters
ShareData
Shearson-Lehman
T. Rowe Price
US Federal Reserve Bank
US Treasury Department
Visa
Wells Fargo Wells Fargo
WF-Nikkei Investments

Medical and Healthcare

Alegent Healthcare
American College of Physicians
Angeion
Beckman Instruments
Boeringer Manhheim
California Cancer Registry
CareFX
Cogito Learning Media
CollabRX
Compulink
Eastman Kodak
Emtek
Epocrates
Equilibrio
Healthmarket
Healinx
Kaiser Permanente
Lawrence Berkeley Lab, Human Genome Project
LiveProcess
McKesson Health Solutions
Medtronic
National Institutes of Health
National Library of Medicine
Nellcor

On-Lok Healthcare
Sanofi-Diagnostics Pasteur
Stanford Medical Informatics
Sunquest
Vitalcom

Mobile/Telecom

Aspect Telecommunications
AT+T
Cisco (Internet phones)
Compuserve
DTS
Epocrates
Equilibrio
Garmin
HP Labs: Mobile and Media Systems Lab
Intelsat
Livescribe (previously, Anoto)
Microsoft
Motorola
Motorola Israel (Israel)
Nokia (Finland and UK)
Pacific Bell
Qwest
Samsung (South Korea)
Samsung Research Lab (Israel)
San Jose Police Department
SAP
Siemens (Germany)
Springer (UK)
Tiscali (Italy)
T-Systems (Germany)
Ubitrotech (South Korea)

Travel, Auto

BMW (Germany)
Daimler Chrysler
Ferrari (through DHS Ireland)
Ford

GM.Buick
IBM, Government Systems,
FAA Project
Motorola, Government Fleet Systems
Motorola, In-car Vehicle Systems
Orbitz
Sabre for Travel agents
Sabre Business Solutions
San Jose Police Department
Siemens Technology-to-Business
Travelocity
Virgin America